WOMAN SUFFRAGE & POLITICS

THE INNER STORY OF THE SUFFRAGE MOVEMENT

CARRIE CHAPMAN CATT
AND
NETTIE ROGERS SHULER

DOVER PUBLICATIONS
GARDEN CITY, NEW YORK

Bibliographical Note

This Dover edition, first published in 2020, is an unabridged republication of the work originally printed by Charles Scribner's Sons, New York, in 1923.

Library of Congress Cataloging-in-Publication Data

Names: Catt, Carrie Chapman, 1859–1947 author. | Shuler, Nettie Rogers, 1865–1939 author.
Title: Woman suffrage and politics : the inner story of the Suffrage Movement / Carrie Chapman Catt and Nettie Rogers Shuler.
Description: Garden City, New York : Dover Publications, [2020] | Includes index. | Summary: "With the approach of the one hundredth anniversary of the ratification of the 19th Amendment, this book offers an important aid to understanding how women won the right to vote and the extensive debt we owe to those who fought for it for seventy years. Written by Carrie Chapman Catt and Nettie Rogers Shuler, two leaders of the movement, this landmark work reveals the inside story, tracing the struggle for women's suffrage from 1848 to 1922. They argue that there was not a lack of public sentiment supporting woman suffrage, rather that certain interests in the American political system controlled public sentiment and deflected information in order to delay the passage of the amendment that would give women the right to vote. They note that twenty-six other countries gave women the right to vote before the United States and offer their own insights as to why this might have been the case"— Provided by publisher.
Identifiers: LCCN 2019041084 | ISBN 9780486842059 (trade paperback) | ISBN 0486842053
Subjects: LCSH: Women—Suffrage—United States.
Classification: LCC JK1896 .C3 2020 | DDC 324.6/230973—dc23
LC record available at https://lccn.loc.gov/2019041084

Manufactured in the United States by LSC Communications Book LLC
84205302
www.doverpublications.com

2 4 6 8 10 9 7 5 3
2021

THIS BOOK IS DEDICATED
ON BEHALF OF THE WOMEN
WHO HAVE GONE BEFORE
TO
THE WOMEN WHO COME AFTER

Contents

Contents

Why the Book Is Written

The campaign for woman suffrage in America long since ended. Gone are the days of agitating, organizing, educating, pleading, and persuading. No more forever will women descend on State Legislatures and the national Congress in the effort to wrest the suffrage from State and national legislators. The gates to political enfranchisement have swung open. The women are inside.

In the struggle up to the gates, in unlocking and opening the gates, women had some strange adventures. They learned some strange things. Especially startling became their experiences and their information when woman suffrage once crossed the devious trail of American politics. It is with that point of intersection that this book concerns itself. We have left it to others to write the details of suffrage history. Those details fill six huge volumes. We have left it to others to tell the immortal story of the services of individual suffragists. Here we eliminate names to emphasize work. We have left it to others, too, to synthesize American politics. This book's essential contribution must be sought in its revelation of the bearing of American politics upon the question of woman suffrage.

It is impossible to make that revelation adequately without a summary of the seventy-two years of campaign for the enfranchisement of women in the United States, together with a survey of American politics for the last fifty-five years of that period. The two are interlocked, neither story is complete without the inclusion of the other, and this story is not comprehensible without the inclusion of both. But our summary of the woman movement will be brief. Our survey of American politics will be brief. Our emphasis will lie where woman movement and American politics met in mutual menace. Our revelations will illumine political crises with which the suffrage cause was closely identified and over whose motivation suffragists had to keep sharp watch.

Throughout the suffrage struggle, America's history, her principles, her traditions stood forth to indicate the inevitability of woman suffrage, to suggest that she would normally be the first country in the world to give the vote to women. Yet the years went by, decade followed decade, and twenty-six[1] other countries gave the vote to their women while America delayed.

Why the delay?

It is a question that was the despair of two generations of American women. It is a question that students of history and national psychology will ponder through generations to come.

We think that we have the answer. It was, not an antagonistic public sentiment, nor yet an uneducated or indifferent public sentiment—it was the control of public sentiment, the deflecting and the thwarting of public sentiment, through the trading and the trickery, the buying and the selling of American politics. We think that we can prove it. Suffragists consider that they have a case against certain combines of interests that systematically fought suffrage with politics and effectively delayed suffrage for years. We think that we can make that case.

We find it difficult to concede to the general opinion that, because of the tendency to overestimate the importance of events with which they are most familiar, those who have been a part of a movement are disqualified to write its history. We are sure that history would be worthless if it took no account of the observations made within a movement by those who have been a part of it. That is why we, who have had an opportunity to become acquainted with facts which throw light upon the political aspects of the woman suffrage question, feel impelled to pass our knowledge on to others.

The sources of all our information when not otherwise indicated are the archives of the National American Woman Suffrage Association, which contain continuous reports and other data from 1848 to 1922. Documents of this kind decline in interest for the general public as the movement they chronicle recedes into the past, but the facts and deductions drawn from them, and here assembled, should prove of significance to the advocates, perhaps especially the women advocates, of each recurring struggle in the evolution of democracy.

CARRIE CHAPMAN CATT.
NETTIE ROGERS SHULER.

CHAPTER 1

How the Woman Suffrage Movement Began

When, during the last decade, the great suffrage parades,—armies of women with banners, orange and black, yellow and blue and purple and green and gold,—went marching through the streets of the cities and towns of America; when "suffrage canvassers," knocking at the doors of America, were a daily sight; when the suffragist on the soap box was heard on every street corner; when huge suffrage mass meetings were packing auditoriums from end to end of the country; when lively "suffrage stunts" were rousing and stirring the public; when suffrage was in everybody's mouth and on the front page of every newspaper, few paused to ask how it all started, where it all came from. It was just there, like breakfast.

To the unimaginative man on the street corner, watching one of those suffrage parades, the long lines of marching women may have seemed to come out of nowhere, to have no starting place, no connection with his grandmother and his great grandmother. To the same man the insistent tapping of those suffrage canvassers, the commotion of the suffrage mass meetings, the repetition of those suffrage stunts, the incessant news of suffrage in the daily press, may have seemed unrelated acts, irrelevant to social history. Yet it was all part of social history, and had immediate connection with other phases of social history. For the demand for woman suffrage was the logical outcome of two preceding social movements, both extending over some centuries: one, a man movement, evolving toward control of governments by the people, the other a woman movement, with its goal the freeing of women from the masculine tutelage to which law, religion, tradition and custom bound them. These movements advanced in parallel lines and the enfranchisement of woman was an inevitable climax of both.

Neither the man movement nor the woman movement had a dated beginning. In the struggle upward toward political freedom, men were called upon to overthrow the universally accepted theory of the Divine Right of Kings to rule over the masses of men; women, the universally accepted theory of the Divine Right of Men to rule over women. The American Revolution forever destroyed the Divine Right of Kings theory in this country, but it left untouched the theory of the Divine Right of Man to rule over woman. Men and women believed it with equal sincerity, the church taught it, customs were based upon it, the law endorsed it, and the causes which created the belief had been so long lost in obscurity that men claimed authority for it in the "laws of God." All opposition to the enfranchisement of women emanated from that theory.

Students of human progress might have predicted at the inception of the American Republic that, should it continue, universal manhood and womanhood suffrage would become inevitable. The official announcement of the causes that led the American patriots into revolution emphasized two maxims as explanatory of all their grievances, namely, "Taxation without representation is tyranny" and "Governments derive their just powers from the consent of the governed." Although in the minds of the Colonists these aphorisms undoubtedly were limited in application to the relation which the Colonies bore to their Mother Country, it was as clear to individual men and women then, as to hundreds of thousands of them a hundred and forty years later, that a nation that proclaimed these principles upon the one hand and denied them upon the other, applied them to men and refused to apply them to women, presented so untenable an inconsistency that sooner or later professions and deeds would have to be squared.

Yet not only was the battle for woman suffrage fought longer in the United States, it was fought harder. It engaged the lifelong energies of a longer list of women, called into action a larger organization in proportion to population, and involved a greater cost in money, personal sacrifice and ingenuity, than the suffrage campaign of any other land. And when, in 1920, the final victory came to the woman suffrage cause in the land of its birth, the rejoicing was sadly tempered by the humiliating knowledge that twenty-six other countries had outdistanced America in bestowing political liberty upon their women. More, American suffragists knew that their victory had, even then, been virtually wrung from hesitant and often resentful political leaders, while the vote had come to the women of many other lands as a spontaneous and liberal concession to the common appeal for justice; and that, too, without serious effort on the women's part.

The delay in America was not due to the retarded growth of the general woman movement, for the rate of progress of that movement had been more rapid in the United States than in any other country, as a brief review will show.

Taking the year 1800 as a fixed point from which to measure progress, the investigator will find the civil and legal status of women practically the same as that of several preceding centuries, although there were signs of a coming revolt, and in North America the personal liberty of women had been much extended under the influence of the freer institutions of the Western Hemisphere. Married women at that date were not permitted in any country except Russia to control their property nor to make a will; to all intents and purposes they did not own property. The Common Law in operation in Great Britain and the United States held husband and wife to be "one, and that one the husband." The legal existence of the wife was so merged in that of her husband that she was said to be "dead in law." Not only did the husband control the wife's property, collect and use her wages, select the food and clothing for herself and children, decide upon the education and religion of their children, but to a very large extent he controlled her freedom of thought, speech and action. The husband possessed the right to will the children, even unborn children, to other guardians. If the wife offended the husband, he possessed the legal right, upheld by public opinion, to punish her, the courts interfering only when the chastisement exceeded the popular idea of appropriate severity. Humane, affectionate husbands treated their wives as loved companions, and there were happy wives and homes, but upon the wives of fickle, ignorant, brutal husbands, always numerous, the oppression of the law fell with crushing force.

Although single women were legally as independent as men, it was contrary to accepted form for them to manage their own business affairs. What women were unaccustomed to do the world believed them incapable of doing, and they had in consequence neither confidence in themselves nor public encouragement to attempt ventures of independence. Very few occupations were open to women and these were monopolized by the poor. It was accounted a family disgrace for women of the middle or upper classes to earn money. The unmarried woman of such classes, dubbed "old maid," forbidden by public opinion to support herself, even were work and wages available, became a dependent in the home of her nearest male relative. Pitied because she had never "had a chance," regarded with contempt as one of the world's derelicts, she was condemned to a life of involuntary service, and the fact that she legally possessed property enough to insure her independence did not greatly alter her status.

In the church, then a far greater power in the making of opinion than now, women with few exceptions were not allowed to preach, sing, pray, testify or vote. During church services women were seated upon one side, and men upon the other in order that "men might commend themselves to God without interruption."

It was "indelicate" for a woman to appear upon a business street without a male escort or to go to a bank to transact business, and any woman seen unattended upon the street after dark was regarded with suspicion. No college in the world admitted women, and there were no high schools for girls. It was the universal belief that Greek and higher mathematics, then the two chief corner stones of the collegiate curriculum, were utterly beyond the capacity of women. Convents and boarding schools wherein girls of wealth were educated taught nothing more than the rudiments of learning, with so-called "accomplishments." The daughters of the poor received no education at all.

The recital of the legal and social disabilities of women at the beginning of the Nineteenth Century is shocking to modern thought, but it conveys only a partial understanding of the timid, self-distrustful, untrained character of the average woman of the day. Taught that it was unwomanly to hold opinions upon serious subjects, that men most admired clinging weakness in women, and that woman's one worthy ambition was to secure men's admiration, it is no wonder that women made little effort to think for themselves.

An English book which appeared at this time, Dr. Gregory's "Legacy to My Daughters," and which was much read on both sides of the Atlantic and recommended by the clergy as expressing the correct attitude for women, said: "If you happen to have any learning, keep it a profound secret, especially from men, who look with a jealous, malignant eye on a woman of great parts and a cultivated understanding." The author counseled girls "not to dance with spirit when gaiety of heart would make them feel eloquent, lest men who beheld them might either suppose that they were not entirely dependent on their protection for their safety or entertain dark suspicions as to their modesty."

The philosophy of Jean Jacques Rousseau, which had largely influenced the thought of France during the closing years of the eighteenth century, was still representative of thought and feeling in the beginning of the nineteenth. With regard to women Rousseau had said: "The education of women should always be relative to that of man. To please Us, to be useful to Us, to make Us love and esteem them, to educate Us when young, to take care of Us when grown up, to advise, to console Us, to render Our lives easy and agreeable; these are the duties of women at all times and what they should be taught from their infancy."

In reply "The Vindication of Women" was wrung from Mary Wollstonecraft. Her eloquent appeal for larger opportunities for women was received in the hostile spirit with which the world receives all new ideas, and Horace Walpole doubtless reflected public opinion when he called her a "hyena in petticoats."

In the Western World there were more robust signs of coming change. Mistress Brent, a relative of Lord Baltimore and the owner of a vast estate in Maryland, not only demanded a voice in the State Assembly, composed of land holders, but defended her contention with so much spirit and logic as to create a lively if unsuccessful debate in that body and all of its constituencies. In March, 1776, Abigail Adams wrote her husband, when he was sitting with the Continental Congress, "I long to hear you have declared an independency, and, by the way, in the new code of laws which I suppose it will be necessary for you to make, I desire you would remember the ladies and be more favorable to them than your ancestors. Do not put such unlimited power into the hands of husbands. Remember all men would be tyrants if they could. If particular care and attention are not paid to the ladies, we are determined to foment a rebellion and will not hold ourselves bound to obey any laws in which we have no voice or representation."

In New Jersey, tax-paying women were granted the vote by the constitution of July 2, 1776, two days before the Declaration of Independence was declared. In 1790 and 1797 legislative enactments confirmed them in the right. The vote was taken from them by the Legislature in 1807, and the explanation was that although qualified women had used the vote quite generally, they had not supported the right candidates in the election. The legislators therefore sought and won a party advantage by the disfranchisement of electors who had voted against them!

It was upon such signs and portents that the curtain of the nineteenth century rose; the century which the prophetic voice of Victor Hugo proclaimed the "Century of Women."

Of special significance were the indications of a definite movement in the United States for education for girls. School Districts taxed their own residents for the maintenance of schools. As it cost more to build school-houses large enough for both boys and girls than for boys alone, the discussion was at once precipitated as to whether "schools for shes" should be maintained, the liberal-minded contending for them and the conservative and ungenerous against them.

Many districts compromised by permitting girls to attend school in summer months when boys vacated seats to work on the farms. In Boston, from 1789 to 1822, girls were allowed to attend the public schools under this rule, although for a portion of the time an exception was made and they were admitted for two hours in the afternoon after the boys had gone home. In 1826, Boston, amid a storm of opposition, opened a high school for girls, but yielded to hostile clamor and closed it in 1828. It had been an "alarming success"; the school had been full and not a girl had quitted it in the eighteen months of its existence, in spite of the persecution of doubters.

The discussion of educational opportunity for women received a fresh impulse when it was proposed to include geography in the instruction of girls. The proper schedule for girls was held to be confined to the three R's, "Readin', 'Ritin' and 'Rithmetic," with some knowledge of a fourth R, Religion; so a battle royal was fought around geography. Girls whose parents approved the innovation were chased from the schoolhouse to their homes by bands of rollicking boys, throwing dirt, stones or snow balls, and shouting in tones of derision—"Geography girl, Geography girl! There goes a Geography girl."

It was not uncommon for a teacher to give private instruction to girls after school hours, and consequent "Dame Schools" for girls, that is, teaching by women in their own homes, sprang up in all parts of the country in response to the demand. In time women began teaching in country districts during summer months when schools were small, one dollar a week and "boarding round" being considered good terms for such teachers. In 1821 the Troy Female Seminary was opened by Mrs. Emma Willard, the first institution in the United States offering "higher education" to women. It became an immediate storm center of abuse. The complainants charged that time was wasted in teaching girls two subjects utterly nonsensical for them to know, physiology and mathematics. A struggle similar to that which brought geography into the list of subjects permissible for a girl's education was next waged around physiology. As late as 1844, when an exceedingly gifted woman, Paulina Wright Davis, attempted to lecture on physiology and used a manikin for illustration, she reported that so "indelicate was the theme considered that women frequently dropped their veils, ran out of the room or even fainted." Mary Gore Nichols, another gifted woman, also gave lectures on anatomy and received similar condemnation for the "indelicacy" of the act. A graduate of Troy Seminary[2] gave evidence in after years of the custom, inaugurated during the controversy, of pasting thick paper over illustrations of the human body in text books on physiology, in order that the modesty of young girls might not be shocked. The graduates of Mrs. Emma Willard's school seem to have felt the responsibility of extending the study of physiology, for they introduced it later into their own schools, yet several reported that visiting mothers on examination day left the room in a body when the examination in physiology was called. Of two clergymen visitors at the Willard school one was as incensed as the other at the "unwarranted attempt to teach girls higher mathematics." But their reasons were different. One contended that as the female mind was incapable of comprehending mathematics, any effort to teach it to girls was opposing nature and God's will. The other declared, as vehemently, that young women might become so enamored of mathematics that they would employ all their time in solving abstruse problems in algebra and geometry, to the exclusion of proper attention to husband and babies.

Thus, popular ideas concerning education for girls slowly evolved from the zero point of no education to the acknowledgment of a girl's right to acquaintance with the four R's to be gained in free public primary schools; from the four R's to the inclusion of geography; from geography to physiology; from physiology to higher mathematics and high schools,—each new step being an outpost around which intolerant and bitter controversy raged.

After 1800 the legal disabilities of women also began to receive attention. In 1809 Connecticut gave married women the right to make a will. From that date legislative changes concerning the civil status of women were frequent. Southern states deserve the honor of a share in the leadership of the advanced legislation. The first of all States to grant the married woman the right of control of her own property was Mississippi. The third State to give married women the right to make a will was Texas (1840); the fourth Alabama (1843); and the first suffrage for women in the United States, after New Jersey, was the school suffrage granted by Kentucky to widows with children in 1838.

Possibly the most permanent factor in giving impulse to the woman movement came with the announced and undisputed discovery by Von Baer, a German scientist, that the protoplasm of the ovule, the reproductive cell of the maternal organism, contributed at least half to the structure of the embryo child. Before that date it had been held that the mother had no essential share in the formation of the child, the comparison being usual that "man was the seed and woman the soil." The proof of "at least" equal physical responsibility of parents opened the question of the extent of the mental and moral responsibility resting upon the mother, and by degrees this reversal of theory concerning fatherhood and motherhood changed the attitude of educated men toward all phases of the woman question.

At about this date Margaret Fuller upset the conventions of the staid City of Boston by sitting down at a table in a public library to read a book.

Meanwhile two great reforms were rapidly pressing forward, propelled by the controversy of earnest, consecrated protagonists on the one hand, and bitter, hostile antagonists on the other—the anti-slavery and anti-liquor movements. Both appealed strongly to the humanitarian sympathies of the better educated women. Whether the effort of women had any appreciable effect upon either movement between 1800 and 1850 may be doubted, but it is certain that these reforms furnished the most impelling motive that led women to come forth from their seclusion to take part in public affairs. They came timidly at first, but with the discovery that the majority of men not only did not want their help but expressed their antagonism in phrases and tones of bitter contempt the spirit of many was stung into resentment. They chafed at the restraint of individual liberty, and the bravest boldly defended the right of any woman to give service to any cause and in any manner she chose. The controversy by degrees inevitably spread to all movements, churches and philanthropic societies.

In 1833, Oberlin College in Ohio was opened, admitting boys and girls, black and white, on equal terms. It was the first college in the world of modern times to admit women, but as the feeling of hostility against Negro rights was even more intense than that against women's rights, the advantage won was lightly regarded by the nation. The Negroes, too, shared the common view concerning women, and when colored students unfitted to enter the college were organized into preparatory classes they rebelled against being taught by Lucy Stone, one of the earliest students. After being persuaded that it would be better to receive education from a woman than not to have it at all, they resigned themselves to destiny and became eventually her loyal supporters, even saving her at one time from the savage threats of a mob.

Two courageous and remarkable women, the Grimke sisters of South Carolina, had freed their slaves in 1828 and gone North. They began speaking publicly in favor of abolition and were mobbed many times. They contended for the rights of women as well as of the slaves. Abby Kelly, "the most persecuted of all the women who labored in the anti-slavery cause," also began speaking at about this time, and these three fearless women blazed a trail, through a fusillade of rotten eggs, brickbats and vile abuse, to an acknowledgment of the right of women to speak on public platforms. Independence Hall in Philadelphia was torn down and set on fire while Angelina Grimke was speaking in it in 1837, and mobs were frequent incidents in the career of the sisters, but they were unafraid. Many men and women were expelled from their churches for having listened to the pleadings of these women for justice to the Negro. The persecutions continued for years and only ceased with the triumphant acknowledgment by the public of the right of women to organize, speak and work for public causes.

As an outcome of these events the National Female Anti-Slavery Society was formed in 1833. It is claimed as not only the first organized women's society but also as the first effort of women to affect a political question. In 1835 at a meeting of the Boston Female Anti-Slavery Society, auxiliary to the National Society, from six to ten thousand men, many being "gentlemen of property and influence," gathered about the hall to demand the adjournment of the meeting composed of fifteen to twenty women. The mayor appeared and ordered them to adjourn, as "he could not guarantee them protection any longer." The society adjourned to the home of its president, and the mob turned upon William Lloyd Garrison, who was in his office on the same floor, carried him out and tore off his coat. The authorities were obliged to place him in jail for safety. What proportion of this intolerance was aimed at the anti-slavery movement and what at the pro-woman movement, the mob itself probably did not know.

Women abolitionists were far from being intimidated by the public attitude. Eight hundred women in New York petitioned Congress for the abolition of slavery in the District of Columbia, a radical act at the time, as it was generally believed that the right to petition was confined to electors. John Quincy Adams, in his famous congressional campaign to establish the right of petition for all, introduced in 1837 several additional anti-slavery petitions from women. The National Female Anti-Slavery Convention met in New

York that same year, the first representative body of women ever convened. Seventy-two delegates were present.

It was in 1837, too, that Catherine Beecher published an Essay on Slavery, with reference to the "Duty of American Females." It was answered by a pastoral letter, issued by the general association of the Congregational Churches of Massachusetts, in which all attempts of women to do public work were bitterly condemned. The letter included the following: "We appreciate the unostentatious prayers and efforts of women in advancing the cause of religion at home and abroad and in leading religious inquirers to the pastor for instructions; but when she assumes the place and tone of man as a public reformer, our care and protection of her seem unnecessary, we put ourselves in self-defense against her. She yields the power which God has given her for protection, and her character becomes unnatural. We say these things not to discourage proper influence against sin, but to secure such reformation as we believe is Scriptural."

In that unveiled resentment that male protection of the female should be found unnecessary, in that threat of self-defense, lies the world-old revelation of man's naive need to appear strong in his own eyes, even if he can do so only by making woman appear weak!

The women doing public work at that time promptly took issue with the letter. Sarah Grimke, in spirited defense of her sex, said: "The business of men and women who are ordained by God to preach the unsearchable riches of Christ to a lost and perishing world is to lead souls to Christ and not to pastors for instruction." John Greenleaf Whittier poured out his indignation, and Maria Weston Chapman her amusement in verse which traveled far. Sarah Grimke threw a bomb into the established views of society when in vigorous English she said: "If sewing societies, the fruits of whose industry are now expended in supporting and educating young men for the ministry, were to withdraw their contributions to these objects and give them where they are needed, to the advancement of their own sex in useful learning, the next generation might furnish sufficient proof that in intelligence and ability to master the whole circle of sciences, woman is not inferior to man, and instead of a sensible woman being regarded as she now is—a lapse of nature—they would be quite as common as sensible men."

The controversy raised the Woman's Rights agitation into general notice and made it a burning question in all abolition societies, splitting some of them wide asunder.

The Men's and Women's Anti-Slavery Societies united in 1839, and a resolution endorsing the work of women in the anti-slavery field was passed, but left an embittered minority still unconvinced. Already many "tracts" written by women were in useful circulation, while the propagandistic effect of the public addresses of the increasing number of women speakers was unquestioned. The next year, it was proposed in the same society to name Abby Kelly on a committee, whereupon the defeated minority of the year before vented its wrath upon all women workers. No question of the value of women's work was raised, the opposition to their participation in the work being based upon the claim that they were disobeying God's will. The women were sustained by a large majority, but two clergymen refused to serve upon the committee with a woman, and others left the Society.

In the same year (1840), the British Anti-Slavery Societies issued an invitation to all "friends of the slave" to join in a World's Anti-Slavery Convention to be held in London in July, and all American Anti-Slavery Societies were especially urged to send delegates. Eight women were among those named.[3] A stormy debate began in the very first session, in which it was vehemently declared that "all order would be at an end" if "promiscuous female representation be allowed" and "God's clear intention violated." The debate will

14

always stand as a landmark showing the world's opinion of the capacities and rights of women at that date. It ended by a vote to bar out the women delegates. William Lloyd Garrison and Nathaniel P. Rogers, arriving after the convention had taken action, refused to take their places as delegates and sat behind the bar with the rejected women.

Lucretia Mott, delegate, and Elizabeth Cady Stanton, the wife of a delegate, with indignation thoroughly aroused by this experience, agreed to call a convention upon their return to the United States, to be devoted exclusively to the Rights of Women. Thus the unwarranted rejection of properly accredited delegates by the World's Anti-Slavery Convention, solely because they were women, gave impulse to the organized demand of women the world around for justice in every sphere of action.

Meanwhile women in larger numbers and bolder fashion kept on engaging in public work, and in unexpected fields individual women kept on startling the world by achievements generally believed impossible. Men of vision began to perceive that a powerful movement was under way. But few ventured at that date to predict either the direction it would take or its ultimate aim.

CHAPTER 2

The Averted Triumph

(1848–1860)

It was not until 1848 that the compact, made in 1840 by Lucretia Mott and Elizabeth Cady Stanton, to call a woman's rights convention was carried out. Mrs. Mott was occupied with religious and reform obligations, Mrs. Stanton with a family of young children. The project was revived while Mrs. Mott was visiting her sister, Martha C. Wright, in Seneca Falls, New York, where Mrs. Stanton also had become a resident. Action followed so shortly upon the decision to call a convention that the news had not spread through the neighborhood when an astonished public read a notice in the town paper on July 14 that a Woman's Rights Convention would be held in the Wesleyan Chapel on the 19th and 20th of the month. The program of the first day as announced was to be exclusively for women, and of the second day for the general public, when "Lucretia Mott and others" would speak. The call was unsigned.

The five days intervening were busy ones for the four sponsors, Mrs. Lucretia Mott, Mrs. Elizabeth Cady Stanton, Mrs. Ann McClintock and Mrs. Martha C. Wright. Having called the convention, they set themselves at work to compose a program and policy for it. In the McClintock parlor, around a small table now in the Smithsonian Institution, they discussed women's wrongs and how to lay them before the world in orderly fashion, until finally they hit upon the happy idea of framing their grievances against the nation in imitation of the Declaration of Independence. Finding as many grievances against the government of men as the Colonists had against the government of King George, they promptly drew up the Declaration of Women's Rights. Fortified by this document and four speeches, for each of the four had prepared one, they were on hand at the appointed hour.

Although the hurried and timid call had not been heard far away, the small Chapel was filled. At first the women were disconcerted to find that men had not taken their exclusion seriously and were present in considerable numbers, but when they reflected that no woman had ever presided over a convention they welcomed the men cordially and elected one of them, James Mott, chairman. The Declaration was adopted. It named as the first of the grievances, "the denial of the elective franchise," and it was signed by one hundred men and women. So inadequate did the two days prove for the discussion of a subject so extensive that the convention adjourned to meet in Rochester two weeks later. There the Declaration was again adopted and signed by large numbers of influential men and women.

These two conventions had in no sense been national in scope but newspapers throughout the country regarded them as an innovation worthy of comment and full press accounts were carried far and wide. Preceding events had prepared the country for controversy centered upon the subject of woman's rights apart from the anti-slavery and temperance causes, and a widespread discussion for and against the long list of liberties claimed was inaugurated by the two conventions.

Never in all history did so small a beginning produce so great an effect in so short a time.

17

Emily P. Collins immediately formed a local suffrage society at South Bristol, New York, the first in the world, and the baby club, wasting no time, sent a woman suffrage petition to the New York Legislature in January, 1849, with sixty-two signatures. Encouraged by the knowledge that other women were rising, organized groups sprang into being in all parts of the country with no other incentive than the ripeness of the time, and no other connection with the original movers than the announcements of the press.

Meantime year by year, and State by State, the legal disabilities of women had been yielding to attention. Between 1844 and 1848 the Legislatures of Maine, Mississippi, New York and Pennsylvania, in the order named, granted property rights to women. The right to make a will had been granted in some States.

In the educational realm the graduation of Dr. Elizabeth Blackwell from the Geneva Medical College made a tremendous sign-post for the year 1848. Public hostility to her course may be measured by the fact that the women at her boarding house refused to speak to her during her three years of study; on the streets they drew aside their skirts if they chanced to meet her, lest they be contaminated by contact. The controversy created by the events of the year was excited and widespread. Clergymen were alarmed and very generally denounced the "masculine, strong-minded women" who were attempting to drive men from their God-ordained sphere. The press took sides and contributed, as usual, both understanding and confusion to the discussion.

From that date, some new wonder was continually emanating from the woman's camp to give fresh impulse and direction to the agitation. Three young women had been graduated from Oberlin in 1841, and each year brought the announcement of more graduates. Women were lecturing in all parts of the country on slavery, temperance, physiology, and woman's rights, and were drawing and edifying large audiences. The most reckless escape from traditional discipline occurred in 1846, when, the license law having been repealed in New York, women alone or in groups entered saloons, "breaking windows, glasses, bottles, and emptying demijohns and barrels into the streets. Coming like whirlwinds of vengeance, drunkards and rumsellers stood paralyzed before them."[4] These episodes continued spasmodically for some years. A lively total abstinence movement conducted by men had been in progress for fifty years and out of it had grown the demand for various reforms, including legalized prohibition. Women circulated and presented petitions to town councils and the Legislatures, asking revision of liquor laws. What was called "the wave of temperance excitement" passed over the country in 1852-1855, beginning in Maine, which passed a prohibition law.

In 1840, the Sons of Temperance were organized and the Daughters of Temperance quickly followed. Argument on woman's place in human society was passing from the anti-slavery to the temperance societies. The Sons of Temperance, meeting at Albany in 1852, gallantly admitted delegates from the Daughters of Temperance, but when one of them, Susan B. Anthony, arose to speak to a motion, the chairman informed her that "the sisters were not invited there to speak but to listen and learn," a fact which led the women to withdraw and form the Woman's State Temperance Society, with Elizabeth Cady Stanton as president, and Susan B. Anthony as secretary. It held important meetings during the next two years and was addressed by many distinguished men and women. The example set by New York was followed in other states and several similar societies came into existence.

Later in the same year, a New York State Temperance Convention was held in Syracuse. Susan B. Anthony and Amelia Bloomer, accredited delegates from the Woman's State Temperance Society, were refused admission, after a debate described as "a perfect pandemonium." The women had an unintentional revenge; a liberal clergyman publicly offered his church for a meeting and announced that the two rejected delegates would speak there; whereupon the convention was deserted and the church was packed.

In 1853 "the friends of temperance" met in New York at the Brick Church to arrange for a World's Temperance Convention. Women delegates were present and were accepted by a vote. A motion was made that Susan B. Anthony should be added to the business committee, whereupon a discussion arose upon the right of women to such posts. The discussion was marked by the usual vituperation and insult and ended by the appointment of a committee to decide the matter. The committee recommended that the women be excluded from the convention and the report was adopted. Thomas Wentworth Higginson at once requested all persons who wished to call a *whole* World's Temperance Convention to meet elsewhere. The ten women delegates and a number of liberal-minded men left the room. After their departure a further discussion followed, condemning all public action of women, one reverend gentleman expressing pleasure at being "now rid of the scum of the convention."

It therefore happened that there were two World's Temperance Conventions held in New York in September, one arranged and attended by men and women and the other held under the auspices of the Brick Church meeting. Antoinette Brown was sent by two societies to the last named convention. The credential committee omitted her name from the list of delegates, whereupon it was moved that she should be admitted. A furious discussion followed, in which every phase of the "Woman's Rights movement" was given attention. The discussion covered the greater part of two days, ending in a vote upon the question. By a small majority Miss Brown was admitted. It was then moved and carried by the same majority that she be given ten minutes in which to address the convention. She came to the platform, cheered by a "Take courage!" from Wendell Phillips, and a

"God bless you!" from Rev. William Henry Channing. The minority, however, were not to be overcome so easily. She was greeted with sneers, hisses, shouting and stamping. The confusion, appropriate only to a mob, continued for three hours, at which time the convention adjourned. During this period the courageous young woman stood firm and unshaken, although the fingers of men from all over the house were pointing at her and shouts of "Shame on the woman!" assailed her continually.

When asked why she went to the convention, she replied: "I asked no favor as a woman or in behalf of women; no favor as a woman advocating temperance; no recognition of the cause of woman above the cause of humanity; the endorsement of no issue and of no measure; but I claimed, in the name of the world, the rights of a delegate in a world's convention." A clergyman (nearly all the delegates were clergymen) when asked why the convention acted as it did, replied that "it was the principle of the thing." Practically the whole time of this World's Convention was expended in rude and quarrelsome discussion over the question of permitting women to speak and work for temperance.

An Ohio Woman's Temperance Convention was called at Dayton the same year. The Sons of Temperance permitted the use of their hall, "provided no men were admitted to their meeting." No sooner had the first session opened than "A column of well-dressed ladies, very fashionable and precise, marched in two and two and spread themselves in a half circle in front of the platform, requesting to be heard." Permission being granted they informed the delegates that they had come to read a remonstrance against the unseemly and unchristian position assumed by women who called conventions, "taking places on platforms and seeking notoriety by making yourselves conspicuous before men." They condemned the disgraceful conduct of Antoinette Brown at the New York convention and, having presented their views, turned and walked out.

The convention went right on.

The right of women to work for temperance was now a dominating question of the temperance movement, as a decade before it had been a mooted question of the abolition movement. The conflict over women's rights, however, was by no means confined to these two great reforms. The same year Susan B. Anthony attended the New York Teacher's Convention in Rochester. Although a member on equal footing with others, she caused a sensation by rising to speak to the question, "Why the profession of teacher was not as much respected as that of minister, lawyer or doctor," which had been discussed for some hours. It had been the custom in these conventions for men to discuss all motions and to vote upon them, although women composed a large portion of the membership. "At length President Davis of West Point, in full dress, buff vest, blue coat, gilt buttons, stepped to the front and said in tremulous mocking tone 'What will the lady have?'—'I wish, Sir, to speak to the question under discussion,' Miss Anthony replied. The Professor, still more perplexed, said, 'What is the pleasure of the convention?' A gentleman moved that she should be heard, another seconded the motion, whereupon a discussion pro and con followed, lasting fully half an hour, when a vote of the men only was taken and permission granted by a small majority."[5] Miss Anthony arose and said: "Do you not see, gentlemen, that so long as society says a woman is incompetent to be a lawyer, minister, or doctor, but has ample ability to be a teacher, that every man of you who chooses this profession tacitly acknowledges that he has no more brains than a woman?" For this speech she was bitterly denounced by nearly all the men and women present, but the next morning's Rochester *Democrat* said: "Whatever the schoolmasters may think of Miss Anthony, it is evident that she hit the nail on the head."

While much discussion within other organizations was centering about Woman's Rights, the movement was rapidly solidifying into an organization of its own. The first National Woman's Rights Convention was held in Worcester, Massachusetts, October, 1850. Unlike that of 1848, which was not heralded as national, it was carefully arranged and well advertised. The call was signed by eighty-nine prominent men and women. Eleven States were represented at the convention, which provided for another the following year. The importance of the persons connected with it, and the high tone of all its deliberations secured widespread comment. A report of the convention reaching England, Mrs. Taylor (afterwards Mrs. John Stuart Mill) sent an account to the Westminster *Review*, from which dates the organized woman suffrage movement in England.

From 1850 to 1860, a national suffrage convention was held in the United States each year, with one exception.[6] State conventions, attended by some of the leading spirits, were held in Ohio, Indiana, Pennsylvania, New York, Massachusetts, out of which grew State organizations with local auxiliaries. Indiana boasts the first State organization.

The New York convention of 1853 was afterwards called the Mob Convention. The week had begun with an anti-slavery meeting, opened on Sunday morning when Antoinette Brown addressed five thousand people, and the fact that she had done so "called out the denunciations of the religious press." During the week many meetings devoted to reforms were held, public condemnation growing in hostility until it broke in rampant violence upon the suffrage issue, which was last of the series. The mob was present at every session and met each motion and each speaker with hisses, yells and stamping of feet. The suffragists themselves said that "owing to the turmoil we have no fair report of the proceedings" and even "the representatives of the press could not catch what was said."

The contrasting comment on the convention was well presented by the *Tribune* and the *Herald*. Said the *Tribune* (Horace Greeley),

September 7, 1853: "It was never so transparent that a hiss or a blackguard yell was the only answer that the case admitted of, and when Lucy Stone closed the discussion with some pungent, yet pathetic remarks on the sort of opposition that had been manifest, it was evident that if any of the rowdies had had an ant hole in the bottom of his boot he would inevitably have sunk through it and disappeared forever." Said the *Herald* (James Gordon Bennett) September 7, 1853: "The assemblage of rampant women which convened at the Tabernacle yesterday was an interesting phase in the comic history of the Nineteenth Century . . . a gathering of unsexed women, unsexed in mind, all of them publicly propounding the doctrine that they should be allowed to step out of their appropriate sphere to the neglect of those duties which both human and divine law have assigned to them. Is the world to be depopulated?" There was one immediate redeeming feature of the occasion for, at twenty-five cents per admission, the mob had not only paid the entire expenses of the convention, but it had left a surplus in the treasury with which to continue suffrage work.[7]

The experiences of that week had not intimidated the women but had, instead, stirred their minds to clearer conviction and united their hands to more constructive action. Mobs seem a divine instrument for the furtherance of good causes. No mob ever destroyed an idea, but many a mob has given one a fresh impulse, and this one sent every delegate home with her soul afire.

Lucy Stone, silver-voiced, gentle to look upon but with the courage of a lioness, had graduated from Oberlin in 1847 and started forth single-handed and alone to conquer the world for Woman's Rights. She now went through Massachusetts from town to town engaging the town hall, nailing up her own advertising and conducting her own meetings. Her auditors came "to scorn and went away to praise." The press gave her such titles as "she hyena"; the clergy thundered at her; the average man and woman regarded her as a freak; but the liberal-minded listened and endorsed. In time she formed committees to carry the work forward. From Massachusetts as a center, lecturing and organizing spread all over New England, and in 1854 a New England convention was held in Boston, and became an annual feature of the May anniversaries for sixty years thereafter.

In the period from August, 1854 to 1855, Miss Anthony had held meetings in fifty-four of the sixty-one counties of New York, and conventions at Saratoga, then a favorite summer resort of the leisurely well-to-do, had already become an established and exceedingly popular feature. In 1854, the first convention designed to influence suffrage legislative action was held in Albany, and petitions of ten thousand names asking for woman suffrage were presented from two counties alone, Onondaga and Warren. Mrs. Stanton addressed the Legislature with so masterly a speech that the legislators pronounced it unanswerable. In 1856, Legislative Committees in Ohio and Wisconsin reported favorably "right to suffrage" bills, recommending that they "do pass," and legislators in many other States publicly pronounced their conversion.

Lecture courses were organized in many States by these women, in which Slavery, Temperance and Woman's Rights were presented, the speakers endorsing all three. Theodore Parker, William Lloyd Garrison, Wendell Phillips, George William Curtis, Ralph Waldo Emerson, Henry Ward Beecher, were among those who spoke.

After one convention, Grace Greenwood, a distinguished writer, said: "Lucretia Mott may be said to be the soul of this movement, and Mrs. Stanton the mind, the swift, keen intelligence. Miss Anthony alert, aggressive and indefatigable, is its nervous energy, its propulsive force." All three were at work, lecturing, inspiring, organizing, planning, raising money. There were many others—Paulina Wright Davis, Ernestine L. Rose, Clarinda I. Nichols, Lucy Stone, Frances D. Gage, Hannah Tracy Cutler,—all able advocates of the cause. On the Anti-Slavery and the Temperance platforms still other women were speaking, and giving sledge-hammer blows at the old prejudices. There were few towns of consequence which were not reached by one or more of these resolute souls in the North and West. One by one the States were fast amending the "woman laws." Wisconsin, California, Minnesota, Oregon and Kansas, coming into statehood during this period, began with liberal codes of law for women and their example proved so infectious that no new State thereafter went back to the old legal sources for its guidance concerning women.

At the tenth annual national suffrage convention held in New York, May, 1860, Miss Anthony, chairman of the Finance Committee, made an elaborate report and announced that "the press has changed its tone. Instead of ridicule we now have grave debate." She reported the many legal changes already made, the aroused and sympathetic public opinion, and predicted that New York would "enfranchise its women when it revises its constitution six years hence." Already, said she, the State had been thoroughly canvassed and "every county visited by lecturers, and tracts and petitions by the hundreds of thousands have been sent to the Legislature asking for the right to vote, the right to her person, her wages, her children. During the past year we have had six women lecturing in New York for several months each. Conventions have been held in forty counties and one or more lectures delivered in one hundred and fifty towns and villages."

Many bills for women's rights had by now been passed by State Legislatures, including women's right to their earnings, their property and their children. Men of prominence in large numbers had publicly espoused the cause, and hope for continued triumph of the movement was exuberant.

No cause ever made such rapid strides as that of Woman's Rights from 1850 to 1860. Women had proved their value as reform propagandists, and apparently all the leaders of the abolition and temperance movements were at length united in recognizing that fact, and all espoused their cause. "The more reflection I give, the more my mind becomes convinced that in a Republican Government, we have no right to deny to woman the privileges she claims," wrote a member of the New York Legislature, and his views were reported by suffrage workers as becoming common. Anti-Slavery and Anti-Liquor had fought their way to the center of the nation's thought, and Woman's Rights had sprung from the two "full armed" and exceeded both in legislative concessions.

Jubilant with success, despite the hard work and unhappy experiences of the early days, suffragists pushed on expectantly. The goal was in sight. The race was all but run. Few of this generation, even among suffragists, realize how close to victory were the women of that earlier suffrage crisis. Through disrepute and abuse and mob violence, they had brought the woman suffrage question out upon a new plane. The rotten eggs, the jeers, the hisses and vile epithets of the beginning were bygones. Able and widely influential men had come to the support of the suffrage cause. Suffrage meetings wherever held were calling forth enthusiastic crowds and favorable reports by the press, with editorials pro and con. The whole world had grown friendly and tolerant. In political interest woman suffrage was ranking second only to the question of slavery. Both were fairly up to the doors of the national congress. Had the nation moved forward in the mood of those times, women assuredly would have been enfranchised soon, consistently with the Declaration of Independence, the Constitution, and the liberal progressive spirit which inspired the period.

Alas, before the date for the next annual suffrage convention the nation was plunged into the tragic depths of Civil War over the slavery issue; and thereafter woman suffrage was so hopelessly enmeshed in the politics of the Negro question as to be inextricable for long years to come.

CHAPTER 3

That Adjective Male

(1866)

Before the Civil War, there was no movement in the United States to secure Negro suffrage. Of the "thirty-seven States which composed the Union at the time of the ratification of the Fifteenth Amendment, all save six used the word 'white' as descriptive of the elector. Five of the six were in New England, and the sixth was Kansas."[8]

The war aftermath presented two imperative and difficult problems which demanded immediate attention; one, the re-instatement of the seceding States in the Union, the other, the determination of the status of the Negro. Both led inevitably to the discussion of questions involved in the right to vote. Representation in Congress had been apportioned to the Southern States by the federal constitution (Article I, Section 2) according to the number of free persons, plus three-fifths of all other persons, meaning slaves. It was clear that no such apportionment could continue. Slaves *within the seceding States* had been freed by the Emancipation Proclamation issued by President Lincoln as a military emergency, January 1, 1863. Some months before the close of the war, the Thirteenth Amendment to the federal constitution, forever abolishing slavery throughout the entire Union, was submitted to the several Legislatures and was proclaimed as ratified, December 18, 1865, some months after the close of the war.[9]

The Congress then asked itself what is now the status of the Negro, and answered its own question in lengthy debate, the crux of which was that "He is no longer a chattel, but although a freeman, he is neither alien nor citizen." The Republican party, "the party that had won the war and freed the slaves," felt keenly that the Negro was a charge upon it. Many proposals were offered in that Congress for the settlement of these two momentous problems, each involving almost endless subsidiary controversies. Each proposal was defended and opposed by earnest, sincere groups, and into every discussion the question, "Shall the Negro be enfranchised," injected itself. At no time since the convention which drafted the Declaration of Independence had political debate reached so high a level. The rights of man had again come into the foreground of the nation's chief consideration. The principles of human rights were quoted, analyzed and applied. Rights, freedom, liberty, and, most frequently of all, the "consent of the governed," were the expressions which marked the trend of the debate.

The Northern victors were in a forgiving and magnanimous mood. The nation's orators painted fascinating pictures of a restored and contented nation, with slavery abolished, with full and complete justice given all races, classes, and both sexes, and with a patriotic unity of service for the common welfare. To be sure, the details were blurred or wanting, but the picture was heartening and inspiring. Despite the oppressively high cost of living, the looming burden of taxes and the many homes of mourning, a comforting belief was widespread that great and amazing good had come to the nation out of the terrible suffering and sacrifices of the war. A very definite impulse to extend to all a far greater need of justice than the world had yet dreamed possible seized the people. They were inspired to this end by the great men upon whose leadership the country had learned to rely with confidence. Negroes were justified in trusting for protection to the party that had freed them, nor was it to be altogether a concession of the strong to the weak, for during the war a quarter of a million black men had been enlisted and trained for the Union Army. Women were equally justified in the hope that the lofty expressions of sentiment and frank admissions of gratitude for their war sacrifices would be written into law. They too had not only served in the hour of danger but their services had frequently been decisive in character. As in all modern war, women had quietly taken the places of men in stores, shops, factories and fields, and kept the nation's needs supplied by their unremitting, although often unskilled toil. Dr. Elizabeth Blackwell, returning to the United States from England where she had engaged in practice, had organized the scattered efforts of women into a nationwide constructive force. This had been accomplished in June, 1861, under the name of *The Sanitary Commission,* which was placed under Government authority. Scraping lint, making bandages, packing boxes and gathering materials to go to the front, had absorbed the time of thousands of women. The organization had been supported entirely by women's work and during the war had raised ninety-two millions of dollars to aid in the care of the sick and wounded of the army. It was the forerunner of the Red Cross, and its work was so much more thoroughly done than anything before attempted by women as to call forth expressions of astonishment from foreign observers.

While the Sanitary Commission had been supporting the Union, the women of the South had been as devotedly and ably supporting their side of the nation's controversy. Nurses in the army hospitals—North and South—knew no respite and gave all the possibilities of their strength to temper the suffering of the wounded men.

Nor had the war work of women been confined to these usual feminine services. During the early years of the war a constant demand had been made by the abolitionists for the emancipation of the slaves. The replies of President Lincoln indicating that the country had given no mandate for such an act, Mrs. Elizabeth Cady Stanton and Susan B. Anthony, the woman suffrage leaders, organized a National Loyal League and set themselves the task of supplying that mandate. When Senator Charles Sumner presented the first instalment, one hundred thousand signatures, he said: "I offer a petition now lying on the desk before me. It is too bulky for me to take up. I need not add that it is too bulky for any of the pages of this body to carry." The petition eventually presented to Congress numbered three hundred thousand signers and was acknowledged by President Lincoln and members of Congress as furnishing an authoritative public demand for the Emancipation Proclamation.

The Civil War developed military heroines, too, though the greatest of them died unacknowledged by her nation. Anna Ella Carroll proposed, urged and finally persuaded the military authorities to substitute the Tennessee River for the Mississippi as the base of operation and this strategy was generally admitted as having more speedily won the war. Colonel Scott, Assistant Secretary of War, pressed upon Judge Evans, a friend of Miss Carroll, the necessity of keeping the origin of the Tennessee campaign a secret while the struggle lasted. Men of high positions in military affairs of the government, including President Lincoln, also made it clear to Miss Carroll that it would be dangerous to success to make known the fact that the Government was proceeding under the advice of a civilian and especially a woman civilian." The war over, the story leaked out, but before a demand was made for congressional recognition of her service, death had claimed those who knew it best.

Women had also participated in the civic and political life of the nation in ways hitherto unknown. Women for the first time were appointed, during the war, to positions in federal departments of government and filled them with credit. The Freedman's Bureau upon which Congress first tried to build the reconstruction measures was the idea of Mrs. Josephine Griffing. In the second Lincoln election there was grave anxiety on the part of Republicans as to the outcome, since loyal voters were at the front. Then Anna Dickinson entered the campaign, young, eloquent and soul-stirring, speaking "as if her lips had been touched with a live coal from the altars of Heaven." Numerous Republican leaders gave her frank credit for having turned some of the doubtful States.

And the climax of the men's gratitude?

In the midst of this early after-war period, so pregnant with hope for the future, wherein speeches, interviews and press articles were common and fulsome in praise of the unexpected but admittedly decisive help that women had given to the Civil War, Susan B. Anthony was visiting her brother in Leavenworth, Kansas. One day, while quietly perusing the morning paper, she received a shock. She read that a proposal had been made to introduce the word "male" into a forthcoming amendment to the federal constitution. The Thirteenth Amendment was not yet ratified. Another amendment was predicted. What form it might take no one knew, yet she was quick to see that if this phrasing went into it, it would stamp women as a definitely disfranchised class throughout the land and degrade them to a political status inferior to the one they then occupied. Still wearied from the constant toil and anxiety of war work, she waited to learn no more but hastened at once to her home in Rochester, New York, stopping at several points on the way to confer with men and women who before the war had been sincere champions of the cause of woman suffrage. Nowhere did she find encouragement that the earlier zeal for women's rights could be revived, but her intrepid soul was undaunted. She arrived at her home September 23, 1865, and the next morning began a campaign that was not to end until a proclamation announced the ratification of a woman suffrage federal amendment, fifty-five years later.

She visited every town where before the war there had been an influential group who stood for women's rights, held meetings, aroused old friends and inspired new ones into activity, secured favorable press comment and everywhere started the circulation of petitions to Congress. When Congress convened on December 4, petitions were already arriving, protesting against the introduction into the constitution of the word "male." Few Senators or Representatives escaped a bombardment of letters and petitions urging that the nation should take no such backward step as to write the word *male* into the constitution.

Throughout the winter the congressional debate in Washington continued, often much jumbled and wandering far afield, but with the Fourteenth Amendment very slowly and very definitely emerging from the chaos of thought as the final congressional deduction.

Miss Anthony without respite traveled, planned and aroused, Mrs. Stanton wrote and inspired, and the women at home sought signers to the petitions, which poured into the Congress incessantly. Groups of women, watching and working, followed the debate from every great center of population, and higher and higher rose the justifiable expectation that the noble expressions of faith in the just application of sacred American principles made by Congressmen, party officials and leaders of popular thought were to be written into law. The climax of hope was reached when Senator Charles Sumner, long a tried and supposedly true friend of the woman's cause, delivered a speech which literally "rang around the world." "Equal Rights for All" was the theme, and every possible plea for the ballot was reviewed, unanswerably, eloquently and passionately. Indeed in after years he replied to an appeal for a message on woman suffrage as follows: "Take that address," said he, "substitute sex for color and you have the best speech I could make on your platform."

The great speech did not definitely mention women but no word excluded them, and those who believed he meant *all* when he said so, found in it nothing to shake their faith.

A few days later, while the noble and stirring appeal of this address was still ringing in their ears, each watching group of women was chilled to the soul with the apprehension of coming disaster. Senator Sumner, in presenting a petition for suffrage for women constituents led by Lydia Maria Child, one of the most gifted and cultured women in the land, apologized for it as "untimely and injudicious." That this advocate of "Equal Rights for All," and longtime defender of "woman's rights" would repudiate the women's claims at the first opportunity to translate theory into reality was an outcome no woman had suspected. Did his defection signify apostasy of other friends, the women asked each other in alarm, and worked the harder to avert that possibility.

In May, 1866, the first Woman's Rights Convention since that of May, 1860, was held in New York. Suffrage forces had been reorganized, and new recruits had taken the places of defections. At the opening of the convention, resolutions were adopted calculated to fix the purpose of the convention, which was to plead with Congress to consider suffrage for women as a question of immediate importance, and if nothing more could be achieved to protest against putting the word male in the constitution as defining electors. Twice resolutions were passed and delivered to Congress, fortifying the appeals that were being sent in by petition. An address to Congress prepared by Miss Anthony was also read, adopted and later laid upon the desk of every Senator and Representative. In part, Miss Anthony said:

"Men and parties must pass away, but justice is eternal; and they only who work in harmony with its laws are immortal. All who have carefully noted the proceedings of this congress, and contrasted your speeches with those made under the old régime of slavery, must have seen the added power and eloquence that greater freedom gives. But still you propose no action on your grand ideas. Your joint resolutions, your reconstruction reports do not reflect your highest thought. The constitution in basing representation on 'respective numbers' covers a broader ground than any you have yet proposed, but the only tenable ground of representation is universal suffrage, as it is only through universal suffrage that the principle of 'Equal Rights to All' can be realized. With you we have just passed through the agony of death, the resurrection and triumph of another revolution, doing all in our power to mitigate its horrors and gild its glories. And now think you, we have no souls to fire, no brains to weigh your arguments; that after education such as this, we can stand silent witnesses while you sell our birthright of liberty? . . . Our demand must ever be: 'No compromise of human rights. No admission in the constitution of inequality of rights, or disfranchisement on account of color or sex.'"

Three conspicuous figures upon the program at this convention were Theodore Tilton, Henry Ward Beecher and Wendell Phillips. There were no men who exercised a more compelling political leadership than they at that moment. No voices in the land were so eloquent as those of Beecher and Phillips, and their influence was enormous, with the people, with Congress and the Republican party. In the light of what happened afterwards, their speeches were fraught with historic significance. Said Henry Ward Beecher:

"I can scarcely express my sense of the leap the public mind and the public moral sense have taken within this time. The barrier is out of the way (slavery abolished). That which made the American mind untrue logically to itself is smitten down by the hand of God; and there is just at this time an immense tendency in the public mind to carry out all principles to their legitimate conclusions, go where they will. There never was a time when men were so practical, and so ready to learn. I am not a farmer, but I know that the spring comes but once a year. When the furrow is open is the time to put in your seed if you would gather a harvest in its season. Now, when the red-hot plowshare of war has opened a furrow in this nation, is the time to put in the seed. If any man says to me 'Why will you agitate the woman question, when it is the hour for the black man?' I answer, it is the hour for every man, black or white. When the public mind is open, if you have anything to say, say it. If you have any radical principles to urge, any organizing wisdom to make known, don't wait until quiet times come. Don't wait until the public mind shuts up altogether. Progress goes by periods, by jumps and spurts. We are in the favored hour. I, therefore, say whatever truth is to be known for the next fifty years in this nation let it be spoken now— . . . I therefore advocate no sectional rights, no class rights, no sex rights, but the most universal form of right for all that live and breathe on the continent. . . . I propose that you take expediency out of the way, and that you put a principle that is more enduring than expediency in the place of it—manhood and womanhood suffrage for all. You may just as well meet it now as at any other time. You never will have so favorable an occasion, so sympathetic a heart, never a public reason so willing to be convinced, as today."

So far, splendid!

But the speech of Wendell Phillips sounded alarm anew for the women. His had been the staunchest, most uncompromising soul among the many great men friends of women's rights. Now he pleaded with the same culture and eloquence for ultimate justice that always characterized his addresses, but he seemed to put the date afar off, subtly and skillfully skirting around the practical questions of immediate policies.

Interviews with Congressmen, begging them to heed the petitions which were pouring in, followed the convention. The work did not cease until June 16, 1866, when Congress submitted the Fourteenth Amendment. It was an omnibus and a compromise amendment covering all the mooted points and contained the word male three times.[10] Nationwide protest was expressed by press and platform. Said the *Springfield Republican:* "No one can deny that it was a mean thing to put the word male into the Fourteenth Amendment, it was an implied denial of suffrage to women."

Thaddeus Stevens, author of the amendment and majority leader of the House, had based representation upon the number of legal voters in the original draft,[11] but conservatives made such vigorous protest that he was forced to introduce the word male. These protests were especially vigorous from California, Oregon and Nevada, where the possibility of Chinese preponderance was feared. Charles Sumner afterwards confessed that he had covered nineteen pages of foolscap in his effort to formulate the amendment so as to omit the word male.

The truth was that the congressional mind was much disturbed by the political situation and the popular mind was much divided in opinion. The biennial congressional election was approaching and the Republican party could not face it with calmness. The steadying influence of President Lincoln had been removed by his assassination in April, and Vice-President Andrew Johnson, a pro-war Democrat, had taken his place. The President and the Congress held incompatible theories of reconstruction. A consequent feeling of rancor had arisen which made the next election an appeal to the voters to decide between the President and Congress. A genuine fear lest President Johnson should make connections with Democrats, North and South, and thus produce a party strong enough to overthrow the Republicans was entertained by many. The reception of the Fourteenth Amendment was uncertain and the suffrage phase of reconstruction was the particular point where moral courage yielded to political timidity. Most congressional abolitionists were firm in their conviction that the Negro freemen would not be able to protect themselves against their former masters unless they were equipped with the vote. Their efforts to convert their fellow members were making progress, much stimulated by continual rumors of the mistreatment of the Negroes in the South.

But Nevada, received into statehood (1864) after the ratification of the Thirteenth Amendment, had audaciously specified a denial of the vote to Negroes in her constitution. In the autumn of 1865 Negro suffrage had been submitted to popular vote in Connecticut, Wisconsin, Minnesota, the Territory of Colorado, and the District of Columbia and had been defeated in all of them, although the Republicans were in power in them all. Urgent pleas were hurriedly issued by national leaders of the Republican party to those in control of State party organizations to start activities which would hasten the removal of this handicap to national action.

State party leaders returned excuses for delay in taking further referenda upon the ground that public sentiment was opposed to the entire question. Leaders in the Congress began to sense a baffling struggle ahead. The combination of this hesitancy on the part of the North to enfranchise the Negro, the vexatious conflict between the President and the majority in Congress, the convincing proof that freedom for the Negro was not an accomplished fact in the South, tended to increase timidity and conservatism. Expediency was being rapidly substituted for principle. Although abolitionists were urging Negro suffrage, and although several amendments of the Fourteenth Amendment had been proposed to this effect, no endorsement of Negro suffrage had yet passed Congress.

Every argument which could be made for Negro suffrage applied to women. There was no escaping that fact. The Negro was making little demand for the vote. The women were making an unprecedented one. How to get the Negro in and keep the women out constituted an ever present conundrum.

The reason for the growing sordidness of attitude was twofold. The politician held fast to the idea that if the surrendered States were to be retained in obedient and humble mood, the Negro with his certain tendency to vote in conjunction with northern ideas must be enfranchised; the average abolitionist, that the Negroes must have the vote to protect themselves from their late masters, and both politician and reformer united in the conviction that if Negro suffrage was ever to come, the North must endorse the act which extended it. Yet the North not only showed no desire to take this step but anti-slavery men were not entirely united as to the wisdom of such demand. Mr. Garrison himself, though foremost for the abolition of slavery, was not quite ready to join this advanced movement.[12]

The Fourteenth Amendment merely presented an option to the South to enfranchise the Negro or subtract the colored man from the basis of representation; it did not confer the vote upon the Negro, yet it threatened to punish States if they allowed him to remain unenfranchised. In after years James G. Blaine wrote: "Under the strain and anxiety of finding the way to carry the next election and to hold the South in line, the outspoken moral courage, which a few months before had exalted the nation, withered and left the nation wondering, doubting and depressed."

The Congress adjourned and entered the campaign of 1866 with confused misgiving.

In the common sacrifices made necessary by war the people of all nations are united by sympathetic ties rarely existent at other times. The Civil War was no exception to the rule and men had sincerely felt and honestly expressed their gratitude to women for the part they had performed, but as the victory receded further and further into the past, and vexatious problems continually injected themselves in ceaseless procession for solution, the gratitude faded, the services themselves were forgotten. In the next mood, the question of the extension of suffrage to either Negroes or women made the nerves of politicians tingle and filled them with exasperation.

CHAPTER 4

The Negro's Hour

The elections of 1866 resulted in an overwhelming victory for the Republicans. The two-thirds vote of both Houses needed to over-ride any veto of the President had been returned to Congress, and the Northern Legislatures had sufficient majorities to insure the ratification of the Fourteenth Amendment. There still remained the rasping inconsistency which had put the North in the position of thrusting Negro suffrage on the South while it had taken no action on Negro suffrage itself, but the majority in Congress had been rendered bolder by its size and the emphatic expression of public confidence. Moreover, it had been further aroused by the disturbing reports of Negro persecution in the South. So it determined upon radical action. A bill was promptly introduced to confer suffrage upon the Negro men of the District of Columbia, with the sole qualification of one year's residence. Thereupon Senator Cowan of Pennsylvania, an extreme conservative and a Democrat, moved to strike out the word "male" from the bill, thus making the suffrage apply equally to women and Negroes.

It took three entire days of debate to dispose of Senator Cowan. He had invariably opposed change of any kind, and was accused of insincerity and a desire to hector the Republicans. He confessed that he believed in neither woman suffrage nor Negro suffrage, but "Negro suffrage will come," said he, "because the majority here is strong enough to bring it," but, "if I have no reason to offer why a Negro man shall not vote, I have no reason to offer why a white woman shall not vote." He asked Charles Sumner how he would answer the challenge to the United States Senate "when made by women of the highest intellect perhaps on the planet, and women who are determined, knowing their rights, to maintain them and to secure them." How can such Senators explain their attitude, especially those "who desire to keep themselves in the front of the great army of humanity which is marching forward just as certainly to universal suffrage as to universal manhood suffrage"?

This gauntlet thrown down to the Republican leaders brought out a paradoxical debate, many supporters of woman suffrage stoutly opposing the amendment, and many opponents defending it. Former suffragists not only acknowledged the justice of the woman's claim to the vote but admitted as well that it was a proper reconstruction demand. They contended, however, that while woman and Negro suffrage were both just and logical, the nation would not accept two reforms at one time; therefore the question of suffrage must be divided and the first chance be given to the Negro. "This is the Negro's hour" became the universal response to the woman's appeal. Opponents of both woman and Negro suffrage, chiefly Democrats, played at friendliness and contended that white women were far better qualified to vote than Negro men. They held that if the suffrage must be extended at this time the ballot given to educated white women would offset the illiteracy of the black man, and therefore women should be given the first chance.

Republicans charged Democrats with insincerity and a desire to embarrass the party in power. Democrats in turn charged the Republican leaders with insincerity, since they seemed determined to put aside the woman suffrage cause which they had long advocated and to substitute this newer proposition of Negro suffrage. Time proved that the diagnoses of motives made by the rival parties against each other were both correct. Both parties had carried the Civil War into politics and each was sparring for immediate party advantage. At the end of three lively days of discussion, the vote revealed nine Senators for the amendment and thirty-seven against, the vote in opposition including many convinced advocates of woman suffrage. It was the first vote taken in the United States Congress on the subject of woman suffrage. The historic date was December 13, 1866.

On December 14 (1866), the Congress conferred the suffrage upon the Negroes of the District of Columbia. President Johnson vetoed the bill, January 5, 1867, upon the ground that the voters of the District had rejected Negro suffrage at the polls by an almost unanimous vote.[13] On January 7 the Senate, and, on January 8, the House passed the bill over the veto.

The Congress followed this act by another, equally revelatory of Republican intentions toward Negro suffrage. On January 25, 1867, it passed a bill providing that "in the territories thereafter organized, the right to vote should not be denied on account of race, color or previous condition of servitude." Thus the Congress had extended Negro suffrage wherever it had jurisdiction so to do. This bill became law without the President's signature. Under its provisions Nebraska was admitted to statehood after agreeing that the franchise should be allowed to Negroes. It promptly ratified the Fourteenth Amendment and thereby became an historic bone of contention, the Republicans being immediately charged by the Democrats, and by members of their own party, with "gross irregularity" in their haste to secure another Legislature to ratify the Fourteenth Amendment, then pending. Whether the charge was true or false, the amendment was ratified by Nebraska, June 15, 1867.

Meanwhile the irritable political situation in Washington was growing still more acute. While the Republican party included a controlling majority of the people outside the South, there were ominous signs of a split, or at least damaging defections. Leaders began to sense the possibility that all that had been gained by the conflicts of war might be lost by the conflicts of peace, and the instinct of self-preservation pushed all other motives into the background. The lofty expositions of the principles of human justice, which, as pronounced by great leaders, had uplifted the nation a few months before, were heard no more. The Congress ceased to talk of the rights of man and occupied itself with plans for saving the party. Under the threat of disruption from within, the party deserted logic and consistency and drove forward with the power of political might. Senators Sumner, Stevens, Wade, Wilson and Pomeroy, woman suffrage advocates in the Congress, made peace with their own consciences by the agreement that the Negro's chance must come before all else. Outside Congress, Wendell Phillips, Gerrit Smith and Horace Greeley adopted and disseminated that view. Thinking is always a laborious and painful process for the average human being, and the great leaders had simplified it for him by giving him an answer for every query,—"the Negro's hour."

From statesman to editor, from editor to people, the maxim passed, easy to remember, soothing to troubled consciences and comfortably postponing any necessity for further mental exertion. A successful maxim has ever been the most effective oil for troubled political waters. Political leaders stopped discussing woman suffrage; abolitionists declined further aid; political papers stopped publishing suffrage letters; editorials ceased; and in Congress former friends either withheld petitions for woman suffrage or dishonestly introduced them as petitions for universal suffrage which, in the parlance of Congress at the time, meant Negro suffrage. Abolitionists, like Gerrit Smith, who had always

44

decried mistaking policy for principle, now refused to sign a petition to the Constitutional Convention of New York urging that in the extension of suffrage no distinction between men and women be made. Horace Greeley pointed out to the women: "This is a critical period for the Republican party and the Nation. It would be wise and magnanimous in you to hold your claims, though just and imperative I grant, in abeyance until the Negro is safe beyond peradventure, and your turn will come next."

The women replied: "No, no, this is the time to press the women's claim; we have stood with the black man in the constitution for half a century and it is fitting that we should pass through the same door now opened to his political freedom." "Well," said Mr. Greeley, "if you persevere in your present plan, you need depend on no further help from me or the *Tribune*." At that moment, the national political leaders had definitely turned their backs upon woman suffrage and were devoting all their energies to the first division of the suffrage question, the enfranchisement of the Negro. The women, surprised and grieved as they certainly were, did not yet comprehend what had happened. Miss Anthony said at this time: "Some think this is a harvest time for the black man and seed-sowing time for women; others, with whom I agree, think we have been sowing the seed of individual rights, the foundation idea of a republic for the last century, and that this is the harvest time for all citizens who pay taxes, obey the laws and are loyal to the Government." The great party leaders had given the women staunch promises that their turn would come next, and although the latter keenly felt the humiliation of this discrimination, they still believed in the promises and trusted the leaders who made them.

So, when the doors of Congress closed, suffrage leaders, discomfited but still undaunted, turned with brave hopes to New York and Kansas which offered fields for immediate work. In New York, Negroes owning $250 worth of property had long been permitted to vote and as Negro suffrage was no novelty in the State, New York was expected to lead in the movement for their full enfranchisement.

Although all the referenda on Negro suffrage had failed, party leaders believed that the great State of New York would give a fresh impulse to the proposed change, and therefore the Constitutional Convention of the State was watched by anxious men in all parts of the country. The New York Legislature had promptly ratified the Fourteenth Amendment upon the convening of the Legislature in January, 1867, which added strength to their expectations.

The woman suffragists were filled with as urgent a hope. On January 23, Mrs. Stanton by arrangement appeared before the crowded Assembly chamber in Albany where she made a masterly plea on behalf of allowing women to vote for delegates to the Constitutional Convention, basing her argument upon the precedents already established by the State. The Legislatures of 1801 and 1821 had each extended the right to vote for delegates to the Constitutional Convention of those years to all disfranchised classes of men. They had "swept away property qualifications and color barriers" upon the principle that constitutions must emanate from and be representative of *all* the people. Mrs. Stanton begged the Legislature to continue that precedent in the provision about to be enacted for the election of delegates. "Your laws degrade rather than exalt women; your customs cripple rather than free; your system of taxation is alike ungenerous and unjust. Just imagine the motley crew from the ten thousand dens of poverty and vice in our large cities, limping, raving, cringing, staggering up to the polls, while the loyal mothers of a million soldiers whose bones lie bleaching on every Southern plain stand outside, sad and silent witnesses of this wholesale desecration of republican institutions."

Logical, eloquent, soul-stirring was that marvelous address. The legislators afterwards declared that no such complete and unanswerable argument had been heard in the Capitol for many a year, but their answer was, "The time is not ripe for woman suffrage; this is the Negro's hour." A resolution to give women the vote for delegates to the Constitutional Convention was promptly introduced, but only nine members voted in its favor.

Meanwhile an active woman suffrage campaign had been in progress for some months in all parts of the state. Committees had been formed, meetings had been held and petitions had been circulating. From the first, the women workers met the maxim "this is the Negro's hour" at every turn. Clergymen, newspapers, abolitionists, Republicans, who once favored woman suffrage and still professed to do so, refused to help and repeated the well-nigh universal aphorism. Not a letter came to the suffrage headquarters that did not recount experience with advocates of the "Negro's Hour" and the refusal of many suffragists to cooperate with any campaign for woman suffrage until the Negroes were enfranchised.

The Constitutional Convention met on June 1, 1867. The first petition presented was for woman suffrage, and introduced by George William Curtis. Every day the petitions for woman suffrage poured in until the total of signatures was twenty-eight thousand, a remarkable demand for those days. Horace Greeley was chairman of the Elections Committee. Seven days before the convention opened, he had written editorially in the *Tribune* another endorsement of the principle of woman suffrage and predicted victory in Kansas. But he, it will be recalled, was among those who were willing to sacrifice the principle of woman suffrage to the expediency of the Negro's Hour.

On June 28, Mr. Greeley, as chairman, rendered the report for the Elections Committee. Just before he arose, suffrage petitions were presented, a few for Negro suffrage but many for woman suffrage. By request of the women the last to be handed in was presented by

George William Curtis. It was a petition from Mrs. Horace Greeley and three hundred other women of Westchester County. Mr. Greeley was visibly embarrassed and irritated. His report recommended universal manhood suffrage for blacks and whites. It included the following:

> "Your committee does not recommend an extension of the elective franchise to women. However defensible in theory, we are satisfied that public sentiment does not demand and would not sustain an innovation so revolutionary and sweeping, so openly at war with a distribution of duties and functions between the sexes as venerable and pervading as Government itself. . . . Nor have we seen fit to propose the enfranchisement of boys above the age of eighteen years."

As no one had made a suggestion that boys be enfranchised, while thousands of the best known men and women of the State had petitioned for woman suffrage, the allusion to boys was received as an additional and unnecessary offense.

Although the subject of woman suffrage was debated several times, the convention refused to submit an amendment to give the voters of the State an opportunity to express their opinions upon it, but, acting under party instructions, it submitted a Negro suffrage amendment. The friends of woman suffrage in the New York Convention admitted that a majority of women might not want the vote but declared that proportionately many more women than Negroes were asking for the suffrage. The opponents as frankly acknowledged the truth of this assertion, but with shrugs of the shoulder dosed the debate with the finality,—this is "the Negro's hour."

The Negro suffrage amendment, though clear of any entanglements with woman suffrage and though supported by the urgent influence of the party in power, was lost at the election.[14]

With the door closed to further action in New York, Mrs. Stanton and Miss Anthony hastened to Kansas where the Republican Legislature of 1867 by a large majority had submitted two State constitutional amendments, one for woman suffrage and one for Negro suffrage. This was the first referendum for woman suffrage in the world, and the hearts of the women leaders were again light with hope and anticipation. Lucy Stone and her husband, Henry B. Blackwell, had already been at work in the State for some months. They had sent optimistic telegrams to the annual national suffrage convention in May predicting victory, and the convention raised a special fund to aid the campaign. Elizabeth Cady Stanton, writing about the campaign afterwards, said:

"With no greater faith did crusaders of old seize their shields and start on their perilous journey to wrest from the infidel the holy sepulcher, than did these defenders of a sacred principle enter Kansas and with hope sublime consecrate themselves to labor for woman's freedom; to roll off her soul the mountains of sorrow and superstition that had held her in bondage to false creeds and codes and customs for centuries. There was a solemn earnestness in the speeches of all who labored in that campaign. Each heart was thrilled with the thought that the youngest civilization in the world was about to establish a government based on the divine idea—the equality of mankind."

They journeyed westward confident of victory, for the amendment was a Republican measure sponsored by a Republican Governor and advocated by the leaders of the party in Kansas and as they believed in the nation. The New York *Tribune*, with Horace Greeley at its head, the *Independent*, edited by Theodore Tilton, and the *Anti-Slavery Standard*, edited by Wendell Phillips, all circulated widely in the State, and their support was confidently expected.

Fourteen of the twenty papers in the State were already supporting the amendment; why should they not have been lighthearted?

Alas! they were to see the Sumner episode in Congress paralleled again and again. Men who had stood shoulder to shoulder with the women leaders in their convention before the war when the women were serving men's causes, men who had earnestly and eloquently espoused in return the woman's cause when it was in a purely academic stage, now at the first opportunity to put theory into practice boldly chided the women for their selfish intrusion upon this, "the Negro's Hour." The eastern papers upon which they had depended were stolidly silent.

When all was over Mrs. Stanton said:—"The editors of the New York *Tribune* (Greeley) and the *Independent* (Tilton) can never know how wistfully from day to day their papers were searched for some inspiring editorial on the woman's amendment, but naught was there; there were no words of hope and encouragement, no eloquent letters from an Eastern man that could be read to the people; all were silent. Yet these two papers, extensively taken all over Kansas, had they been as true to woman as to the Negro, could have revolutionized the State. But with arms folded, Horace Greeley, George William Curtis, Theodore Tilton, Henry Ward Beecher, Thomas Wentworth Higginson, Wendell Phillips, William Lloyd Garrison, Frederick Douglass, all calmly watched the struggle from afar, and when defeat came to both propositions, no consoling words were offered for the woman's loss, but the women who spoke in the campaign were reproached for having 'killed. Negro suffrage.'" Mrs. Stanton testified further that the loss of friends and sympathy just when they were most needed was the hardest experience the suffragists had yet been called upon to bear. Again and again to the very end of the suffrage campaign half a century later this same history repeated itself, for human nature is timid and looks out upon the world through small windows.

The women had expected stalwart help from Republicans and Abolitionists in Kansas. They found that Eastern Republicans had urged the Central Committee to do its utmost for Negro suffrage, which was a party measure although it had not been endorsed in a national platform, and not to entangle itself in the "woman question." The State Central Committee had been called by its chairman, T. H. Drenning. It had issued an address to voters on behalf of Negro suffrage but had said nothing about woman suffrage. It had summoned ten Republicans who were known opponents of woman suffrage and engaged them to canvass the State for Negro suffrage, permitting them "to express their own sentiments on other questions." The Committee had taken pains to summon no Republicans who advocated woman suffrage, although such Republicans were numerous and the list included as gifted speakers as those who were called.

The Republican campaign committee therefore officially sponsored and campaigned for the Negro suffrage amendment and as officially repudiated the woman suffrage amendment, which their own party Legislature had submitted. Negroes were encouraged to speak on their own behalf and were aroused against the woman's amendment as an impediment to the success of Negro suffrage. They commonly said that "the black man has the woman question hitched on him."

Before election day the report had traveled eastward that the Republican managers had so incensed the early settlers that they were likely to lose the Negro amendment, whereupon a list of prominent Eastern Republicans issued an appeal to "Voters of the United States" urging them to apply the principles of the Declaration of Independence to women, but the appeal came too late. The news had reached Kansas that the commission appointed by the Michigan Legislature to consider Negro and woman suffrage had submitted Negro suffrage only, and that Horace Greeley, well known as an advocate of woman's rights before the war, had reported the recommendation from the Elections Committee of the New York Constitutional Convention that Negro suffrage should be submitted to the voters but not woman suffrage. That the national party stood for Negro suffrage and not for woman suffrage was therefore accepted in Kansas.

The suffrage workers in the Kansas campaign were unanimous in their conviction that had the old time friends stood steadfast the woman suffrage amendment could have been won. As it was, it fell behind the Negro amendment by one thousand votes, though the latter had been supported by the full party influence of the State and nation. Both were lost. The Republicans were dismayed and irritated that Negro suffrage had failed in the two States upon which they had most depended; the Democrats were rasped by the entire reconstruction program; and white women were hurt by the apostasy of former friends and the failure of the party of which most, if not all of them, were supporters to uphold the principle of equality and justice.

The nation had receded from the exalted unity of sympathy which marks any war period, and public thought had reached that chaotically distrustful, suspicious and divided state which accompanies any reconstruction period.

In the matter of Negro suffrage the Congress was not, however, to be deflected from its purpose of completing the ratification of the 14th Amendment, although completing it meant the coercion of at least four of the seceding Southern States, all of whom save Tennessee had rejected ratification. It is written in imperishable history that they were coerced, just the same, and that the Negro was temporarily enfranchised in the ten rebellious States by statutory act of Congress, the measure carrying the penalty that until this act was respected by the States and acknowledged in their constitutions, military supervision would be in force. The

Fourteenth Amendment was adopted by no less than seven States under military compulsion and the threat that military supervision would continue until they did.

Thus it came about that under the threat of the bayonet, resolved upon by the majority party in Congress, the black man was enfranchised in the Southern States; under the instructions of the same party, the Congress declined to consider woman suffrage and the New York Constitutional Convention refused to the voters of the State their constitutional right to decide the question; while in Kansas that same party used its enormous influence to secure the adoption of Negro suffrage and the defeat of woman suffrage at the polls.

CHAPTER 5

Negro Suffrage as a
Political Necessity

It was with troubled minds that Republican leaders faced the presidential election of 1868. Negro suffrage had already been temporarily imposed upon the South by the Military Reconstruction Act which also stipulated that the seceding States must include Negro male suffrage in their new constitutions. These acts were in operation and must be defended. Of all the referenda on Negro suffrage in the North, none had been won.[15] Senator Henry Wilson of Massachusetts had warned his party in January that the insistence upon Negro suffrage had cost a quarter of a million votes. Similar expressions of doubt were common. The Fourteenth Amendment was still pending, waiting for five more ratifications. These were certain to be supplied and were in fact supplied by the States reconstructed under military supervision.

On July 28 the Legislatures of Florida, North Carolina, Louisiana, South Carolina, Alabama and Georgia having ratified the Fourteenth Amendment, it was proclaimed. (Mississippi and Texas ratified later.) While the Military Reconstruction Act had declared that military governments should continue in control of the South until those States had adopted a constitution with Negro suffrage in them, the Fourteenth Amendment seemed to speak in a softer tone and to say to the South: take your choice, grant suffrage to your male Negroes or lose a portion of your representation in Congress. The harmonizing of these two acts required explanation not easy to make.

Speaking of the general sentiment concerning Negro suffrage at this period, James G. Blaine commented as follows:

"Political leaders with few exceptions shunned the issue (suffrage) preferring to wait until public sentiment should become more pronounced in favor of so radical a movement. But a large number of thinking people who gave more heed to the absolute right of the question than to its political expediency could not see how with consistency, or even with good conscience and common sense, the Republican party could refrain from *calling to its aid* the only large mass of persons in the South whose loyalty could be implicitly trusted. To their apprehension it seemed little less than an absurdity to proceed with a plan of reconstruction which would practically leave the State Governments of the South under the control of the same men that brought on the Civil War."

The Republican Convention, meeting in Chicago in May, 1868, had unanimously nominated General Ulysses S. Grant. The platform included a plank dealing with the question of suffrage. "The guarantee of Congress of equal suffrage to all loyal men of the South (meaning Negroes) was demanded by every consideration of public safety, of gratitude, and of justice, and must be maintained; while the *question of suffrage in all the loyal States properly belongs to the people of those States.*"

The Democratic Convention meeting in New York in July, 1868, had declared that "The privilege and trust of suffrage belong to the several States." The real difference in these platforms hinged on the fact that Republicans were regarding the seceding States as conquered provinces and as such subject to a federal control of suffrage not imposed on loyal States.

In an old diary kept by Miss Anthony one finds this entry under date of January 1, 1868: "All the old friends, with scarce an exception, are sure we are wrong. Only time can tell, but I believe we are right."[16]

There were two reasons for this expression of doubt and anxiety. First, many of the friends with whom the suffragists had worked side by side before and during the war, with no differences of opinion as to policy, had now not only deserted the ranks of woman suffrage workers but were also engaged in bitterly denouncing the women for not repudiating their own cause. Second, the suffragists now had a paper of their own, the *Revolution*, and it was causing a new outbreak of hostility from old friends.

George Francis Train, a wealthy and eccentric Democrat, had volunteered as a helper in the Kansas campaign and had stirred up much irritation among Republicans by his witty and pungent comparisons of the relative qualifications for the vote of white women and black men. One day he had asked Miss Anthony what would give the woman's cause most aid, and she had answered —a paper. That night he announced upon the platform, without further consultation with her, that when the Kansas campaign was over there would be a woman suffrage paper with Miss Anthony as manager, Mrs. Elizabeth Cady Stanton and Parker Pillsbury as editors. Its name would be the *Revolution*; its motto "Men, their rights, nothing more; women, their rights, nothing less."

With Mr. Train and David M. Mellis, financial editor of the New York *World,* as financial backers, the paper appeared on January 8, 1868. It was the first paper of national scope the movement had had. Challenging the sincerity of both political parties in their attitude on suffrage and advocating Negro suffrage when and if included with woman suffrage in the extension of universal suffrage in many a brilliant editorial, it became at once a power in the political field. In the words of Mrs. Stanton: "Some denounced it, some ridiculed it, but all read it."

Since the two men who had become its financial sponsors were Democrats, Mrs. Stanton and Miss Anthony were charged with deserting the slave and enlisting with "copperheads and traitors." The *Revolution* took the position held by the great leaders of the Republican party in 1865, but from which they had later receded. Its editorials were based upon the impregnable principles of human rights and its pleas were set forth in terms no logician could challenge. It proved terribly embarrassing to the peace of mind of those who admitted the justice and logic of woman suffrage, and who being unable to deny the accusations of inconsistency, retreated behind the defense, universal under similar circumstances, of attacking the accusers. In the tone of derision with which naughty boys had once screamed "Geography girl," former comrades in reform now inconsistently hurled at these two consistent leaders the word Democrat, a term of opprobrium to all loyal citizens at that time.

The *Revolution* held fast to the position it had assumed. Upon one occasion it said: "Charles Sumner, Horace Greeley, Gerrit Smith and Wendell Phillips with one consent bid the women of the nation stand aside and behold the salvation of the Negro. Wendell Phillips says: 'One idea for a generation, to come up in the order of their importance. First, Negro suffrage, then temperance, then the eight-hour movement, then woman suffrage.' Three generations hence, woman suffrage will be in order. What an insult to the women who have labored thirty years for the emancipation of the slave now, when he is their political equal, to propose to lift him over their heads."

Upon another date it said:

"Because we make a higher demand than either Republicans or Abolitionists, they in self-defense revenged themselves by calling us Democrats; just as the church at the time of its apathy on the slavery question revenged the goadings of Abolitionists by calling them infidels. If claiming the right of suffrage for every citizen, male and female, black and white, a platform far above that occupied by Republicans or Abolitionists today, is to be a Democrat then we glory in the name, but we have not so understood the policy of modern Democracy."

The American Equal Rights Association held its annual meeting in New York in May, 1868. Lucretia Mott, its president, was detained at home by illness in her family; Elizabeth Cady Stanton was vice-president. So vindictive had the feeling of Abolitionists become toward Mrs. Stanton and Miss Anthony, that Thomas Wentworth Higginson attempted to persuade them that Mrs. Stanton, whose official duty it was to call the meeting to order, should give way to another. Miss Anthony would not yield this point and Mrs. Stanton presided over the convention. The public meetings of the convention were as crowded as ever, the speeches as eloquent, but a spirit of dissension never before present prevailed, owing to the determination of the men advocates of woman suffrage to compel the women to admit the wisdom of all working for Negro suffrage at that time, let woman suffrage come when and if it would. The slightest hint that the Fourteenth Amendment was not a perfect solution of reconstruction problems brought forth hisses.

The convention, however, did not surrender to these attacks but made plans to bombard Congress with more petitions, this time for a woman suffrage constitutional amendment and for the inclusion of woman suffrage in the proposed revision of government in the District of Columbia.

A group of the more radical members organized a special committee which sent a memorial to the National Republican Convention, urging it to include a woman suffrage plank in its platform. Apparently it found its way into the mysterious oblivion which received so many similar pleas in after years.

During the convention, Theodore Tilton presented a resolution half jocularly requesting Miss Anthony to attend the Democratic convention as a delegate appointed by the American Equal Rights Association, and to secure in the Democratic platform a recognition of woman's rights to the elective franchise. The resolution was intended as a gentle gibe at the alleged Democratic leanings of women who would not postpone work for woman suffrage. Miss Anthony accepted the instruction as sincere and with Mrs. Stanton prepared a memorial to the Democratic convention.

The effect of this news upon the country was to harass the Republicans and disturb the Democrats. The Republicans were in absolute control of the political situation in the nation, yet many leaders feared for the permanency of this control, since the Republican attitude toward Negro and woman suffrage could not stand the test of reason. For the first time since 1860, Southern Democrats would sit with Northern Democrats in the coming convention. Many Northern Democrats had taken the attitude that if suffrage was to be given to illiterate Negro men, it should not be denied to educated white women. Would Southern Democrats support this position? Would the voters insist upon logic instead of expediency? Alarm that "abolition women should associate with copperhead enemies of the nation" to the extent of presenting them with a memorial was common. The Democrats, unwilling to extend suffrage to any class, asked themselves equally disturbing questions, and the press found the incident a call for a surprising amount of editorial comment. The New York *Herald* said (July, 1868):

> "The Democrats have a splendid opportunity to take the wind out of the Republican sails on 'womanhood suffrage' against manhood suffrage and for white women especially as better qualified for an intelligent exercise of the suffrage than the thousands of black men just rescued from the ignorance of Negro slavery. The Democratic convention can turn the radical party out of doors upon this issue alone if only bold enough to take strong ground upon it."

The Republicans were greatly relieved when the Democratic delegates, after hearing the memorial read by the Secretary,—with Miss Anthony seated upon the platform,—far from showing any sign of comprehending the opportunity pointed out by the *Herald,* received the petition with "yells, shrieks and demoniacal, deafening howls."

Whether silent contempt, as shown by the Republicans, or audible contempt, as shown by the Democrats, is more damaging to a cause was a question women discussed through the next generation. They had numerous after experiences with both varieties of treatment.

Meanwhile the presidential campaign moved onward.

Francis Newton Thorpe[17] emphasizes the extension of the suffrage to the Negro as the great political issue of the campaign. Braxton[18] says that "Negro suffrage for the South was a paramount issue." While John Mabry Matthews in his history of the Fifteenth Amendment takes the position that Negro suffrage, as the subject of a possible Fifteenth Amendment, was not recognized as a campaign issue at all.[19]

James G. Blaine throws a strong light upon these three contradictory statements.[20] "The evasive and discreditable position in regard to suffrage taken by the National Republican Convention was keenly felt and appreciated by the members of the party when subjected to popular discussion. There was something so obviously unfair and unmanly in the proposition to impose Negro suffrage on the Southern States by national power, and at the same time to leave the Northern States free to decide the question for themselves, that the Republicans became heartily ashamed of it long before the political canvass had closed."

Even when there is no deliberate intent to deceive, it is inevitable, owing to the enormous size of the United States and its division into States each of which has its own political point of view, that party policy, interpreted by a great number of campaign speeches, be expounded with varying meaning. The campaign of 1868 was no exception to this rule.

Speakers pressed the view in the East that the Negro needed and must have the vote for his own protection; in the Middle West, that those States, having very small colored populations, should enfranchise the Negro by referenda in order to support the policy of insistence upon Negro suffrage in the South; and assured the far West, where fear of Chinese domination was professed, that Negro suffrage was intended only for the South. In all parts of the country campaigners took the ground phrased by Senator Carl Schurz of Missouri, "For Negroes, suffrage is of right, for rebels of grace."

Throughout the campaign, the term "impartial suffrage" was employed to denote Negro suffrage. "Universal suffrage" could not be used as that would include women, and the frank words, "Negro suffrage" were offensive to many. "Impartial suffrage" had come into use to express the delicate discriminations intended, the inclusion in the electorate of Negroes and the exclusion of Northern white women and Southern white traitors. The word "impartial" could scarcely be construed by any known definition as explanatory of this unique political policy, and it therefore served to confuse rather than clarify the general understanding.

The fact that the Southern States had accepted the Fourteenth Amendment was announced, however, with a heartening assurance that political turmoil would now end, and this had more effect than any other point in the discussion. "The stoical submission of the South to the provisions of the Fourteenth Amendment" was seized upon by its northern advocates as confirmation of the justice and wisdom of the measure,"[21] and the election closed in victory for the Republicans, with the national tension much relieved.

The Republican Congress, triumphantly re-elected, returned to Washington determined to forget all inconsistencies and to make Negro suffrage secure in the South by further action. Many proposals were made and debated and the entire subject of suffrage became again a consideration to Congress.

The first move toward insuring suffrage to the Negro by means of another federal amendment was made by Senator Pomeroy of Kansas in December, 1868. His proposal based the suffrage on citizenship, thus including women. George W. Julian of Indiana introduced a similar amendment in the House; also three other bills, one to give the vote to women in the District of Columbia, another to grant it to women in the territories, and later one to give it to the women of Utah. The first two of these bills followed the precise lines taken by the Congress relative to the Negro.

While Congress was making ready to submit a 15th amendment, the first suffrage convention held in Washington took place in January, 1869. A new feature at women's rights conventions was the attendance of several colored men who were given the opportunity of free speech. All denounced the women for jeopardizing the black man's chances for the vote and one, standing by the side of that saintly superwoman, Lucretia Mott, presiding officer, declared that "God intended the male should dominate the female everywhere." Abolitionists too were there to defend the black man's prior claim and the spirited debate ran on for many hours, the women contending that it was never expedient to deny justice, and white and black men uniting in the declaration that justice in this particular case must yield to expediency.

Elizabeth Cady Stanton made another masterly speech which incidentally expressed the sentiments of suffragists in regard to the proposed Fifteenth Amendment. Said she: —

"While poets and philosophers, statesmen and men of science are all alike pointing to women as the new hope for the redemption of the race, shall the freest Government on the earth be the first to establish an aristocracy based on sex alone? to exalt ignorance above education, vice above virtue, brutality and barbarism above refinement and religion? Not since God first called light out of darkness and order out of chaos, was there ever made so base a proposition as 'manhood suffrage' in this American Republic, after all the discussions on human rights in the last century. . . . In our Southern States women were not humiliated in seeing their coachmen, gardeners, and waiters go to the polls to legislate for them; but here in this boasted Northern civilization women of wealth and education who pay taxes and obey the laws, who in morals and intelligence are the peers of their proudest rulers, are thrust outside the pale of political consideration with minors, paupers, lunatics, traitors and idiots, with those guilty of bribery, larceny and infamous crimes."

The first Congressional Hearing ever secured for suffrage followed this convention. Mrs. Stanton addressed the District Committee of the Senate with women representatives of nineteen States at her back in a powerful plea to save the women of the District from being debarred from the exercise of their right of suffrage.

In and out of the Congress the debate concerning the further extension of suffrage continued at white heat. President Grant recommended the ratification of the Negro suffrage amendment in his inaugural address, in March, 1869, saying: "The question of suffrage is one which is likely to agitate the public so long as a portion of the citizens of the nation are excluded from its privileges in any State. It seems to me very desirable that this question should be settled now." Commenting privately upon the political situation he said, however:[22] "I could never have believed that I should favor giving Negroes the right to vote but that seems to be the only solution of our difficulties." Petitions poured in from many States to refer the question to referendum or to submit it to conventions called for the purpose.

Throughout the angry contentions over Negro suffrage, the women quoted often the well-known suffrage letter of the martyred Lincoln. His influence lay over the country like the spirit of a benediction, but although the letter helped the women's cause, it rasped the Republicans. Lincoln's letter read as follows:

"New Salem, June 13, 1836.

"To the Editor of the 'Journal':

"In your paper of last Saturday I see a communication over the signature of 'Many Voters,' in which the candidates who are announced in the 'Journal' are called upon to 'show their hands.' Agreed. Here's mine. . . .

"I go for all sharing the privileges of the Government who assist in bearing its burdens. Consequently, I go for admitting all whites to the right of suffrage who pay taxes or bear arms, by no means excluding females.

•　•　•　•　•　•　•

"A. LINCOLN."

The Fifteenth Amendment was submitted on February 27, 1869.[23] Whereupon the phrase "The Negro's Hour," on all tongues from 1865 to 1868, was cast aside and immediately forgotten. In its place there came a new slogan, "A Political Necessity," which served as effectively to explain the inexplicable as its predecessor; under its suggestion loyal voters were cautiously led to overlook the fact that the amendment was not only in direct contradiction to the suffrage plank in the platform by which the Republicans had been charged with national power, but also to the solemn pledges made by campaigners in the West. As has been shown above, the Republican platform had firmly relegated all authority for Negro suffrage to the States, with the exception of those recently in rebellion, and had not mentioned women at all. Yet out of the maze of politics, with no emphatic change of public opinion, the proposed Fifteenth Amendment had emerged as a "political necessity" with a united party behind it. And so carefully had the preparations been made that eleven States ratified the amendment within the first month.

On March 15, 1869, Mr. Julian of Indiana introduced a Sixteenth Amendment which copied the phraseology of the Fifteenth Amendment and substituted "sex" for "race, color or previous condition of servitude." The women, of course, were back of this amendment, which was a federal woman suffrage amendment; but though supported by a ceaseless succession of petitions and an unanswerable plea, it was utterly ignored. The congressional friends who had introduced the suffrage bills, Senators Pomeroy of Kansas and Wilson of Iowa, and Mr. Julian of the House, were all regarded as "irregular" by the party majority, which had decided that Negro suffrage, superseding all other considerations, had become an imperative "political necessity."

The Fifteenth Amendment made the rounds of the Legislatures in a year and a month and was proclaimed as ratified by the necessary three-fourths of the States on March 30, 1870. The States of California, Delaware, Kentucky, Maryland, Oregon and Tennessee, having gone Democratic, rejected the amendment. The State of New Jersey ratified subsequent to the Proclamation by the Secretary of State. The ten reconstructed States of Virginia, North Carolina, South Carolina, Florida, Georgia, Alabama, Mississippi, Texas, Arkansas, Louisiana, where Negroes, carpet-baggers and a minority of loyal Southern men directed the government, are counted in the list of ratifying States.

New York ratified in a Republican Legislature April 14, 1869, and a Democratic Legislature the following year withdrew her consent, January 5, 1870. The Democratic Legislature of Ohio rejected the amendment, May 4, 1869, and a Republican Legislature ratified it, January 27, 1870. The federal Secretary of State ruled that a State once ratifying an amendment could not reverse its action and reject it, but that a State rejecting an amendment could reverse its decision and ratify it. The ratifications of both States were, therefore, counted in the total. These points were never reviewed by the Supreme Court.

The Fourteenth and Fifteenth Amendments had been submitted by Congress and ratified by a strictly party vote, the Republicans voting solidly for them and the Democrats against them. With the ratification of the Fifteenth Amendment, the United States became the first country in the world to elevate all men to the sovereignty of voting citizenship. In all other countries there were certain classes of men excluded with the women. The discrimination had been advertised and emphasized by the Fourteenth Amendment and its triply reiterated adjective "male." This political degradation put upon women would have been less humiliating had there been promise of relief, but the prediction of

Mr. Beecher was completely realized; the public mind had indeed "shut up altogether."

Appeals to party leaders who had faithfully pledged their help to women when the Negro's hour should have passed fell upon deaf ears and resisting minds. Many Republicans were disturbed by the realization that the reconstruction measures had violated logic, justice, consistency and common sense. They were irritated by the fact that these measures had not brought peace and stability, but it was too late to reconsider, too late to be logical, and, obeying a psychological rule, they began to hate woman suffrage and woman suffragists,—incidentally the occasion of the self-accusation of their own consciences. In the South, an antipathy toward the Negro race as the cause of the Southern humiliation, which was very different from the pre-war variety, was manifesting itself in a new and portentous form. The North had enfranchised the Negro; the South had capitulated in form, but the sheeted Ku Klux Klan, riding by night, had established a reign of terror over the ignorant and superstitious freedmen compared to which their former slavery was comparative freedom. The political future looked dark and troubled. The moral courage of statesmen, but recently contending in exalted phrase for human liberty and equal rights for all, had utterly surrendered to the politician's eternal plea of expediency.

Once Mrs. Stanton, lecturing in California, met Senator Bingham of Ohio stumping the State on behalf of the Fourteenth and Fifteenth Amendments which that State had declined to ratify. Mrs. Stanton gently charged him with insincerity, since every argument he was presenting applied equally to woman suffrage. "With a cynical smile he replied that he was not the puppet of logic but the slave of practical politics."[24]

Victimized by "practical politics" and its slaves, the politicians, suffragists pushed forward, just the same, with their national and state programs.

CHAPTER 6

The First Victory

(1869)

In the midst of the baffling discouragement politics had wrought, a tiny flickering star of victory arose out in the great mysterious West. So unimportant did it seem at the time that the *Revolution* gave but three lines to the announcement, and that in an inconspicuous corner. The map of the United States of America as represented in the geographies used in the public schools of the day denoted most of the territory lying between Nebraska and the Rockies as the Great American Desert. Out of this vastness the federal government had carved a section large enough to accommodate an empire and called it Wyoming. A sparse and shifting population of adventurous men, sometimes with families, was scattered along the trails which led from Council Bluffs to Oregon or California. The Union Pacific Railroad was completed half-way across Wyoming in 1867, and a City of Tents sprang up as if by magic at the last stop, called Cheyenne. Thousands of men poured in where dozens had been before, trappers, hunters, miners, prospectors, but all seekers of adventure. Saloons, dance halls, houses of prostitution, always numerous in frontier settlements, increased to such an extent that crime became rampant. Neither life nor property was respected, and robberies, hold-ups and murders were every day occurrences.

The better element petitioned the Congress for the protection of an organized government. The Congress immediately granted the request by a bill providing for a territorial government and President Johnson signed the bill. The conflict between the President and Congress was then at the climax of its bitterness and Congress refused to confirm the President's appointees for the new territorial administration. The Wyoming government, therefore, was not organized until May, 1869, when appointees of President Grant took charge. During the two intervening years lawlessness had grown even more audacious and the town of Laramie, established as another outpost on the Union Pacific, was duplicating the experiences of Cheyenne.

The first election took place in September, 1869, its purpose being the choice of delegates to the first Legislature. At South Pass City, the largest town in the State, a settlement consisting of rows of shacks stretching along a ledge of the Wind River Mountains, the call for an election found three thousand persons washing gold and dreaming of fortune. The "blue and the gray," the loyalist and the copperhead, with bygones laid aside, were amicably following the common lure of gold hunting. Politics offered an acceptable diversion and they promptly fell in line as Republicans and Democrats, each group prepared to nominate candidates and defend them to the death.

At this point, twenty of the most influential men in the community, including all the candidates of both parties, were invited to dinner at the "shack of Mrs. Esther Morris, who had followed her husband and three sons into the trackless West." She was a newcomer with a complete understanding of the Eastern political treatment of Negro and woman suffrage. In her ears were still ringing the words of Susan B. Anthony, one of whose public lectures she had heard just before setting out upon her Western journey. To her guests she now presented the woman's case with such clarity and persuasion that each candidate gave her his solemn pledge that if elected he would introduce and support a woman suffrage bill. The election resulted in the choice of Wm. H. Bright, Democrat, who was elected president of the Council when the Legislature met, October 1, 1869. Many years after, in order that justice should be done the memory of Mrs. Morris, Captain Nickerson, the Republican candidate defeated in 1869 but elected in 1871, wrote the story, giving entire credit to Mrs. Morris for the act of the Territory, and filed his documentary evidence at the County Seat of Sweetbriar County.

The Wyoming September election reflected the hostility to Negro suffrage common in the country and was conducted in a manner to be expected of a turbulent population but recently brought under the discipline of law. In the words of Hon. J. W. Kingman, associate justice in the territory: "There was a good deal of party feeling developed, and election day witnessed a sharp and vigorous struggle. The candidates and their friends spent money freely, and every liquor shop was thrown open to all who would drink. Peaceful people did not dare to walk the streets in some of the towns during the latter part of the day and evening. At South Pass City, some drunken fellows with large knives and loaded revolvers swaggered around the polls, and swore that no Negro should vote. When one man remarked quietly that he thought the Negroes had as good a right to vote as any of them had, he was immediately knocked down, jumped on, kicked and pounded without mercy and would have been killed had not his friends rushed into the brutal crowd and dragged him out, bloody and insensible. There were quite a number of colored men who wanted to vote,[25] but did not dare approach the polls until the United States Marshal, himself at their head and with revolver in hand, escorted them through the crowd, saying he would shoot the first man that interfered with them. There was much quarreling and tumult, but the Negroes voted. This was only a sample of the day's doing and was characteristic of the election all over the territory. The result was that every Republican was defeated and every Democratic candidate elected."

Mr. Bright, the newly elected president of the Council, was described by those who knew him as "a man of much energy and good natural endowments but without much school education." His wife was reported to be a woman of unusual attainments and Mrs. Morris completely converted them both to woman suffrage. Mr. Bright is quoted by ex-Governor Hoyt as saying to his wife: "Betty, it's a shame that I should be a member of the Legislature and make laws for such a woman as you. You are a great deal better than I am; you know a great deal more and you would make a better member of the Assembly than I. I have made up my mind that I will do everything in my power to give you the ballot."

Arrived at Cheyenne, Mr. Bright set himself to the task of converting to woman suffrage the twenty-two men who composed the two Houses of the Legislature. He reminded his fellow members that the Legislature was unanimously Democratic and that, should it vote suffrage to women, it would show the world that Democrats were more liberal than Republicans who confined their extensions of the vote to Negroes; and that, should the Republican Governor veto the bill, it would give the Democrats a decided advantage. With all he argued the justice of the cause and pointed out that such an act would advertise the territory as nothing else could. Meanwhile, men and women in different parts of the territory wrote their delegates, urging support of the bill. On the 27th of November, Mr. Bright, having secured the necessary number of pledges, introduced the suffrage bill. The Council (territorial Senate) without discussion passed the measure by a vote of ayes 6, nays 2, absent 1. In the House, the bill found an opponent as determined as was Mr. Bright— Mr. Ben Sheeks. A lively and acrimonious debate followed, and many amendments designed to kill the bill were introduced and voted down, one being that the word "woman" be stricken out, and the words, "all colored women and squaws, be substituted." The original bill named eighteen years as the qualified age of the woman voter. A proposal to substitute twenty-one for eighteen was the only change made, and thus amended the bill passed, ayes 6, nays 4, absent 1, the Council concurring.

Several of those who had voted for the bill, smarting under the gibes of outsiders who looked upon suffrage for women as wholly ridiculous, soon regretted having done so. Friends and foes alike turned to John W. Campbell, the unmarried Republican Governor, and pleaded with him, some to sign, some to veto the bill. Women also called upon him, pleading for his signature to the bill. His interviewers found him vacillating and doubtful as to his duty. The determining factor proved to be a memory rising in the background of his mind, and growing each hour more vivid and persistent. In that memory he saw himself and other young boys, nineteen years before, acting under the impulse of curiosity tempered with mischief, stealing into the back seats of the Second Baptist Church in Salem, Ohio, his birthplace. The attraction was a Woman's Rights Convention which the entire village agreed was an unheard of innovation, a few of the elders defending it, but more condemning it. The convention was the first in the State and differed in one respect from others at that period. It was entirely officered by women and "not a man was allowed to sit on the platform, speak or vote." The women issued an "address to Ohio women," a "memorial to the State Constitutional Convention" about to sit, and passed twenty-two resolutions, "covering the whole range of woman's political, religious, civil and social rights." Although greetings of encouragement were received from many of the chief leaders of the movement, the convention speakers were all Ohio women. When it was over, the men who had been in attendance met together and "endorsed all the ladies had said and done."

An episode so remarkable had not failed to make its impression upon the boy, although in the intervening years no occasion had arisen to transform the impression into conviction. Now the boy, grown to man, heard the voices once more, listened again to the arguments and knew no answer to their appeal. With his mind made up, in the words of ex-Governor Hoyt, "he saw that it was a long deferred justice and so signed the bill as gladly as Abraham Lincoln wrote his name to the Proclamation of Emancipation of the slaves."

"Of course," continues Mr. Hoyt, "the women were astounded! If a whole troop of angels had come down with flaming swords for their vindication, they would not have been much more astonished than they were when that bill became a law and the women of Wyoming were thus clothed with the habiliments of citizenship."

The two years which intervened before the next legislative election were eventful ones to the woman's cause in the territory. Soon after the passage of the bill, Mrs. Esther Morris was surprised by an appointment as Justice of the Peace at South Pass City. Owing to the fact that the population was sparse and regular courts were not yet numerous, a Justice of the Peace was an important officer and frequently heard cases which in after years would have gone to other courts.

The rowdies of the place undertook to intimidate Mrs. Morris and thus force her resignation—and incidentally prove that women were unequal to the performance of political duties—but they retired humiliated and discomfited from the contest. Nearly forty cases were brought before her and so justly did she administer them that not one was appealed to a higher Court. Justice Morris and her court at South Pass City aroused widespread comment throughout the nation, the reports being both true and false, favorable and unfavorable.

At the first term of the District Court held after the first Legislature women as well as men were drawn for grand and petit jurors. The enemies of woman suffrage had caused this action, intending thereby to make the whole cause of women in politics so obnoxious to the public that it would prepare the way for a repeal of the woman suffrage measure at the next Legislature. On the contrary, the woman jurors were continually complimented and praised by judges and press.

"The first mixed Grand Jury was in session for three weeks during which time bills were brought for consideration of several murder cases, cattle and horse stealing and illegal branding, all of the bills strangely commencing, 'We, good and lawful male and female jurors, on oath do say.'"[26] When Justice Howe addressed this jury, and incidentally a packed court room, he assured the women that there was not only no impropriety in their serving as jurors but that their service was needed in the effort to secure a law-abiding community. Said he: "You shall not be driven by the sneers, jeers and insults of a laughing crowd from the temple of justice as your sisters have been from some of the medical colleges of the land."

When the Grand Jury was discharged, Judge Howe complimented the women upon "the service rendered during this first term of the territorial court," saying that women would make just as good jurors as men, if not a great deal better.

A petit jury soon thereafter tried a murder case, the indictment having been brought in by the Grand Jury. Six women and six men composed the jury. When the case was referred to the jury, it was unable to come to a decision and the jury, as is customary, was locked up. This was the possibility that had done duty in all lands as a decisive reason why women should never serve as jurors. The Sheriff of Albany County, Wyoming, solved the problem easily enough upon this first occasion. The jury was retired in two rooms at the chief hotel; a man bailiff was placed on guard at the door of the men's room, and a *woman bailiff* at the door of the women's room. There was still another incident new in the history of juries. While the men, in the effort to while away a few weary hours, were engaged in playing cards, smoking and drinking beer, their attention was arrested by the notes of a hymn coming from the women jurors' room and easily heard through the thin walls. Presently they heard the minister's wife ask the jurors to kneel with her in prayer "while she asked the Highest Court to give them guidance in arriving at a just verdict."

For two and a half days and nights the jury labored to reach a decision. Fifty years after, when the secrets of that jury's action could be told, it was learned that the six women voted from the first for conviction, and that the delay was occasioned by three men who voted for acquittal. The verdict was manslaughter and was signed with a pen fashioned from an eagle's quill.

The news of these women jurors spread far and wide. "King William of Prussia sent a congratulatory cable to President Grant upon this evidence of progress, enlightenment and civil liberty in America."[27]

While arousing much discussion and winning approval among the law-abiding, women jurors were less popular among other classes, as was evidenced in the second Legislature. The Legislature of 1871 contained a minority of Republicans. Nine days after the Legislature convened, a bill to repeal woman suffrage was introduced. The leader of the suffrage opposition in 1869, Ben Sheeks, was the only man in either house who had been returned, and he was elected as Speaker of the House. He devoted his entire attention to the repeal bill which passed the following day, ayes 9, nays 3, absent 1, every vote for repeal being Democratic and every vote against being Republican. On November 28, the bill passed the Council by a vote of ayes 5, all Democratic, and nays 4, all Republican. Governor Campbell (Republican) promptly vetoed the bill, saying in his message that "to repeal it at that time would advertise to the world that women in their use of enfranchisement had not justified the acts of the members of the previous session and that such an imputation would be false and untenable." The House passed the repeal over the Governor's veto by the required two-thirds vote, ayes 9 (Democrats), nays 2 (Republican), with two absentees who had paired their votes. In the Council the repeal did not secure a two-thirds vote, ayes 5 (Democratic), nays 4 (Republican). Thus woman suffrage was preserved by a single vote, for had one Republican deserted and voted with the Democrats, the two-thirds vote for repeal would have been secured. No effort was ever again made to repeal woman suffrage in Wyoming.

Twenty years after (1889), a constitutional convention met in September to frame a constitution preparatory to statehood. In the preceding June, a woman's convention had been called and a hundred of the most prominent women of the Territory had attended it. The purpose of the convention had been carried out in the adoption of the following resolution: "Resolved, That we demand of the constitutional convention that woman suffrage be affirmed in the State constitution."

Not a single delegate in the constitutional convention opposed woman suffrage, but one delegate proposed that the question be submitted to the people separately from the constitution, as it was likely to prove difficult for the state to get into the Union with woman suffrage in the constitution. The proposal brought out a staunch and unyielding protest and the woman suffrage clause was included in the constitution.

The Committee on Territories in the House of Representatives recommended the admission of Wyoming, but William M. Springer, Democrat, of Illinois brought in a minority report "consisting of twenty-three pages, twenty-one devoted to objections because of the woman suffrage article."[28]

The Territory was Republican and would send two Republicans to the Senate. The battle fiercely waged against its admission as a State was therefore led and chiefly supported by Democrats, woman suffrage furnishing a convenient excuse for opposition. The ghosts of reconstruction came forth from their hiding places and stalked the aisles of the United States Senate and House once more, off and on making their presence known whenever the bill came up during a period of six months. Lengthy speeches by representatives from Alabama, Arkansas, Delaware, Georgia, Tennessee, Missouri and Texas, vituperative and ignorantly hostile, marked the opposition. "Woman suffrage will result in unsexing womanhood." "It is a reform against nature." "Let her stay in the sphere to which God and the Bible have assigned her." "They are going to make men of women, and the correlative must take place that men become women." During the debate, when it seemed impossible that Congress would consent to the admission of Wyoming with woman suffrage in its constitution, Delegate James Carey telegraphed the Wyoming Legislature then in session and asked advice. The answer came back: "We will remain out of the Union a hundred years rather than come in without woman suffrage." This staunch response stiffened the faith of the friends and won votes of Republicans who were not yet ready to approve of woman suffrage. The bill of admission passed the House March 28, 1890, by a vote of 139 ayes to 127 nays.

The procedure was repeated in the Senate, action being postponed several times. The effort to amend by striking out woman suffrage having failed there also, the bill of admission was passed June 27, 1890, by 29 ayes, 18 nays, 37 absent.

In the Congress Republicans opposed to woman suffrage had held quite unitedly that the State should have the right to decide who should vote within it. The Democrats, always contending that suffrage was a matter for the consideration of States, now refused to accept the principle and demanded a federal veto on state action. The Bill passed by a party vote, Republicans voting for admission and Democrats against.

From the year 1869, every Governor, Chief Justice and many prominent citizens of Wyoming have given endorsements of the beneficence of woman suffrage. "Not one reputable person in the State said over his or her own signature that woman suffrage is other than an unimpeachable success in Wyoming."[29] At one time, suffragists in the East were dismayed because Boston papers carried an interview with a "Prominent Gentleman from Wyoming" who declared that all the beliefs of the opponents of woman suffrage had proved true in that State. A telegram to the Mayor of Cheyenne asking for particulars concerning this "prominent gentleman" brought back the quick response, "A horse thief convicted by a jury half of whom were women."

For fifty years Wyoming served as the leaven which lightened the prejudices of the entire world. She pronounced false every prediction of anti-suffragists and gave so much evidence of positive good to the community arising from the votes of women that she became the direct cause of the establishment of woman suffrage in all the surrounding States. Amid the gibes and the jests, the ridicule and the ribaldry, Wyoming stood fast through the generations, until the nation acknowledged that she was right and stood with her.

CHAPTER 7

Politics after the War

The enfranchisement of the Negro did not have the effect upon the politics of the nation that was expected.

General Grant had been elected in 1868 with a "handsome majority" but, said Mr. Blaine:[30]

> "An analysis of the vote gave food for serious reflection. Six of the reconstructed States gave Grant their electoral vote. Georgia and Louisiana gave theirs to Seymour, the Democratic candidate, and it was believed that this had happened through fraud and intimidation of the Negro. If these conditions had obtained in all the States and Mr. Seymour had received the electoral vote of the solid South, he would, in connection with the vote he received in the North, have had a majority over General Grant in the Electoral College."

Many Southern men had fought in the Northern army, risking their lives for the cause of the Union and had proved effective leaders of the Negroes in the first days of reconstruction, but by degrees when Negro suffrage became the test of loyalty the strongest of them deserted the Republican Party and joined the secessionists' standard. The remnants of the various political parties which had existed in the South before the war drew together under the banner of the Democratic party, whose watchword in that section was "white supremacy." The so-called carpet-baggers from the North were driven out, intimidated, or their views modified. Few white men remained as leaders and the black man was far too inexperienced to command his own forces.

The Fifteenth Amendment was proclaimed on March 30, 1870, and on May 31, 1870, the Congress passed what was familiarly known as the Force Bill in the effort to quiet southern disturbances, overthrow the Ku Klux Klan and insure Republican control over the South. The bill "was based upon the idea that until the colored man should have reached the point at which he could compete on even terms with the white man, his undeveloped powers must be reinforced."[31] "These Southern State governments proved a source of angry contention inside the Republican Party in the North,"[32] and the military supervision of Southern elections, with its need of continual defense was waxing more and more unpopular. The strong characters who had unceasingly striven for Negro rights were passing out, and new men, whose convictions had not been formed in the long and hard-fought abolition struggle, were less ardent. As once the "political necessity" of enfranchising the Negro "to save the party" had been urged, the advancing years brought forth talk of "unloading the Negro" in the interest of the salvation of the same party. The Pacific Coast continued to be alarmed by the possibility of Chinese political domination[33] and this state of the public mind in that section was aggravated by the presence of large numbers of Southern men who, lured by the greater promise of the undeveloped resources of the West, had migrated there after the war.

The Negro vote proved annoying to Republicans in other ways. The gentleman's game of battling on the floor of presidential conventions for the nomination of favorite candidates lost much of its interest and thrill in the presence of full delegations from all the Southern States, mostly colored, few of whose members were competent to play their part on the plane of mental and ethical equality with other delegations. Their expenses were usually paid and they demanded favors not easy to confer. Candidates earliest in the field or with most money at their command had an unfair advantage which further increased the irritation. All in all, the Northern conscience became easier and less determined to protect the Negro in his right to vote. Negro suffrage had proved a load to carry instead of an added strength. It became odious to Northern Republicans to give military protection at elections to men the majority of whom could neither read nor understand; as odious to them as the intimidating Ku Klux methods had become to the better classes of the South. Any mention of further extensions of suffrage affected the average Republican politician with mental nausea.

Meanwhile, the hands of Northern suffragists were stretched across Mason and Dixon's line and accepted by Southern women, timidly at first, but after the lapse of twenty-five years with friendly loyalty to the common cause. "How I hate Susan B. Anthony," exclaimed one Southern woman in 1895 to an astonished visiting suffragist from the North. "Why? Do you know her?" No, the lady had never seen her, but Susan B. Anthony was an Abolitionist, the Abolitionists had won the war, and had sent Sherman marching across Southern plantations, one of which had belonged to her father. The same Abolitionists had devised Negro suffrage and the Force Bill. Therefore all of them and all of their ideas were gall and wormwood to the South. Fearless Southern women in time, within the locality whose peculiar prejudices they knew and understood, waged unremitting warfare against these prejudices, and no stronger characters did the long struggle produce than those great-souled Southern suffragists. They had need to be great of soul. As late as 1920, the average Southern Democrat was filled with explosive rage at any mention of woman suffrage. He would not and could not argue the question. His response to all appeals was a scornful, sputtering ejaculation, "Negro *women!*"

For years, Southern white women demonstrated by Census reports that, when enfranchised, white women would outnumber black men and women in all save two Southern States, yet the invariable answer was that of the Mississippi Senator, though less rudely given: "We are not afraid to maul a black man over the head if he dares to vote, but we can't treat women, even black women, that way. No, we'll allow no woman suffrage. It may be right, but we won't have it." A Southern woman, pleading with a Congressional Committee for the submission of the Federal Suffrage Amendment in 1918, was publicly chided by a Congressman for having deserted the traditions and the political creed of her section.

As no action had ever been taken by the Republicans to enforce the penalty of loss of representation on account of the flagrant violation of the Fourteenth Amendment, the State of Mississippi in 1890 called a constitutional convention for the frankly avowed purpose of restoring white supremacy. It accomplished the purpose by establishing an educational and poll tax qualification. No federal penalty being enforced, Louisiana called a convention in 1898, with the determination to go farther. She adopted all the Mississippi handicaps and added the "grandfather clause" which limited the vote to those who had it before the Civil War "and their legitimate descendants." As the Republicans still took no action, other Southern States followed with constitutional conventions in quick succession, until in the "black district" the Negro was almost completely disfranchised. In after years the Supreme Court, upon an Oklahoma case, declared the "grandfather clause" wholly unconstitutional, but to this day no political action has ever been taken to reduce Southern representation as provided by the Fourteenth Amendment.

Southern Democratic States disfranchised the Negro by as unconstitutional processes as the Republican Northern States had employed in enfranchising him. Whether the Negro, enfranchised a generation before his time, or the woman, enfranchised two generations after her time, suffered the greater injustice, it may take another century to demonstrate. Certainly both paid heavy penalties for the political blunders of the "white male."

"The real reason behind the attitude of both Congress and the Courts" concerning the enforcement of the amendments, "is the apathetic tone of public opinion which is the final arbiter of the question. In the technical sense, the amendment is still a part of the supreme law of the land. But as a phenomenon of the social consciousness, a rule of conduct, no matter how authoritatively promulgated by the nation, if not supported by the force of public opinion, is already in process of repeal."[34]

In the year 1872, the Republican Party suffered a split over financial problems. A convention of delegates calling themselves Liberals met in Cincinnati and nominated Horace Greeley for president. The women, led by Miss Anthony, were there to ask endorsement of woman suffrage, but although many of the old and true suffrage friends were delegates, they would not heed the appeal "to load the new party" with issues other than those which called it into being. The Republicans met in Philadelphia in June, anxious and distressed by the defection of the so-called liberals. They needed all the help possible and for the first time put a woman's plank in the platform—a plank that deserves to go down in song and story as the ablest effort to say something and give nothing that was ever indulged in.

"The Republican party is mindful of its obligations to the loyal women of America for their noble devotion to the cause of freedom; their admission to wider fields of usefulness is received with satisfaction; and the honest demands of any class of citizens for equal rights should be treated with respectful consideration."

Suffragists spoke of it not as a plank, but as a splinter!

The Democrats, meeting in July, made no mention of women. A strong pressure was now put upon suffragists to throw all their forces into the Republican side of the balance and many did, believing with Henry Blackwell that the "recognition of 1872 would be endorsement in 1876." The chairman of the National Republican Committee wired Miss Anthony to come to Washington, but as there was serious illness in her home she was unable to reach Washington until five days later, and then in response to a second telegram. Said the chairman:—"At the time we sent our first telegram we were panic-stricken, and had you come then you might have had what you pleased to carry out your plan of work among the women; but now the crisis has passed and we feel confident of success."

The same change of front was soon noticeable in the press. "When it looked as if Greeley might be elected, the Republican newspapers were filled with appeals to the women, and the plank was magnified . . . but as the campaign progressed and the danger passed, it was almost wholly ignored by press and platform."[35]

Horace Greeley was defeated and for 48 years the Republicans, with restored confidence, not needing women's help, made no further pronouncement concerning woman suffrage in a national platform.

CHAPTER 8

Two Amendments and Many Women

At the annual woman suffrage convention of 1872, Miss Anthony led a lively discussion as to whether the 14th and 15th amendments[36] could be interpreted as extending the vote to women as well as to Negroes. Strong resolutions were adopted in favor of a declaratory act of Congress to affirm this interpretation. A hearing was granted before the Senate Judiciary Committee, and Mrs. Stanton, Miss Anthony and Isabelle Beecher Hooker, on behalf of these resolutions, made arguments which could not have failed to leave conscientious Senators with disturbed peace of mind.

Many Senators, Representatives of Congress and eminent lawyers in all parts of the country interpreted the Fourteenth Amendment as securing the vote to Negroes *and* to women. The Attorney General of Nebraska ruled that women were voters under that amendment. In order to test this possibility, and acting under legal advice, women in several States, inspired by the action of their national leaders, attempted to register and vote in 1871 and 1872.[37] Usually their right either to register, or to vote after having registered, was denied by election inspectors, and the method pursued was to bring action against the inspectors for that refusal. Learned and able counsel volunteered in most instances to conduct the defense of the inspectors.

Four cases surpassed all others in importance, three drawing an opinion from the Federal Supreme Court. In chronological order these were:—(1) The case of seventy women in the District of Columbia appealing from the decision of the District Supreme Court, decided December, 1871, chief counsel Senator Matthew Carpenter of Wisconsin; (2) The case of Myra Bradwell, only indirectly bearing upon the subject but testing the meaning of the Fourteenth Amendment, appealing from the Supreme Court of Illinois which had denied her admission to the bar, decision given, December, 1872; (3) The case of Virginia L. Minor, appealing from the Supreme Court of Missouri, chief counsel Francis Minor, an eminently able lawyer of that State, decided October, 1874; and (4) The case of Susan B. Anthony and thirteen other women who, November, 1872, registered and voted in one ward in Rochester, New York. This case did not reach the Federal Supreme Court but attracted the widest comment of all the cases.

The tendency of judges and counsel to turn aside from the consideration of the legal points involved in these cases, in order to deliver lectures upon the proper sphere of women, was a noticeable feature common to all of them, and that prejudice seriously affected the judicial decision will be manifest to readers of the literature of the cases. Manifest, too, will be the muddle in which Court opinions left the Fourteenth Amendment. Even to this day it is doubtful if any exposition, explanation or interpretation of that amendment has been given which is capable of being clearly understood by an average American mind.

Said Albert G. Riddle, counsel for the women voters of the District of Columbia:

"Colored male citizens now vote constitutionally and rightfully, although the word 'white' stands as before in most of the State constitutions; and yet they vote in spite of it. Some potent alembic has destroyed the force of that word. We are at once referred to the Fifteenth Amendment for a solution. The Fifteenth Amendment does not confer anything. It is a solemn mandate to all concerned not to deny this right which is clearly recognized as having existed before. . . . You see in a moment this does not confer anything. It uses no words of grant. . . . It expressly recognized, as an already existing fact, that the citizens of the United States have the right to vote. . . . It is absolutely certain that colored male citizens do not claim their admitted right to vote from the Fifteenth Amendment. Whence did they derive it? From the Fourteenth Amendment? If so, then did women acquire it by the same amendment?"

Francis Minor, also counsel in the same case, picked up the argument at that point and carried it forward.

"Clearly, the Fifteenth Amendment does not confer any right of suffrage. Clearly, prior to the Fourteenth Amendment colored men had no right to vote. The Thirteenth Amendment gave them no such right. But between the Thirteenth and Fifteenth Amendments in some way or other, the colored man came into possession of this right of suffrage and the question is, where did he get it? If he did not get it under the Fourteenth Amendment, by what possible authority are they voting by hundreds of thousands? The legislative and constitutional provisions that prohibit their voting still remain unrepealed upon the statute books of many States, but yet they do vote. There is no way by which they legally can vote except by the operation of the Fourteenth Amendment."

Chief Justice Cartter delivered the opinion of the Court, the main point being, "This clause (the first) of the Fourteenth

Amendment (see page 41) does advance them (women) to full citizenship and clothes them with the capacity to become voters. The constitutional capability of becoming a voter created by this amendment lies dormant, as in the case of an infant, until made effective by legislative action."

Judge Cartter turned aside from his opinion on the legal points under consideration to discourse upon the failure of universal suffrage for men and by implication betrayed his own doubt of the wisdom of universal suffrage. The decision was quoted with ridicule in the press as meaning "that women were voters but had no right to vote."

The most important phase of the Myra Bradwell case is the explicit evidence that popular opinion at the time so governed the views of the Supreme Court of Illinois and of the Federal Supreme Court as completely to control their verdict. The Illinois Court discoursed at great length upon the sphere of women and whether it would "promote justice to permit women to engage in trials at the bar." Mrs. Bradwell's qualification was admitted but her petition was denied because she was not only a woman, but a married woman. Illinois denied to women the right to hold office, and to a married woman the right to make contracts. Mrs. Bradwell had pointed out that a woman, a married woman, under precisely the same conditions, had been admitted to the bar in Iowa, but this precedent fixed by a neighboring State made no impression upon the mental operations of either the Illinois or the Federal Supreme Courts, which were molded by older custom. Justice Miller rendered the judgment of the Federal Supreme Court, denying that "privileges and immunities" protected by the United States include the practice of law; and Justice Bradley, concurring, gave a further opinion in which he delivered a long address on the historic sphere of woman in which "man is or should be woman's protector and defender."

The Minor case traveled somewhat farther. Francis Minor, Mrs. Virginia Minor's husband, joined with her in the appeal as required by the Missouri law, and served as chief counsel. Said he:

> "While the Negro votes today in Missouri, there is not a syllable of affirmative legislation by the State conferring the right upon him. Whence then does he derive it? There is but one reply. The Fourteenth Amendment conferred upon the Negro race in this country citizenship of the United States, and the ballot followed as an incident to that condition. Or to use the more forcible language of this Court in the Slaughter house cases (16 Wall, 71) 'The Negro having by the Fourteenth Amendment been declared a citizen of the United States, is thus made a voter in every State of the Union.' . . . If the Fourteenth Amendment does not secure the ballot to women, neither does it to the Negro; for it does not in terms confer the ballot upon any one."

In summing up, Mr. Minor claimed that the plaintiff was entitled to any and all the "privileges and immunities" guaranteed to all citizens by the first section of the Fourteenth Amendment, and that the elective franchise is a privilege of citizenship in the highest sense of the word.

The decision delivered by Chief Justice Waite was long and indefinite. The chief points were: "The constitution does not define privileges and immunities of citizens." "The amendment did not add to the privileges and immunities of a citizen." "No new voters were necessarily made by it." "The constitution has not added the right of suffrage to the privileges and immunities of citizens." Since "The constitution of the United States does not confer the right of suffrage upon anyone," the constitution and laws of the several States which commit that trust to men alone "are not necessarily void." "If suffrage was one of these privileges and immunities, why amend the constitution to prevent its being denied on account of race?"

Neither Judge nor Court has yet been able to point out in terms comprehensible to the average man on the street, wherein lay the "potent alembic" cited by Mr. Riddle in the District of Columbia case which had granted the vote to Negro men. The laws of no State had conferred the vote upon them. The Federal Supreme Court before 1884, in all cases seeking interpretation of the two amendments, held that the constitution of the United States, including the new amendments, conferred the vote upon no one. If neither State nor federal constitutions nor laws had conferred the vote upon colored men, where did they get it? The military reconstruction act had given the Negro the vote in disloyal states, but that act did not apply to the loyal States and presumably was intended as a temporary measure. No other act of any kind had been passed.

Justice Miller in the case of *ex parte* Yarborough, in 1884, delivering the opinion of the Federal Supreme Court, declared:

> "While it is true, as said in the Reese case, that the Fifteenth Amendment gave no affirmative right to the colored man to vote . . . yet it does substantially confer on the Negro the right to vote, and Congress has the power to protect and enforce that right."[38]

In bewilderment, the public asked, "How may an amendment substantially confer a right when it does not confer it?" Just why the Congress, in which sat many of the ablest men of the nation, was unable or unwilling to write amendments which could be understood by those who read them is difficult of comprehension, but the explanation is undoubtedly to be found in the fact that the Fourteenth Amendment was a compromise of many conflicting views.

A participant in the controversy, in writing its inner history, throws light upon the puzzling situation. He quotes Alexander Stevens, the father of the reconstruction measures and leader of the majority in the House of Representatives, as saying:

"Don't imagine that I sanction the shilly-shally, bungling thing that I shall have to report to the House tomorrow."[39]

Replying to a protest following the public announcement of the provisions of the amendment, Mr. Stevens wrote:

"In the course of last week the members from New York, from Illinois and from Indiana, held, each separately, a caucus to consider whether equality of suffrage, present or prospective, ought to form a part of the Republican program for the coming canvass. They were afraid, so some of them told me, that if there was 'a nigger in the woodpile' at all (that was the phrase) it would be used against them as an electioneering handle, and some of them—hang their cowardice!—might lose their elections. By inconsiderable majorities each of these caucuses decided that Negro suffrage, in any shape, ought to be excluded from the platform; and they communicated these decisions to us. Our committee hadn't backbone enough to maintain its ground. Yesterday the vote on your plan was reconsidered, your amendment was laid on the table, and in the course of the next three hours we contrived to patch together—well, what you've read this morning."[40]

The Fourteenth Amendment extends certain rights to the Negro, but not the suffrage. It merely threatens to cut down the representation of States which deny the vote to any male inhabitants. The Fifteenth Amendment declares in stern tones that the right to vote *shall not be* denied on account of race, color or previous condition of servitude and gives the Congress power to enforce the provision.

It takes a careful reading of the long congressional debates on the subject to reveal the "potent alembic" that was challenged by Mr. Riddle as destroying the force of the word "white" as one of a voter's qualifications. It was politics. The National Republican party passed on to the State Republican parties an interpretation that was not written in the law: The Negro must have the vote in the South to protect himself from the domination of white men. The Republican party must have the support of loyal men in the secession States if there is to be peace, and the loyal men are the Negroes. The right of the State to make its own suffrage laws shall be respected, and therefore no conferring of the vote upon the Negro shall be done by federal act. These amendments mean however that the Negro shall have the right to vote in your State. They do not confer the vote, they merely threaten you with penalties if you deny the vote.

Politics, therefore, put into the amendments the meaning not clear to the reader of the text, and over whose obscurity courts and lawyers tripped. The Negro voted by the authority of the federal law forbidding the States to deny him the right to do so, but not conferring the right upon him. The States accepted this political order and allowed him to vote, although no State law conferred the vote upon him. This strained attempt not to offend State's rights sensibilities, when considered in connection with the methods of ratification, including "the crack of the party whip" at the North and the threat of the bayonet at the South, offers a curious example of State's rights in theory and centralized autocracy in practice.

It was in connection with the controversy and confusion over the 14th and 15th Amendments, that one of the most spirited chapters of all suffrage history was enacted. It was the last and most noteworthy of the four cases enumerated above through which the women of that day tried to get into the electorate by way of the door opened by the 14th amendment. On November 5, 1872, Susan B. Anthony and thirteen other women voted in a ward of Rochester, New York, in an effort to test the provisions of the amendments as applying to women. The Supreme Court of the nation had already passed upon the District of Columbia cases, and the decision had not only aroused keen criticism and comment but many lawyers charged the Court with prejudice and failure to meet squarely the question involved. Other cases were pending and Rochester gave a fresh impulse to the popular discussion as to what the Fourteenth and Fifteenth Amendments really meant.

At this juncture politics, directed by Washington, took a hand in the Rochester proceedings. A few days after Miss Anthony's vote, a Deputy United States Marshal appeared at the various houses of the Rochester women voters and arrested them in the name of the United States government, upon the criminal charge of "having voted without having a lawful right to vote." Authority for the United States government to take charge of the alleged violation of State election laws was laboriously drawn from the so-called Ku Klux Klan law which had been passed by Congress to prevent disfranchised rebels from exercising the suffrage before being pardoned. *The women were gathered, fitly enough, in the same office where before the war fugitive black men and women had been examined and returned to slavery.* Bail of $500 each was ordered for their appearance at the Albany term of the United States District Court in January, 1873. Miss Anthony refused to give bail and petitioned for a writ of habeas corpus, her petition being presented by Judge Selden, one of the most eminent attorneys in the State of New York.[41]

On January 16 and 17, 1873, the annual national woman suffrage convention met in Washington. Miss Anthony named the possible methods of securing the vote for women as: by State constitutional amendments, to be adopted by electors at the polls, by a federal constitutional amendment to be adopted by a two-thirds vote of both Houses of the Congress and ratified by three-fourths of the State Legislatures, or, by taking "their right under the Fourteenth Amendment." She pointed out that court decisions permitting women to avail themselves of this right, or a declaratory act of Congress, were necessary. "The vaults in yonder Capitol," said she, "hold the petitions of one hundred thousand women for a declaratory act; and the calendars of our courts show that many women are already testing their right to vote under the Fourteenth Amendment. I stand here under indictment for having exercised my right as a citizen to vote at the last election, and by a fiction of the law I am now in custody and not a free person."

The convention passed resolutions declaring its confidence that the Fourteenth Amendment enfranchised women as certainly as Negroes, and again called upon Congress for a Declaratory Act.

Miss Anthony hastened from Washington to Albany, where her petition was denied by United States District Judge N. K. Hall and her bail increased to one thousand dollars with orders for appearance at the May term in Rochester. This was in January. Again she refused to give bail, but Judge Selden, her counsel, against her wishes and without her knowledge, went on her bond. When she learned that by this fact "she had lost her chance of getting her case before the Supreme Court by writ of habeas corpus, she tried to have the bond cancelled but to her chagrin her counsel pronounced this impossible."[42] Immediately after Judge Hall's decision, all the women and the three inspectors were indicted by a Grand Jury. Between the hearing before Judge Hall and his decision, Miss Anthony had time, accompanied by her counsel, to appear before the Commission on Amendments to the New York State Constitution, then sitting in Albany, and make a powerful plea to include woman suffrage in the proposed changes.

Before the May term of Court, Miss Anthony held a meeting in every post office district of her county (Monroe), twenty-nine in number, speaking upon the subject, "Is it a crime for a United States citizen to vote?" The United States District Attorney, Richard Crowley, notified her that if she did not desist he would have the case moved to another county when the Court met, and made good his threat. Claiming that no jury could be drawn which might not be prejudiced in her favor, he asked and secured a change of venue to the United States District Court at Canandaigua, Ontario County, allowing just twenty-two days before the trial. The change was ordered on Friday, and on Monday she held her first meeting in Ontario County and followed it by twenty-one other meetings. Matilda Joslyn Gage came to her aid and held sixteen meetings. When on June 17, 1873, the trial took place, the court room was filled by politicians, lawyers and prominent citizens, among them ex-President Fillmore and Judge Hall who had denied the writ of habeas corpus. The jury was sworn in, with Judge Ward Hunt presiding, United States District Attorney Crowley appearing for the United States government and Henry R. Selden and John Van Voorhis for the women voters.

Some hours were consumed in the arguments presented. The one point which stands out most conspicuously after the lapse of half a century was this statement of Judge Selden's:

"Miss Anthony believed and was advised that she had a right to vote under the provisions of the Federal Constitutional Amendments. She was advised as clearly that the question of her right could not be brought before the courts for trial without her voting or offering to vote. Her motives were pure and noble and carried no intent of fraud or crime. If by the laws of her country she shall be condemned a criminal for taking the only step by which it was possible to bring the great constitutional question of her right before the courts for adjudication, it adds another reason to those I have advanced to show that women need the ballot for their protection."

When the last word had been spoken, those assembled were shocked to see the presiding Judge draw from his pocket a written opinion, clearly prepared before he had heard evidence or argument. He directed the jury to bring in a verdict of guilty, and when Judge Selden protested at this unwarranted act, he refused to have the jury polled and in the midst of the controversy discharged it!

The character of Judge Hunt's previously prepared opinion was equally astonishing. Said he: "Miss Anthony knew that she was a woman and that the constitution of this State prohibits her from voting." Since Miss Anthony based her claim to a vote upon the fact that she was a citizen of the United States and upon the belief that the vote was included among the "privileges and immunities" which the Fourteenth Amendment, as a part of the federal constitution, forbade any State to abridge, this point of view begged the whole question. Quite possibly this curious failure even to comprehend what the contention was about would not have been expressed had the Judge waited to hear the case before he wrote his opinion.

He further held that although she might have believed that she had the right to vote and voted in good faith, and that she had been advised that such right was hers, nevertheless she was guilty of a crime because she had had no legal right to a vote, the motive having no bearing upon the question.

There was widespread condemnation of Judge Hunt's conduct of the case, and none were more outspoken than some members of the jury who boldly declared that had they had the opportunity they would not have voted guilty. The Albany *Law Journal,* though scornfully disapproving woman suffrage, admitted that the Judge usurped power in taking the case from the jury, and editorial discussion of the question "Can a judge direct a verdict of guilty" was frequent. Those who had sympathy neither with woman suffrage nor the effort to test the Fourteenth Amendment, pronounced Judge Hunt's assumption of authority a dangerous and menacing threat to free government.

A motion for a new trial was denied. A fine of one hundred dollars and the costs of the prosecution were the penalties imposed. Miss Anthony responded with the declaration that she would never pay a penny of the unjust penalty, whereupon Judge Hunt said that the Court would not order her committed until the fine was paid, and although this procedure was contrary to the custom and the law, the fine was neither paid nor remitted.

Had the Judge demanded the penalty or imprisonment, Miss Anthony would have gone to prison and could then have taken her case directly to the Supreme Court of the United States by writ of habeas corpus. Lawyers claimed that the fact that she had been denied a trial by jury would have made her discharge certain. Had this case been permitted to find its way to the Supreme Court, or had the jury at Canandaigua been allowed to perform the ordinary function of jurymen, history might have been decisively changed.

The trial of the inspectors which followed attracted little attention by comparison, but it was in reality an even more unwarranted usurpation of authority. The inspectors served under the laws of New York and any failure to perform their duty in accordance with that law was clearly an offense against State, not national, law. Yet they were arrested by officers of the United States and tried by a Judge of the Federal Supreme Court for the crime of violating a New York law! The inspectors were found guilty, although it was made quite clear that they believed it to be their duty to accept the women's votes and that they acted in good faith and without criminal intent. This time the jury was permitted to act, although counsel was denied the privilege of addressing it, and the judge virtually directed it to bring in a verdict of guilty, which it did.

In February, 1874, about nine months after their trial, the three inspectors were seized by the United States authorities and thrown into jail because they had not paid their fines. As was well known, they had been advised not to do so. Senator Sargent of California promptly presented a petition to President Grant who at once remitted their fines. They were, however, in jail a week, during which time the best of meals were furnished them by the fifteen women voters; hundreds of citizens called to pay their respects, and the entire city regarded the proceedings as a joke.

The press gibed at United States District Attorney Crowley unmercifully for prosecuting the young men and being afraid to attack the woman "who shrinks not from any of the terrors of the law," but she was neither arrested nor approached again in reference to her fine. She was importuned to allow an appeal to be made to President Grant, for whom she had voted, to remit her fine, but this she refused to do. Instead, by the advice of Judge Selden she addressed an appeal from Judge Hunt's decision to Congress in her own name. Her petition was presented in the Senate by Senator Sargent of California, afterward Minister to Germany, January, 1874, and was referred to the Judiciary Committee, which through its chairman, Senator Edmunds of Vermont, asked to be discharged from consideration, as Congress had no authority to act.

Senator Matt H. Carpenter of Wisconsin, acknowledging that Congress could not remit the fine imposed, nor secure a new trial, yet condemned the injustice of the trial, denouncing it as without precedent, and called the attention of Congress to the need of an amended system of jurisprudence, since "a citizen may be tried, condemned and put to death by the erroneous judgment of a single judge, and no court can grant him relief or a new trial." In the House the petition was reported adversely by the Judiciary

Committee, a letter being incorporated in the report from District Attorney Crowley urging the Committee "not to degrade a just judge and applaud a criminal." As Judges Hall and Hunt and District Attorney Crowley were appointees of the Administration, political considerations assisted the committee in arriving at its conclusions.

Benjamin F. Butler, however, offered a minority report recommending that the prayer of the petitioner be granted. He too declared that she had had a mistrial, and though both Senator Carpenter and Mr. Butler had been careful not to accuse too boldly the motives or the qualifications of Judge Hunt, their subtle comments were recognized as a severe reproof.

Although the women failed to secure an opinion from the Federal Supreme Court that the Fourteenth Amendment included women under its provision concerning "the privileges and immunities of citizens," the conviction remained with suffrage leaders and many able lawyers that the words of the law could be only so interpreted. Again and again in after years eminently qualified lawyers with briefs in hand begged suffragists to make further appeals to the Court for affirmation of their rights as set forth in the amendment, but the women knew that the "potent alembic" of politics would not be made to operate in their case, and they steadfastly refused to waste any more time in efforts to get favorable judicial decisions to support their claim to the suffrage under the provisions of that amendment.

CHAPTER 9

The Woman's Hour
That Never Came

Three years were consumed in the process of writing the word male into the Federal Constitution, two more in completing the enfranchisement of the Negro. Both were strictly Republican party measures and were achieved by the combined political force of a majority party and the military power of the nation. The demand to include women in any further extension of the suffrage, although supported at the time by men of great influence in party and nation, was effectually evaded all along the way by the proposal to "let the women wait—this is the Negro's hour,—the woman's hour will come."

To get the word male in effect out of the constitution cost the women of the country fifty-two years of pauseless campaign thereafter. During that time they were forced to conduct fifty-six campaigns of referenda to male voters; 480 campaigns to get Legislatures to submit suffrage amendments to voters; forty-seven campaigns to get State constitutional conventions to write woman suffrage into State constitutions; 277 campaigns to get State party conventions to include woman suffrage planks; thirty campaigns to get presidential party conventions to adopt woman suffrage planks in party platforms, and nineteen campaigns with nineteen successive Congresses. Millions of dollars were raised, mainly in small sums, and expended with economic care. Hundreds of women gave the accumulated possibilities of an entire lifetime, thousands gave years of their lives, hundreds of thousands gave constant interest and such aid as they could. It was a continuous, seemingly endless, chain of activity. Young suffragists who helped forge the last links of that chain were not born when it began. Old suffragists who forged the first links were dead when it ended.

During this long stretch of time, the dominant political parties, pitted against each other since 1860, used their enormous organized power to block every move on behalf of woman suffrage. The seeming exceptions were rare and invariably caused by breaks or threatened breaks in party ranks. Strong men in both parties and in all States championed the woman's cause in Legislatures and in political conventions, and eventually the number of these became too large to be ignored. But it was not until public opinion, far in advance of party leaders, indicated that a choice between woman suffrage and party disruption must be made that organized party help was given, and even then it was neither united nor whole-hearted.

Between the adoption of the Fifteenth Amendment (March 30, 1870), which completed the enfranchisement of the Negro, and 1910, lie forty years during which women watched, prayed and worked without ceasing for the woman's hour that never came. The party whips had cracked to drive the nation to enfranchise the Negro. They cracked, and cracked again, to prevent the enfranchisement of women. Whenever there was an exception and the parties stood by woman suffrage in a referendum, success came to the woman's cause. Most victories were won, however, in spite of party opposition.

It was with amazing courage that the 480 campaigns to secure the submission of State constitutional amendments from

Legislatures were conducted. In these campaigns millions of names were presented to the several Legislatures in the form of petitions, party endorsement was sought in political conventions, candidates were interviewed—hundreds of whom gladly gave their pledges of support—press aid was solicited, and, in most States, a majority of the newspapers were won over to support the submission and adoption of the question. These campaigns were conducted in all the thirty-three States and territories lying outside the original pro-slave district, in some continuously through the half century, in some intermittently. Yet in forty years, as a result of the 480 campaigns, only seventeen referenda[43] were secured. As Oregon submitted the question four times in those years, and Washington, South Dakota, and Colorado twice respectively, the number of States wherein the voters expressed their opinion upon State amendments was eleven only. Since no Legislature or constitutional convention possesses the authority to extend or withhold suffrage from women, and has only the right to pass the question on to the voters or to refuse to do so, the autocracy of this record makes impressive legislative history.

The strongest suffrage organizations were in the East where the movement began and where the ablest of the early leaders lived. It was these States which had furnished the initiative and the insistence which enfranchised the Negro by bayonet. Yet in Massachusetts, New York, New Jersey, Pennsylvania, Ohio, Indiana, Illinois and Iowa, where the woman suffrage appeal was continual during those forty years, no suffrage referendum was secured. Of the seventeen referenda in those years, all were in States west of the Mississippi except three. Four referenda, Michigan 1874, Colorado 1877, Nebraska 1882 and Oregon 1884, were normal by-products of the Negro suffrage agitation; ten were the direct result of the defection within the dominant parties, chiefly Republican, which was produced by the Populist uprising which reached its crest between 1890 and 1900,[44] and the three remaining (Washington 1889, Rhode Island 1887 and New Hampshire 1902) were due to local causes. Two States only were won in these seventeen referenda, Colorado and Idaho; in both cases the party organizations were broken wide asunder and each faction endorsed the amendment. In the fifteen other States where amendments were submitted there were disturbed political conditions in nine, but in no case did the opposing factions endorse the amendment, and the regular party organization used its power to defeat the amendment.

A cursory review of these referenda campaigns, State by State, makes clearer and clearer the character of the opposition that piled higher and higher in the path of suffrage workers.

Michigan—In 1874 a special session of the Michigan Legislature submitted a woman suffrage constitutional amendment. The debate indicated that the action was an attempt to do justice to the women who had been made political inferiors of the recent slaves. Forty thousand men voted in favor but the amendment was lost and little record of the campaign has been preserved.

Nebraska—In 1869 the Legislature failed to submit the question of woman suffrage by a single vote in one house. In 1871 the Legislature memorialized the constitutional convention sitting that year, urging it to submit woman suffrage, and it did so, but the entire constitution was defeated. It was never charged that the woman suffrage provision caused the defeat of the constitution. In 1882 the Legislature, by the required three-fifths vote, submitted a woman suffrage amendment. The State constitution stipulates that an amendment shall receive a majority of all the votes cast in the election at which it is voted upon, a handicap so serious that most amendments submitted under this condition, however popular, have gone down to defeat. Liberal promises of help had been received from many men of prominence. For that day the organization was good, the campaign carefully planned, and more efficient than any yet conducted, but as election day approached the women were mystified because so many men failed to fulfill their promises and developed a sudden aloofness.

The reason for this defection was soon apparent. "The organ of the Brewers Association sent out its orders to defeat the amendment to every saloon, bills posted in conspicuous places by friends of the amendment mysteriously disappeared or were covered by others of an opposite character, and the greatest pains were taken to excite the antagonism of foreigners by representing to them that woman suffrage meant prohibition."[45] "Judge O. P. Mason, who had agreed to give ten lectures for the amendment and whose advocacy would have had immense weight, was engaged to speak for the Republican Party and at every place but one the managers stipulated that he should be silent on the amendment." There was a large German vote, thoroughly aroused over the "menace of prohibition," and prejudiced against and afraid of the woman vote. Nebraska was a State where men voted on first papers, and with the appearance of evidence of possible organized opposition threatening candidates and parties, politicians flew to safety like a frightened covey of ducks. The Republican party machinery, set in action against the amendment, defeated it two to one. Fraudulent ballots with no mention of the amendment on them were found in large numbers. Ballots with wording differing from that prescribed by the Legislature were also numerous. All these were counted in the total number of votes at the election, of which the amendment must secure a majority, and were therefore virtually counted as against the amendment. The correct returns were never known and many suffragists had justification for the belief that had the election been an honest one, the amendment would have been won. The vote for woman suffrage was 25,756; against, 50,693. The suffragists learned in this campaign that they had an insidious enemy which was not public opinion.

Nebraska announced that this was the German's hour!

Rhode Island—The Legislature of Rhode Island in 1887 submitted an amendment, leaving just twenty-nine days for a campaign. In that time the women held ninety-two public meetings, but the two political parties passed the word along the line that the amendment was to be defeated. No secret was made of the bi-partisan order which, combined with normal conservatism and prejudice, brought the heaviest defeat yet recorded, or more than three to one; 6,889 against, and 2,195 in favor.

Washington—In 1883 the territorial Legislature of Washington had followed the example set by the Legislatures of Wyoming and Utah, and extended full suffrage to women. The women voted in large numbers at every election. In 1887, a man named Harlan Young, convicted by a jury composed in part of women, contested the verdict upon the ground that women were not legal voters. Grover Cleveland had come into the presidency in 1884 and, adhering to the spoils system common to both parties, had filled the Supreme Court of Washington with Southern Democrats whose prejudices against woman suffrage were impregnable. The Court declared the suffrage law invalid because its object had not been properly described in its title. The next Legislature, 1889, promptly re-enacted the law, free from the defects of the former one, and women continued to vote. Washington Territory was agitating for statehood and the enemies of prohibition were determined that women should not vote on the constitution soon to be drafted. They arranged that the judges of the spring municipal election in a district of Spokane should refuse to accept the vote of Mrs. Nevada Bloomer, the wife of a saloon-keeper. She then brought action against them, the case was speedily rushed through, and on August 14 the Supreme Court decided that the Act of January 18 was invalid, as a Territorial Legislature had no authority to enfranchise women. Mrs. Bloomer refused to appeal and no one else could. The women were therefore debarred from participating in the next election.

The decision of the Court was certainly an illegal one, for the following reasons: (1) The Act of Congress authorizing the organization of the Territory had stated clearly that "all persons should be allowed to vote upon whom the Territorial Legislature might confer the elective franchise." (2) The women of Wyoming had voted under such a law since 1869 and in Utah since 1870. (3) When Congress, in 1887, disfranchised the women of Utah in order to strike a blow at polygamy, that act admitted the right of the Territorial Legislature to enfranchise women. Yet Congress, which had enfranchised the Negro by bayonet and defended his vote with military force, admitted Washington to statehood on a constitution framed by a convention whose members had been elected by voters of whom a considerable number had been illegally restrained from voting. Moreover, the constitution had been adopted by the same illegal electorate!

The liquor forces, having thus illegally disposed of the woman vote, conducted a successful campaign to elect a convention that would represent their wishes. The convention submitted a separate suffrage amendment to male voters only, and both parties, under direction of the liquor interests, used the power of their organizations to prevent its passage.

There was no doubt in any mind that 1889 was the saloon's hour in Washington.

These four referenda in the twenty years from 1869 to 1889 represented the sole results of efforts to secure full suffrage for women.

In the year 1890 a farmer's party, later called the Populist party, emerged from earlier farmers' organizations,—the Farmers' Alliance, the Grange, and others,— in Western agricultural States, and as it held the "balance of power" it exercised an enormous influence upon American politics for the next decade. As all these States were controlled by large Republican majorities, the new party drew its chief support from that party. The minority Democratic party, fusing with the Populists, produced a combination which either wrested power from the Republicans or shared it with them.

Simultaneously a movement arose in Western mining States, caused by the low price of silver and aiming to correct it by giving silver a place with gold, at the "ratio of 16 to 1," as the basic standard of money values. The silver movement split the Republican Party in most of the mining States, and the Populists, fusing with Democrats and silver Republicans, became an even more important political factor in those States. As the result of these political changes, Grover Cleveland was elected in 1892. The free silver coinage movement reached its climax in 1896 and the Fifty-fifth Congress (1897–1899) contained six Populist Senators and twenty-seven members in the House, while in all the Western States many Populist or Fusion members were elected to the Legislatures, and in some instances were in control.

In Washington the Fusionists were so successful that the 1897 Legislature was made up of reform elements. That Legislature submitted a woman suffrage amendment to the voters of 1898. It was defeated but the adverse majority was only half as great as in the election of 1889.

South Dakota—The splitting and fusing of political groups had direct bearing upon the suffrage referendum in South Dakota in 1890. The Territory of Dakota, created in 1861, was later divided, and North and South Dakota were admitted into the Union in 1889. The Dakota Territorial Legislature of 1872 came within one vote of extending full suffrage to women, and in 1885 it did so, following the example of Wyoming, Utah and Washington, women at the time voting in all three. The Republican Governor, Gilbert

A. Pierce, vetoed the bill of 1885, upon the ground that Congress might not welcome Dakota into statehood with woman suffrage in operation, since Congress had taken no steps to enfranchise women, which it had a right to do.

The constitution accepted by Congress when South Dakota was admitted to statehood provided that the first Legislature at its first session should submit a constitutional woman suffrage amendment to the voters. But the Constitutional Convention submitted a prohibition amendment which went to vote in 1889, at the same election which adopted the constitution. After a bitterly fought battle, prohibition was carried and an immediate campaign was undertaken by the liquor forces for its repeal. They regarded, as the first outpost to be taken, the defeat of the suffrage amendment which, according to plan, was to come to vote the following year—1890.

Before the campaign began suffragists anticipated victory in South Dakota. The Farmer's Alliance was a large and powerful body and its officers had not only agreed to exert the full influence of their organization for the amendment, but had urged Miss Anthony to come to South Dakota to conduct the campaign in person in order that it might the more certainly be won. The Knights of Labor had agreed by resolution to support the amendment "with all our strength." These two organizations later decided to form an Independent or People's party, and at the convention called for the purpose of adopting a platform and nominating a ticket, the leaders repudiated their pledges, having decided that the new party would be overloaded should it endorse woman suffrage. When this group of professed friends refused endorsement, nothing could be expected of the regular parties, weakened by the defection of those who composed the new party.

The Republican party, recognizing that three hundred Sioux Indians would vote in the State by the act of the federal government, invited three blanketed representatives to sit on the floor of the convention with the delegates, but refused to allow any women so honored a position. The suffrage amendment was ignored in the platform.

It was the Indian's hour.

When Susan B. Anthony addressed the Democratic convention, a delegation of illiterate Russians wearing large badges "Against Woman Suffrage and Susan B. Anthony" were carefully seated where their presence announced the party attitude. As the delegates came out of these two conventions, men at the door thrust into their hands a paper called the *Remonstrance,* published by ladies in Boston who were not yet courageous enough to indicate their responsibility by printing their names on the sheet. The men who distributed the papers were saloon men, and the sight of their dirty hands and degenerate faces would have made the gentle remonstrants squirm. The outstanding feature of this campaign was the employment for the first time in a large way of the foreign vote as a bloc, voted under direction and paid for the assistance it rendered. South Dakota permitted foreigners to vote on their first papers, and there were thirty thousand Russians, Germans and Scandinavians in the State. Very many thousands had been there from six months to two years only. Unable to read or write in any language or to speak English, these men were boldly led to the ballot boxes under direction of well-known saloon henchmen, and after being voted were marched away in single file, and, within unmistakable sight of men and women poll workers, were paid for their votes. The movement to curb the practice of buying votes, which led in after years to laws in all States more or less strict, had scarcely begun and in the new State of South Dakota there was no redress. The amendment was lost—22,072 ayes; 45,682 nays; majority opposed 23,790.

It was the Russian's hour.

The Legislature again submitted the question in 1898 and again the Russians were mobilized "like dumb driven cattle" and paid to defeat the amendment.

Suffragists drew the following conclusions from this campaign: (1) That non-English speaking, illiterate men who were voted by the thousands did not go to the polls voluntarily, nor had they offered their own services. Some power had enlisted them, voted them, paid them. What was it?

(2) Whatever that power was, it had either commanded the political parties to do its bidding, or the political parties had called it to their aid.

Colorado—In 1893 Colorado had inaugurated a Populist Governor, and the Legislature, with Republicans in control in the House and Populists in the Senate, submitted the question of woman suffrage to the voters, most Populists voting for the measure and the majority of Republicans against.[46] This was not the first experience with suffrage referenda in Colorado. The constitutional convention of 1876, preparing for statehood, had submitted a separate amendment which had come to vote in 1877. The debate had indicated that the details of Negro enfranchisement were fresh in the minds of the delegates and that some amends were due the women. A hurried organization had been effected and a creditable campaign conducted. The amendment was lost, but the effects of the campaign persisted and the organization had never entirely lapsed.

Old friends and new now united in preparing for the contest of 1893. There was no State election that year. The State political machines were not in operation, and the rank and file of the voters received no orders. County nominating conventions were held, and in most counties one or more party conventions endorsed the amendment, all Populist conventions and many Republican conventions taking this stand. Very many individual Republicans and Democrats frankly espoused the amendment, and assisted in the campaign. A factor everywhere manifest was the influence of Wyoming. No imaginative prediction of baneful results to arise from woman suffrage was allowed to travel far, for a man from Wyoming was certain to come forward with a scornful denial.

Although there were many women who labored long hours, hard and earnestly, and although the consecrated central committee was wise and alert, the campaign, as compared with those that came after, was neither elaborate nor thorough.

No organized opposition appeared until the eve of election day. The Denver Brewers' Association then gave hurried orders to the saloons, assessing them for funds. Dodgers were issued, bearing the imprint of the Brewers' Association on the first few issued, which found their way into circulation. The imprint was soon removed, however, and the thousands later distributed from door to door carried no evidence of their origin. Fortunately a newspaper came into possession of some of the first dodgers issued and revealed the character of this eleventh-hour attempt to defeat the amendment.

Tricks with which suffragists afterwards became sickeningly familiar were also used. A lawyer was employed to discover ways of throwing ballots out of the count on "technicalities." Influence with election officials, wielded by some of the opponents, secured ballots bearing the words "For the Amendment," "Against the Amendment." The question to be voted upon was not an amendment. By the provision of the constitution of 1876 woman suffrage could be granted by the Legislature if confirmed by referendum. The women of the State had been enfranchised by the Legislature, and the voters were now being asked to confirm or deny. The Attorney General gave a prompt opinion which was published by the State authorities to set the voters right. At the polls the measure was carried by a majority of 6,347.[47] The counties that had gone Republican and

Democratic in the previous election gave a majority of 471 against the measure. The counties that had gone Populist gave the favorable majority.

Startled by their own victory, the women wanted to do something in celebration which would remain forever after in their memories. A crowd gathered in the suffrage headquarters and they talked it over, but being unable to devise any unique plan, someone started "Praise God from whom all blessings flow," and people passing by outside heard a great chorus of song. After which the tired workers went home quietly with praise God singing in their hearts.

Informed suffragists derived two convictions from the Colorado campaign which stayed with them to the end:

(1) That which was achieved in the State would not have been possible had there been no break in party control.

(2) That which had been done in Colorado could be done in any Western State were voters free to vote their own convictions.

Kansas—The Populist contest in Kansas was particularly aggressive and bitter. In 1892, the Populists swept the State and the following election was regarded as the test of strength. As both Populists and Republicans carried planks favoring the submission of a woman suffrage amendment in their platforms, the Legislature of 1893 submitted the question. The Kansas Equal Suffrage Association was one of the most alert in the United States, its president, Mrs. Laura M. Johns, one of the ablest of presidents. A series of county conventions by way of preparation had been held in all the more thickly populated sections. Kansas was a State where women were trained in politics. In 1861, school suffrage had been extended to women. There had been a woman suffrage referendum in 1867 that had aroused public opinion and its effects were still manifest. In 1887, the Legislature had granted municipal suffrage to women. Kansas was a prohibition State and municipal politics had centered largely upon the enforcement of this law. The women, because they were voters, had been drawn into the party campaigns and yet by the exercise of rare good sense had kept their organization non-partisan. Mrs. Johns was a Republican, but Mrs. Annie E. Diggs, a Populist, was made vice-chairman of the Kansas Auxiliary to the National American Woman Suffrage Association.

Work without ceasing was now the order of every day. More able, well-trained women were engaged in the campaign than in all the preceding ones put together. All agreed that should the Republican and Populist parties endorse the amendment, as they had the question of submission, there was no possibility of defeat. The Republican convention met on June 6. The leaders had already decided to throw woman suffrage overboard "to save the party." There were no saloons in Kansas but there were "wets." There was also a conservative Southern element which had come in before the war to make Kansas a slave State. Ex-Governor C. V. Eskridge, an active opponent of woman suffrage since 1867, was chairman of the Committee on Resolutions, Mrs. J. Ellen Foster, a national Republican lecturer, and Mrs. Johns addressed the Committee. It was reminded that by common admission women municipal voters had kept the State of Kansas Republican. Yet Committee and Convention ignored the amendment.

The women now awaited the Populist convention with dread. The Populist candidate for Governor, Mr. Llewellyn, declared that he would not stand for re-election on a platform that contained woman suffrage. Genuine disapproval of woman suffrage there was, but it was rendered powerful by the accession of those who feared for the party's safety.

This convention proved to be one of the most thrilling experiences in the long suffrage struggle. The Resolutions Committee sat most of the night, and, worn and haggard, its members brought in next day a report which omitted the expected suffrage plank.

There was one woman member, Mrs. Eliza Hudson, who brought in a minority report signed by herself and seven men members. Then began a parliamentary tilt to keep the minority report from being heard. It was however brought to debate, and four hours were consumed in as tense and earnest a combat of words as had ever been heard in Kansas. A Negro delegate with halting language declared that woman suffrage would mean party defeat and that in any event women did not know enough to vote. This called forth wild and scornful laughter, and the floor was dotted with delegates who sprang to the defense of the women voters of the State. The minority report was adopted by a vote of 337 ayes to 269 nays, but only after it had been amended by the addition "but we do not regard this as a test of party fealty!"

Suffragists sitting on the platform, glad to get even this much of an endorsement, applauded the vote, whereupon the editor of the chief Republican newspaper, the Topeka *Capital*, with eyes flashing, hastily left the platform and, in the heat of temper, incited an editorial which called upon all Republicans to understand that the amendment was now a Populist measure and no Republican need support it.

A campaign followed which acquainted women with new phases of American politics. Jealousy and suspicion were aroused between the parties. Jealousy and suspicion guided the campaign. The Populists believed that women in the cities, being more numerous than those in the country, would make the State Republican. The Republicans held that, there being more women in the country than in the cities, women voters would make the State Populist! Both were unchangeable. No one expected victory to emerge from a situation so utterly unreasonable. The amendment was lost by 34,837 votes,—95,302 ayes and 130,139 nays. An effort was made to keep a record of the vote by parties and much careful work and tabulation of returns was done. The estimated result showed that

38½ per cent of the Republicans, 54 per cent of the Populists, 14 per cent of the Democrats and 88 per cent of the Prohibitionists voted for the amendment.

This was the most heart-breaking defeat of the suffrage struggle. The majority of the people of Kansas were earnest advocates of suffrage, as was apparent to anyone making a canvass of the State, yet the moral conviction of Kansas men had been utterly surrendered to imagined party advantage.

Idaho—As both Populists and Republicans had declared for suffrage in their State platforms, the submission of a woman suffrage amendment was passed by the Idaho Legislature of 1895, unanimously in the Senate and by thirty-three to two in the House. The National Suffrage Association made itself responsible for the traveling forces that covered the State during the campaign. In August, 1896, four State political party conventions met in Boise; the Republicans splitting into Regulars and Silver Republicans, the Populists and Democrats fusing. All four endorsed the suffrage amendment and many of the campaigners of all parties spoke for it. The campaign was simple and normal, costing only $1,800. The amendment carried without organized opposition by a majority of 5,844—12,126 for and 6,282 against.

California—The Republican Legislature of California, carrying out the declaration in its platform, submitted a woman suffrage amendment, which was voted upon in 1896. Participants have always remembered the campaign as the best conducted, liveliest and most enthusiastic of their experience. All meetings were crowded, jubilant and heartily in sympathy. The press was friendly. No opposition appeared. The hospitable Western spirit of freedom for all seemed to control the situation.

Four days before election day, the chief Republican newspaper, the *Chronicle,* burst forth in a vituperative frenzy of hostility and used its utmost powers to arouse opposition. Election day brought the unique sight of Chinese voters, in "pigtails" and sandals, at the polling booths. Chinese are denied naturalization by the United States but those born in this country are citizens by the provisions of the 14th Amendment and some five thousand were thus qualified voters. Faithful watchers reported that these men were rarely informed enough to mark more than one item on the ballot, in which case their vote was invariably marked against the amendment. When the voter was intelligent enough to mark two items he voted for McKinley electors and against the amendment. The Pacific Coast, and especially California, had made a vigorous protest against the 14th and 15th Amendments because of the fear that the Chinese under unscrupulous direction would dominate politics, and for these reasons the State had rejected the 15th Amendment. By a curious cynicism Chinese voters now, with the possible knowledge of those who had once protested against them and certainly with the aid of their fellow partisans, directed their votes to deny self-government to American women.

It was the hour of the Chinese!

The entire State was carried for the amendment with the exception of San Francisco and Alameda counties. Ayes 110,355, nays 137,099. Majority against 26,744. The majority against in San Francisco County was 23,772, in Alameda 3,627. Both counties returned the Republican ticket.

Oregon—In 1882 the Oregon Legislature submitted an amendment which was voted on in 1884. A notable list of prominent men and women were scheduled to speak and work for the amendment. Abigail Scott Dunniway, the leader, reported that "suddenly, in the midst of the enthusiastic and promising campaign, politicians were seized with alarming reticence. They ceased to attend meetings, made excuses for breaking speaking engagements and dodged their suffrage friends." On election day, "railroad gangs were driven to the polls like sheep and voted against us." Although 11,223 votes were cast for the amendment it was lost by more than two to one. The women were astounded that anyone should care enough about holding them in disfranchisement to pay men to vote against the amendment as had been done. They were bewildered, too, by the discovery that an enemy supplied with money and strong enough to intimidate a political party had been working against their amendment.

Oregon Legislatures thereafter submitted woman suffrage amendments in 1900, 1906, 1908, 1910 and 1912. In each election the women found public sentiment strong and effective, but on election day they discovered the presence of the same mysterious foe that had scattered their forces in 1884.

In 1906 evidence appeared to indicate its character. A secret circular, sent out by the Brewers' and Wholesale Liquor Dealers' Association of the State to every retail liquor seller, fell into the hands of the press and was reproduced in several newspapers. It read in part:

"It will take fifty thousand votes to defeat woman suffrage.

"There are two thousand retailers in Oregon.

"That means that every retailer must himself bring in twenty-five votes on election day.

"Every retailer can get twenty-five votes. Besides his employees, he has his grocer, his butcher, his landlord, his laundryman and every person he does business with. If every man in the business will do this, we will win.

"We enclose twenty-five ballot tickets showing how to vote.

"We also enclose a postal card addressed to this Association. If you will personally take twenty-five friendly voters to the polls on election day and give each one a ticket showing how to vote, please mail the postal card back to us at once. You need not sign the card. Every card has a number, and we will know who sent it in.

"Let us all pull together and let us all work. Let us each get twenty-five votes.

"Yours very respectfully,
BREWERS' & WHOLESALE LIQUOR DEALERS'
ASSOCIATION."

The postcard enclosed for reply was addressed: "Brewers' and Wholesale Liquor Dealers' Association, 413–414 McKay Building, Portland, Oregon."

The reverse side of the card bore this reply:

"Dear Sirs:

I will attend to it.

" .... twenty-five times.

"00000"

Instead of a signature, a number was appended.

Despite the publicity given the plan of the brewers, the campaign of 1906 followed its predecessors to defeat, Mrs. Abigail Scott Dunniway finding the cause in the "slum vote."

Another referendum was secured in 1908, but again the brewers assigned to saloons the number of voters necessary to defeat the Amendment and again the foreign-born were organized to defeat the native woman's plea for the suffrage.

It was the hour of the foreign-born in Oregon.

New Hampshire—One campaign took place in the East during this period. In 1902, New Hampshire held a constitutional convention and the suffragists, following their custom of appeal to all constitutional conventions, conducted a preliminary campaign of preparation which was to culminate in a hearing before the convention. The Grange of the State was a popular and thoroughly established organization. One hundred and forty local Granges and all Pomona or District Granges were addressed before the convention met, and 145 delegates pledged their support. The amendment was submitted by a vote of 145 to 92. This was in December and the vote took place on March 10, leaving little more than two months for a campaign in a bitterly cold winter. Yet two hundred meetings were held. The total previous vote in the State had not exceeded eighty thousand voters and these voters were circularized, material was furnished weekly to the press, and seventy-five ministers preached sermons in favor of the amendment.

So alarmed did the opponents become that an anti-suffrage meeting was arranged on March 4, with Rev. Lyman Abbott as chief speaker; it was followed by a suffrage meeting the next evening, the largest and most enthusiastic of the campaign. The amendment received 14,162 votes for and 21,788 against. The State suffragists considered the result excellent for so conservative a State, but outside workers had come in contact with a new factor in campaigns. The electorate of New Hampshire was utterly demoralized by corruption, and this sad fact was generally admitted. The chairman of the Republican and Democratic Committees both frankly acknowledged that a group of voters called "floaters" had to be paid even when they voted their own party ticket.

This completes the roster of the seventeen referenda in eleven different States and brings the suffrage story forward to 1910. That year found full woman suffrage established in four States, Wyoming and Utah, won in their territorial days, and two, Colorado and Idaho, won on referendum. These four States, composing a great territory in the heart of the West, stood for fourteen years (from 1896 to 1910) like a democratic oasis in a desert of pretension, without another acquisition.

There had been hours for the Indian, the Russian, the German, the Chinese, the foreign-born, the saloon, hours when each had decided the limits of woman's sphere, but no woman's hour had come.

Meantime the possibilities of gains for woman suffrage in the Territories had not been overlooked by suffragists. Territories had the right to grant full suffrage to women by act of their Legislatures without a referendum to the voters, and many suffrage lecture and organizing tours had been made in the early days into each and all of them.

Wyoming had led the way to victory in 1869; Utah followed promptly in 1870. The Mormons practiced polygamy and defended it as a tenet of the church. In 1869 George W. Julian of Indiana had introduced a bill to enfranchise the women of Utah with the expectation that they would in some undefined manner make an end of polygamy. Possibly this initiative prompted the Utah Legislature to enact a woman suffrage measure in 1870, under which the women of Utah territory voted for seventeen years. Observers agreed that they availed themselves very generally of the privilege and voted in the interest of good government; but they did not eliminate polygamy, which was a church and not a state institution. In 1887 Senator Edmunds of Vermont caused the introduction and passage of a congressional bill to disfranchise the women of Utah in order to strike a blow at polygamy. The Territory, and especially its women, made heroic protests, in vain. Utah regarded this act of Congress as a discriminatory one and that fact tended to keep alive and to strengthen the suffrage sentiment in the territory. After many efforts to secure statehood, an enabling act was signed by Grover Cleveland in 1894. Both parties dominant in the State placed woman suffrage planks in their platforms, and the women presented a memorial to the Utah Constitutional Convention asking that they should be recognized in the constitution. Their plea was granted. The constitution, like that of Wyoming, declares that the right to vote shall not be denied on account of sex. The vote of the convention on this clause was ayes 75, nays 6, absent 12. Every member signed. Cleveland affixed the presidential signature January 4, 1896, and Utah was admitted to statehood with woman suffrage in its constitution, the women having been deprived of their vote by act of Congress for nine years.

Arizona and Oklahoma were the two remaining territories, and after the successful Utah denouement in 1896 the Organization Committee of the National American Woman Suffrage Association promptly marked both for suffrage onslaughts. In both there proved to be as frank revelations of the nature of the opposition and its methods as were encountered anywhere along the line of suffrage march. In the nineties suffragists were not as familiar with this nature and these methods as they came to be later, and they were left gasping by developments on both battlefields.

In Arizona they saw a complete *volte face* on the part of the Council (or Senate) from a strong favorable majority to an insidious opposition that filibustered the suffrage bill of 1899 into innocuous desuetude; they heard the popping of corks and the clinking of glasses that accompanied the barter and sale of senatorial votes to the proprietors of the prosperous saloons of the State; and they were the legatees of the confession of the young president of the Council who told them, with tears in his eyes, that the saloons of Prescott had elected him and had made him their attorney, that now their representatives not only threatened to repudiate him politically and take from him their legal work but to "break him" completely if he dared to vote for woman suffrage. He was under promise to his mother not only to vote but to work for suffrage; he had told his masters of the promise; and they had assured him that the blame should be neatly laid upon the committee which would never report the bill. And which never did report the bill.

Working in this same devious way, the saloons of Arizona for eleven years successfully checkmated every effort to secure woman suffrage by territorial legislative act.

In Oklahoma the story was the same—almost down to chapter number and line on page. There, too, in the year 1899, advocacy of suffrage by legislators changed overnight to opposition. There, too, the saloons worked hard and furiously against suffrage, having organized themselves into a "Saloonkeepers' League" with the purpose of "protecting our interests from unjust legislation." There, too, corks popped and glasses clinked while the vote for the political freedom of women was bartered away; and there, too, in the face of marked evidence that the people wanted woman suffrage the legislative filibuster checkmated all efforts to secure it for Oklahoma women.

The women of two territories lost the vote through the veto of Republican Governors, one through the decision of a Democratic Supreme Court, two through the direct intervention of an organized saloon power and one through an act of Congress. Wyoming alone stood the test of years unchallenged.

It is clear that the attempts to win the territories were little more effective than the campaigns with State Legislatures to get them to submit the woman suffrage question to the voters of the States. Territory or State, it was work of a heart-breaking slowness, this pitting of suffrage against politics in State and territorial Legislatures. Had there been encouragement from Washington, Republican or Democratic, the entire West in its territorial days would assuredly have extended the vote to women and would have defended it as gallantly as did Wyoming, but politics was not yet willing to allow this act of inevitable justice to prevail.

Reviewing this forty years of effort between 1870 and 1910 and comparing the carefully filed reports of all the States year after year, the suffragists of 1910 arrived at some more conclusions:

(1) The more favorable public opinion was and the more numerous the pledges of State Senators and Assemblymen, the more certain were suffrage amendments not to pass Legislatures. (2) The better the campaign, the more certain that suffrage would be defeated at the polls. (3) The majorities which defeated amendments were clearly composed of ignorant Americans and foreigners, controlled, that is organized, persuaded or bought, by some master mind. (4) The rank and file of men in the dominant parties accepted platforms and tickets as framed by party leaders without question and voted as advised. (5) The average party leader played "the game of politics," using these voters as pawns, and the big stakes were power, patronage and graft. (6) The real influence which dictated platforms and tickets were monied interests which made gigantic contributions to party treasuries or their candidates' campaign funds. (7) Here and there a statesman, "fair as a star when only one is shining in the sky," kept faith with the people.

The outlook in 1910 was dark. To win without party support seemed impossible, and behind the lack of party support there was now uncomprehending public opinion which had largely lost its earlier zeal for governments by majorities.

The crucial deduction drawn from all the facts at hand was that public opinion must be made to understand, to arise and to exert its power, not only to secure justice for women but to save the nation from the threatened peril of elections controlled by invisible influences.

CHAPTER 10

The Invisible Enemy

Those invisible influences that were controlling elections; that invisible and invincible power that for forty years kept suffragists waiting for the woman's hour; for forty years circumvented the coming of suffrage; that power that made Republican leaders hesitate to fulfil their promises to early suffragists; restrained both dominant parties from endorsing woman suffrage; kept Legislatures from submitting suffrage amendments; and organized droves of ignorant men to vote against suffrage amendments at the polls when its agents had failed to prevent the submission of the question, was, manifestly, the power that inhered in the combined liquor interests.

The vested interest in human slavery exerted a controlling influence over American politics for more than half a century, but the public was never deceived concerning that fact, for its battles were fought in the open and its political compromises were frankly acknowledged. But when the vested interest in liquor arose to dictate terms to parties and politicians it executed its strategical moves in secret. The political wires, laid with purposeful care to trip the feet of men, were unseen by the public. The action of men, Legislatures and parties had the appearance of being the reflection of public opinion.

Victorious movements record their history; vanquished ones rarely do. The men who buy or sell votes do not confess. Political leaders do not acquaint their own party following with the deals they make. Full knowledge, therefore, of the extent to which the liquor trade exercised a dominating influence over the politics of the United States for a generation will probably never be revealed. But enough indisputable evidence has been accumulated to establish the fact that it did wield that influence and to reveal also much of the general plan by which results were achieved.

In 1862, while the nation was absorbed in the life and death struggle of the Civil War, the United States Brewers' Association was quietly organized. Although other reasons for organizing were afterwards given by the Brewers, the weight of evidence indicates that the main object of the Association was the political protection of the trade. It is a fact that this organization continued to be the chief directing power in the political defense of the liquor interests until the end of the struggle.

At its convention in 1867 the Association boldly warned political parties to take due notice that it would declare war upon all candidates of whatever party who were favorably disposed toward the total abstinence cause.[48] Although no more resolutions of this character were passed, and no public pronouncements of this nature were made by the leading brewers in the years that followed, there was no break in carrying out that policy. When the first decision was made to include woman suffrage as an indirect menace to the liquor cause is unknown, but in 1867, when the Kansas suffrage campaign was on, suffragists noted that in all parts of the State local liquor men were conspicuous workers against the suffrage amendment.

It was in 1869 that the Legislature of Wyoming extended the vote to women. It was in that same year that the Prohibition Party was organized. These unrelated but outstanding events may have called the attention of the trade to a possible connection between the two reforms, but far more definite causes for fear of women on the part of the liquor interests soon appeared. In 1873-4 an uprising of Christian women against the saloons of Ohio startled the church, the saloon and the nation. Groups of women, well known for their virtue and piety, appeared before the doors of saloons, or at times entered, read passages of Scripture, sang hymns and, kneeling, prayed fervently for the abolition of all "rum shops." Out of this "crusade" the Woman's Christian Temperance Union emerged in 1874. It grew in size and influence with astonishing rapidity, spreading to all States of the Union and carrying with it much of the crusade spirit that had created it.

Women thus became an unmistakable factor in the movement which was rapidly pressing forward the demand for "total abstinence for the individual and prohibition for the State." Their meetings filled churches, bridged denominational differences, enlisted the clergy and influential churchmen. More than all else, the organization aroused women and trained them for public work as no movement had yet done. Soon the Woman's Christian Temperance Union became the largest organization women had yet formed in any country. Its leader for many years, Frances Willard, was one of the world's greatest women, beloved by her followers and honored by all. She captivated audiences, disarmed their prejudices and enrolled them in her cause. Under her inspiration a great army of women, recruited chiefly from orthodox Protestant churches, rapidly mobilized.

It was doubtless because of these things that the press reports of the Brewers' Convention of 1881 included the account of the adoption of an anti-suffrage resolution to the effect that the Brewers would welcome prohibition as far less dangerous to the trade than woman suffrage, because prohibition could be repealed at any time but woman suffrage would insure the permanency of prohibition. Thirty-two years afterward, President Ruppert of the United States Brewers' Association denied that the brewers had ever taken such action, but suffrage scrap-books preserved the resolution and the brewers confessed to the Judiciary Committee of the Senate, in 1918, that they had kept no minutes.

Meanwhile evidence had accumulated to prove conclusively that whether the brewers had stated their hostility to woman suffrage in resolutions or not, they had ceaselessly demonstrated it in practice. Three official investigations into the political activities of the brewers have been made and four large volumes of the evidence have been published. On January 9, 1915, the Attorney-General of the State of Texas filed suit against seven breweries in the State charging "the use of their corporate means and assets in politics and elections" contrary to the laws of the State. In March, 1916, indictments were brought against one hundred Pennsylvania brewing companies and the United States Brewers' Association by a Federal Grand Jury. The indictments charged the brewing companies with the unlawful expenditure of money in the election of federal officials. Rather than have the investigation proceed, the brewers chose to plead guilty and pay a fine of a million dollars.

In September, 1918, the United States Senate called for an investigation by the Judiciary Committee into the charges of German propaganda by German brewers in association with the United States Brewers' Association. The charges included the following:

"The United States Brewers' Association, brewing companies and allied interests have in recent years made contributions to political campaigns on a scale without precedent . . . and in order to control legislation in State and nation have exacted pledges from candidates to office . . . have subsidized the press and stipulated when contracting for advertising space with the newspapers that a certain amount be editorial space, the material to be furnished by the brewers' central office . . . they have set in operation an extensive system of boycotting of American manufacturers, merchants and railroads, etc. . . . have on file political surveys of States, tabulating men and forces for and against them, and that they have paid large sums of money to citizens of the United States to advocate their cause, including some in government employ."

The press reported that some tons of documents were taken on subpoena from various offices and bureaus. Although the evidence was fragmentary, it made clear that a national political agency, set up by the combined interests, had long existed and that it supervised or was active in both prohibition and suffrage campaigns throughout the United States.

This evidence, combined with the circumstantial and direct evidence supported by affidavits carefully preserved by the National American Woman Suffrage Association during a period of fifty years, shows the liquor interests in active opposition to woman suffrage on the following counts:

1. The same man or men who conducted the anti-prohibition campaign directed the anti-suffrage contests in Legislatures, constitutional conventions and referenda campaigns.

2. Money to oppose woman suffrage was taken from the funds placed in the hands of the political committees organized by the liquor interests to fight prohibition.

3. A given quota of votes to be secured against woman suffrage was customarily assigned each saloon in referenda campaigns.

4. By definite agreement, in secret conferences, the liquor forces determined to conceal their opposition to woman suffrage so far as possible.

5. The liquor interests applied the boycott to men favoring woman suffrage as they did to those favoring prohibition.[49]

6. By the same coercive means they sought contributions for anti-suffrage campaigns from firms with which they dealt.

7. In States reputed strong for both suffrage and prohibition, the attitude of Congressmen and State legislators on both questions was reported to the national political committees of the liquor interests with equal care.

8. The allied organizations that were set up to oppose prohibition opposed woman suffrage by the same methods.

To carry on these numerous campaigns required great sums of money. An attempt was made by the attorneys for the Senate Judiciary Committee to ascertain how much money had been raised annually by the liquor forces, from what sources it had been derived, and how it had been expended. These efforts brought forth little that was new. The Brewers' officers, called on subpoena by the Government, admitted as little as possible and remembered nothing of importance, yet the evidence confirmed many suspicions and beliefs that had been based previously upon hearsay. It confirmed, for example:

1. That the United States Brewers' Association and the Pennsylvania Brewers' Association kept no minutes of their official proceedings.[50]

2. That the practice of the United States Brewers' Association to destroy check stubs and cancelled checks with each bank balance was customary with State brewers' associations.[51]

3. That a working agreement had existed for many years whereby the brewers furnished two-thirds and the distillers one-third of the campaign funds.[52]

4. That the United States Brewers' Association and the State Brewers' Associations each levied an annual tax of one-half cent to one cent per barrel on the output of member brewers,

the amounts thus derived being dues, chiefly expended in administration of the national and State associations.[53]

5. That a custom existed whereby contributions made to State political campaigns by the national liquor organization were based upon the stipulation that the State interests would raise an equal fund, although exceptions were doubtless made in the States with comparatively few liquor resources.[54]

6. That funds for political campaigns were secured by making additional assessments as needed. In 1913 a contract was made whereby the brewers agreed to assess themselves three cents per barrel annually for a term of five years, the agreement to become operative when brewers representing twenty-five millions of barrels had subscribed. As more than that number entered into the agreement, the plan was carried out until the prohibition amendment was submitted.[55] This plan supported a national fund only. The State associations also assessed their member breweries according to State agreements in order to secure State campaign funds. The treasurer of the brewers' political committee of Nebraska in 1913 reported that the breweries of that State for eight years had never paid less than sixty-five cents per barrel and from that up to $1.10.[56] It was admitted that an assessment of twenty cents per barrel for State campaign funds was not unusual and that sixty cents per barrel had been assessed in several States. The Texas brewers assessed themselves sixty-five cents per barrel.[57]

7. That the largest known deposit of the United States Brewers' Association in any one year was $1,400,000 in the year 1914, and its known deposits from 1913 to 1918 were $4,457,941, although the records for a portion of this time were lost, so that the total was more.[58]

It is probable that few persons, if any, knew how much money was actually raised and spent by the liquor forces in any given year.

The money did not pass through one treasury, and the trustees of the different funds made no acknowledged reports to each other. Each State conducted an independent campaign, raised its own money and spent that contributed by all the national liquor organizations. As State laws became more and more drastic in their demand for public reports of campaign receipts and expenditure, it became increasingly necessary, from the liquor viewpoint, to conceal as far as possible both the source and amount of receipts and the nature of expenditures. This was easily done by dividing the funds among the different committees or bureaus, many being totally unknown to the public and therefore never called upon for reports.

Some facts are known, however, and from them a fair estimate of the amount of money raised annually for campaigns may be made. It is a known fact, for instance, that $1,400,000 was deposited by the United States Brewers' Association in 1914.[59] Let us start with that and beat back to its likely sources. It is true that the total number of barrels from which campaign funds, as well as the assessment levies, were collected is a secret buried with destroyed bankbooks, but the usual half-cent per barrel for dues, plus the three cents per barrel assessment for campaign purposes agreed to in 1913, would bring in that $1,400,000 if the assessment had been levied on only forty millions of barrels. Forty million barrels formed not more than two-thirds of the total barrelage of the country for that year. Allowing $100,000 for national administration expenses, the amount available from the brewers for campaigns was $1,300,000. At that time the agreement in operation was that the brewers should furnish two-thirds and the distillers one-third of the campaign fund, so the brewers' quota of $1,400,000 was augmented by a distillers' quota of over $700,000, making a total of $2,100,000 plus, raised by the national liquor organizations.

Now it was the rule that the manager of each State campaign must raise within the State a sum equal to the sum given to that

State's campaign fund from the national fund. If each State, therefore, merely duplicated its quota from the national fund, the total funds, national and State, available for campaign purposes reached the vast sum of four million dollars. As a matter of fact, though some States may not have raised more than the necessary amounts to secure the national contribution, other States raised funds far in excess of those amounts. We know this because assessments of five cents upwards to $2.00 per barrel were admitted, and twenty cents was not unusual.

In Ohio, where the hardest fought battle between the prohibition and liquor forces was waged and where woman suffrage was caught in the imbroglio and held fast for a dozen years, the annual output was about five millions of barrels, and it was admitted that that State paid twenty cents per barrel regularly during the years of its main struggle. Such a State assessment alone would have netted an annual fund of a million dollars. If State assessments of twenty cents per barrel applied on the total forty million barrelage from which was raised the $1,400,000 known to have been deposited as the tribute from the two national liquor organizations, the result would have been eight millions of dollars, instead of the mere two millions plus, necessary to match the national contributions. That the State funds approached this amount is supported by considerable evidence. For example, the manager of the anti-prohibition campaign in Texas wrote Adolph Busch, in 1913, that plans to raise *five and a half millions of dollars* for their campaign had been completed and that it *ought* to be enough.[60] Mr. Beis of Ohio in a secret conference said[61] that the State Brewers' Association had spent half a million dollars in 1913 and would spend another in 1914.

From all of which it seems fairly clear that the liquor funds spent in the political campaigns of the country ranged from four to ten millions of dollars a year.

It was against such a Croesus foe as this that suffrage, with its pitiful but consecrated dimes and dollars, dared raise its head. — "I will pledge my car fare," said a shabby little woman at an upstate suffrage meeting in the New York campaign of 1915, when pledges of money to the suffrage campaign were being made. "I will pledge my car fare. I can walk to and from my work."

There were other sources of money-raising than the assessments upon the output of the liquor manufacturers. In a fervid speech made at a closed session of the United States Brewers' Association in 1913 by Percy Andreae[62] it was said that the *allied interests* of Ohio had paid out a million dollars in five years to perfect an organization which he declared performed campaign work with "unerring accuracy."

A National Retail Liquor Dealers' Association, organized in 1893 with auxiliaries in each State, was also a political and financial ally. A system of assessment upon the sales of local dealers in order to secure campaign funds was the rule in this organization. The liquor retailers invented a new method, which was later adopted by the manufacturers and wholesalers. When paying bills for any and all supplies, such as plumbing, furniture, crockery, glassware, groceries, it became their custom to withhold a small per cent, with the explanation that should prohibition obtain they would no longer be able to buy, and as their creditor would lose trade to that extent he surely ought to be willing to assist in the campaign to continue his own business.

Although the liquor management of anti-suffrage campaigns was subrosa so far as possible, this same method of raising funds for the direct purpose of opposing woman suffrage was used in several States,—several of the covering letters were turned over to suffrage workers. In Montana, such a letter was sent out while the suffrage measure was pending in the Legislature, and again after it had been submitted to the voters. That letter blithely connected the liquor interests and anti-suffrage in these words, "The local wholesalers and retailers are working unanimously to maintain for Montana the proud position of being the wettest State in the Union. This takes money. We are preparing a Statewide campaign against woman suffrage in this State. Our local retailers are doing all they can but the burden is too heavy for them to carry alone and it is only right that those who are enjoying and making a profit from the sale of their goods should help us in conserving for them their accounts and goods."

A National Hotel Men's Association became an active and open opponent of prohibition and an active but secret opponent of woman suffrage. Druggists and other dealers in various kinds of liquors, and tobacco manufacturers and dealers were also organized opponents of both movements. The money raised by these organizations was probably expended in their own activities and no estimate of the amounts so used can be made, though they swelled the unknown total of the anti-prohibition and anti-suffrage campaign funds.

Reports on woman suffrage were held to be as vital to the liquor interests as those on prohibition, as the minutes of several secret conferences secured on subpoena revealed. At a conference between the "Interstate Conference Committee" and the Board of Trustees of the United States Brewers' Association, held at the Hotel Kimball, Springfield, Massachusetts, October 13, 1913, Oscar Schmidt, a Milwaukee brewer, said:

"Mr. Chairman and gentlemen of the committee: . . . I have been in this game fighting prohibition for about thirty years and I want you to know that I learn something all the time. . . . For the State of Wisconsin I will have only a few words to say, that we are fortunate in having a good organization. . . . In the last campaign . . . we had the usual bills, like every other state-county option, women's suffrage in about six different forms and we had everything else,

which were all defeated; and I can say that can be done only
by organization and by active work of the brewers being on
the job all the time and not leaving it to somebody else. . . ."

Wisconsin's only referendum on suffrage was defeated in 1912.

"I am also a delegate from Nebraska. . . . For eight years
I have been treasurer of the so-called Executive Committee
consisting of three brewers from Omaha and two smaller
brewers from the State. These five brewers have been doing
all the work. . . . The women's suffrage in the State we
defeated two years ago at a tremendous expense and we won
in the State by about nine thousand votes. If they had carried
the election, of course the State would have been dry."[63]

The Nebraska referendum on woman suffrage was defeated in
1914.

Mr. Doyle of the Illinois State Brewers' Association wanted "to
suggest" and "to implore" that "female suffrage" be defeated at all
hazards.

"As the result of experience we have had with two different
subjects, I want to suggest to the gentlemen who are here
a very serious matter, that if you are living in liberal states
which have not the initiative and referendum and have not
female suffrage, I want to implore you to defeat these two
things at all hazards."[64]

Mr. Schlighting, South Dakota brewer, said:

"We have some possibility of winning if we get plenty
of assistance. . . . So far we have been able to cope with these
things; we have defeated county option by the vote of the people
at four different times. We have defeated women's suffrage at
three different times, and I want to say that this association, the

United States Brewers' Association, through the efforts of one gentleman, Mr. Edward Dietrich, has been able to cope with it, and he has always been fortunate in winning."[65]

A report on Iowa was presented to the Interstate Conference Committee of the United States Brewers' Association by Henry Thuenen, General Counsel of the Iowa Brewers' Association, on June 10, 1915, in which he said:[66]

"We are of the opinion that Woman's Suffrage can be defeated, *although we believe that the liquor interests should not be known as the contending force against this amendment.* (Italics ours.) Action of some kind should be taken to assure a real and active campaign against this measure.

To sum up, what Iowa needs at your hands, if you are disposed to interest yourselves in the State, is —

First, A contest on Woman's Suffrage at the Primary, in 1916.

Second, A contest for liberal Senators at the election, in 1916, and if this fails, then

Third, a contest at the polls on the prohibitory amendment which will be held at the general election in 1917 unless otherwise provided by the Legislature."

The brewers *were* disposed to interest themselves in the State. They sent the assistance, and woman suffrage was announced as defeated in Iowa in 1916—although suffragists believed it was won.[67]

The struggle between temperance and liquor forces had reached its height in 1913. Local option authorized by the Legislatures of most States had thrown large expanses of territory into the "dry" column. Statewide prohibition had been established in several States and the issue was a crucial one in the politics of many others. Court decisions were notably more friendly to the temperance side of legal contests, but a far more important factor in the situation was the addition of many powerful manufacturers to the prohibition forces. The labor unions had striven long for employer's liabilities in cases of death and accident of employees, and such laws had been passed by many States. Manufacturers now discovered that accidents happened more often when men were under the influence of intoxicants and sought to protect themselves from this risk by advocating the legal removal of the cause. Another cogent factor pushing them toward prohibition was the argument that working forces would not be so depleted at the beginning of each work-week if working men had no Saturday night and Sunday sprees to sleep off on Monday morning. A tremendous impulse was given prohibition through the addition of this new ally. Legislators, sensing a changed public opinion, became more independent and daring. The liquor traffic recognized the need of more money and more intensive campaigning than ever before. Onlookers saw the final battle emerging from the half century struggle.

The brewers promptly entered into the five years' agreement previously noted to provide more money, and accepted the proposal of Percy Andreae, chief of a publicity bureau for the Brewers' Association, to increase organization. It was in an executive session of the United States Brewers' Association, held in Atlantic City in October, 1913,[68] that he urged this new policy. He announced that arrangements were already completed whereby the venture would be made operative under his direction. He did not take the brewers into his confidence as to how the plan was to be put into execution. "I must have a free hand," he said. "No one who realizes the character and the magnitude of the work I have undertaken will believe that it could be accomplished under any other conditions. An army—and it is an army if you please, that is to be called into existence—must have a leader. . . . What hope would there be for the success of an undertaking . . . involving alliances which the slightest misconstruction . . . of our intentions would place in jeopardy if I were obliged to herald all details . . . to the world, which I would be doing if I confided them to the knowledge of several hundred men." The general plan, however, was made clear and involved two main features:

1. To rely no longer upon contributions and favors as the sole means of controlling parties and politicians, but to add the threat of large blocks of voters which would go for or against the party or candidate who did not do the bidding of the trade.

2. To build up organizations, chiefly to be recruited from the foreign population, having the appearance of voluntary bodies with public-spirited aims, but in reality existing solely to defend the trade. These organizations were designed not only to join in the general propaganda, but to provide the army of voters which was expected to awe parties and politicians into a proper degree of subservience.

Mr. Andreae was authorized to proceed upon the policy that the foreign vote should be organized in order to control elections and legislation. The experiment about to be tried was not new, and had already proved itself. It had organized the Russian vote against woman suffrage in the Dakotas, the German vote in Nebraska, Missouri and Iowa, the Negro vote in Kansas and Oklahoma, the Chinese vote in California.

The most important organizing done along this line was that which resulted in the National Association of Commerce and Labor. Mr. Andreae organized it and became its president. It appeared to be a business man's organization and exerted great influence in consequence upon national and State political parties. Its staff salaries were forty-six thousand dollars per year and its workers were mainly ex-State Senators and Representatives.

With these precedents to encourage similar activities, innumerable societies sprang up. Every State with a prohibition or suffrage campaign had its inevitable accompaniment of Home Rule

Societies, Personal Liberty Leagues, Traveling Men's or Merchants' Leagues, Men's Anti-Suffrage Associations, *ad infinitum*. With object and sponsorship concealed, the seemingly spontaneous outburst of public protest exerted an influence, often widespread and effective.

The allied organization that performed the deadliest work in woman suffrage campaigns was the German-American Alliance. It was organized in 1901 and chartered in 1907, and although the leading German brewers were influential members from the beginning, it is probable that it was not organized originally either for the purpose of defending the liquor traffic or for pro-German propaganda. Its charter was taken away by unanimous vote of Congress in 1918 upon proved charges that it was in part supported by the brewers and that some of its officers were engaged in dangerous pro-German activities, yet the rank and file of the membership, however obedient to the "systematized direction" of their votes, were probably quite unaware of the illegal part the organization was playing in American politics.

At the national convention of this German organization in San Francisco in 1911, a membership of 2,500,000 persons and ten thousand branches were claimed. There were at the time seven hundred German newspapers in the country. The *National Bulletin*, the national organ of the Alliance, was resuscitated by the brewers, its organizing committees in Ohio, Iowa, Texas, Indiana and probably other States[69] were assisted financially by the brewers, and when in 1914 a headquarters and a lobby were established in Washington, the brewers paid the rent.

Each State German Alliance had a political committee which received direct from the liquor campaign managers a ticket to be supported at each election. Meanwhile, an active campaign by letter and circular, as well as through meetings, was maintained in States holding elections, to persuade all Germans to register and vote. In Texas, Missouri, Iowa, North Dakota, South Dakota,

Nebraska, Wisconsin, Michigan, this organized German-liquor vote was hurled into woman suffrage referenda campaigns with the unerring accuracy claimed for it, the combination of the German-American Alliance with the liquor trade making a well-nigh all-controlling political power in these States.

An important feature of the plan for utilizing the foreign-born vote was the subrosa campaign to increase naturalization, the fees often being paid by the liquor forces. Under subpoena, documents and proceedings showed that this had been done in several States. In Texas, where foreign citizens were allowed to vote on first papers, the campaign took the direction of urging Germans to pay their poll-tax in order that they might vote. Joseph Keller, Chairman of the Propaganda Committee of the German-American Alliance, reported to Percy Andreae that the anti-prohibitionists had gained seventy thousand votes through the payment of the poll tax.[70]

Probably the most ambitious venture along this line was in Pennsylvania, where special headquarters were established for the purpose of giving the appearance of labor offices with names of leading labor leaders on the doors. Thither men were urged to go, and their naturalization was facilitated by liquor money for the purpose of gaining more votes under control. Upon cross-examination, Mr. Gardner, president of the Pennsylvania Brewers, admitted that the electorate had been increased there by two or three hundred thousand votes, although "Jim said he could do better than that."[71]

The liquor trade was non-partisan and made its combination with any or all parties. Henry Thuenen, general counsel of Republican Iowa's Brewers' Association, reported to Percy Andreae, June, 1914, that the Republican nominations for governor and lieutenant-governor were very satisfactory, as were the Democratic nominations. The Democratic nominations for United States Senator and for Congress were equally gratifying. For all the big offices, "we won in every instance."—"This being the first time that the so-called Andreae system of organization was put into practice in Iowa, you are to be congratulated upon results. . . . With the continued application of the system of organization we have commenced in Iowa, it cannot be more than one or two battles until we will find ourselves in possession of the fort. I am sure that if we continue this work through another, or at least two more campaigns, we will be practically in a position to dictate legislation on the liquor question."[72]

It should be plain by now why it was that when suffragists turned from the closed doors of Congress to seek justice by State action, they found that legislative doors were also closed; nay more—mysteriously locked! Suffragists approached their task with the exaltation of a belief that theirs was a righteous reform demanded by the great destinies of the human race. In the beginning they regarded the opposition they met as normal inertia to be overcome, but in later years the end of many campaigns left them prostrated with amazed despair, for with the years came the clearer comprehension of the invisible and devious but monstrous force against which suffrage was contending.

The legislative anti-suffrage work of the liquor interests began by simple processes. The first move was to "fix" the committee to which a suffrage bill was referred and this they, or some other mysterious power, were able to do in nearly three-fourths of the suffrage legislative campaigns. An overworked committee, a crowded legislative calendar, were the explanations given to women workers, while the bargains which brought the result were made without witnesses behind closed doors. If the suffrage bill was likely to be reported out by the committee to which it had been referred, work was begun on the legislators.

Very often the legislative campaign was confined to the Senate, the smaller body where a single man or small group of men could be a sufficient balance of power to insure an adverse vote. The liquor lobbyist worked with economy and concentrated his efforts on a few men who held key positions in the Legislature. The member who believed that his political future depended upon getting a bill through the Legislature often traded his vote on suffrage for that of a liquor or railroad man who favored his pet measure.

Men who could not be bought were definitely influenced by the knowledge that generous contributions were made to the State and national campaign committees of their party by representatives of the trade, and that blocks of voters alienated from party support would mean party defeat. With these thoughts in their minds, they were readily persuaded that women could wait for the vote. Cajolery, promises of assistance in coming campaigns, presents to wives, attentions to relatives and friends, business, financial and political preferment, were all among the methods employed. If the legislative poll showed a majority by these means, no others were applied. If, however, a few votes were still necessary to make the majority, the "third degree" of politics was brought to bear. Intimidation, threats "to make or break men" and out-and-out bribery were the methods used at this stage.

The women in time learned to know the signs, but they had incomplete proof to offer. The public neither knew nor wanted to know. After every legislative term, the reports of State suffrage auxiliaries to the National Suffrage Association bore a remarkable similarity of testimony. The full force of the statements of any one became apparent only when taken in connection with all the others. Men who wanted to go straight compromised with their consciences in that shady political borderland lying between honesty and dishonesty. An illustration chosen from many on file explains the difficulties of such men. It came from a State wherein manufacturers, railroads and liquor interests had each their great political battles and where all three worked together to secure the desired aims of any one. Wrote the State suffrage officer February, 1917:

"That the Senators meant to vote for the suffrage bill when they first came to ——, we believe. They said to us and to each other that they were pledged to it. The women anti-suffragists who appeared at the hearing seemed to have made no impression. Various Senators told us so repeatedly. Yet gradually Senators began to weaken. One Senator, who spoke and voted for our bill, said 'You know, I suppose, that it was the liquor interests which were responsible for the death of the bill.' Many others said the same thing, but no man will come out in the open and make a charge against the wet interests and back it up, for they are too afraid of those interests.

"A Senator who had openly espoused the bill in this Legislature and pledged himself to vote for it, not only voted, but made a speech against it. This was a matter of frequent occurrence, but this Senator gave an interview to the women to whom he had pledged his support, unusual for its frankness. Said he: 'The client giving me most business is a manufacturer who is tied up with the liquor interests. The most powerful newspaper in the town gives me all its legal business but the newspaper is wet in policy and also opposed to woman suffrage. If I become too pronounced as a champion of woman suffrage, the liquor interests would put the screws on the manufacturer and he in turn would notify me that he had found it convenient to seek legal counsel elsewhere. The newspaper would let me know that my services could be dispensed with. I have a nice home, a little Ford for business and pleasure, and two sons to educate. I cannot afford to lose the patronage of my two best-paying clients.' He added that he had often regretted that he was not a man of wealth and thus could be independent."

Nowhere does the rule, "Self-preservation is the first law of nature," show itself more conspicuously than in politics. The liquor trade's representatives systematically proceeded with faith in the claim that "every man has his price." From that base were projected the methods by which Legislatures were controlled.

The liquor trade also made allies of other special interests seeking legislative protection or privilege, and successes were frequently due to this combination. Liquor, railroad, manufacturers', cattle, sheep, and packers' lobbies were among the allied interests. None had "trouble" in every State nor in every Legislature but all had their big political campaigns, which frequently resulted in regularly employed counsel for the liquor interests being nominated as representatives of the people by the controlling party—and being elected by unsuspecting voters to seats in the Legislature. Within the legislative forum such men fought the battles of those who paid them. When two or three were engaged upon measures in the same Legislature, each having a group of legislators at command, it was usually easy to effect a union of forces whereby the trading of votes secured more certain results for all. By no other theory is the opposition to woman suffrage by railroad lobbies, for instance, to be explained; and for many years railroad lobbies were a hostile factor that suffragists constantly encountered.

To illustrate: An investigation into railroad political activities by the New Hampshire Public Service Commission in April, 1916, was summed up in a public report. It revealed that men employed for the purpose of defending the interests of the Boston and Maine Railroad had also the secret purpose of opposing woman suffrage, and one of these men, while drawing a salary from the railroad, drew another from the State as delegate to the Constitutional Convention of 1913, where *he served as floor leader against woman suffrage.* While the Investigating Commission was unable to present a complete account of the political activities of the railroad, since no minutes, contracts or financial reports could be found, and the railroad representatives refused to remember, yet enough was revealed to establish the fact that the Boston and Maine expended considerable money in the effort to prevent the submission of woman suffrage by the New Hampshire "Constitutional Convention of 1912. The suffrage workers of the State reported at the time that three agencies opposed their measure, a railroad lobby, a liquor lobby and a manufacturers' lobby. The resolution to submit a woman suffrage amendment was defeated, 208 to 149. But not until the revelations of 1916, four years later, was the part taken in the campaigns by the railroad lobby made manifest.

After the State of Washington, in 1910, and California, in 1911, had slipped into the suffrage column, an apparent challenging of the national brewers' admonition to keep to an underground policy on woman suffrage appeared in many States and the liquor forces more boldly displayed their hostility to woman suffrage. In the following year, 1912, when six States[73] had referenda campaigns on suffrage amendments, the trade so far abandoned its previous policy of "the still hunt" as to become the most conspicuous opponent in each State. Consternation was aroused in the liquor camps when the press headlines, the morning after the first election in which women had participated in Illinois, announced that woman suffrage had closed one thousand saloons. Public expressions of liquor resentment became instantly bolder.

At the annual meeting of the National Retail Dealers' Association that year, Neil Bonner, the president, said in his address:

"We need not fear the churches, the men are voting the old tickets; we need not fear the ministers, for the most part they follow the men of the churches; we need not fear the Y. M. C. A., for it does not do aggressive work, but, gentlemen, we need to fear the Woman's Christian Temperance

Union and the ballot in the hands of women; therefore, gentlemen, fight woman suffrage."

In 1914 there were seven[74] State amendment campaigns, five of which were lost. It is noteworthy that all trade papers within those States openly opposed the amendments. The general character of their pronouncements may be set forth in a few examples. *Progress,* the official organ of the Wisconsin State Retail Dealers' Protective Association, published at Watertown, Wisconsin, and describing itself on its editorial page as "An educational Journal covering every phase of the retail, wholesale liquor and brewing industries," devoted much space and energy in 1912 to the suffrage campaigns then in progress in Wisconsin and Michigan and was a fair example of many liquor trade papers. One editorial caption was: "Give ballots to women and industry goes to smash." The article continued:

> "If women get the ballot it means prohibition. It means that the farmer must stop growing corn, must stop growing rye and must stop growing barley. It means that the breweries must suspend business, it means that the saloons must close. . . . The condition is serious. Woman suffrage means prohibition.
>
> "It is the duty of all men of this State who love their home, their family, their liberty, their rights and their citizenship, to go to the polls on November 5 and vote against this constitutional amendment."

The *Champion of Fair Play,* chief liquor organ of Illinois, kept a standing article urging every member of the Liquor Dealers' Association of that State to bring all possible pressure from every quarter to defeat the woman suffrage bill which passed in 1913. The *National Forum* of Butte, Montana, was particularly aggressive that year. In the April number an article, "A Little Plain Talk," urged more activity against woman suffrage:

"Right now the question of woman suffrage is before the people of this State. If it carries, the saloons and breweries are doomed. If suffrage carries, the advocates of the movement will not be to blame. The blame will be at the door of the saloon man and brewer. It will not be a case of homicide, but it will be a clear case of suicide. Together we assist, and by united effort woman suffrage can be defeated, but divided, the saloons and breweries of Montana will be matters of history within a few years."

Meantime the old policy of cloaked activity was not entirely abandoned. On January 14, 1914, H. T. Fox, Secretary of the United States Brewers' Association, wrote the Fred Miller Brewing Company of Milwaukee, in answer to an inquiry as to what was being done "in regard to woman suffrage and the spring elections of Illinois":

"In regard to the matter of woman suffrage, we are trying to keep from having any connection with it whatever. We are, however, in a position to establish channels of communication with the leaders of the Anti-Suffrage Movement for our friends in any State where suffrage is an issue. I consider it most dangerous to have the retailers identified or active in any way in this fight, as it will be used against us everywhere. The Illinois brewers had a meeting last week, and while I have no definite particulars, I understand that they have made plans for a very active campaign in connection with the Spring elections!"[75]

As the suffrage and prohibition campaigns whirled faster and faster, a change of position on suffrage was advocated for the liquor interests. In 1914, M. Michelson proposed to Hugh T. Fox, Secretary of United States Brewers' Association, plans for placing "the brewers squarely on the side of progress . . . the ally of the social reformer," and proceeded, under the head, "woman suffrage," as follows:

"Nothing, it seems to me, can be more short-sighted than the policy of the brewers in some States in actively opposing, and, therefore, arousing the hostility of what is undoubtedly the most fanatical of all groups in American politics today. . . .

"By leaving out of consideration its indirect power, there can be no question that suffrage will be extended to many more States within the next year. This means that the voting population of those States will be doubled. In some of the suffrage States prohibition will come and there will be the question of compensation to the brewer. Why arouse the antagonism of one-half the voters? Why not educate them—and before they have the vote? . . .

"I think the answer is to be found in the *New Republic* of August 21. The *New Republic* does not believe in the methods employed by the Texas brewers who, masquerading under the name of Farmers' Union et al, attack woman suffrage. 'The methods of the Texas Business Men's Association furnish an excellent example of how public opinion is poisoned against woman suffrage.' . . .

"The *New Republic* is . . . quoted in newspapers throughout the country, is opposed to prohibition, yet publishes editorials that can be used by the prohibitionist, and refuses to get material from the brewers because of the position taken by the brewers towards woman suffrage. . . . It is true that in some States the Brewers may be able to successfully fight woman's suffrage for years, but those few should not be allowed to sacrifice the industry in other States where suffrage is strong. . . ."

M. MICHELSON.

The *New Republic's* reference to the Texas Business Men's Association, quoted above, bore on a line of anti-suffrage activity that developed in 1915 and was especially directed to the four eastern States, New York, Pennsylvania, Massachusetts and New Jersey, where suffrage campaigns were in progress. Investigation revealed that in Texas a Farmers' Union had gained a large membership and then extended itself into a National Farmers' Union. Peter Radford and W. D. Lewis were successive presidents, and apparently engaged in a private enterprise by establishing a publicity bureau paid for by those who desired to distribute propaganda. A "Texas Business Men's Association" was operated by these same men and the publicity activities of the two organizations were interchangeable. The evidence made clear that contributions from railroads, brewers, retail liquor-dealers, telephone, telegraph, electric, oil, gas and packing companies supported the publicity. Free plate was issued to rural papers. It carried propaganda favorable to all its supporters and against woman suffrage. The investigation led to the repudiation of the men by the Farmers' Union. In a short time the same service was again instituted under the name of the Agricultural and Commercial Press Service. Under different direction a National Council of the Farmers' Co-operative Association, with Headquarters in Nebraska, and a Grain Dealers' Association, with Headquarters in North Dakota, were instituted and issued similar press services.

The open campaign of self-defense conducted by the liquor forces can be respected as the unquestioned privilege and right of all who seek to convince public opinion. The point at issue is that the liquor interests did not rely upon open propaganda but upon secret maneuvers for results, and in this field no moral law, no democratic principle, no right of majorities was recognized. While its activities were suspected by all observers of political events, proof was lacking, and its power was so intricately bound up with partisan politics that none but the Prohibitionists, and not all of them, dared proclaim the truth.

The party machine was an instrument perfectly suited to the uses of the liquor trade and the "boss" was a powerful ally. The boss and the machine made the trade secure for many years and the trade lengthened and strengthened the rule of the boss and the machine. Together they disciplined parties and dictated platforms and tickets. No party dared inaugurate war on this power; to do so meant its own certain defeat, since the trade would make an inevitable alliance with its rival. Neither dominant party has ever endorsed either prohibition *or its enforcement* in a national platform.

The power of this gigantic political machine, allying itself with the Republican organization in Connecticut, Massachusetts and Pennsylvania, with the Democratic organization in Texas, Oklahoma and Nebraska, making connections with both in Iowa, Missouri, Illinois, New York, and choosing candidates from both tickets when no alliances could be made with party managers, recognizing loyalty to none and serving no cause but its own, will never be measured. In the end it defeated its own purposes. Men who conscientiously believed in moderate drinking found themselves aligned with a political condition they could not tolerate. Men who believed in total abstinence, but not prohibition, found their position equally untenable; women were aroused and made resentful by the attitude of the trade on the question of their enfranchisement. In the long run, the prohibition forces were augmented by the addition of thousands of men and women who came in protest against the corrupt influences of the saloon in politics. The methods it employed became the boomerang that gave the liquor power its final and mortal blow.

CHAPTER 11

Special Handicaps and Hazards

No reform of government can be written into law in America until it has run a gauntlet of handicaps and hazards peculiar to this country. Some are inherent in the range and quality of our electorate; some are incidental to the operation of our laws, especially our election laws, as already written. In the case of woman suffrage each and all of them proved so particularly crippling as to be entitled to a chapter of their own.

To begin with, woman suffrage came up to one of its first great moments just after the Civil War. The War had done two things to the immediate detriment of suffrage, along with all other idealistic causes. It had swept into their graves thousands of idealistic American men and it had opened the doors of America to thousands of unidealistic immigrants from Europe.

The appalling figures of the war show that one hundred thousand young men, the flower of the manhood of North and South, gave up their lives in the contest. The vacancies created in population and electorate were ultimately filled by immigrants, who, fleeing from European conscription and lured by the promise of high wages or profits, flocked to our shores in great numbers. Their muscles were as tense, their thrift as constant, their industry as profit-producing as those of the men who had gone. But there were differences which affected the entire history of the nation.

In the veins of many thousands of the dead, both North and South, flowed the blood of the heroes of the Revolution. They were men who had been educated in American schools and knew the ideals and principles upon which the young Republic had been founded. Their idealism had been supported after the European uprising of 1848 by a considerable number of European exiles or disappointed idealists, who, possessing as intense a love of political liberty as any American, found refuge in the United States, and not only gave gallant service in the Northern Army, but made the supreme sacrifice. Such additions were, of course, all to the good in a nation striving for democracy. So, too, was the fact that immigration immediately after the war came from the North of Europe where education and movements toward political freedom had made most progress.

But later that tide from the North was checked, and another set in from the South of Europe where illiteracy was most prevalent. By the naturalization law, immigrants were granted the privilege of citizenship after a five years' residence. Male citizens became voters in all States when qualified by age and residence in accordance with their laws. Fifteen States, impatient to attain numbers and prosperity, offered to foreign-born settlers the inducement of a vote before citizenship had been acquired, the declaration of intention to become a citizen, or "first papers," being the sole qualification required in addition to those of residence. Thus it came about that immigrant voters, who took the places of the men that had gone, had neither understanding of American principles nor a heritage which easily acquired it. Immigrants from each European nation generally joined the party advocated by earlier immigrants of their nationality, the Germans, Scandinavians and Italians usually allying themselves with the

Republican party, and the Irish, Greeks and other southeastern nationals with the Democratic party.

The newcomers furnished so fruitful a field in which to recruit party voters before an election that no party could afford to neglect it. The new voters were not tutored in American history, principles or traditions; they were not made to understand that votes mean responsibility for the common welfare; instead they were urged to support a party because that party would do most for the men of their nationality. The method used was to pay leading men, usually called key men, to round up their nationalities on election day. If the pressure was great and competition strong, votes were bought, yet a loyalty to the party chosen was often beyond purchase. An illiterate Italian bootblack in the national suffrage headquarters building in New York often said that he had been offered a political job as street cleaner, but, said he, "I didn't take it because I would have to vote the Democratic ticket."

Until the closing years of the struggle, when the suffrage army grew vastly larger and was recruited from all classes, its leaders and members were women of American birth, education and ideals. A remarkable number were daughters of Revolutionary fathers and in their childhood homes had learned the meaning of political freedom and had inherited other ideas of progress. Such women, turning to the States to seek enfranchisement, were driven to beg their right to have their opinions counted from Negroes, newly emancipated, untrained, and from foreign-born voters, mainly uneducated, with views concerning women molded by European tradition. No other women in the world suffered such humiliation nor worked against such odds for their political liberty.

Yet the woman suffrage movement in the United States was a movement of *the spirit of the Revolution which was striving to hold the nation to the ideals which won independence.*

All women of other lands now enfranchised (1923) received their vote by act of a single parliament, with the exception of two provinces of Canada where the question was put to referendum. In the United States, no State Legislature possessed authority to extend more than a restricted vote to women and some could not do that. Woman suffrage within the States meant approval by a majority, and in several States more than a majority, of the electors voting on the question. The necessary procedure was to secure an amendment to the State constitution by "striking out the word male." Thousands of voters did not know what a constitution or an amendment meant and were easily persuaded that striking out the word male "would take the vote away from men and give it to women!"

In the year 1915, the suffrage committees of four campaign States, New York, Pennsylvania, Massachusetts and New Jersey, united in the publication of literature. One flier, setting forth simple principles, was illustrated by a cartoon in which a cradle labeled "political liberty" was being rocked by a big foot, labeled "the Spirit of '76." In all four States these had to be withdrawn because of the voters who did not know the meaning of those phrases and interpreted the cartoon as meaning that when women vote men will have to rock the baby's cradle.

The enfranchisement of the black man by bayonet turned into the electorate a vote, enormous in some States, which in every referendum campaign became a solid bloc, under the direction of white men, with which to club back the advancing suffrage forces. The Negro vote proved to be an exceedingly venal one and even though Negroes usually voted the Republican ticket, they were often able to exact pay for their loyalty. A professor at Princeton, suspecting that a certain colored factotum sold his vote, said to him the day after election,—"Well, George, what did you get for your vote yesterday?"—"Five dollars, sah."—"Well, which ticket did you vote for?"—"Republican, sah, but de Democrats offered me more."—"Well then, why didn't you take the highest bid?"—"Well, sah, I specs de Democrats be de corruptedest."

The Negro should not be too much blamed for his political weaknesses; he was untrained and ignorant and leaned upon the advice of the white man who freed him from slavery, much as a child leans upon an elder. Those upon whom he leaned were not the great men who advocated human rights, but small men who lived by prostituting human rights.

With the enfranchisement of the Negro, the last man in the United States was enfranchised except the Indians living on reservations. As these were reclaimed from primitive habits and established in civilized customs, they too were enfranchised by the federal government and were given their chance to vote against extending the right of suffrage to white women, which they proceeded to do in several States.

After the war the Negro, and the foreign-born, together with the illiterate American voter, offered continual temptation to unscrupulous interests within and without the party, whose privilege or profit was affected by an election or the fate of a legislative bill. "Wherever there is money, there will be corruption," says James Bryce,[76] and wherever there is a large portion of an electorate too ignorant to understand party differences or the nature of political issues, a combination is created which will never fail to produce an extreme variety of corruption. Prosperity after the war was stimulated by the protective tariff, by city, State and national franchises, and various commercial concessions. Questions involved in these matters became issues of campaigns, and men whose profits thus depended upon Legislatures or elections were induced to invest a portion of their profits in politics in order that more profits might be forthcoming. A corrupted minority of the monied interest, combined with a corruptible minority of the electorate, produced the inevitable, and a balance of power was created which at times dictated legislation and won elections.

This vicious combination caused the State Legislatures to elect so many United States Senators in bold shamelessness that the dominant parties took up the challenge of the Populists and secured the adoption of a federal amendment providing for the popular election of Senators. This same combination ruled the large cities with such utter disregard for honor or honesty that campaigns by reform elements were constantly waged "to put the rascals out" and that, too, with more defeats than successes. Neither party was clean; the "shame of the cities" has been Democratic in New York and Boston, Republican in Philadelphia and St. Louis. Votes have been bought in elections by both parties, and, although the long struggle for the restoration of decency has removed the baser forms of corruption, the end is not yet. An occasional judge has been proved corruptible, juries have been often suspected and legislation not infrequently has borne the signs of purchase. Corporations, with need for political protection, made large contributions to parties and candidates, expecting political favors in return, until the public made so loud a protest that such contributions were forbidden by law. Individual stockholders could do what their collective corporation was forbidden to do, however, and thus the law was easily evaded. Manufacturers, railroads and the liquor trade kept sharp men on watch over all Legislatures and Congress, in order that no legislation inimical to their interests should be passed without their knowledge, and when measures affecting them came up, flocks of professional lobbyists descended upon the Legislature. A man thoroughly versed in all the intricacies of parliamentary law and legislative procedure, informed as to the history, the ambitions and the weaknesses of every legislator, affable, plausible, well-mannered, was an ideal chief for these lobbies. He was often a lawyer and usually a far abler man than the majority of the legislators he was expected "to handle."

The pay of legislators has always been so small that men ambitious for business success would not give the time necessary to legislative service. The State custom of selecting representatives from the residents of districts often limits the selection of candidates to people ill-fitted for the duties involved. Every Legislature is likely in consequence of these conditions to include a number of men low in mental and moral qualities, easily moved by flattery and tempted by money. "What sort of a Legislature have you got?" was asked in one State.[77] Quick came the answer, "As good as money can buy."

In the second election of Abraham Lincoln in 1864, loyal men at the North, sincerely believing that the fate of the nation would be endangered should the election be entrusted to the free will of an electorate from which loyal men had gone to the front, leaving a disproportion of disloyal ones at home, bought votes to save the day, conscientious Christian gentlemen contributing to this end. The corruption thus begun, or continued from prewar days, was kept alive by elements which were wholly selfish and sordid. New Hampshire furnishes a well-known example of the methods which robbed many States of all but the form of democratic government. Soon after the war a contest began between the Boston and Maine Railway and the Concord Railway for control of the State. It continued before the voters, the Legislature and in the courts for nearly twenty years. Legislators were bought in each succeeding Legislature, the price climbing higher each year, and when the contest grew most intense, agents of the two railroads selected candidates satisfactory to their respective sides, and bought votes at the polls to elect them. Even at that, they were obliged to pay for the loyalty of the successful candidate.

The bitterness of the contest overshadowed all partisan interests. Electors, observing that others were being paid for their support, excused themselves with the philosophy that one railroad was bound to win and the winner ought to pay for the privilege, and joined the list of the purchasable. The Concord road was finally beaten in the struggle and its representatives made no secret of the fact that the contest had cost it a million dollars. The successful Boston and Maine never divulged the secret of the cost of its victory, but in after years was merged with other railroad interests, thus offering circumstantial evidence that it had impoverished itself in the contest. United States Senator William E. Chandler was outspoken in his condemnation of the methods employed, and was promptly punished by the loss of his seat. The electorate was utterly demoralized by this wholesale purchase of votes. Even in ordinary elections electors insisted upon being paid for their time, even when supporting the party of their choice. Other men were frankly for sale to the highest bidder. "Floaters," as the purchasable voters were called, gathered around the polling places and refused to sell their votes until closing time approached, when prices went up.

"Why," asked a suffragist of the Republican State Chairman, "do not the Republican leaders agree with Democratic leaders to buy no more votes and thus rescue the State from its shameful degradation?" With a whimsical smile, he replied, "It was tried once in the town of C——, and when the announcement was made that no votes were to be bought the floaters called a convention, nominated a ticket and elected it." Thus had the right of voters to be bought been firmly established!

When in 1919 the National Suffrage Association sent women into New England to help the local workers in polling their Legislatures, preparatory to the ratification of the Federal Suffrage Amendment, several members quite frankly responded with the confession that they were not at liberty to promise their votes upon any question without consulting the "man who put me in." Similar demoralizing conditions were constantly found throughout New England, New York, New Jersey, Pennsylvania and Ohio, and spasmodically in other Northern States. Few States, if any, have escaped this corrupting influence, which everywhere has lowered political standards and subverted democratic freedom of choice.

Yet at no time have honest majorities entirely surrendered to criminal minorities and many a hard battle between the two has been fought, and sometimes won. In response to public opinion, laws curbing the practices which had aided corrupt minorities have been passed, and although these have been difficult of enforcement, they have exercised a restraining influence.

"In the United States," said Mr. Bryce,[78] "the swift growth of prodigious fortunes and the opportunities for increasing them by obtaining favors from the governments of States and cities had coincided with the building up of party organizations through whose help these favors could be obtained. The influence of what is called 'Big Business,' wealth concentrated in a few hands and finding its tools in politicians and party organizations, was for many years a fruitful source of mischief, exploiting the resources of the country for its selfish purposes. These abuses provoked a reaction. 'Big Business' began to be bitted and bridled, and though it still shows fight, can hardly recover the dominance it enjoyed thirty years ago, for public opinion has grown more sensitive and vigilant."

The effect of corruption upon the political history of the nation has been to drive many of the best equipped men out of politics and to render those who accept office conservative and exceedingly cynical toward "the rights of the people." Men have long warned women of the "dirty mire of politics" and many have been in truth pessimistic concerning the permanency of self-government. "Wait," they said, "until manhood suffrage has proved itself, money has been eliminated, and politics has become a fit place for women." This plea was conscientious and sincere and served to discourage many women of their class from aiding the campaigns for the vote. "We know woman suffrage is just and that it will come, but this is not the time," said men and women in large numbers in *every* suffrage campaign, and held themselves fastidiously aloof from co-operation.

Still other hazards, hazards of a legal nature, beset the path of suffragists and balked their efforts. For instance, an amendment to a State constitution must, in most States, pass two consecutive Legislatures, the campaign to secure submission thus covering a period of three or four years. Several States require more than a majority of the Legislature on the second passage. States requiring passage through one Legislature only usually call for more than a majority vote, three-fifths, three-fourths, two-thirds, being the usual provisions. And when a majority vote of one Legislature only is required for passage, additional handicaps are imposed over the election, it being usual to require the majority of all the votes cast at the election, instead of the majority cast on the proposition. The suffrage referendum in Oklahoma was the only one ever carried under this requirement. In many States a single vote in one House has prevented submission of suffrage amendments. In referenda elections illegal ballots have been counted in the total of which the suffrage amendment must secure a majority. If, therefore, the tricks of suffrage opponents failed to insure defeat in the Legislature there were always many others to be applied at the election.

Again, a referendum on a non-partisan issue has none of the protection accorded a party question. The election boards are bi-partisan and each party has its own machinery, not only of election officials but watchers and challengers, to see that the opposing party commits no fraud. The watchfulness of this party machinery, plus an increasingly vigilant public opinion, has partly corrected the election frauds which were once common. When a question submitted to referendum is espoused by both dominant parties it has the advantage of the watchfulness of both party organizations and is doubly guarded. But when such a question has been espoused by no dominant party it is at the mercy of the worst forms of corruption, precinct election officers often aiding its defeat by running in illegal votes against it, or uniting to count it out.

Women have been eligible as watchers in few States. Moreover, non-partisan questions, even when submitted at elections, are not entitled to separate watchers. A suffrage amendment unsponsored by political parties, as was usual, had no protection within the election precinct and when unscrupulous enemies were on hand was sent to certain disaster. Under the theory of our government, election officials, respecting "the will of the majority" as the sovereign of our nation, are expected to maintain honesty in elections, but in suffrage referenda theory and practice were frequently unacquainted.

"If suffrage amendments are defeated by illegal practices, why not demand redress?" the novice in suffrage campaigns used to ask. There was the rub. In twenty-five States, no provision is made by the election law for any form of contest or recount on a referendum. Political corrupters could, in these States, bribe voters, colonize voters and repeat them to their hearts' content and redress of any kind was practically impossible. If clear evidence of fraud could be produced, a case might be brought to the courts and the guilty parties might be punished, *but the election would stand.* In New York in 1915, the question was submitted to the voters as to whether there should be a constitutional convention. The convention was ordered by the ludicrous plurality of 1,300 out of New York's millions of voters. On recount in a few precincts, it was estimated that about eight hundred fraudulent votes were cast. Leading lawyers discussed the question of effect upon the election, and the general opinion was that, even though the entire plurality, and more, was found to be fraudulent, the election could not be set aside. The convention was held.

The election law is vague and incomplete in most States and if fraud has been committed it is practically impossible to discover what an honest count of the vote would come to. Thirty-two States in clear terms disfranchise (or give the Legislature power to disfranchise) bribers and bribed, but few make provision, for the method of actually enforcing the law, and, upon inquiry, the Secretary of State of many of these States reported that no man had ever been disfranchised for this offense. This was true of States which have been notorious for political corruption.

With a vague law of uncertain meaning to define his punishment in most States, and no law at all in twenty-five States, the corrupt opponent of woman suffrage amendments found many additional aids to his nefarious acts. A briber must make sure that the bribed carries out his part of the contract. Whenever it is easy to check up the results of the bribe, corruption may reign supreme with little risk of being found out. Ways of checking up on bribes have been the chief study of the corrupt politician. It was attained in Wisconsin in 1912 by using a small pink ballot for the suffrage ballot. In North Dakota in 1914 the regular ballot was long, the suffrage ballot, small and separate, although of the same color. In Iowa in 1916 the suffrage ballot was separate and yellow. In New York in 1915 there were three ballots. Party emblems easily distinguished the main ballot. The other two were exactly alike in shape, size and color, and each contained three propositions, one group coming from the Constitutional Convention and the other from the Legislature. Party orders went forth to vote down the constitutional provisions and it was done by a plurality of 482,000, nearly three hundred thousand more than the plurality against woman suffrage. On the ballot containing the suffrage amendment, No. 1, there was No. 3, which all political parties wanted carried. Yet so difficult was it to teach ignorant men to vote "no" on suffrage, No. 1, and "yes" on No. 3 that, despite the fact that orders had gone forth that No. 3 was to be carried, it barely squeezed through.

In the early years of State effort so few referenda were secured that women did not learn the difficulty of securing honest elections. With experience, however, they knew that when their cause had overcome the obstacles imposed by the constitution it immediately entered upon the task of surmounting the infinitely greater hazards of the election law. They became aware that an unscrupulous body stood ready to engage the lowest elements by fraudulent processes to defeat suffrage. They learned that the place on the ballot, or the kind of ballot, exposed it to criminal manipulation; that there was no protection against fraud on election day for a measure unsponsored by a dominant political party, and that after the fraud was committed there was no redress.

Through the handicaps and hazards created by these indefensibly unjust conditions, women were forced to fight their way to political liberty. On the outside of politics, with no vote to help, they waged their battle against sharp, shrewd groups of men who, on the inside of politics, served no God but Mammon. To their aid such men called the foreign-born, the Negro, the Chinese, the Indian, mobilized into an army at their back, and in this position of vantage commanded just and liberal-minded men to silence, and many obeyed. There were men who nobly helped the suffrage cause, but in the main the decades came and the decades went, and the women went forward, but alone. No party whip was cracked, no bayonet was drawn in their behalf, They steered their course by their unshakeable faith in self-government and its ultimate redemption from the menaces which threatened it. They despaired, not so much at the postponement of their own vote, as over the wild chaos which the strife of parties had wrought and into which their own enfranchisement would plunge them.

Why did they not give up? Many, very many, did; but the eternal destinies of the human race drove others on.

CHAPTER 12

A New Impulse

There was light ahead. The influence of the Populist Party had disappeared and politics had settled back into the old rut in the late '90s, but within the decade that followed there were premonitions of another outburst against "invisible government." Old party bonds were straining again. Making the most of conditions, the National Suffrage Association focused first on the State of Washington, where an intelligent, earnest campaign was conducted by the National Association's Washington auxiliary, assisted by organizers sent by the National. In the result the Legislature of Washington submitted a suffrage amendment in 1909, to be voted upon in 1910. In spite of a regional rivalry that split the State into two separate suffrage camps, one on its eastern slope, one on its western, the campaign moved straight forward to victory and astounded the nation with a twenty-four thousand majority. A prominent liquor campaign manager in disgusted tone said the result "was solely due to the fact that the brewers were off guard, thinking there was no danger."

A few contributions from individuals and State associations were sent to Washington, but the cost of the entire campaign did not exceed six thousand dollars. The brewers were undoubtedly misled by the quiet character of the campaign. To their inaction and to the incipient political uprising the suffrage movement owes the first great impulse on the "home stretch."

California was the next center of activity. In 1910 a new political party was organized in California and was called Progressive, the forerunner of the national party of 1912. Five parties, in consequence, had tickets in the field that year. Each carried a plank pledging submission of a woman suffrage amendment. The Legislature of 1911 carried out the political promises given and submitted woman suffrage, one of twenty-three propositions, the vote to take place at a special election on October 10, 1911. All parties supported it at the polls.

Northern and southern California, which like eastern and western Washington, do not always dwell in brotherly love, conducted each its own campaign. But the competition thus stimulated was friendly. Southern California, having been carried in the campaign of 1896, was on its mettle to save its record. Northern California, remembering that Sacramento and San Francisco had lost the State in 1896, was determined to prevent a repetition of that catastrophe. Inspired by the victory in Washington, all the liberal-minded elements of the State worked unitedly and effectively. The political parties, all women's and most men's organizations, the churches, the educational institutions, the press, all pulled together under the direction of an able and energetic central committee. The National Suffrage Association and its auxiliaries in other States helped with money, speakers and material. Every village had at least one meeting and the cities had a succession of rallies crowded to the doors, with overflows to take care of late comers. Millions of pages of literature were disseminated, hundreds of thousands of suffrage buttons were distributed, and plate matter was provided the press. In addition to suffrage news, the papers carried controversial articles on suffrage, while suffrage pennants and posters covered the State in every direction.

Ten thousand suffragists worked early and late throughout the six months of campaign, confidently carrying the slogan, "We are going to win," to the remotest corners of the State. So omnipresent was the insistent suffrage propaganda that the twenty-two other constitutional amendments were thrust into the background and thousands read and talked of woman suffrage only, day after day. No previous campaign had been so thorough-going, so triumphant in spirit from the first. Its participants to this day recall it with sparkling eyes and say, "Ah, it was a great campaign!"

Yet the victorious majority in the election was only 3,500.[79]

San Francisco again went heavily against the amendment, all voting Chinese being again rounded up against it as in 1896. The adverse city vote had to be, and fortunately was, overcome by the outlying districts. It was evident that no opponent had been "off guard" in California. When it was over, few took time to note the fact that Washington with a small campaign had won by a big majority, while California with a big campaign had won by a small majority.

Washington had given the suffrage movement a decided impulse. California gave it a veritable boom. Suffragists in all the States were amazed at the distinct change of attitude occasioned by the action of California. In November, 1912, suffrage amendments were submitted to the electors in six States (Arizona, Kansas, Oregon, Michigan, Wisconsin and Ohio) to be voted on. In several other States, where the action of two successive Legislatures was required, amendments passed the first stage.

When Arizona prepared for statehood the women had made a statewide and stirring appeal for either the inclusion of woman suffrage in the constitution, or the submission of a separate suffrage amendment. The vicious interests of the State held so decided a balance of power that the convention that was drafting the constitution refused both appeals. The women made their appeal to every Legislature thereafter, to no avail. Even the Legislature of 1912, with a public sentiment much aroused by the action of its neighbor, California, the year before, followed its predecessors in refusing the women's petition. But when the initiative and referendum had once been established in Arizona, the women turned from the recalcitrant Legislature to this new weapon of democracy. The petitions for a referendum on woman suffrage were filed July 5, 1912. The election took place in November. Republicans and Democrats had persistently refused to endorse even the submission of suffrage, the Legislature had carried out the same policy of ignoring it, but there was a complete *volte face* after the National Progressive Party, with Theodore Roosevelt as its standard bearer, had adopted a suffrage plank. Both parties not only endorsed the amendment but rendered hearty support to the campaign. With every party carrying a plank in its platform, every county was carried and the State gave a majority of 7,240 for the amendment.

In Kansas, by 1912, the bitter partisanship of 1894 had long since disappeared, scars only showing where it had once raged to the undoing of the reason of the State. The women had continued voting in the municipal elections in numbers nearly equal to those of men. The Legislature, as a long overdue act of justice, submitted the suffrage amendment to vote in 1912. The campaign was a quiet, uneventful and modest one, but directed by able women whose self-sacrifice was conspicuous. The amendment was carried by a majority of 10,787.

Oregon had in all six referenda on woman suffrage. The campaign in 1906 had been desperately fought by all the vicious elements of the population. After that date the women took the matter into their own hands and secured a submission by initiative and referendum petitions in 1908, 1910 and 1912. In 1910 they decided to ask suffrage for tax-paying women, since under the

State law a woman owning nothing but a suit of clothes could pay a voluntary tax of a few cents on her clothes and thus make herself a voter. By mistake the amendment was so worded in the initiative petition as to cover full suffrage and neither the women nor the thousands of voters who signed the petition perceived it until a short time before election. Both suffragists and antis appealed to the officials to have the description of the amendment on the ballots made to conform to the fact, but in vain. It was printed as a full suffrage amendment with a tax suffrage heading. Had the amendment carried, it would have established full suffrage unless the courts had thrown it out. The women had believed that less hostility on the part of the combined vice interests would be shown to suffrage for tax-paying women, but the usual campaign was waged, each saloon getting out its regular quota. The following year, the women returned to the usual suffrage amendment.

In 1912, however, the suffragists of Oregon had a new argument. "Since Oregon is bounded on the north by Washington where women vote, on the south by California where women vote, on the east by Idaho and Wyoming where women vote, why should not the women of Oregon vote?" The voters answered at the polls with an affirmative majority of 4,161.[80]

There was great rejoicing over these three victories of 1912, both within and without the triumphant States. Church bells were rung, processions carrying tokens of victory passed through city streets, sermons were preached, speeches made, and a greatly enlarged sale of text books on government followed. In Pittsburgh, Kansas, two hundred women gathered around a big bonfire to celebrate, with thousands assembled to see the sight. At a given signal they threw old bonnets into the fire as a symbol of the passing of the old fashion in politics and the coming of the new.

The other three campaigns of 1912 met a different fate. The story of Ohio is so remarkable that it is told in a separate chapter.

In Michigan and Wisconsin the campaigns were as ably conducted, as enthusiastically supported, the favorable sentiment as generally manifest through the press, resolutions of organizations, expressions of prominent men, quite as pronounced as in the winning States. But suffrage was defeated. A review will suffice to show what defeated it in both States.

From 1874, when the first referendum was submitted, suffragists of Michigan had continuously appealed to each successive Legislature for the submission of a suffrage amendment. The only variation was between the years 1883 and 1893 when an effort was made to secure municipal suffrage, which was granted in 1893, though the Supreme Court declared the law unconstitutional before it was put into effect. Centering their efforts thereafter upon an amendment, the women had supported their demand in all the known ways of giving evidence of public sentiment—petitions of constituents, meetings, hearings, press and literature appeals. A petition of 175,000 had been presented to the constitutional convention of 1907-8 as part of an extensive campaign, but even that body, whose sole business it was to submit amendments to the constitution to the electors of the State, had denied the voters the right of an expression of opinion. The Legislature of 1911 had followed its predecessors with the same refusal.

A special session of the same Legislature, however, was called in March, 1912, and Gov. Osborn included in the call the recommendation that a constitutional amendment relative to the right of women to vote should be submitted to the electors. Meanwhile several other States had submitted the question. Moreover, the coming schism in the Republican party was showing unmistakable evidence. The Republican Governor was a friend of woman suffrage. The Republican party had been in full control of the Legislature since the Civil War, and the Legislature now concluded that thirty-eight years was an overlong record for continual refusal to allow the electors the right to express themselves upon the question. The same Legislature that had refused submission in 1911 granted it in 1912.

The campaign that followed was triumphant in character. No unfortunate or unpleasant incidents occurred. But when the time came to print the ballots an altercation arose as to method. It was the duty of each county clerk to print them for his county, always a dangerous provision, but in this case the opportunity for irregularity was much increased by two facts, one because the ballots were to be separate and the other because the Legislature had given three suggestions for printing the question, to one of which the ballots must universally conform. In response to queries from bewildered clerks and anxious suffragists, the Secretary of State issued instructions to all clerks to follow the uniform plan of printing the full text of the amendment on the ballot. The situation produced was well suited to political chicanery. Many clerks ignored and many jumbled the instructions. Suffragists familiar with methods of juggling election returns faced election day with dread.

The early returns showed favorable figures and the suffrage majority steadily climbed to eight thousand. But many scattered precincts mysteriously withheld their returns without explanation. One by one these were released, cutting the majority to five thousand, where it seemed established and Michigan was announced to the world as another suffrage State. Then the delayed precincts began sifting in their returns, each with a suspiciously large adverse majority, until the favorable majority became a slightly adverse one. Many weeks had been consumed in the process and nerve-racked suffragists, knowing precisely what was taking place, stood helpless before the deliberate theft of an election.

The well-known method by which crooked politics counts out candidates and measures by withholding returns from controllable precincts, until returns from the rest of the State show how large an adverse vote is required to wipe out the favorable one, had been brazenly applied, the withheld precincts being finally released with a sufficiently large adverse vote to accomplish defeat. The better elements of the entire State arose in protest. Suffragists engaged counsel and filed petitions for recounts in suspected sections, notably the large cities. Though the hand that had performed the trick was well hidden, it became evident that some power in collusion with local election officials of both parties had accomplished by fraud what could not be done by an honest vote. Saloon-keepers, bar-tenders, pool-room managers, the puppets of political directors who had connived at the misprint of the ballots, now came forward with writs of mandamus to compel injunctions restraining the boards of canvassers from counting these ballots. Great irregularity was revealed in five counties. Without these counties the State had been carried by a large majority. Governor Osborn issued a ringing denunciation of the liquor interests which were clearly attempting to defeat the will of the people, in which he said:

> "If the liquor interests defeat the amendment by fraud,
> proved or suspected, the people of Michigan will retaliate in
> my opinion by adopting statewide prohibition; the question
> seems to be largely one as to whether the liquor interests
> own and control and run Michigan."

Thirteen precincts in Detroit were still withheld but after the Governor's charge of trickery, nine came in with large adverse majorities. The count was still further delayed to get an opinion from the Supreme Court which finally declared that all the ballots must be counted as printed. A recount was now demanded by press and public. A conference of public men was called to consider the situation and was attended by prominent men from different parts of the State, including many eminent lawyers. The conference demanded a recount, but it also declared for a resubmission of the question by the Legislature, the election to take place at the spring municipal election in the event that the recount proved that the amendment was lost.

Despite the many obstacles imposed, the recount was finally secured, the entire nation watching the result, for it had now become less the question of woman suffrage than the honor of Michigan that was at stake.

So skillfully had the party election officers managed their frauds that the official count of Saginaw County, which on the original report showed 1,300 majority against, now increased it by 1,200; that of Ottawa County, first reporting 2,130 majority against, increased it by 561; and St. Clair County doubled her adverse majority of 530. The Wayne County (Detroit) recount showed twelve thousand ballots not initialed by election officers as required by law and an application was made to the Circuit Court to determine the status of these ballots. The court denied the application to have them thrown out. A cry went up from all parts of the State to take an appeal to the Supreme Court.

Michigan was in a turmoil of political excitement. It was rumored that the county clerks would be arrested and tried on the charge of falsely printing the ballots with malicious intent. A story went the rounds that the saloons had been assessed in proportion to their sales and that the liquor interests had worked under common direction. In after years the brewers confessed that this had been long their established custom, but at the time the liquor representatives loudly denied both charges and the Michigan public was still unconvinced that the politics of their State was under control of the wets. Many citizens, not suffragists, were convinced that the bipartisan election officials had connived at a miscount, whoever might have paid the bill, and joined in the demand for investigation.

Party politics also entered the lists. The Chairman of the National Progressive Committee, Senator Dixon, wired the national committeeman of Michigan, Henry M. Wallace, the "situation appears suspicious" and asked him to prevent the amendment from being defeated by corruption. Thereupon Mr. Wallace gave out a public statement charging that the Republican party controlled the election machinery and that "the same elements are now fighting the suffragists that opposed us. They are crooked business and crooked politics, the saloon element allied with machine politicians." The Republicans replied with denials. Meanwhile the weeks passed by, the Legislature met and no end was in sight. It had become clearer each day that the discrepancies and irregularities were so numerous, yet so tangled, that the truth concerning the election would never be uncovered by recount or court decision and that the best plan was to hold another election.

The election returns finally agreed upon as official, although under the suspicion of fraud, were: Yes, 247,375; No, 248,135, an adverse majority of 760.

The State Suffrage Association held its annual convention in Lansing, January 16, 1913. The newly inaugurated Governor Ferres had urged resubmission in his message, and the Lieutenant-Governor and the Speaker of the House not only invited the convention to visit the Legislature but both Houses adjourned in order to receive it. The entire convention (150 delegates) accepted the invitation and its representatives addressed the Legislature "amid thunderous applause."

The women had sworn statements of ballots not given out to voters; of ballots missing in the final count, of contents of ballot boxes burned before the recount could be taken; of suffrage ballots refused to voters when called for; of ballots marked both yes and no, of amendment ballots taken out and brought back two hours later, and that thirteen precincts in the city of Detroit had held back their count for one month. With such an arraignment of an election, few Legislatures would have taken the responsibility of refusing a resubmission. But suffrage opponents had frankly announced that they would be able to postpone any action by the Legislature until after the date of the April election, and legislators who had shared in the conspiracy to secure false returns in their constituencies now boldly advertised that, their constituency having gone against the amendment, they would vote against resubmission. Yet on February 20, the House resubmitted the amendment, 74 to 21; the Senate in March, 25 to 5. The vote was set for April 7, 1913, leaving a month for the campaign.

The State had been so completely aroused, the press and the people had so poignantly felt the disgrace of an election so clearly fraudulent, that the tired suffragists rested in a false security. Not so the opponents. Rumors were soon afloat that cash prizes were offered saloon men for increasing their quota of the anti-vote, and the Republican and Democratic machines were suspiciously uninterested.

The German-American Alliance, Carl Bauer, President, in March, 1913, circularized the members of the "Staatsverbund Michigan" telling each "German brother" just how to vote no on the woman suffrage amendment on April 7. Said the leaflet:

> "If the suffrage would be laid into the hands of the native-born American woman only, the results, which surely will follow, can easily be predicted. Narrow-mindedness will triumph everywhere; fanaticism will flourish; prohibitionists and their refuse, the Anti-Saloon League, will easily set up for dictators in the State of Michigan."

There is no allusion in the leaflet to the temperance issue and it showed no connection with the brewers whose decoy the Alliance was.

The returns from the April election were: Yes, 168–738; No, 264,882. The total vote in November had been 495,510; the total vote in April was 512,257, the votes being increased by 16,747. Curiously, the number of "no votes" was increased by precisely 16,747. The "yes votes" fell off to the astounding number of 78,637. The municipal election was of small interest to rural voters, which accounted for a considerable loss. Some rural precincts recorded no vote at all on any issue. The over confidence of suffrage men that the amendment was certain of an enormous vote accounted for a further loss. Twenty-five counties had fewer "no votes" than in the first election and sixteen had not to exceed one hundred increase in the "no vote." Of the 16,747 increase of the "no votes," thirteen thousand were gained in counties where a wet and dry contest was in progress. The wet interest in the question was evidenced by the fact that the next heavy vote fell forty-seven thousand behind the total suffrage vote.

By what means the wets increased the adverse vote will never be known; but that it represented honest public opinion few believed. One point stood forth nakedly startling: All the frauds, irregularities and delays of the first election could not have been possible without the collusion of the local bi-partisan election officers, and these under direction of "higher ups." Two questions were therefore raised—and never answered: 1. Did the State Central Committees of these two parties join in the conspiracy, or could a marauding band within the parties carry on its steal of an election without the knowledge or the reproof of their leaders? 2. Did not the same boards, in charge in 1913 as in 1912, do the same things in the same way?

A grave suspicion remained in the minds of the public which went far to deepen the prevalent pessimism concerning the possibility of achieving honest campaigns and elections in this country.

Governor Osborn's prophecy was fulfilled and in 1916 prohibition was established in Michigan by popular vote, many voters being actuated by the patriotic desire to free the elections and legislation from control by the liquor traffic.

The State of Wisconsin stood second among the States in its output of malt liquors. The brewing industry was one of enormous importance to the State, the capital stock valuation being eighty-five million dollars. Several cities were brewing centers with large populations dependent upon liquor prosperity, yet there as everywhere the prohibition movement was threatening the overthrow of the trade. These facts should have warned suffragists that Wisconsin was not an auspicious point for a referendum on their question, but they did not understand, and in 1912 continued the campaign of a generation to secure the submission of an amendment.

The Legislature that passed the question on to the voters discussed at length and with apparent sincerity the best means of securing a general expression of opinion on amendments, with the result that an order was passed providing that all future constitutional amendments should be printed on separate pink ballots. This project was introduced by a wet legislator and all wet members voted for it. The bill was passed before the suffrage amendment was actually submitted and the Attorney-General, who collaborated with the liquor interests, ruled that the suffrage amendment *only* should be printed on the pink slip as other amendments passed by the same Legislature, and to be voted upon at the same election, had been passed before the new order had been voted! The isolation of the suffrage amendment on a ballot the most sub-normal voter could distinguish furnished corrupt agencies with an ideal weapon with which to compass its defeat.

The liquor trade did not rely upon election methods alone, however, but emphasized in the trade press of Wisconsin, Michigan and Ohio, through press communications and press advertisements, and by the word of mouth of numberless workers sent out to canvass voters, that all who did not want prohibition must vote against woman suffrage as women would be certain to bring it. More, every voter who did not want to see the absolute destruction of all the trades dependent upon the manufacture and sale of liquor, such as coopers, bottle and cork makers, farmers who grow the barley and corn used, must also vote against the amendment. They pictured thousands of men thrown out of employment, with starving families a charge upon charity. The effect of this propaganda was insidious and with many classes overpowering. There were cities in Wisconsin, so suffrage workers reported to the National Suffrage Association, where practically every man's business was dependent upon the good will of the big breweries and where "no business man dared allow his wife to come out for suffrage."

The women waged the best campaign they could and spent time and money in the effort to acquaint all friendly voters with the fact that the suffrage ballot would be found on a pink slip. In Racine and vicinity where they expected the largest suffrage vote, they were filled with consternation when, on election day, they discovered that the suffrage ballot was not pink, but *white*. "The calibre of voting intelligence in many cases is not equal to straightening out such a complication," wrote one observer.

The usual tricks which accompany the separate ballot were not forgotten by the opposition. The suffrage ballots had not arrived when the early voters came to some polling places; they had been exhausted when the late voters came to others, and clerks forgot to hand them to voters in still others. The total votes thus lost were many. The responsibility for these irregularities was obscured in the mysterious maze created by the joint action of a bi-partisan board, each member disclaiming knowledge and referring the query to another official equally surprised and ignorant.

As Oscar Schmidt, Milwaukee brewer, said on October, 1913, to the Interstate Conference Committee and Board of Trustees of the United States Brewers' Association:[81]

"In the last campaign we had . . . woman suffrage, etc., which were all defeated; and I can say that can only be done by organization and the brewers being on the job all the time."

The vote stood, Yes, 135,545; No, 227,024; adverse majority, 91,479. The pink ballot did it, reported the suffragists, but the federal investigation pointed to a power behind the pink ballot.

Thus the year 1912 closed with three victories to inspire suffragists, and three defeats to comfort opponents. All the world knew now that a political war was being waged which was not likely to end until women were the victors.

CHAPTER 13

Illinois: a Turning Point

After 1912 woman suffrage prospered with the fortunes of the Progressive party. The Progressives in 1912 elected fifteen members of the House of Representatives, one United States Senator and many members of Legislatures, especially in the West. The division in the Republican party was credited with the election of the Democratic President, Woodrow Wilson. The year 1913 showed the effect of this break in party regularity by concessions to progressive demands in many directions. Seven States submitted woman suffrage amendments, with the vote set for November, 1914. And there were other significant victories, notable among which was the grant of suffrage in Alaska.

The first Territorial Legislature of Alaska met in Juneau in 1913. The National American Woman Suffrage Association had circularized each legislator with "Five reasons why Alaska should adopt woman suffrage," and had corresponded with some of the leading men of Alaska. There was no suffrage organization in Alaska and no other campaign, yet the first bill introduced was one extending full suffrage to women, and it passed unanimously, one member only absenting himself from roll call. It was the first bill approved by the Governor and was signed March 21, 1913, thus becoming the first act of the newly organized Territory.

This victory at the North, however, was completely over-shadowed by a greater one, the victory of the "Illinois law" in the great Middle West.

Two outstanding forms of limited suffrage characterized this law. One, municipal suffrage, had been in operation in Kansas since 1887, and its operation had been uniformly commended by all except the liquor sympathizers. Its constitutionality had never been tested. Michigan, in 1893, after ten years of continued effort on the part of the suffragists had passed a similar law but a case had been immediately filed to test its constitutionality and the Supreme Court had declared that "the Legislature had no authority to create a new class of voters." After 1893 the legislators of no other State could be persuaded to extend municipal suffrage, the example of Michigan being held universally applicable.

The other form of limited woman suffrage covered by the Illinois law was presidential suffrage, the right to vote for the electors who vote for the president of the United States. Separately and in combination with municipal suffrage it was to play a great part in the ultimate triumph of full suffrage. Presidential suffrage inhered in Article II, Section 2, of the federal constitution. That section reads in part:

"Each State shall appoint, *in such Manner as the Legislature thereof may direct,* a Number of Electors, equal to the whole Number of Senators and Representatives to which the State may be entitled in the Congress."

For years women had been growing more and more certain that under its terms a State Legislature had the power to give the women of the State the right to vote for the president of the United States, as well as for certain less significant officials. Indeed, woman suffrage for presidential electors was introduced in the Rhode Island Legislature for the first time in 1892, and a brief defending the claim that authority for such action existed in the federal constitution was ably and, as time proved, unanswerably prepared and presented. It was left to Illinois women to make the application.

While never failing to appeal for the submission of a constitutional suffrage amendment at every legislative session, Illinois suffragists had also striven to gain municipal and presidential suffrage, separately and combined. By 1913 they had begun to formulate the idea of adding to a combined bill for municipal and presidential suffrage a clause covering the right to vote for any State officers not especially named by the State constitution as to be voted for by *male* electors. As the Governor of Illinois refused to allow any but an initiative and referendum amendment to be submitted to the voters of 1913, there was nothing for it but for the suffragists of the State to bend their energies that year to the task of finding a form of suffrage which could be granted women by the Illinois Legislature. In that body the Progressives, happily for suffrage, held at the moment a balance of power on all legislation.[82]

A bill was finally drawn up by women lawyers of the suffrage association and introduced in the Legislature. The chief of the wet lobby directed the opposition to the measure and every conceivable parliamentary maneuver was resorted to in an effort to keep it from coming to vote. Hundreds of men came to Springfield from Chicago and other cities to entreat Speaker McKinley to prevent the bill from reaching a vote. "Haggard and worn," he begged suffragists to give him a demonstration of sentiment on the other side. Immediately, letters, telegrams and telephone messages poured in upon him in such an avalanche that he was satisfied that the mandate of the State lay with the suffragists. The bill was allowed to go to vote, and when the vote came up women captains made themselves responsible for the presence of members of the Legislature, stayed on duty through the five hours' debate and saw to it that every pro-suffrage legislator was in his seat on the final count. The Senate voted, ayes 29, nays 15. The House voted, ayes 83, nays 58.

Illinois women stood possessed of the right to vote for the president of the United States, for municipal officers and for those State officers not named in the State constitution as eligible by the votes of male electors only.

The effect of this victory upon the nation was astounding. Suffrage sentiment doubled over night. When the first Illinois election took place in April, the press carried the headlines that 250,000 women had voted in Chicago. The States thus far won were those of comparatively small population, but Chicago was the second city in size in the United States. In the previous presidential campaign it had been generally noted, without making much impression, that the women of the first four full suffrage States had helped choose seventeen members of the Electoral College, and that Washington and California had added twenty more electoral votes which the votes of women affected. It was noted again after the elections of 1912 that that year's victories had added eighteen more electoral votes to the women's list. Illinois, with its large electoral vote of twenty-nine, proved the turning point beyond which politicians at last got a clear view of the fact that women were gaining genuine political power.

The day following the Illinois municipal election, newspaper headlines announced that "women had closed more than a thousand saloons" in local option elections, chiefly in the small towns. The liquor trade papers threw "We told you so" at their readers, and showed their angry disapproval in hysterical injunctions to stop woman suffrage before it wrought any further damage. That brought prohibitionists over to the suffrage side by the thousands, and hundreds of thousands of the indifferent observed for the first time that two great movements were in progress and were unconsciously pushing each other forward.

The wets at once began a series of contests to declare the Illinois law unconstitutional. It was estimated that fifty unsuccessful cases were brought in local option contests by the liquor interests, each based upon the constitutionality of the woman suffrage act. As these contests did not question the entire act but merely the right of women to vote for some specific officer or issue, the constitutionality of the entire law was not upheld by the Supreme Court until 1914. Failing to overturn the law in the courts, the opponents, now openly led by the liquor forces and allied interests, attempted to secure a repeal of the law by the Legislature, which necessitated another all-winter campaign on the part of the suffragists in order to keep what they had won.

The Illinois victory was not only tremendous in itself; it initiated a program of tremendous importance to the suffrage cause. Although the National Suffrage Association had urged presidential suffrage for twenty years, its State auxiliaries had not been able to persuade their legislators of its constitutionality. Now all was changed. Not only presidential but additional suffrage rights by legislative action became a possible aim in all States and, since the courts had established beyond doubt the right of women to vote under the Illinois law, that law became a model for other States to copy. An outstanding feature of the annual suffrage convention at Atlantic City in 1916 was a plan formulated by the president of the National American Woman Suffrage Association to secure presidential suffrage State by State as fast as possible. Delegates to the convention went home and put that program into telling effect, as will be seen later.

Meantime seven suffrage referenda took place in 1914. The States were Montana, Nevada, North Dakota, South Dakota, Nebraska, Missouri and Ohio. Of these two only were won—Montana and Nevada.

The liquor interests were particularly and vindictively active in Montana, as recorded elsewhere, and suffragists regarded the winning of the State as a brand snatched from the burning. The young president of the State auxiliary to the National Suffrage Association, Miss Jeannette Rankin, the first woman to go to Congress, won the confidence of the voters by her campaign of "Tell the people." Nevada's mining interests were aligned against suffrage, but the Nevada suffragists used a map showing the State colored black and the surrounding States white, for Nevada was now bounded by States where women voted, and the suggestive injunction, "Out, damned spot!" had a notable effect.

Yet the campaigns in these two States were probably not more efficiently conducted than those in the other western States where defeat was the portion of suffrage. In North and South Dakota the German-Russian vote was again organized against the amendment, although both Legislatures had readily submitted the amendments. In Nebraska the suffragists overcame legislative obstruction by resorting to the initiative and referendum law. The campaign followed the usual lines. It was ably conducted and supported by the best elements of the State. The German-American Alliance fought the amendment privately and publicly and the brewers made no secret of their opposition during the campaign nor, afterwards, of the fact that they had defeated it.

In Missouri the Legislature had proceeded to the date fixed for taking the vote on the suffrage amendment, when the amendment was mysteriously taken from the calendar, referred back to committee and pigeon-holed. The suffragists, however, had a weapon in reserve, and next invoked the initiative and referendum, filing on June 27th the necessary petition of thirty-eight thousand voters' names. Woman suffrage was, however, rejected at the Missouri polls.

The seventh State to vote on woman suffrage in 1914 was Ohio, which is another story, pointed enough to be told in a separate chapter.

There was a tedious similarity in all seven campaigns. Some of them were more effective than others, and some were doubtless not big enough to overcome normal indifference when flanked by a secretly working, thoroughly organized and well-financed opposition. The decisive feature of each campaign was the mobilization of the foreign vote against suffrage under the direction and probable pay of the liquor interests, and with the collusion of local bi-partisan election officials, if not that of State central committees. Wherever there were Negroes to recruit, they were recruited. Mr. Andreae's allied organizations, supported by the brewers, were now in full swing. The German-American Alliance passed resolutions in its conventions, and circularized its membership, urging no man to fail in his duty on election day. Despite the loss of five State campaigns, the year 1914 closed with spectacular suffrage activity throughout the nation, and climaxed in a spirited effort in Washington to secure the submission of the Federal Suffrage Amendment.

CHAPTER 14

The Story of Ohio

The States of Ohio and Iowa furnish a curious comparative study for the suffrage record. Ohio was a wet State wherein a powerful movement was urging its people to "go dry." Iowa was a dry State wherein a well-nigh controlling force was urging it to "go wet." In both, yearly political campaigns were waged by the prohibition forces and the liquor interests. In Ohio referenda were held under the county local option law which provided that when a majority of the voters had so indicated the county became dry. In Iowa the referenda were held under the Mulct law which provided that when a majority of the voters so declared the territory concerned might become wet.

Standing at opposing poles of their own struggle, the two factors, wet and dry, had exactly the same effect in nullifying the woman suffrage struggle. The wets were opposed to suffrage, but trying to keep their opposition subrosa. The drys were in sympathy with suffrage but restraining their sympathy from open expression lest they overload their own question. Balancing between wets and drys swung the political parties, afraid, because of the large blocks of voters on each side, to be committed to any phase of the questions at issue between liquor forces and prohibition forces. So that the women of both States were reduced to the position of political supplicants with no organized bodies to support them. Their organized friends were all muzzled.

In Ohio, despite the desperate efforts of suffragists to present their question to the public upon its own merits, it was so inextricably drawn into the more bitterly fought "wet" and "dry" contest that it was never possible to do so.

Ohio was referred to by both sides of the controversy as "the cradle of prohibition." It was here that the woman's "crusade" was initiated, out of which issued the Woman's Christian Temperance Union (1874). The Prohibition party (organized 1869) had had an energetic branch in Ohio, and the first Anti-Saloon League was organized in Ohio in 1893, and for twenty-five years thereafter assumed directorship over all prohibition campaigns. While the two preceding temperance forces had been drawn almost entirely from the church, the Anti-Saloon League attracted large numbers of business men. Before 1910, county, municipal and township local option laws had been enacted, local campaigns conducted, and a considerable portion of the State outside the urban regions had "gone dry."

On the other hand, Ohio was one of the seven largest brewing States, standing fifth in the list."[83] In 1912, when for the first time the wet and dry contest was sent to the voters of the State for arbitrament, Ohio listed 125 brewers, 14,210 retail liquor dealers (or one dealer to each sixty-nine men in the State) and 4,742,665 barrels, as the State production of fermented liquors. These forces, united in support of a common plan, composed a powerful organization that could, and did, produce nearly a million and a half dollars for a year's campaign purposes.

It was in Ohio that Percy Andreae had first carried out the plan of the organization of *allied interests* which before 1913 had spent a million dollars to perfect an organization warranted to produce political results with "unerring accuracy." It was here too that the brewers first aided the German-American Alliance to extend its organized voting strength in support of the liquor cause.

The head of the brewers' State political committee reported, in secret session in 1908, that the liquor candidate for Governor had been elected, "the result of months of organized effort on the part of all our interests and the Ohio Personal Liberty League, the Manufacturers' and Dealers' Clubs of Cleveland and Cincinnati . . . the Ohio Traveling Men's Liberty League. The result is very gratifying because it marks the collapse of the Anti-Saloon League as a factor in Ohio politics."[84]

The Ohio constitution had not been revised since 1851 and in 1910 all factions and both dominant parties agreed upon the necessity of such revision. The Legislature submitted the question, the voters ordered the convention, the delegates were elected, and the convention was held in 1912.

Concerning that election, Mr. Beis of Ohio reported[85] at a secret conference of the brewers in 1915 as follows:

"In 1912 an election was held under a resolution which was introduced by our friends in the Legislature. . . . The Andreae organization so called was put into the field there. We selected a majority of the delegates to that convention. That convention wrote licenses into the constitution of the State. Something that no other State has done."

Ohio dated its suffrage organization from 1850 and that portion of the State known as the Western Reserve was renowned for its liberal and progressive tendencies. Yet it was not until 1894 that Ohio women were granted school suffrage. An attempt to repeal even this law had been made in 1899 but had been thwarted through the influence of a petition bearing the names of forty thousand Ohio citizens.

Suffragists had made a thorough canvass of the State and knew before the Ohio constitutional convention met in 1912 that very nearly a majority of delegates would support the submission of a suffrage amendment. The directors of the suffrage campaign declared that "interests, vicious and commercial, opposed the suffrage submission at every turn," yet in the end it was accomplished, passing the convention by a vote of 76 to 34 on March 7, 1912. The paragraph defining voters in the original constitution read: "Every white male citizen, etc." The proposed amendment eliminated the words "white male." Although Ohio Negroes had not been denied the vote claimed for them under the Fifteenth Amendment, the word "white" had remained in the Ohio constitution, which thus nominally forbade what the federal constitution granted! The liquor lobbyists, in ugly temper because the suffrage amendment had been allowed to go to the voters, lost no time in planning a strategy to prevent a favorable vote.

Suddenly they became deeply solicitous for the rights of the Negro whom they found to be unworthily tied to the "women's apron strings," and in the hope of entirely alienating the Negro vote from support of the suffrage amendment, not a difficult task, they secured the submission of a separate amendment that merely eliminated the word "white." For their own purposes they were able to secure an amendment providing for the licensing of the sale of liquor. Their next effort was to place the suffrage amendment alone in a column next to the liquor amendment which, at the request of those promoting it, occupied a column by itself. Thus arranged, ignorant voters could have been easily instructed to mark one amendment for defeat and the other for victory. But the women were able to foil this plan, and the suffrage amendment was placed on the ballot with other amendments.

The convention also submitted an initiative and referendum amendment, which was supported by all reform forces in the State and not vigorously opposed by anyone. Through the submission of these four amendments, the convention had neatly balanced the distribution of political favors, granting two amendments the liquor forces wanted, and two that they did not want.

The vote was to be taken at a special election on September 3, 1912, and for three months prior thereto a vigorous and exciting campaign was waged by all interested groups.

The Ohio Woman Suffrage Association reported that it had just twenty-three dollars on hand when the suffrage measure passed the convention, but it closed the campaign with three thousand dollars with which to "carry on." "More than fifty workers came into Ohio and remained for varying lengths of time. . . . Picnics, county fairs, family reunions, circuses, teachers' institutes, summer schools, all furnished ready-made audiences, while tens of thousands of men and women were gathered together on street corners in the cities, on the public squares, in the small towns, before the general store at the country cross-roads, night after night, by our dauntless campaigners."

The campaign developed such strength that predictions that the suffrage amendment would carry were generally made. One prominent politician, mayor of a large city, basing his estimate on careful investigation, estimated that the measure would carry by forty thousand. The press and friends of the measure generally grew confident that the amendment would be carried.

But election returns revealed some curious facts. The amendment to eliminate the word "white" was lost, the wets having given it no election support. The anomaly resulted that by vote of the people "white" remained in the State Constitution as a qualification for voters, although in reality the right of colored men to vote was and remains unquestioned. The initiative and referendum amendment, being opposed by no one, and supported by many, was carried. The liquor license amendment was carried by a majority of 84,536.[86] The suffrage amendment was lost by a majority of 87,456. Its total vote was 586,296—249,420 voting yes and 336,876 voting no. The total vote cast on the suffrage amendment was 124,000 *votes more than the total vote cast on the liquor amendment.* Had each of the fourteen thousand retail liquor dealers secured twenty-four votes, according to the usual plan, the total would have composed the 336,876 noes. With the aid of the allied forces, this "systematized voting" would not have been difficult of achievement.

The allied wets did not hesitate to accept responsibility for the result. "At a meeting of the German-American Alliance held in Youngstown, a short time after election, John Schwab, the president, in his address boasted as one of the achievements of the Alliance the defeat of the suffrage amendment at the special election September 3, 1912."[87]

At the Fifty-third annual convention of the United States Brewers' Association held in 1913, President Ruppert repudiated the charge that the brewers were fighting woman suffrage, but acknowledged that Ohio was an exception.

After 1912 both suffragists and prohibitionists saw hope in the new initiative and referendum law, since they could now initiate a referendum of their respective causes to the voters without facing the problem of consent from a Legislature badly frightened by the big totals of votes rolled up on both sides of these two questions. In 1913, the president of the Ohio Woman Suffrage Association approached the president of the Anti-Saloon League with the plea that suffragists should be permitted to conduct a suffrage amendment campaign unembarrassed by any prohibition measure. The request was granted and suffragists hopefully undertook a house-to-house canvass for the 130,000 voters' signatures required by the law to secure the referendum.

The law was new, and authorities differed as to the procedure. An attempt was made to secure an official opinion, but with delay here and obstruction there an entire year passed before the petitions approved in form by the Attorney-General were ready for circulation. More than the required 130,000 men voters wrote their names on the suffragists' petition, in the presence of a circulator who then on oath declared the signature genuine. This work was done by women volunteers and every county was represented in the total. In July, 1914, the petitions were presented to the Secretary of State, a representative from each of the eighty-eight counties bearing its petition. The work involved had been enormous—but the result was a free expression of public opinion.

When the liquor interests comprehended that woman suffrage was certainly going to the voters with no other entangling question, they hastily held a conference with Mr. Andreae at Cincinnati and determined to throw confusion into the election by initiating a repeal of the county local option law, under the title "Home Rule Amendment."

The entire force in the Andreae department was withdrawn from various fields and thrown into the State. These workers, "augmenting the force already at the disposal of the Ohio campaign manager, secured 304,000 voters' signatures to the petitions[88] in less than thirty days' time."

The Anti-Saloon League, considering that their pledge to the suffragists should not be kept under these circumstances, circulated petitions for a referendum on a prohibition amendment. Thus woman suffrage, full prohibition and repeal of county local option (called Home Rule Amendment) were placed on the same ballot for 1914. An intensive campaign was conducted on each of the three amendments by its respective friends. The wets again waged their campaign against the two reform amendments with the same fund and the same workers, while suffragists and prohibitionists conducted as always an unconnected campaign. The prohibition and suffrage amendments were lost;[89] the Home Rule Amendment was carried by forty-six thousand majority.

In 1916 Ohio suffragists turned their attention to local campaigns, and after a hard campaign won municipal suffrage in East Cleveland on a referendum.

Meanwhile the national Republican and Democratic party platforms of 1916 had adopted suffrage planks and the two Ohio party conventions, never before brave enough to express an opinion on woman suffrage, confirmed the national platforms. Supported by these platforms, the Legislature of 1917 extended presidential suffrage to Ohio women. The dry House passed the measure on February 1 by a vote of 72 to 50. The wet Senate passed it on February 14 by a vote of 20 to 16. The action was at once recognized by the old foe as a dangerous wedge, and soon a curious thing happened: No other than the wet leader of the Senate introduced a bill providing for the submission of a full suffrage amendment. Now ensued an utterly anomalous situation: opponents of woman suffrage urging the Legislature to submit a bill for full suffrage for women, advocates of woman suffrage trying to block any such submission. None but those on the inside could possibly have understood the mystery of the motives at work. But on the inside there was no mystery at all.

The opponents of woman suffrage had two objects in view: one to obscure the issue; one, the ultimate rejection of the women's presidential suffrage bill. The suffragists, on their side, had a clear perspective. For fifty years they had been trying to get the Ohio Legislature to submit a suffrage amendment, but now the time for it had gone by. Full woman suffrage was coming and coming fast by the federal route. Over in Washington a federal suffrage amendment was drawing near to victory in Congress. Ohio women wanted their energies left free to help speed ratification on its way. They did not want, at this critical moment in the federal fortunes of suffrage, to be engulfed in the whirlpool of political trickery within the State that always had engulfed them when woman suffrage was brought to the Ohio polls. Yet here were the wets proposing submission of a State suffrage measure. The women antis asked for a hearing. The women antis and the wet men occupied seats en bloc and both pleaded for submission; the suffragists opposed. The bill was passed in the Senate February 14, 19 to 17, but the opposition of suffragists stayed its course in the House.

Just within the time limit prescribed by the law, ninety days, petitions for a referendum were filed on presidential suffrage. The suspicious suffragists immediately began a thorough invest-igation of the petitions. The first to be examined were those of Trumbull County. Of fifteen petitions, containing 584 names, it was discovered that twelve were circulated by proprietors of saloons. Five of these men, not being able to write, had made their marks in attesting the petition. No petition was circulated in dry sections of the county, and many irregularities were discovered. This preliminary examination gave direction for other county investigations. Alert groups of women in forty-four counties searched the voters' rolls for names appearing on the petitions and took note of other possible sources of fraud. The petitions to the county courts of Common Pleas presented by these women showed a remarkable uniformity. Thousands of names signed to the referendum petition as registered voters were not to be found on the poll lists and the same name was signed more than once. Affidavits that sponsors for petitions were volunteer workers when facts indicated that this was unlikely was a common charge. For example, "six petitions in Clinton County were circulated by a man who has no visible means of support, has frequently been employed by the wets, and had been arrested for bootlegging."[90]

"Between 75 and 90 per cent of the petitions were circulated by saloonkeepers, bartenders, brewers, and recognized county wet leaders" was the testimony of the president of the Ohio auxiliary to the National Suffrage Association. Signatures were secured in saloons, German clubs and other wet centers. Hundreds of petitions were kept so closely within saloon circles that business men, lawyers, doctors, teachers, did not learn that they were in circulation, and they were finally filed without the name of a single representative man of the community.

All this chicanery resulted in one advantage for the women: it aroused Ohio opinion to the issue of the square deal to such an extent that when the women of Columbus appealed to the men voters for the municipal suffrage, they got it.

So notorious had become the control of both dominant political parties by wet influences, that dry Democrats held a special convention in Columbus in May, 1917, and the dry Republicans in June. Suffrage representatives attended both conventions for the purpose of calling attention to the fact that the petitions filed on presidential suffrage were "reeking with fraud." The presentation of facts was unnecessary, as the press had already made them common knowledge. Resolutions were introduced by delegates and passed by both conventions, urging the rejection of the petitions.

Meanwhile the suffragists carried their evidence to election boards, which, after examining the evidence, referred them to the county courts. They were able to secure a hearing in four counties only, Scioto, Trumbull, Mahoning and Cuyahoga. Out of 9,964 names in these counties, the courts threw out 8,661 as fraudulent! The women in charge of the investigation insisted that a similar portion would have been thrown out in every county. Yet for various excuses other courts would not grant the hearings. In the words of the Akron *Times:*

"If there is anything that should strengthen the cause of woman suffrage in Ohio it is the disclosure that the petitions of the antis for a referendum on the Reynolds Act abound in frauds. Fraud is a confession of weak cause. It ought to condemn its perpetrators in the eyes of all fair-minded voters."

An attempt was then made to lay the entire evidence before the Secretary of State. He too refused the suffragists a hearing and, to the lasting dishonor of Ohio politics, the question went to referendum upon a petition "reeking with fraud."

In their circular to the voters of the State, the suffragists thus summed up their case:

"Do these petitions represent the people? No! They represent a special interest. Five hundred and eighty-one petitions were circulated by saloonkeepers and bartenders; 246 were circulated by employees of the breweries, the Personal Liberty League (a wet propaganda group) and by others more closely allied with the liquor interests. This referendum is the work of the organized liquor ring. Nearly one-quarter of all the names were obtained in Cincinnati alone (the great brewing city). Circulators had to resort to fraud and forgery to get the petitions filed. Though these petitions were formally filed by the Association Opposed to Woman Suffrage, not one woman circulated a petition."

By November 6, 1917, while over the boundary line New York State voters were giving a tremendous majority for full suffrage for women, the wets had succeeded so well in organizing a vote against presidential suffrage in Ohio that they defeated it by 144,000 majority. The prohibition amendment was also lost, but with so small a majority as to fill the drys with hope and the wets with dread.

In 1918, the drys initiated a prohibition amendment. The wets, following their usual tactics of a countering proposition, initiated a constitutional amendment to the effect "that the people reserve to themselves the legislative power of the referendum on the action of the General Assembly ratifying any proposed amendment to the constitution of the United States."

It may not be easily evident on its face but what this meant was that the Ohio people were to take precedence over the constitution of the United States. That constitution provides that the Legislatures of the different States shall have the power of accepting or rejecting any federal amendment submitted by Congress. Here was a state constitutional amendment proposing that a State's people and not its Legislature should have these powers of ratification. It was aimed, of course, at the federal prohibition and suffrage amendments, the first of which had by then been submitted by the Congress, while it was already apparent that the other was going to be, as sure as doom.

The Ohio Woman Suffrage Association recognized the significance of this measure and attempted to arouse prohibition opposition to it. But the prohibitionists were completely absorbed by the demands of their own campaign and refused to regard the referendum amendment as worthy of attention. The National American Woman Suffrage Association came to the aid of its Ohio auxiliary and financed the attempt to prevent the question from being placed on the ballot. The suit was brought in the name of a leading citizen of Columbus, Edgar L. Weinland, who as taxpayer protested against the unnecessary expenditure of money for printing ballots and other costs to provide for putting the question to the voters, since it was clearly unconstitutional. The brief presented by the attorney for the National Suffrage Association, Mr. Frank Davis, Jr., set forth precisely the same plea which a year later led the Federal Supreme Court to declare this law unconstitutional, but the Ohio Supreme Court avoided a decision on the ground that it had "no jurisdiction in advance of the election."

At the November election (1918) the State prohibition amendment won by a majority of twenty-five thousand; while the amendment making referenda on federal amendments possible won by a majority of 193,000.

With generous though secret contributions to political party funds and with their known ability to deliver votes of organizations one way or the other, as their interest was aroused, "the Liquor Ring" had for years intimidated political leaders but the long and bitterly contested prohibition victory brought relief to the political situation. Conscientious men who did not endorse prohibition, accepted it as a liberation from the tentacles of the liquor incubus and breathed easier after the winning of the prohibition amendment at the Ohio polls. The 1919 Legislature of Ohio at once restored the presidential suffrage lost to women by the referendum of 1918, so that in the event of the nation's failure to complete ratification before the presidential election of 1920, Ohio women would be qualified to vote for president.

The liquor forces, however, were still unconquered. They filed a referendum petition on ratification of the prohibition amendment under the authority of the State amendment they had carried the year before, bringing it to vote in the November election of 1919. They filed petitions also to repeal the State prohibition amendment; to authorize 2.75 per cent beer; to repeal the State Enforcement Act.

Another wet and dry struggle rocked the State of Ohio from capitol to boundary. The November election of 1919 recorded that ratification of the federal prohibition amendment had been lost by a wet majority of five hundred votes. The repeal of the State prohibition amendment had been defeated by a dry majority of 41,849, but the Prohibition Enforcement Act, which alone could make it effective, had also been defeated by a wet majority of 26,838, while 2.75 per cent beer had been defeated by a dry majority of thirty thousand. The liquor forces had won two points and the temperance forces two, and again the electorate stood bewildered by its own acts.

The wets all over the nation were elated that the ratification of prohibition in one State had been repudiated on referendum. Apparently the four wet measures were considered a sufficient undertaking for one Ohio election, for though petitions to refer the Ohio Legislature's ratification of the Federal Suffrage Amendment and the grant of presidential suffrage were also circulated by the same wet army that circulated the others, the time of filing was carefully planned so as to fall short of the required sixty days before election. This was to bring the two suffrage referenda to vote in 1920, a fact which the wets hoped would prevent a proclamation of ratification of the Federal Suffrage Amendment before the presidential election of 1920.

The suffragists, tired and defrauded, set to work, not with cheerful hope but with grim determination, to prepare for a referendum if one should come, by enrolling the women who wanted the vote as a plea to the voters. In the midst of these endeavors an event occurred that was scarcely noted in the midst of the political, industrial and social excitement at the time. A group of Ohio suffragists stole away to the little town of Newburg. Once Newburg had been a center of that fiery devotion to free thought and human liberty which had marked the early settlement of the Western Reserve. In it a vigorous suffrage organization had lifted up its voice in 1874. Women had refused to pay taxes there unless they were represented and had allowed the authorities to sell property to meet the bill. There they had offered their votes and had been refused. There this early group had planted an acorn in commemoration of their faith. The acorn had been growing for forty-five years and was now a sturdy oak. Under its branches the Newburg Memorial Association received the visiting suffragists, and together they held a service of honor for the women whose vision had seen the coming victory afar off. They listened to the stories of the fearlessness of those early workers, their hope and their faith. Led by the grandsons of the pioneers, they laid wreaths upon their graves. In the little chapel where President Garfield, Lucy Stone, Theodore Parker, Louisa M. Alcott, John B. Gough and Robert Collyer had spoken, they spoke.

Forty-five years of ceaseless work lay between that movement and the beginning of the suffrage movement in Ohio. Still unfinished; and still that faith!

Wearily the women returned to the tedious and uninspiring toil of rolling up numbers of women who wanted to vote, in the event the Ohio referendum should take place. Halfheartedly they did the work, for their thoughts now centered on Washington. While they worked they were hoping and waiting for the Supreme Court of the United States to speak and declare the unconstitutionality of the Ohio amendment that had given to Ohio voters the right to supersede the federal constitution at the Ohio polls.

Exhausted by their ten years of ceaseless campaigning, prohibitionists and liquor forces also turned to the Federal Supreme Court and awaited its fateful decision.

CHAPTER 15

The Story of Iowa

The woman suffrage campaign in Iowa is remarkable for what it failed to achieve. Its interest lies in the accomplishments of the foes of suffrage.

The State was populated by a people of high average intelligence, and a school system that dotted the prairies with schoolhouses in every four square miles was early established. All public institutions of higher learning were co-educational. The State was a staunch defender of the Union, as a soldiers' monument in nearly every county seat testifies, and its traditions made it normally a one-party State, its history recording only one Democratic Governor. The State motto, "Our liberties we prize, our rights we will maintain," reflected in truth this high-spirited sense of freedom.

The suffrage agitation was begun in 1854, but in Iowa as elsewhere the movement paused during the Civil War. The submission of the 15th Amendment by the Congress in 1869 induced action on behalf of woman suffrage in Iowa, and a number of suffrage clubs under influential leadership were organized in the larger cities.

These new groups made an appeal to the incoming Legislature which ratified the 15th Amendment and passed a resolution providing for the submission of a woman suffrage amendment to the voters of the State. This action was widely commented on by the nation, as the Iowa Assembly had for the first time elected a woman engrossing clerk and it became her duty to carry the victorious suffrage resolution from the House to the Senate, a fact which called forth many editorials upon the new opportunities of women, many warmly endorsing woman suffrage.

In the spring of 1869, delegates from the organized suffrage clubs met in convention and organized the Iowa State Woman Suffrage Association with the object of preparing for the expected referendum. Lecturers hastened hither and yon, leaving suffrage societies behind them, which presented their plea at meetings and in interviews with clergymen, editors and politicians. The most historic of these was the Polk County Woman Suffrage Society, located at the capital. This society not only never failed to hold its monthly meeting from October, 1870, to August, 1920, when all suffrage work in the nation came to an end, but it served for many years as the director of the State legislative campaigns. It never failed to make its appeal to every Congress for the submission of the Federal Amendment and to each Legislature for suffrage action, usually the submission of a State amendment. Whenever the State organization threatened to collapse as the result of disgusted disappointment the Polk County group stood steadfast and bolstered it up again.

The Iowa Legislature meets biennially and the constitution provides for amendment by the submission of any proposition to the voters after its passage through two successive Legislatures. When the Legislature of 1872 met, the organization was ready, the press friendly, the leaders of the Republican party outspokenly favorable, the Governor announced his endorsement of the amendment and the House voted its second passage by 58 to 39. The Senate, after a spirited debate, voted to engross the bill for third reading, 26 to 20, and hopes ran high. Yet a few minutes later the final vote stood 23 to 23.

That record was the prototype of the fate of suffrage in various encounters with Iowa Legislatures to come: First a legislative opinion reflecting an unmistakable public opinion in favor of suffrage, then a sudden overnight shift that lost the pending suffrage measure by the scantiest margin, but lost it just the same.

The Republican State Convention of 1874 adopted a clear-cut pledge to submit to the voters a woman suffrage constitutional amendment. When, in 1876, the Legislature elected on this platform met, Governor Carpentier in his message said:

"When all America is celebrating achievements inspired by the doctrine that taxation and representation are of right inseparable, it is recommended that you give the people of Iowa an opportunity to express their judgment upon the proposed amendment at the ballot box."

The House promptly passed the measure, 54 ayes; 40 nays. A careful canvass of the Senate, made by friendly Senators as well as by the women, showed a suffrage majority of ten on both polls. The vote was taken—and suffrage lost by one vote. Not a known enemy had appeared. No reason was given for the sudden change of front.

Undismayed, the women rallied for the legislative campaign of 1878 and Governor Newbold wrote a recommendation favoring submission in his message, but some unexplained influence induced him to suppress it. The House passed and the Senate defeated the resolution.

The Legislature of 1880 submitted to the voters a prohibitory amendment for the first time. The woman suffrage amendment was lost by an error on engrossment. From that time on suffrage was buffeted about in the fight of the wets and drys for the political control of Iowa, the wets fighting it subrosa, the drys masking their sympathy for fear of overloading the prohibition fight.

For years the State vacillated from one side to the other, now wet, now dry. A type of politician developed which was afterward familiar in many States, known as the "damp dry" and the "dry wet," a delicate difference existing between these two terms. Such men could be depended upon to vote neither dry nor wet if it were possible to avoid action. It was in this State that the term "stand pat," afterwards adopted nationally, was inaugurated.

Meanwhile the suffrage association continued to be one of the ablest of those early days. The '70s and early '80s was a period of lectures and lecture courses and every man or woman who spoke on woman suffrage made the rounds of the State. The press was circularized over and over, as were the clergy. The press was extremely favorable and the churches of all denominations were remarkably liberal-minded on the question. Iowa "woman laws" by comparison were unusually fair.

Iowa claims the first woman dentist (1863) in the country and also the first woman to be admitted to the bar (1871). Woman physicians found hospitable welcome in the State, while forced in the East to bear little short of persecution from their male rivals. Many women ministers, also, who would not have been tolerated at the time in the East, presided over large and flourishing churches. In the early '80s, the Patrons of Husbandry grew with rapidity and at one time had two thousand local granges. Each, being founded upon the principle of the equality of the sexes, was a center of woman suffrage education among the farmers. The first woman county superintendent of schools was elected in. 1869, and women superintendents were numerous thereafter. These and many similar facts demonstrate not only the liberal attitude of the people toward the woman question, but the fact that the State was a leader in the movement.

When politics was not involved the Legislature made quick response to this advanced public opinion by voting eligibility to women for the office of county superintendent of schools and Recorder of Deeds, when few States granted the first privilege and none the last. It made women eligible to most State boards and commissions and defended their equal rights under the law in numerous ways. It is also claimed that the Republican party, dominant in the State, was the first to introduce the innovation of women campaign speakers. Yet among this public-spirited, progressive people where suffrage was advocated to a notable degree, forty-three years of unceasing work was necessary before a well-organized, intelligent suffrage association could get the question to the voters who alone possessed the right to render decision.

An extraordinary effort was put forth by suffragists in 1900 in order to convince the legislators that a public demand existed for submission of the question, and petitions numbering one hundred thousand signers were presented to the Legislature. The Committees of both House and Senate reported the bill favorably and unanimously. The House defeated the measure 44 ayes; 55 nays. Further work by suffragists secured a promise of reconsideration and the certain passage of the measure, provided the Senate should first pass it. This information was given the Senators. The resolution was lost in the Senate by *one vote.*

The women knew of nothing further that could be done to strengthen their demand. They had exhausted all methods known for giving a mandate to a Legislature concerning the desires of the people except through the expression of party platforms. The Republican party was as evasively friendly as the Legislature, the Democratic was frankly wet and "anti." The suffragists had not yet learned that the stronger the demand and the more efficient the organization, the smaller the chance of getting submission! Under the State suffrage motto "Never give up" the workers were again rallied, and in the hope that a new Legislature might prove to be a more liberal one they urged submission again in 1902. The bill was passed by the Senate and lost by the House. In 1904 and 1906 the amendment was lost in the House and did not come to vote in the Senate.

The constitution being amended, the legislative year was changed from even to odd years, and the Legislature met again in 1907. It was now time to reverse political responsibility, so the measure was lost conveniently in the Senate, and did not come to vote in the House. In 1909 and 1911, for the first time in forty years, it was lost in both Houses.

In 1913, the Legislature, having the first dry majority in some years, passed the resolution, the Senate voting 31 ayes, 15 nays; and the House 81 ayes, 26 nays. In 1915, under similar conditions, the resolution was again passed by the Senate, 38 ayes, 11 nays; and by the House, 84 ayes, 19 nays. Thus after twenty-four campaigns stretching over forty-five years, the Legislature, having no power itself to decide the matter, permitted the voters the right to express their opinion. The first suffrage leaders who, exalted by the spirit of liberty prevailing in the '60s, had begun the movement in expectation of early triumph, had long been gone. Those who had taken their places and led fearlessly forward for another generation were nearly all gone, too. Mary J. Coggeshall, who for thirty years had inspired the suffragists of the State, had died in 1911, leaving ten thousand dollars to the National and five thousand dollars to the State Suffrage Association with which to "carry on." Her friends in 1913 sorrowed that she was no longer there to share the joy with them when the first triumph broke the long strain of continual discouragement. Many of the faithful remembered how she, the bravest of them all, had turned away from the State House after the last adverse vote with pale face, broken look and trembling lip—a lifetime of work apparently of no avail.

The Legislature passed the amendment on to the voters for the primary election, June 5, 1916. So many times had the suffragists made ready for campaigns that never came that they had had no spirit for preparation for this campaign of 1916, lest it again prove fruitless, and the neglect had left them much to do. While they were holding conferences to make their campaign plans and to compose a campaign budget, calling for a modest campaign fund, another conference was taking place in St. Louis of which they knew nothing.

Henry Thuenen, counsel for the Iowa brewers, gave a report of it to Mr. Andreae, chief of the National Political Committee:[91]

"Fred Kemmerle and I were in St. Louis yesterday to keep an appointment previously made with Mr. August A. Busch, President of the Anheuser-Busch Brewing Association.

"This conference was in pursuance of our agreement and understanding with Mr. Andreae, and was asked in order to give us an opportunity to discuss the future of Iowa."

Mr. Thuenen had already sent a long letter to the Interstate Conference Committee of the United States Brewers' Association,[92] setting forth the political situation and adding:

"We are of the opinion that woman suffrage can be defeated, although we believe that the liquor interests should not be known as the contending force against this amendment. Action of some kind should be taken to assure a real and active campaign against this measure. . . .

"As we view the situation there is a feeling that the fight which has been made by the brewers and the liberal interests of the State is very little short of marvelous in that it has deferred the evil day so long. . . . Our breweries will be closed and the revenue with which we have conducted our past fights will be removed. . . . To sum up, what Iowa needs at your hands, if you are disposed to interest yourselves in the State is: First, a contest on woman suffrage at the primary in 1916; Second, a contest for liberal senators at the election in

1916, and if this fails, then Third, a contest at the polls on the Prohibitory Amendment in 1918 unless otherwise provided by the Legislature."[93]

Before the primaries a mysterious but vigorous campaign for hard paved roads began to make itself seen and heard in Iowa. Nothing seemed more remote from the old familiar wet and dry controversy that had raged for more than a generation in the State than good roads. Farmers Tax-Payers' Leagues—apparently to be sincerely what they purported to be, that is, organized protests against extravagant taxation—had been vigorously urged by the Iowa *Homestead,* the chief farm paper of the State, with a pro-suffrage editor. In answer, such leagues had sprung up like magic, until nearly every county had one. The *Homestead* urged the nomination of W. L. Harding, whom the brewers had called "our man," upon the sole ground that he disapproved of hard roads. The *Register,* chief Republican paper, was urging his defeat as earnestly because of his well-known wet record. Many farmers read the *Homestead* only and, aroused to protest against taxation for hard roads, were won to the Harding standard.

As the campaign drew near its close and the hard roads controversy was at its climax, having been successfully pushed into the forefront of the political discussion of the moment, a connection between the two sides of the contest was made. A rumor—no one knew whence it came—grew into a definite charge, that it was the women in the towns who wanted the hard roads, estimated to cost millions of dollars, in order that they might ride into the country comfortably in their automobiles! Were Mr. Harding nominated and elected there would be no hard roads—he would veto the bill. There followed a further rush of farmers to his support.

At this point the Republicans met in convention. With all the wets, plus a large number of farmers opposed to hard roads, supporting Mr. Harding, his nomination became daily more certain. Then came the final coup. Should Mr. Harding be nominated, and it was evident he would be, he could not be elected should women be enfranchised in the primary! First, they would vote against him because he opposed hard roads which they were alleged to want; second, the probable Democratic nominee was a highly respectable man with a well-known dry record, a curious fact since his party was and always had been frankly wet. Women, said the rumors, would vote for the dry Democrat and against the wet Republican. The only remedy for Republicans therefore who did not want their party to go down to defeat was to kill the suffrage amendment!

The public saw no visible hand, no responsible moving power, yet little "ads" now began to appear in the country press. The last issue of the *Homestead* before the primary carried a page advertisement urging farmers to vote against woman suffrage if they did not want to pay for hard roads. No hint of wet or dry issue was made. When the long-professed suffrage editor was chided for this act of perfidy he could only say feebly, "I got six hundred dollars for the ad."

Certain Republicans were insistent that this mysterious propaganda caused the adverse majority, although they professed not to know whence it came. Was it one of those exasperating cross currents that so often upset political prediction? Not at all. Henry Thuenen, counsel for the Iowa brewers, paid the bills for it; the publicity man who conducted the campaign successfully designed to dupe the farmers said so![94]

On primary day, June 5, 1916, the brewers scored three victories: 1. The woman suffrage amendment was defeated. Mr. Andreae's machine had again worked with "unerring accuracy"; 2. A liberal Senate had been nominated, and 3. The candidate that the brewers wanted for Governor had been nominated.

The results in the primary were not unexpected by suffrage leaders of the State or nation. Some weeks before primary day, the Republicans had met in convention at Cedar Rapids and there it had been decided either by the leaders or by a group within the party to kill the suffrage amendment quietly. From that convention there went home two men who had either reluctantly acquiesced in that plan or had protested in vain. One of these men told his sister of the decision, the other his wife. Both made their confession because the two women were working in the suffrage campaign to the very limit of their endurance, and they wished to soften the coming disappointment. Each man declared to his confidante that, should the fact leak out that he had told, he would swear that he was not the one who had betrayed party confidence.

But had there been no secret information the fact that the amendment had been scheduled for defeat was soon apparent. Like the sudden veering of the wind had come a change in the attitude of friendly Republican leaders. Organizers, speakers, local workers, knowing nothing of the friendly warnings and without knowledge of other points, reported the change as a local symptom. As far away as the New York suffrage headquarters it was known that something sinister had happened. As barometrical changes indicate coming storms so signs as dependable may forecast political action.

The majority against the suffrage amendment at the polls was only 10,341. Four German counties on The Mississippi River where the German-American Alliance was strongest and the wet sentiment had always been constant (Dubuque, Jackson, Clinton and Scott) gave a greater majority against the amendment than did all the rest of the State. The responsibility was thus clearly laid at the door of the brewers but the nature of the secret intrigue that had brought the result is only partially and probably will never be fully known.

Barrels and Bottles, published at Indianapolis, the headquarters of the bureau that pushed the organization of the German-American Alliance for the brewers, commented upon the outcome under the title "Listen, Sisters": "This handicap (of wet opposition) has again and again prevented the granting of suffrage to women, just as it did in Iowa the other day when the suffrage amendment was defeated by a margin so small that it was manifestly only the unpopularity of that proposition in the larger cities, where prohibition is not favored, that prevented its adoption."

Immediately after the election, a third Republican in the upper party ranks, in a moment of disgust, confided to another suffrage State officer that "the amendment would have won had the Republicans not agreed to count it out!" Then he added that should it leak out that he had said this thing he would deny it even though it meant to declare so estimable a lady as his confidante a liar!

Rumors of strange happenings at the polls were already spreading but lawyers advised that the election could not be declared illegal no matter what evidence was found. One lawyer, acting for the W. C. T. U., visited forty-four counties, returning with two hundred pages of affidavits which when summed up revealed many varieties of violation of the election law. A common defense was at once expressed by party workers that such errors occurred in all elections; but there were two which could not be explained away. "The records," ran the lawyer's report, "in the Secretary of State's office disclose that there were 29,341 more votes cast on the equal suffrage amendment than the total cast for all candidates for Governor!" All political experience establishes the fact that in a normal election the head of the ticket receives the largest vote in any given election and amendments or measures the smallest. Where did all these extra votes cast on the suffrage amendment come from?

The achievement could not be charged to the brewers alone. It required the co-operation of bi-partisan election boards in enough precincts to guarantee results. How was it brought about? Was it not the fear of a possible Democratic administration, carefully planted and nursed by the brewers' argument that W. L. Harding would be defeated in the election should women vote, that led to the decision at Cedar Rapids to kill it? Was it not Republican co-operation with wet Democratic election officers long trained in that State to defeat popular opinion at the polls that led the Republican official to use the words "counted out"? The investigator of that election will discover ample evidence of motive for falsifying the returns, and evidence that an honest public opinion was not expressed. What is wanting in the evidence is the testimony of witnesses who saw the compacts made or heard the instruction given. The absence of this conclusive evidence of political corruption has balked the cure of that unmitigated evil for generations.

Conviction was burned into the soul of every suffrage leader that the amendment had been defeated by trickery, but how had it been done? Friendly politicians were put on the grill and asked the question, "What were the tricks and how can we find them?" Numerous lawyers were called upon by anxious deputations and asked another puzzling question:—"If we find the fraud in the election what can we do about it?" The politicians agreed that it was too late to discover actionable evidence of fraud in the election and the lawyers said that were fraud found the law would not warrant the declaration that the election was void.

The law provided that the ballots cast at a special election should be held for six months "unless a contest is pending." Therefore the W. C. T. U. brought an injunction-proceeding against the Executive Council, the Governor, the Secretary of State, the Auditor of State and Clerk of Public Documents, claiming that no legal election had been held. The motive for bringing the injunction was not revealed, beyond its obvious effect to prevent the destruction of the ballots, nor was the character or quantity of evidence given to the press.

It was the intention of the W. C. T. U. to petition the Legislature for an investigation into the conduct of the election and with the evidence collected to press for another election. The Iowa Suffrage Association joined in this request. The law of Iowa, as of many other States, had no suitable provision for a recount on amendments or measures. Frauds once committed were practically beyond discovery.

The situation was without precedent. Public opinion was greatly aroused but divided, many claiming the irregularities unearthed to be the outcome of innocent carelessness, others that they were indications of a statewide criminal conspiracy. It was clear that whether perpetrated by the innocent or guilty, the law offered no easy solution to the problem. No politician wanted an investigation into the election. The evidence proved that an almost unbelievable number of irregularities had been committed by election officials, but it did not reveal whether these had been due to gross ignorance and carelessness or to fraud as defined by the law. Nor did the evidence reveal how or by whom fraud had been committed if fraud there had been.

Iowa suffragists found the wet Legislature of 1917 in irritable mood and professedly resentful of the charge that the men of the State had conducted an illegal election. The legislators made a counter charge that the women were "poor sports" who should know when they were beaten and ask no suffrage favors for a time. A lame compromise was at length agreed to; the women dropped their appeal for a new election and the Legislature resubmitted the amendment. Even this compromise action was secured only after a bitter fight, in the midst of which the wets, following their universal "red herring" policy, introduced an amendment to the constitutional amendment proposing submission of the question to the women for the purpose of sounding their views; and this amendment actually passed the Senate, although the proposal carried no pledge for action even if every woman in the State should vote aye! It was killed in the House and the resolution providing for submission of a suffrage amendment to the legal voters finally passed both Houses.

The dry Legislature of 1919, which had to concur in the submission, was also in unhappy mood. Difficult political problems were demanding attention. The prohibition amendment had gone to referendum in 1918 and had been defeated by a majority of one thousand. Thus the electors had voted down, as a State constitutional amendment, a law that had been on the statute books of the State for thirty-six years. Moreover the first question before the Legislature was ratification of the federal prohibition amendment! The attorney-general and the Governor were in conflict and a movement to impeach the Governor further disturbed legislative serenity. The Legislature, however, ratified the prohibition amendment on January 15, 1919.

When the suffrage amendment, passed by the 1917 Legislature, came up for final passage, it was discovered that no action could be taken because the public notice, as required by law, had not been given by the Secretary of State. The Secretary was a friend of suffrage and professed deep regret for this oversight, the blame falling upon a clerk whose duty it was to attend to such matters. Whether this was another case of Iowa's incapacity for self-government, or whether it was connected with the wet conspiracy, remains as unraveled a mystery as those surrounding the amendments of previous years lost by improper engrossing. The Secretary of State declared, while apologizing for the error, "I have always thought there was something irregular in that election, and

I feel that the women of Iowa did not receive fair treatment at the polls." But again there was no redress. The Legislature made such amends as it could by passing again the resolution submitting a suffrage amendment, which when passed by the Legislature of 1921 would send it to the voters that year. It also willingly added Iowa to the ever-increasing list of States that were by then extending presidential suffrage to women. Friendly members attempted to comfort the impatient women by assuring them that after waiting fifty years for the vote they could not possibly mind a little additional wait of two more years.

Governor Harding, nominated on the primary day on which the suffrage amendment had been defeated, had assured the suffrage leaders in 1917 that he knew nothing of the ruse played upon the tax-payers' leagues and he became conservatively friendly to suffrage. In 1918, he permitted his name to be added to the suffrage advisory committee already adorned by Republican and Democratic names high in party councils. The women declared that he never failed to be frank and honorable with them in every suffrage move thereafter.

In his annual message to the Legislature in January, 1919, he recommended the ratification of the Federal Suffrage Amendment, and when on June 5, 1919, that amendment was finally submitted to the States, he was among the first to respond to the National American Woman Suffrage Association's telegram urging all governors to call special sessions for ratification. The Legislature met in answer to his call on July 2, 1919, at 10 a.m., and by 11:40 a.m. the resolution of ratification had passed both Houses.

The friendly, generous, liberty-prizing spirit of 1870, loosed from the political thralldom which had warped and crippled and held it fast for fifty years, had triumphed. Iowa was herself again.

CHAPTER 16

Woman Suffrage by Federal Amendment

So far the story of suffrage, victory and defeat, has been the story of State referenda. We have been covering the time when for years that state-by-state effort spun the main thread of suffrage activity. "Win more States to full woman suffrage," had been the fell word that the suffragists of earlier days had encountered from friend and foe alike. "Go, get another State," Theodore Roosevelt counseled as late as 1908.

I don't know the exact number of States we shall have to have, said Miss Anthony once in a musing hour, but I do know that there will come a day when that number will automatically and resistlessly act on the Congress of the United States to compel the submission of a federal suffrage amendment. And we shall recognize that day when it comes.

As has been seen, that dream of woman suffrage by federal amendment antedated all the efforts to win woman suffrage by the State route. And it is not to be forgotten that from the earliest days the will and the work to make the dream come true went along concurrently with the work for and in State referenda.

Before the Civil War it seems to have occurred to no one that suffrage for women might be gained through federal action. Public opinion in all parts of the country was strongly resentful of any unusual assumption of authority by the federal government and no precedent existed upon which to base a theory for such action. The Civil War welded the loosely federated States into an "indissoluble Union," the word "nation" for the first time found its way into the list of words frequently used as descriptive of the United States of America, and the Acts of Reconstruction represented a degree of centralized authority which before the war would not have been tolerated. Although apologists for the departure from previous custom explained the Acts of Reconstruction as military necessities and although the conflict concerning the distribution of power between federal and State authorities continues today, the fact remains that hostility to federal legislative supremacy was greatly modified after that period.

After suffragists had made their energetic and heroic struggle to prevent the enfranchisement of the Negro without the inclusion of women in the plan, and when, despite their protests, Negro suffrage was achieved with woman suffrage left out, the Fourteenth and Fifteenth Amendments at least furnished precedents for a federal woman suffrage amendment, and this at once became the ultimate aim of the women's campaign. Observing the frequency with which laws, both State and Federal, were set aside by court decisions, and observing, too, that the Fifteenth Amendment had been declared constitutional, the women of that day took pains to frame a woman's amendment in the same precise phraseology. A group, led by Miss Anthony and Mrs. Stanton, wrote the amendment, designated by the suffragists for many years as the Sixteenth, and it was introduced in the Senate by A. A. Sargent of California on January 10, 1878. Owing to the death of the friendly chairman of the Committee on Privileges and Elections, Senator Oliver P. Morton of Indiana, an adverse report was made, but a minority report, accompanied by a lengthy address, was presented by Senator George F. Hoar of Massachusetts in which he said:

> "No single argument of its advocates seems to us to carry so great a persuasive force as the difficulty which its ablest opponents encounter in making a plausible statement of their objections. We trust we do not fail in deference to our esteemed associates on the committee when we avow our opinion that their report is no exception to this rule."

At that same date President Hayes received a deputation of suffragists, and a petition to the Congress was presented, with speeches on behalf of the amendment.

With so promising a beginning, suffrage hopes centered again on federal action. But between that date and June 4, 1919, when the amendment was finally passed by the Congress, lie forty years and six months, During that period the amendment was continuously pending, having been introduced in the same form in every succeeding Congress. In the Senate it was reported with a favorable majority in 1884, 1886, 1889 and 1893, and without recommendation in 1890 and 1896, and with a favorable majority again in 1913, 1914 and 1916. The House Committee gave favorable reports in 1883 and 1890, and adverse reports in 1884, 1886 and 1894, reported without recommendation in 1914, 1916 and 1917, and favorably in 1918, the Senate Committees making six reports only and the House Committees five in the thirty-five years between 1878 and 1913.

While other influences contributed to this record of inaction, the most outstanding cause was that Southern Democrats, although a minority, held the whip and controlled the suffrage situation. In 1878, when the woman suffrage amendment was introduced, the nation consisted of thirty-eight States and was accordingly represented by seventy-six United States Senators. The constitutional requirement of a two-thirds vote in the Congress for the submission of an amendment and action by three-fourths of the Legislatures for ratification made the support of fifty-one of these Senators and twenty-eight Legislatures necessary to its adoption. To secure this result the vote of five Senators and the ratification of five Legislatures of secession, or border, States had to be obtained, in addition to the united support of all Northern and Western States.

During the earlier portion of this time, Senators from the seceding States would rather have committed hari-kari than vote for any federal suffrage amendment, and the border States were little less pronounced in their vindictive denunciation of suffrage by the federal method. Three prospects only for success appeared: (1) An increase in the number of States, so that the total could outvote the South; (2) A change of attitude on the part of Southern Senators; and (3) A more insistent demand for action by Congress than the nation was then in a mood to give. None offered immediate hope, but in the end all three aids were secured.

The suffragists of 1878 could not believe that the nation would long allow its record of enfranchisement of illiterate men, fresh from slavery, and its denial of the same privilege to intelligent white women to stand unchallenged. They turned to the States, firm in the faith that they would soon furnish a mandate to which popular opinion would yield, and through which the congressional impasse would be broken.

Had Republicans recognized the indefensible discrimination against women created by reconstruction history and given party aid to State amendments, which obvious consistency demanded (without whip or bayonet), woman suffrage would have swept from West to East long before corporate interests had gained sway over party councils. The East and South would have yielded then to the momentum of the triumphant movement, as they did forty years later, and there would probably have been no need of a federal woman suffrage amendment. However, the Republicans, in full control of most Northern and Western States, blocked action in these States as effectually as the Southern Democrats did in the Congress and in Southern States.

So it came about that the dismayed suffragists had to gird on their armor in grim preparation for war with the nation's prejudice, should it take till the end of time. They determined to hold fast the demand established in Congress, to bring to its support such gains among the States as they could wrest from the well-nigh impossible conditions imposed, and then, when politics should indicate the hour, to concentrate their efforts again on a federal amendment with the aim of finishing the task by that method. Formulated at that early day, this remained the policy of the National American Woman Suffrage Association to the end.

When it became plain that no action could be secured in Congress from the committees to which national suffrage amendments were referred, the suffragists attempted to induce Senate and House to establish standing woman suffrage committees with more time and sympathy to give their cause. As a result of much labor for three years, a so-called select committee was obtained in both Houses, the Senate renewing this committee in 1883 and the House declining to do so. The Senate Committee in time became a standing committee and so remained until the end. In the House the amendment was usually referred to the Judiciary Committee. A further attempt to renew the suffrage committee in the House was made in 1884, at which time Miss Anthony said: "This is the sixteenth year that we have come before Congress in person, and the nineteenth by petition."

The early Senate Committee did not prove to be an asset to the women's campaign. In the long list of committees, it was held to be of low rank and during the thirty-five years of Republican control the chairmanship was assigned to a Southern Democrat. Senators from the States of Missouri, North Carolina, Florida, Arkansas, Virginia, and Georgia, to whose people the idea of suffrage by federal act was infuriating, held the post during this period. Said one of these chairmen to a fellow Senator: "There is no man living who can answer the argument of those women, but I'd rather see my wife dead in her coffin than voting, and I'd die myself before I'd vote to submit that amendment."

Upon another occasion, Miss Anthony, bearing her threescore years and ten, closed the hearing with a review of the forty years of effort to secure justice for women and made so pathetic an appeal for action that the great room full of women, with faces drawn and tears running down many cheeks, involuntarily turned their eyes upon the chairman from Virginia. He was clearly perturbed and under the control of emotion. What would he say? What would he do? How could he refuse so unanswerable, so appealing a request? Presently they discovered the source of his emotion—he was in need of the spittoon! And no indication of more sympathetic interest did any of these Southern Democratic chairmen ever show.

During a portion of Grover Cleveland's administration, the Senate became Democratic. Then, the tables being turned, a Republican was given the chairmanship, and that fearless friend of woman suffrage, George F. Hoar of Massachusetts, being appointed, no time was lost in presenting a favorable report.

Based on this favorable report of the Committee in 1886, a vote on the amendment was secured in the Senate in 1887. The vote stood ayes 16, nays 34, absent 26. The debate is a distinct landmark, as Southern Senators laid out with care the argument upon which the Northern opposition was based through the coming years. Already the reaction had set in against the "wholesale and indiscriminate extension of the electorate" and the plea of all opponents for the next generation was "there are too many incompetent voters now, why double them? Let the extension of suffrage stop now."

Said Senator Beck of Kentucky:

"We have been compelled in the last ten years to allow all the colored men of the South to become voters. There is a mass of ignorance there to be absorbed that will take years and years of care in order to bring that class up to the standard of intelligent voters. The several States are addressing themselves to that task as earnestly as possible. Now it is proposed that all the women of the country shall vote; that all the colored women of the South, who are as much more ignorant than the colored men as it is possible to imagine, shall vote. Not one perhaps in a hundred of them can read or write. The colored men have had the advantages of communication with other men in a variety of forms. Many of them have considerable intelligence; but the colored women have not had equal chances. Take them from their washtubs and their household work and they are absolutely ignorant of the new duties of voting citizens. . . . Why, sir, a rich corporation or a body of men of wealth could buy them up for fifty cents apiece, and they would vote, without knowing what they were doing, for the side that paid most."

Said Senator Morgan of Alabama:

"We have now masses of voters so enormous in numbers as that it seems to be almost beyond the power of the law to execute the purposes of the elective franchise with justice, with propriety, and without crime. How much would these difficulties and these intrinsic troubles be increased if we should raise the number of voters from ten million to twenty million in the United States? That would be the direct and immediate effect of conferring the franchise upon the women. ... The effect would be to drive the ladies of the land, as they are termed, the well-bred and well-educated women, the women of nice sensibilities, within their home circles, there to remain, while the ruder of that sex would thrust themselves out on the hustings and at the ballot-box, and fight their way to the polls through Negroes and others who are not the best of company even at the polls, to say nothing of the disgrace of association with them. You would paralyze one-third at least of the women of this land by the very vulgarity of the overture made to them that they should go struggling to the polls in order to vote in common with the herd of men."

No other vote was obtained in the Senate until 1914 and none at all during this period in the House. The years passed with hearings before the Committees of both Houses of every Congress and the circulation of the printed procedure of these hearings, interviews with members, occasional petitions, deputations to the presidents and, every year, a resolution from the national suffrage convention calling upon Congress to submit the suffrage amendment.

Until 1895 all the annual suffrage conventions were held in Washington, in order that suffrage delegates might plead with their representatives in Congress to submit the amendment, but after 1895 the conventions were held alternate years in other cities, meeting in Washington during the first session, of each Congress only. There followed the period between 1896 and 1910 when the business of securing from the country a mandate on woman suffrage made such slow headway. The Congress was accepting the inaction of the country as a cue for inaction in Senate and House, and the inaction in Congress, composed as that body was of the leaders of political parties, was taken as the cue for inaction in the States.

In order to focus the attention of Congress once more upon woman suffrage and that of the country upon congressional obligation to the women of the land, it was voted at the annual suffrage convention held in Buffalo in October, 1908, to roll up another petition calling for the submission of the federal suffrage amendment. This method of agitation had been abandoned many years before, not only because petitions seemed to produce no direct result, but as it was no longer the custom to present such petitions publicly and with speeches, they were robbed of their publicity effect upon the country. It was now proposed to resume the plan, chiefly for its agitational value.

With the view of learning in advance how much effect such a petition would have, the National Suffrage Association asked President Roosevelt to receive a deputation, which he did. The deputation asked whether a petition of a million signatures would influence him to recommend woman suffrage in his annual message to the Congress, as the Association wished to know before going to the labor and expense of such a petition. He replied with a courteous but extremely emphatic assertion that it would neither move him nor the Congress. Asked for advice as to the next step, he promptly gave his memorable dictum, "Go, get another State." When reminded that Republican Legislatures would rarely submit amendments and that when they did his party would not support them at the polls, he failed to sense party responsibility. Reminded that his gubernatorial appointee had robbed the women of Arizona of the vote by veto in 1903, he expressed surprise, although vigorous appeals had been made him for intervention at the time, and he had at the time declared himself powerless to rectify the wrong.

Despite the discouraging interview, the petition work was undertaken, but State suffrage leaders, upon whose interest success depended, had neither faith in the result, nor energy to give in addition to that required to meet the continual State legislature campaigns. An honorary committee of highly influential men and women allowed their names to be joined in the appeal and a nationwide educational campaign on behalf of the federal suffrage amendment was the result. Federal suffrage meetings were held, sermons preached and hundreds of editorials called for the submission of the amendment.

The petition, with 404,000 signatures, instead of the one million intended, was brought to Washington in April, 1910, where the annual suffrage convention was in session. Although there was regret that suffragists had been too much occupied to bring a larger number of names, they recalled that President Lincoln had considered three hundred thousand a sufficient mandate for the Emancipation Proclamation as a war measure. In gaily decorated automobiles, each carrying the petitions of a State and bearing its name on spectacular banners, the procession moved from convention to Congress, where it was met by an honorary committee, and in the State marble room and the House Judiciary room the petitions were handed by each State president to her Senators and Representatives. The custom of no speeches was broken, and an eloquent address to the Senate upon the occasion was made by Senator LaFollette of Wisconsin.

At that convention, for the first time in suffrage history, a President of the United States, William Howard Taft, addressed the national gathering of suffragists, and, among other things, this is what he said:

> "The theory that Hottentots or any other uneducated, altogether unintelligent class is fitted for self-government is a theory I wholly dissent from, but this qualification is not applicable here. The other qualification to which I call your attention is that the class should as a whole care enough to look after its interests to take part as a whole in the exercise of political power if it is conferred."

A hiss was heard. Miss Shaw, who was presiding, arose with a quick "O my children!" Hushed quiet followed, but newspaper headlines carried the news, "Suffragists hiss the President," to the remotest corner of the land. It was denied that the hiss had come from a delegate, and the next day the convention by resolution apologized for the unfortunate lapse in good manners.

Nevertheless delegates agreed among themselves that the word "Hottentot" in connection with their appeal had struck like a whip across their faces, and with this interpretation the press also received the news, some newspapers criticizing the President for his untactful use of words, and the suffragists, for the hissed protest, with equally caustic comment. The entire country found the incident worthy of discussion; editorials, resolutions, sermons, sometimes on one side and sometimes on the other, followed each other, and the wave of publicity started all over again several times. "Hottentot" did not help Mr. Taft but it did contribute indirectly to a curious revival of national interest in woman suffrage.

After the 1910 suffrage convention, once again a Congressional Committee of the National Suffrage Association opened Headquarters in Washington and began the first systematic and complete poll of Congress, including all old and new candidates for election in 1910 and 1912.

The impulse given to the movement that year by the gain of Washington with the astounding majority of twenty-four thousand, followed by the gain of California in 1911, emphasized the question in the public mind to a degree regarded as phenomenal, and had a notable reaction upon the Congress.

The Presidential campaign of 1912 was approaching. The National Suffrage Association had appealed to every dominant presidential convention for a suffrage plank since the first attempt in 1868. After 1900, campaigns had been more thorough, all delegates having been individually memorialized, and more urgent efforts had been made to secure the sympathetic co-operation of leading politicians. Hearings had been usually granted before resolution committees with more or less courtesy, but platforms had remained silent. Democratic presidential platforms carried no expression concerning woman suffrage from 1868 to 1916, and the Republican platforms had had no word since the "splinter" of 1872.

In 1912 there were three candidates for the presidency from the Republican ranks. They were Mr. Taft, Mr. Roosevelt, and Mr. LaFollette. All three were approached by the suffragists for the expression of an opinion on woman suffrage. Mr. Taft answered:

"I don't think we ought to take as radical a step as that without being certain that when we do it it will meet the approval of all those or substantially all of those in whose interest the franchise is extended because if it does not meet their views and they don't avail themselves of the opportunity to exercise the influence which that would give them, then we should be in a bad way because we might lose a substantial proportion of the votes of those that would be for better things. Therefore I am willing to wait until there shall be a substantial, not unanimous but a substantial, call from that sex before the suffrage is extended."

Mr. LaFollette carried a suffrage plank in the platform upon which he proposed to stand. Mr. Roosevelt qualified his statement with so many reservations as to make it as useful for one side as the other.

Amid great excitement and angry dispute over the seating of delegates, the Republican nomination was given to Mr. Taft by a vote of 561, Mr. Roosevelt receiving 107. The Roosevelt delegates, charging fraud in the seating of delegates, met immediately after the adjournment of the convention and nominated Mr. Roosevelt for the presidency—thus bringing into organized form the movement that had been growing in and out of Congress for three years—and called themselves the Progressive Party. A convention to adopt a platform was called for August.

Meantime the Democrats met in Baltimore June 25 to July 3 and nominated Woodrow Wilson. He had replied to the National Suffrage Association's inquiry as follows:

"Allow me to acknowledge with real appreciation your letter in which you put me a very difficult question. I can only say that my own mind is in the midst of the debate which it involves. I do not feel that I am ready to utter my confident judgment as yet about it. I am honestly trying to work my way toward a just conclusion."

Mr. Roosevelt is alleged to have written his own platform for the Progressive convention in August. A group of supporters, paying him a visit, heard it and made loud protest against the suffrage plank it contained. That plank endorsed the principle of woman suffrage but pledged the new party to a practical support only when the question had been submitted to a referendum of the *women* of the United States. His friends persuaded him of the insult of putting upon women a test never made of men, and a straightforward declaration was substituted:

"The Progressive Party, believing that no people can justly claim to be a true democracy which denies political rights on account of sex, pledges itself to the task of securing equal suffrage to men and women alike."

Many women attended the convention as delegates, Several of the Southern States being so represented. Jane Addams seconded Mr. Roosevelt's nomination. State Progressive conventions followed in rapid succession, each endorsing the national platform. Women served on many State Central Committees and very many were listed by the Speakers' Bureau. The great advantage of having the endorsement of a party in the field was quickly manifest. Mr. Roosevelt himself was no longer doubtful, and other men long silent, encouraged by the work women were doing for the Progressive cause, boldly advocated woman suffrage.

The elections of 1912 resulted in "a sweeping Democratic victory by pluralities in so many States as to give that party's candidate the largest vote and largest majority in the Electoral College ever given a party candidate."[95] Mr. Taft carried two States only, Mr. Roosevelt five. Congress was made Democratic and the Republicans lost the Legislatures of nine States. While the Democratic party offered little encouragement to suffrage, the Republican machine was broken or out of repair in most of the States where campaigns were pending and the strong attitude of the new minority party presented a warning to both old parties to treat the suffrage question with fairness.

To emphasize this attitude three more suffrage States were won in the 1912 election, and a controversy, almost as effective, was aroused as to whether three more might not have been added to the suffrage list by an honest count.

Inevitably the new Congress showed far keener interest in the suffrage question. Six representatives insisted upon the privilege of introducing the usual resolution. The Democrats, in concession to changed conditions, gave the chairmanship of the Senate Suffrage Committee to one of their own party, Senator Charles S. Thomas of Colorado. The Committee was favorable. In the Senate body there were now eighteen Senators elected by constituencies wherein both men and women voted.

It was about this time that the suffrage struggle in America began to be complicated by the influence of earlier developments in the suffrage struggle in England. Since 1906 a militant campaign had been raging in Great Britain with demonstrations manufactured by the women to bait the police, the consequent arrests of women duly enlisted to go to prison, followed by imprisonment with hard labor, hunger strikes, forcible feeding and temporary releases for hospital treatment. This shocking story daily repeated had carried an important message to Americans. Many learned for the first time that women in Great Britain had long been voters and only lacked the parliamentary vote to make their suffrage privileges equal to those of men. They learned that no parliamentary suffrage measure could pass unless it became part of the government program and that Premier Asquith, supported by his Cabinet, refused to grant it that assistance.

Women familiar with the home struggle in America perceived that the crux of the British and American suffrage problem was the same, a minority, holding control of a party, was checkmating the majority in that party who were willing to move forward. American men, seeing the injustice of British men, began to apply reason to the home attitude upon the same question. Condemning the women who were deliberately creating the turmoil, and the politicians who met every seemingly ridiculous move of the women with one equally ridiculous, they nevertheless began to think.

Although the militant movement had divided opinion in that country as in all others,[96] it taught many suffragists the world around that spectacular events carried suffrage messages to the masses of the people as suffrage appeals to reason never could, and immediately such features, shorn of militant character, were introduced into State campaigns in America. Many American suffragists including Dr. Anna Howard Shaw, then president of the National American Woman Suffrage Association, had marched in London suffrage parades and were familiar with the helpful as well as the harmful effects of militant tactics. When, therefore, after the annual suffrage convention of November, 1912, Miss Alice Paul, an American who had done prison duty in the English campaign, approached the National Suffrage Association, of which Dr. Shaw was the president, with the suggestion that she be permitted to organize a suffrage parade at the Presidential inaugural in March, 1913, and offered to raise the necessary funds, the Board gladly accepted the offer, gave her the prestige of the chairmanship of its Congressional Committee and provided her with stationery of the Association and the list of its usual contributors.

The Washington suffrage parade was organized with the assistance and co-operation of the entire National Suffrage Association. The preparations were well and elaborately made and between eight and ten thousand women marched. Public interest can be measured by a press story that was carried to the far corners of the nation. "Where," asked one of the incoming President's staff upon the arrival of the presidential party in Washington, "where are all the people?"—"Watching the suffrage parade," the police told him.

As it fell out, the treatment given the parade proved of far more importance to woman suffrage than the parade itself. In the city governed directly by Congress the marching women were shockingly used. "Women were spat upon, slapped in the face, tripped up, pelted with burning cigar stubs and insulted by jeers and obscene language too vile to print or repeat."—"Rowdies seized and mauled young girls."—"A very gray-haired college woman was knocked down."—"The parade was continually stopped by the turbulence of the crowd."[97]

Assistance was called from Ft. Meyer and soldiers brought to the rescue. The parade, however, was largely spoiled. The thousands of men and women who gathered on the sidewalks to see the much advertised spectacle were robbed of a view of the novel floats and colorful costuming, but the failure of the police to maintain order, and not the procession itself, gave the chief contribution to suffrage progress.

Many Senators and Representatives with wives and friends, marched in the procession and saw the treatment accorded the marchers. The Senate promptly voted an investigation and the findings filled a volume. The press united in the declaration that Washington was disgraced, and as an outcome the Chief of Police was dismissed. The dissemination of the news of these events day after day brought discussion on the subject of woman suffrage to every hamlet in the land, but more important than all else it brought debate, live, earnest debate, to the cloakrooms of Senate and House, where it flourished until the end.

In December, 1913, the annual suffrage convention met in Washington and the delegates heard the report of its Congressional Committee with mingled feelings of satisfaction at the lively campaign that had been steadily conducted and surprise over certain facts recorded. Much has been erroneously said and written concerning the breaking away of a smaller body of suffragists from the larger parent body which marked this period. Throughout the last years of the suffrage campaign it was a daily feature of anti-suffrage tactics to scout the National Suffrage Association's oft-repeated assertions that all connection with the new organization had been severed and to try to direct toward the parent body the antagonism aroused by the militant tactics of its offspring. Politicians, too, found it convenient to insist that all suffragists and all suffrage tactics were, subrosa, of the same parent organization, and thereupon used the expedients of the militants as a smoke screen of excuse for opposition to the very principle of suffrage. The facts with regard to the dissociation of the small body of militants from the large body of non-militants in the American suffrage struggle were as follows:

While officially connected with the National Suffrage Association, in charge of its congressional work, and writing on its stationery, the Association's congressional chairman had created a new organization on the plan of the English militant society. The new group called itself the Congressional Union and had launched a paper as its organ. Yet the program of work and disbursements of the Committee of the National had been so interwoven with the work and disbursements of the new organization that the joint chairman of both declared that it was impossible to separate them. After due consideration the Board of the National Suffrage Association decided that it was inadvisable to reappoint Miss Paul chairman of the Congressional Committee Unless she resigned as chairman of the Congressional Union. The constant confusion of the Congressional Committee of the National American Woman Suffrage Association with the Congressional Union, an organized society, was making such action inevitable. But Miss Paul refused to accept these terms.

It had long been predicted that a militant movement similar to that of Great Britain would be reproduced in the United States. Many suffragists hoped to avert this division by adopting the new methods which had helped and discarding those which had clearly harmed the movement. Many delegates to that suffrage convention in 1913 saw in the attitude of the chairman of the Congressional Committee a dark conspiracy to capture the entire "National" for the militant enterprise. Others recognized the inefficiency of disintegrated forces in the closing days of the long struggle and made earnest efforts to prevent a division by persuading the young militants to work under the old banner, but to no avail.

The Congressional Committee of the National American Woman Suffrage Association was a standing committee and thereafter the work went on with renewed energy under a new chairman. The Congressional Union also continued to work with

Congress as an independent body, thus making two committees in Washington working for the same thing but with no plan of co-operation from that time forth.

The Congressional Committee opened a new headquarters in Washington and took a complete poll of Senate and House. The handicaps inevitable when two separate committees are trying to accomplish the same end were soon manifest. To illustrate: The revival of the movement to establish a suffrage standing committee in the House had been begun in 1913 with the approval of the executive board of the National Suffrage Association. Now came the Congressional Union with a petition to the Democrats to caucus on the subject. Vainly the Congressional Committee sought to persuade the Union from thus aligning the Democrats against the project. Aligning the Democrats against the project was exactly what the Union wished to accomplish in order that the Democrats should be put on record as a party in opposition. The Union, following its English model, was preparing to "hold the party in power responsible." In vain did the Committee expostulate that no party can be "the government" in this country as it is in Great Britain, since one party may conduct the national administration and the other control the Congress; one may control the entire national business, executive and legislative, and the other many State Legislatures.

The Democrats were easily enough persuaded to caucus and "not only voted against a standing committee on woman suffrage but Mr. Heflin of Alabama amended the resolution before the caucus so that the members of the caucus were enabled to vote definitely that the woman suffrage question was one to be determined by the States and not by the national government."[98]

The three main differences of policy between the National Suffrage Association and its young offshoot, the Congressional Union, soon developed. The Congressional Union (1) opposed congressional candidates because they belonged to the "party in power" regardless of their personal stand; (2) it opposed an entire "party in power" because some of its individual members of Congress were hostile to woman suffrage; (3) it used so-called militant methods which the National did not endorse.

In accord with this policy it now announced its intention of campaigning against all Democratic candidates in the States where women were enfranchised. Meanwhile, the Congressional Committee, in full realization that the Senate would not give a majority, forced a vote on suffrage on March 19, 1914, resulting in a record of yeas 35, nays 34. Western Democrats were thus given the opportunity to make a public record of their individual attitudes.

The year witnessed the proclamation of the Sixteenth Amendment, the first in forty-three years, authorizing the income tax, and the suffrage amendment lost the place its leaders had so anxiously hoped their amendment would fill. The suffrage amendment was thereafter for a time called the Seventeenth but when the Seventeenth Amendment, dealing with the election of Senators, was adopted, it became plain that the progress of suffrage in the Congress was too slow to hold a numerical place on the amendment schedule, so the suffrage amendment was thereafter called the Federal Suffrage Amendment by the National Suffrage Association.

Shortly after the Senate vote a bomb was thrown into the national suffrage camp by its own Congressional Committee. The poll of the Senate indicated that not only foes but many friends of suffrage were insisting that the question was one that the States should settle, and the Chairman of the Congressional Committee, assisted by her co-workers, conceived a plan to meet this objection. State workers were complaining that they could not secure referenda from Legislatures, and could not win them when submitted, if a majority of votes cast at the election were required. So a new amendment was drawn up, proposing that when an initiative petition, signed by eight per cent of the electors voting at the preceding general election, should request the submission of the question of woman suffrage, such question should be submitted, and a majority on the question should be sufficient for its adoption.

The object was to increase the number of suffrage States and the measure was intended by its authors as a support to the pending Federal Suffrage Amendment. The national suffrage board reluctantly permitted its introduction, although when Dr. Shaw retired from the presidency, she announced that she had never approved it. The amendment was introduced in the Senate by Senator Shafroth of Colorado and in the House by Representative Palmer of Pennsylvania, and was promptly voted out of the committees to which it had been reported. It bore influentially on the annual suffrage convention in November, 1914, where it was voted that every means within the National Suffrage Association's power, in the future as in the past, should be used to further the Federal Suffrage Amendment and "such other legislation as the National Board may authorize and initiate" in support of that amendment. At the mid-year conference of the National American Woman Suffrage Association in June, 1915, a motion to drop work on the so-called Shafroth Amendment was defeated, 21 ayes, 57 nays.

Misunderstanding and confusion in the ranks, occasioned by the charge of the Congressional Union that the National Suffrage Association had substituted a referendum amendment for that which it had been supporting for a generation; the clamor within and without the National Suffrage Association for repudiation of the anti-Democratic policy of the Union; continual complaint from campaign States that Union sympathizers were pulling off workers because "there was an easier way" brought a complexity of troublesome problems which tremendously increased the strain of suffrage leaders and workers.

The Shafroth Amendment was withdrawn just in time to prevent a definite split in the National Suffrage Association. Many suffragists believed that while it had precipitated an agony of differences, on the whole the proposal had been good interim strategy, for the arguments for and against had served to bring the question of suffrage by federal amendment still more prominently to the front. Moreover, State suffrage auxiliaries had been solidified in their allegiance to the National Suffrage Association's policy by the agitation.

The campaigns against Democrats, waged by the Union in the West, aroused the antagonism of voters in the Eastern State campaigns, and many Democrats excused themselves for voting "no" at the polls because women voters in the West were being urged to oppose Democratic candidates. Workers in all referenda campaigns were convinced that this influence swelled the opposition to a considerable degree. On the other hand, the campaign of the Union did not suffice to put the party in power out. Instead of the eighteen Democrats from the suffrage States in the 1913-1914 Congress there were nineteen in the 1915-1916 Congress.

That Congress was reopened in an irritated state of mind. All Republicans and Democrats in Senate or House were outspoken in their condemnation of the "party responsible" plan, and the National Suffrage Association's Congressional Committee was obliged to soothe before attempting to persuade.

But the campaign in Washington went vigorously forward, hearings, interviews and home pressure forming the main aims. The Chairman of the Judiciary was determined that the Amendment should not come to vote in the House; the Democrats caucused and determined to prevent a vote. Nevertheless, the question was at length brought to vote by Representative Mondell of Wyoming, on January 12, 1915, after a ten hours' debate, and resulted in 174 ayes, 204 noes. Eighty-six Democrats and eighty-eight Republicans and Progressives voted yes; 171 Democrats and thirty-three Republicans voted no.

Meanwhile the State campaigns were awhirl with activities undreamt of in earlier days. November recorded the defeat of the suffrage referenda in four Eastern States, New York, Pennsylvania, Massachusetts and New Jersey, but the fact that 1,234,000 Eastern men had voted yes was not overlooked by the Congress.

Then, too, by that hour the great and terrible agency which brought about the downfall of much of the old social and political order and made way for much that was new was having a tremendous effect on woman suffrage by revolutionizing the whole sphere of women. That agency was the world war. From overseas the news kept coming that women, as always in war time, were taking the places of men on farms and in factories, but more than that now, they were doing the work in munition plants, running the railways, keeping the post offices, and managing hospitals. The National American Woman Suffrage Association allowed no Congressman or legislator to remain in ignorance of these facts, should he overlook them in the press. He was reminded of them in conversation, at dinners, and on tennis courts; they were handed to him in typewriting, sent him through the mails and told him by his fellow members in the cloak-rooms. They were to prove a salient part of the education of the American Congress on the subject of the American woman's sphere.

CHAPTER 17

The Crises of 1916

As a presidential election was on its way for the autumn of 1916, early in the year the National Suffrage Association, of which Mrs. Carrie Chapman Catt had become president in 1915, began work to get endorsement of the Federal Suffrage Amendment as a plank in the platform of the two dominant parties. The sentiment of the country was such that a declaration favoring the principle of woman suffrage was not only possible but probable in both platforms, yet careful investigation showed suffragists that neither party intended to endorse the Amendment, the South being politically-minded to block an attempt in the Democratic convention, and the East being like-minded in the Republican convention. The danger was that both conventions would definitely refer the question to the States, thus dismissing responsibility for the nation and the national parties, and continuing upon suffragists the burden and delay of securing action by the State route only.

Under the leadership of the National Suffrage Association's Congressional Committee an appropriate plank for each platform was written, endorsing woman suffrage without reference to the method of securing it. These planks were approved by those Republican and Democratic members of Congress who would be the leaders of their respective conventions. All delegates to the two conventions who were elected in sufficient time for such action were memorialized by letter three times, and the presidential candidates were interviewed, but the major emphasis of the campaign was placed on the work of State suffragists with their own people. As one woman said, "It is harder to dodge home folks." So in each and every State deputations bearing the proposed suffrage plank waited upon the leaders of political policy and visited delegates. Hundreds of pledges of support were thus secured and every delegate knew the question would come before him, and the form of the plank he would be asked to support. The help of the press was urged and hundreds of newspapers joined the suffragists in their demand. Resolutions of State associations of various kinds were secured and presented to the State delegates. Women delegates were numerous in the conventions, and their special activity was sought. To spectacularize the appeal, a suffrage procession, with floats, banners and costuming, was planned for Chicago where the Republicans and Progressives met on June 14, and a golden lane, or "walkless parade," for St. Louis where the Democrats met two weeks later. A public suffrage conference was held in connection with both. In Chicago a memorial to the Republican convention was adopted, to remind the delegates that the women of twelve States were voters, and that the women of six of those had their party affiliations yet to make.

On June 7, for which date the parade of twenty-five thousand women was scheduled, rain descended in torrents and the heavy clouds lifted for no moment during the entire day. Thousands of women pledged to march did not venture forth, but 5,500 did. Those who could secure rubber coats and shoes, did so; those who could not braved the storm without them. The Chicago *Herald* thus described that Rainy Day parade:

"Over their heads surged a vast sea of umbrellas extending two miles down the street. Under their feet swirled rivulets of water. Wind tore at their clothes and rain drenched their faces. Unhesitatingly they marched in unbroken formation, keeping perfect step. Never before in the history of Chicago, probably of the world, has there been so impressive a demonstration of idealism, of consecration to a cause."

Along the route the hotel windows were filled with Republican delegates, dry and comfortable. The procession, neither colorful nor picturesque, with music making discord in the noisy downpour of rain, moved on, carrying its message as no fair weather parade could have done. One delegate to the Republican convention came to the suffrage headquarters to say: "I watched it from a window where men stood eight and ten deep and many had tears in their eyes. They said, these women really mean it and we might as well make up our minds to it." Young and old, "these women" really meant it. As a young girl passed in the procession, a man on the curbstone called, "You ought to be home with your mother." And she called back, "Mother is here, marching with me."

The parade's objective was the Republicans' convention hall and as the women reached it there occurred a coincidence priceless in suffrage annals. Inside the hall a session of the Resolutions Committee of the Republicans was the only convention activity in progress. Its members, seated on the great central platform, were giving a hearing to a group of anti-suffragist women, one of whom was just reaching an effective climax of appeal with, "Women do not want the vote." As if timed to the instant, through the doors of the hall came the drenched and bedraggled marchers for suffrage. They pushed up to the platform, they massed down below it, they scattered out over the hall, and still they came pouring through the doors. To the everlasting honor of a politician's sense of humor let it be recorded that, as the shock of surprise yielded, several of those on the platform smiled in understanding amusement, as if the incongruity of that outworn charge had at last been comprehended.

Meanwhile, the National Suffrage Association's political committee, aided by strong friends on the Republican convention, with no food or rest, kept watch over the Resolutions Committee and lost no opportunity to stress the suffrage claim. At midnight, the night before the parade, a sub-committee had voted down the suffrage plank and refused consent for any mention of suffrage in the platform by a vote of 5 to 4, Senators Lodge of Massachusetts and Wadsworth of New York leading the opposition. But neither the women nor their men allies gave up. Senators Borah of Idaho and Smoot of Utah led the suffrage forces. In an effort to turn the tide, the Republican women delegates gathered together and a staunch appeal signed by them all and urging a suffrage plank was presented to the Resolutions Committee. After hours of work and debate, by a vote of 26 to 21 the committee repudiated its sub-committee's recommendation to shelve suffrage. Within an hour defeat again threatened, for seven absentees demanded a reconsideration. Marion Butler of North Carolina led the opposition and was supported by Murray Crane and Henry Cabot Lodge of Massachusetts, Boies Penrose of Pennsylvania, and James Wadsworth of New York. These men held a special conference in the next room to consider how to prevent any mention of woman suffrage in the platform. Out of the acrimonious discussion, in which North Carolina joined hands with Massachusetts in a determined struggle against a solid West where women were already enfranchised, a compromise emerged. Even this was not achieved until fifteen minutes before the Resolutions Committee was called to report to the convention. The compromise was the price demanded by Senator Lodge of Massachusetts for consent to any kind of suffrage plank. The final vote was 35 to 11 and the plank read:

"The Republican party reaffirming its faith in 'government of the people, by the people and for the people,' as a measure of justice to one-half the adult people of this country favor the extension of the suffrage to women, *but recognize the right of each State to settle this question for itself.*"

The resolution was the one written and presented by the National Suffrage Association with the State's rights rider added.

The Progressive Party meeting at the same time, with women delegates present from nearly all States, adopted a stronger plank than that of 1912. It read:

"And we believe that the women of the country, who share with the men the burden of government in times of peace and make equal sacrifice in times of war, should be given the full political rights of suffrage both by State and federal action."

The National suffragists were disappointed at the results obtained, for the Republicans had given the cue to the Democrats, well knowing that Democrats would not allow Republicans to outdo them in loyalty to their revered State's rights ideals.

On June 16 six thousand women, each under a yellow parasol and encircled by a yellow sash, lined both sides of the street from the Jefferson Hotel to the Colosseum in St. Louis, where the Democratic convention was held. This time smiling sunny skies looked down upon them. Half way up, on the steps of the Art Museum, an impressive spectacle was posed. The figure of Liberty in appealing posture stood guard over three groups of figures, each woman representing a State. The enfranchised States were garbed in red, white and blue, the partial suffrage States in gray and those where no suffrage existed in black. All day long delegates trudged back and forth through the "golden lane," reading its banners and reminded of its appeal.

Several women were delegates to the Democratic convention and an attempt was made to secure a unanimous petition from them to the Resolutions Committee as had been done in Chicago, but two refused to join in the plea, not because they did not want the plank, but because the Congressional Union's campaign against the Democratic party had made them over-suspicious of all suffragists who were working for suffrage by federal amendment. The usual hearings took place before a sleepy committee which had been sitting all night. The committee would not take the plank written by the National Suffrage Association and accepted by President Wilson. Another one was written in the committee as a substitute and his consent to it was obtained over the long distance telephone. The debate on the suffrage plank was not reached by the committee until three o'clock in the morning but the subject thoroughly aroused drowsy committeemen and their voices, in tart and heated controversy, were heard not only in the corridors of the hotel but by passers-by on the street. Three suffrage planks were brought up for consideration. The plank sponsored by the National Suffrage Association was defeated by 24 to 20. In Chicago at the time of the Republican convention the Congressional Union had called a convention of its own and reorganized itself under the name of the Woman's Party. As such it had presented to the Democratic convention a plank pledging submission of the Federal Suffrage Amendment. That plank was voted down 40 to 4. A motion to make no mention of suffrage was lost by 26 to 17. The substitute plank was finally adopted by 25 to 20. As adopted by the convention, it read:

"We favor the extension of the franchise to the women of the country, State by State, on the same terms as to the men."

"My God, fix things so there'll be no debate on the floor," one excited Republican delegate in Chicago had ejaculated to another, speaking of the suffrage resolution, and apparently things had been fixed, for there was no debate. The Democrats were less fortunate. A minority report signed by four men[99] was presented and a consequent discussion could not be avoided. By arrangement Governor James Ferguson of Texas presented the report in a speech of thirty minutes, the same length of time being given for the defense of the suffrage plank. Governor Ferguson quoted much scripture in support of the minority report, declaring that women's place was at home, and that they should be performing the function for which God Almighty intended them. Dozens of men attempted to speak but the time limit prevented the outpouring of views that the delegates desired.

Senator Key Pittman, on behalf of the Resolutions Committee, eloquently defended the suffrage plank, but was early interrupted by jeers and howls from the Texas delegation. When order was restored, the young Senator, in tones that cut through the roar of the big convention, cried, "Are you *men* who cheer every denunciation of women?" Howls of rage were the response of the Texas delegation. And then something startling happened.

The galleries, filled to overflowing with women, burst forth in cheers and shouts. The women were standing; they were waving flags and handkerchiefs; they were unfurling yellow umbrellas that bobbed up and down all around the long sweep of galleries; they were loosening streams of Golden Lane bunting; they were making the galleries a swirl of gold. "It was the first time," recorded the New York *Times*, "that one of the great cheering demonstrations of a National Convention had been a woman's cheer, the first time a gallery menace to a national convention had been a women's menace, and the thought seemed to flash to the minds of that Texas delegation that it would not be the last. They sank into their seats silenced."

When Senator Pittman sat down tumult raged. Outside a sudden thunderstorm had burst in fury directly over the building. The thunder boomed, but over-riding the thunder, the galleries with their bobbing parasols cheered and cheered and possessed the convention. A delegate got the floor and demanded to know what obligation to States the proposed plank carried. He was assured by the chairman of the Resolutions Committee, amid wild confusion in which jeers and cheers each contributed a part, that it carried none! And those golden galleries burst forth again—not in cheers, in unmistakable hisses.

Senator Walsh of Montana, to whom a portion of the suffrage time had been assigned, reminded the delegates of the grim truth that women might control the election of ninety-one votes in the Electoral College and that the women voters of eleven States not only had rights but opinions to be considered. Amid tense excitement the roll call by States was ordered on the minority report. And now something else never before seen in a party convention happened. The women with the yellow ribbons produced roll-call forms and began jotting down each vote as it was cast. Said the New York *Times:* "The sight of them had a most unnerving effect upon the delegates. It was like the French convention of the Revolution, gallery ruled, and the women with the roll-call blanks, noting the way they voted, suggested the knitting women of the Reign of Terror." When a voice from Texas announced 38 ayes for the minority report, 8 nays, the encircling galleries broke forth again "in a long steady stream of hisses." The minority report was lost by a vote of 888½ to 181½. The victory was won and the women quite clearly had won it. By persisting. By not compromising.

Within the next half hour the executive board of the National Suffrage Association was in session and had sent the following telegram to President Wilson:

"Inasmuch as Governor Ferguson of Texas and Senator Walsh of Montana made diametrically opposite statements in the Democratic convention to-day with regard to your attitude toward the suffrage plank adopted by the convention, we apply to you directly to state your position on the plank and give your precise interpretation of its meaning."

To this the President replied on June 22:

"I am very glad to make my position about the suffrage plank adopted by the convention clear to you, though I had not thought that it was necessary to state again a position I have repeatedly stated with entire frankness. The plank received my hearty approval before its adoption and I shall support its principle with sincere pleasure. I wish to join with my fellow Democrats in recommending to the several States that they extend the suffrage to women upon the same terms as to men."

The Board also determined upon two things:

1. To ask and so far as in us lies to insist upon a vote on the Federal Suffrage Amendment in House and Senate before the adjournment of the Sixty-fifth Congress.

2. To declare an emergency and call the regular annual convention of the National American Woman Suffrage Association for August instead of November of 1916.

The issued call announced that the Board felt that the time had come to take a hand in the fall elections, but they were unwilling to dictate an election policy without conference with the workers from all the States. "There is a crisis in our movement," rang the summons, "which no worker can fail to recognize. The wisest, sanest and best balanced judgment is needed to determine the next steps. Suffragists, prepare for the most important meeting in the annals of our movement."

No matter what Republican and Democratic planks said, suffragists were in no mood to go to the States again and beg the vote from Negroes, immigrants and the liquor trade. The first step was to put their own house in order. The Emergency Convention met at Atlantic City on September 4. The candidates of both dominant parties had been asked to address it. Both had been interviewed before their nomination and again after the "nominations. On June 17 a deputation had waited upon Mr. Charles E. Hughes in New York. He frankly espoused the Federal Suffrage Amendment but asked that his views be regarded as confidential until after his official notification of the party platform. On August 1, according to understanding, he issued a public statement approving the Amendment. On the same day a deputation called upon President Wilson in Washington. The news that Mr. Hughes had endorsed the Amendment had just reached the White House as the deputation entered, and the President announced it to the women who had expected to tell it to him. He then reiterated his belief that woman suffrage should come by State action. Candidate Hughes considered his endorsement a sufficient attention to the woman suffrage question and did not accept the invitation to address the National Convention, at Atlantic City, but President Wilson accepted.

The great theatre was filled with the convention delegates and as many others as the seats would accommodate when the President and his staff arrived. A guard of honor composed a line through which he passed to his seat upon the platform where he was received by the standing audience, cheering joyously. Mr. Wilson was not a suffragist when he entered the White House; but he went to New Jersey to vote for the suffrage amendment in 1915 and he had declared his open sympathy with the principle in 1916. Much has been said as to the factors which led to his final conversion to the Federal Suffrage Amendment. The Woman's Party claims that its anti-Democratic policy, its anti-Wilson demonstrations, including the constant picketing of the White House, and the burning of his book "The New Freedom" and his effigy, were the source of his change of attitude. The National Suffrage Association credits him with yielding to the momentum of the movement which was rapidly reaching its climax in his administration and which grew in spite of and not because of these demonstrations. It places the very hour when conversion to the principle became with him conversion to an obligation to join the campaign. Standing before that great audience, four-fifths of which were women, he said, "I have come to fight not for you but with you, and in the end I think we shall not quarrel over the method."

Dr. Shaw, the master orator, was introduced to speak the closing words of that wonderful evening. Said she: "We have waited so long, Mr. President! We have dared to hope that our release might come in your administration and that yours would be the voice to pronounce the words to bring our freedom." With a slightly muffled, rustling sound the great audience was on its feet, with every eye upon the President. On every face was a look that seemed to say, "Oh, Mr. President, we have indeed waited so long, so long." Yet there was no sound. Silent, unmoving, the audience stood, a spellbound living petition to the most influential man in the nation—the President of the United States. Suffragists had planned and staged many a demonstration to prove the reasonableness of their claim and the strength of their demand, but none ever equaled the spontaneous united appeal of that Atlantic City audience. And whether the National Suffrage Association is right or not in believing that then and there the President was transformed from a sympathizer with woman suffrage into a campaigner for it, certainly it was the Association's experience that from that date he never declined to find time for a deputation from it, never refused to grant any request for aid.

The Atlantic City Convention had opened with, a closed session of the Executive Council which proved the most crucial of any session of any convention yet held. The president of the Association, addressing the Council, said:

"The Congressional work in Washington for the last six months cost five thousand dollars. What are the results? An honest, reliable poll of the Congress and the absolute assurance that the Amendment cannot go through! We have gained the long sought planks in all party platforms, but those of the dominant ones tell us to go to the States for our vote. We have brought the demand of a great public opinion, and the achievement of one-fourth of the States won for full suffrage. It should be a sufficient mandate from the country, and the time has come to complete the campaign for the enfranchisement of women by the Federal Amendment. This has always been the plan. The time to turn back from the States to Congress is here. The facts are that the Congress does not recognize woman suffrage as an issue in its own constituencies, and now regards the issue as dismissed from Washington responsibility. Be assured that no committee, however gifted or large, can push that amendment through, nor can it do so with the support of part of our forces. Nothing short of a campaign in every constituency will give our committee in Washington the authority to get the Amendment submitted. There can be no serene, undisturbed army at home resting on its arms and yet expecting victory in the nation's Capitol.

"There is one way to bring the Federal Amendment and only one, a solemn compact signed by the auxiliaries of at least thirty-six States that they will turn the full power of their organizations into the fight to secure the submission of the Amendment and ratification by their Legislatures. Each must secure the pledged votes of its delegation in the Congress and a majority in its Legislature.

"The resolutions passed by twenty-eight Legislatures, calling for a national constitutional convention, forced the submission of the income tax amendment. You must secure resolutions calling upon Congress to submit the Suffrage Amendment. Voting women and the possible power in their hands proved an impressive argument in the presidential campaign. You must increase the number by securing presidential suffrage in as many States. The campaigns pending must go forward to success. We have brought a mandate; but we will bring a bigger one, and before it even the Senate will surrender. That mandate should be a resolution from at least twenty-eight States calling upon Congress to submit the amendment, and presidential suffrage in as many States.

"There must be at least thirty-six State armies, alert, intelligent, never pausing, and they must move in the fixed formation demanded by the national strategy adopted. We already have the members, but many members consider themselves 'reserve forces.' This is the time to call them all out. Do not forget that we cannot win with thirty-five States, it must be thirty-six. What will you do?"

In opening the public sessions of the convention, the president of the suffrage association said:

"Our cause has been caught in a snarl of constitutional obstructions and inadequate election laws. We have a right to appeal to our Congress to extricate our cause from this tangle. If there is any chivalry left, this is the time for it to come forward and do an act of simple justice. The women of this land not only have the right to sit on the steps of Congress until it acts but it is their self-respecting duty to insist upon their enfranchisement by that route.

"But, let me implore you, sister women, not to imagine a Federal Amendment an easy process of enfranchisement. There is no quick, short cut to our liberty. The Federal Amendment means a simultaneous campaign in forty-eight States. It demands organization in every precinct; activity, agitation, education in every corner. It means an appeal to the voters only little less general than is required in a referendum. Nothing less than this nationwide, vigilant, unceasing campaigning will win the ratification.

"A few women here and there have dropped out from State work in the fond delusion that there is no need of work if the Federal Amendment is to be the aim. I hold such women to be more dangerous enemies of our cause than the known opponent. State work alone can carry the Amendment through Congress and through the ratifications. There must be no shirkers, no cowards, no backsliders these coming months. The army in every State must grow larger and larger. The activity must grow livelier and ever more lively. The reserves must be aroused and set to work. Women arise: demand the vote!"

By spectacular demonstration, the difficulties of amending State constitutions were shown at the convention, the different classes being called The Impossibles, The Insuperables, The Inexecutables, The Improbables, The Indubitables, The Inexcusables, The Irreproachables, the last interpreted as the suffrage States. A three-cornered debate on the question of the Federal Amendment, State Amendment or both occupied an afternoon. As a result of these numerous features designed to clarify the Association's own point of view, the convention decided to pursue its time-honored course of bringing the mandate from the States to the support of the Federal Amendment until it should pass, and that the mandate should take the form of presidential suffrage and resolutions as recommended from Legislatures, calling for submission of the Federal Suffrage Amendment. The convention called upon Congress for the thirty-eighth time in *annual* convention to submit the Federal Amendment and called upon the dominant parties to prove the sincerity of their planks by taking immediate action in the campaign States to carry pending amendments to victory.

In a private conference "the solemn compact" was adopted and signed by more than thirty-six States. From that moment there were no defections, no doubts, no differences in the Association. A great army in perfect discipline moved forward to its goal.

While the Republican and Progressive conventions were meeting, the news had flashed over the wires of the Iowa defeat. It came while the Resolutions Committee was discussing the suffrage plank and it had had its deterrent effect upon the minds of the doubtful. Few victories came to stiffen the faith of political friends as the months crept by. On the contrary the Congress returned to Washington in December in petulant mood. Suffragists had witnessed ruffled congressional minds before, but none like these.

The Woman's party in 1916 had again campaigned against all Democratic candidates in Western enfranchised States, and while they had defeated none, they had succeeded in arousing the tempestuous irritation of every candidate to the nth degree. Republicans were in an even more unfriendly frame of mind, for Mr. Wilson had been re-elected by a narrow margin and by common consent that margin was acknowledged to have been furnished by the women voters of California. "Honest John

Shafroth," best of Senatorial friends, calmed the dismay of the suffragists by the admonition: "Take my advice and just hold off a bit. Everybody's sore now and there seems no exception, but they'll get over it, they'll get over it, just wait until they settle down."

The National Suffrage Association took a large house on Rhode Island Avenue, moved its Washington headquarters there and began its work of winning the Congress back to normal mood with regard to suffrage.

The winter wore away and no vote was secured. To the public the federal campaign seemed calm, but the home fires were burning. Ah, how they did burn! The campaign in the States was moving faster and faster. Meanwhile that margin for Mr. Wilson, alleged to have been won by California women voters, served as a leaven in the big prejudiced Democratic loaf. "I had no idea that women would show such intelligent discrimination in political affairs," said one Democrat to another, and that interpretation became widely disseminated until even the Southern press took on a more friendly attitude. Republicans, however, were more offish. They said that women had proved themselves sentimental and had voted for Mr. Wilson because his campaign slogan had been "he kept us out of war."

Alas for slogans. Alas for belief that America could be kept out of war. On April 2, 1917, Mr. Wilson called a special session of the Congress and after a debate in which one hundred speeches were made, mostly on one side, the fateful vote was taken which involved the nation in the Great World War and engaged to send millions of men overseas.

CHAPTER 18

The Fighting Forces

In the struggle from which the final woman suffrage victory was now about to emerge four groups of fighting forces were engaged. They were the Suffragists, the Liquor Interests, the Anti-Suffragists and the Prohibitionists.

In the suffrage army there were over two million women enlisted. The parent body, the National American Woman Suffrage Association, directed the activities of the great mass of them, while the Woman's Party projected its entirely separate and often conflicting program for the group of militants. When victory finally perched upon the banners of the suffragists the National Suffrage Association had direct auxiliaries in forty-six States of the Union and these far-reaching confederated bodies were functioning as one organ through its centralized national board. Extensive headquarters were maintained in both Washington and New York. In Washington congressional activities radiated from the great house at 1626 Rhode Island Avenue. In New York headquarters occupied two entire floors, equivalent to thirty large rooms, of a business building on Madison Avenue. Between forty and fifty women were continuously retained on the clerical staff, and as many field workers were engaged in campaigns. A publishing company prepared and printed literature of various kinds. Publicity, organization, data and educational departments constituted branches of the general administration, and a weekly thirty-two-page magazine, the *Woman Citizen,* was maintained as the Association's official organ and mouthpiece.

Historically, the National American Woman Suffrage Association presents a record of intensive organization probably never paralleled. Through half a century of incessant work that record reaches back to 1869. Even fifteen years before that time suffrage work of an agitational kind had been conducted by local committees or clubs under the direction of a strongly centralized national board. That plan of organization served the purposes of the early time admirably, but when it became clear that the women must for a time go to the States to seek and win their suffrage by referenda campaigns, a different form of organization was found necessary. The workers, therefore, by common consent in 1869, prepared the way for a new body better adapted to the new phase of the struggle. Out of the process, two organizations emerged—The National Woman Suffrage Association and The American Woman Suffrage Association, the first led by Elizabeth Cady Stanton and Susan B. Anthony, the second by Lucy Stone, the differences being more personal than tactical.

The aims of both were the same, to secure suffrage for women whenever possible and by any constitutional method. The National emphasized the federal suffrage method by holding annual conventions in Washington and securing hearings on the Federal Suffrage Amendment, but it maintained, too, the policy of winning woman suffrage State by State until enough States should have adopted it to make women voters an element no longer negligible in the constituencies of United States Congressmen who would someday vote on the Federal Suffrage Amendment. The "American" concentrated on State campaigns with the same end in view, whenever federal action should be possible. The field was wide and by tacit consent the two organizations kept out of each other's way, only a few States having auxiliaries to both.

Twenty years later the younger recruits, perceiving that the two separate organizations at times conflicted, set themselves to the task of union. This they successfully accomplished in 1890, the National-American Woman Suffrage Association resulting, with this announced aim:

> "The object of this Association shall be to secure protection in their right to vote to the women citizens of the United States by appropriate national and State legislation."

Auxiliary to this national body were the State suffrage organizations, known by various titles. They paid dues and sent delegates to the annual conventions where officers were elected, reports heard and plans made. The annual conventions were dated from 1869, although they had been held continuously since 1850, except during the war period.

Elizabeth Cady Stanton, whose "State papers," as Miss Anthony called them, showed a rarer touch of the statesman's genius than those of any other woman have ever shown, was president of the National Association continuously from 1869 to 1890, and although approaching her eightieth year, served the merged associations for one more year.

The National American Woman Suffrage Association had but four presidents, Mrs. Stanton being the first. She was followed in 1891 by Susan B. Anthony who retired in 1900 at the age of eighty, having been the suffrage president only nine years, but the "propulsive force" of suffrage, as Grace Greenwood called her, for forty years— the untiring, intrepid, never discouraged, never defeated, greatest-souled woman of the suffrage movement. Carrie Chapman Catt was president from 1900 to 1904. In 1904 there came to the presidency one who stood unchallenged throughout her career as the greatest orator among women the world has ever known, and who made more converts to the suffrage cause than any other one person— Dr. Anna Howard Shaw, vice-president from 1891 to 1904 and president from 1904 to 1915. Carrie Chapman Catt served again as president from 1915 to 1920, when the final victory came.

Lucy Stone, the leader of the American, was made chairman of the Executive Committee at the union of the two suffrage organizations in 1890, and after her death in 1893 her place in the movement was ably assumed by her husband, Henry B. Blackwell, and her daughter, Alice Stone Blackwell.

After 1890 the composite organization, with its auxiliaries, conducted all the referenda suffrage campaigns in the United States, while at the same time carrying on the campaign for a Federal Suffrage Amendment. An occasional independent society arose here and there, sometimes with special aims, sometimes motived by personalities, but these were spasmodic and short-lived. With a single exception no one of them ever conducted a campaign. The exception was the Congressional Union, organized in 1913 and in 1916 renamed the Woman's Party. Its sole aim was the passage of the Federal Suffrage Amendment. Its tactics being out of harmony with those of the National American Woman Suffrage Association, auxiliaryship was denied it. It therefore conducted a parallel but independent federal campaign.

The early administration work of the National American Woman Suffrage Association was performed in the homes of the officers until 1895, when a part of one room in the World Building, New York City, served as a headquarters for the Organization Committee. That same year an attempt was made to establish a headquarters in Philadelphia as well as in New York, but at the end of the first year the two headquarters were united and located in two rooms in the World Building in New York. In 1898, the headquarters were removed to the Tract Society Building, where they occupied four rooms. In 1902 they were removed to Warren, Ohio. In 1909 they were returned to New York and occupied considerable space in a business building on Fifth Avenue. Before the end of the suffrage campaign "Headquarters" meant the extensive housing arrangements already noted as applying to New York and Washington.

Concurrent with other suffrage work, the organization sponsored a series of suffrage papers that formed a journalistic chain reaching forward from the beginning in 1869 to the end in 1920. As early as 1868 Miss Anthony and Mrs. Stanton launched the lively paper called the *Revolution*. It lasted until 1870. In 1870 Lucy Stone, with money left her by Mrs. Elizabeth Eddy, established the *Woman's Journal*. It was published weekly in Boston and served as the organ for the American Association until the merger in 1890, when it became the official organ of the National American Woman Suffrage Association. Thereafter it had a continuous life until 1917. Mrs. Frank Leslie having in the meantime bequeathed a fund to be used for the furtherance of the suffrage cause, that year, 1917, out of a combination of the *Woman's Journal* and several smaller suffrage papers, the *Woman Citizen* was established, "in the hope," as its prospectus announced, that it might prove "a self-perpetuating memorial to Mrs. Frank Leslie's generosity to the cause of woman suffrage and her faith in woman's irresistible progress." It remained the official organ of the Association until the victory of 1920, since which time it has functioned as an independent magazine devoted to the civic interests of women.

The activities of the second group of the fighting forces in the suffrage struggle, i.e., the liquor interests, have been already fairly covered. When the federal investigation into the political activities of the brewers brought out the minutes of the conferences where political campaigns were reported, it was discovered that the liquor interests' political committees, heavily financed, had directed all campaigns in the nation and that woman suffrage was uniformly included with temperance activities as equally invidious to the liquor traffic. These revelations made clear many a mystifying incident and squared with suffrage experiences that had been carefully filed away after each campaign. That the liquor forces regarded themselves as solely responsible for anti-suffrage campaigns was evident, since each member of liquor organizations, when reporting suffrage defeats in his State, said "we did it." In the closing years of the struggle, the trade added "allied interests and groups of foreign-born voters" as among those who "did it" but all were under the direction of the common master. The liquor organizations were the United States Brewers' Association, the Wholesale Distillers' Association and the Retail Dealers' Association, each with its auxiliary in each State. Collectively these organizations and their allies were designated as the "wets."

The only other organized opposition to suffrage came from the group of women commonly called "the Antis." The name of their organization was the Association Opposed to Suffrage for Women. Its members were mainly well-to-do, carefully protected, and entertained the feeling of distrust of the people usual in their economic class. Their speeches indicated at times an anxious disturbance of mind lest the privileges they enjoyed might be lost in the rights to be gained. The first anti organization appeared in Boston some time before 1890 and was lengthily designated as "The Association Opposed to the Further Extension of Suffrage to Women." It began its work by sending a male lawyer to protest in its name against having the vote thrust upon women, and it issued a small sheet called the *Remonstrance* which withheld the names of editor and publisher.

With the years these ladies grew bolder and made their own protests before committees. By and by similar groups were organized in other Eastern cities but the protestants gained no headway west of

Ohio. Their uniform arguments were that the majority of women did not want the vote, therefore none should have it; that "woman's place was in the home," and that women were incompetent to vote.

After 1912 the women antis were represented in all referenda campaigns, but the manager of their activities was a paid outsider. A few names of women within the State were usually secured and these women were made to do duty as officers of an anti-suffrage association for the State, but they were rarely workers. Speakers were kept in the field and were sent collectively into campaign States. Suffragists learned to regard them, paradoxically, as unfriendly aids. Parlor meetings were their specialty and they frequently drew an audience of conservative women who could not have been persuaded to attend a suffrage meeting; and these women often received an impulse there which led them into the suffrage campaign. The antis recruited from the indifferent, and through an aroused interest many of the indifferent became suffragists. The president of the National Suffrage Association at one time was entertained at luncheon in a conservative city where the table conversation developed the interesting fact that every guest present had been converted to woman suffrage in anti-meetings. In another city a woman became so indignant at what she heard at such a parlor meeting that she presented ten thousand dollars to the suffrage association, the largest contribution any living person had made at that date.

The only time and place when the women antis really aroused suffrage tempers was in legislative hearings. Legislative committees divided the time equally between suffragists and anti-suffragists, and thus the appearance was given of a conflict between two groups of women, each presenting equal claims, before men who had the authority to act as judges. The suffragists represented an unmistakable popular demand for a just cause facing an inevitable final triumph, and the poorest of their speeches no man could answer. Yet when an anti with an ingratiating smile said, "Gentlemen, we trust you to take care of us and the government," almost any legislative committee could be counted on to beam with self-satisfaction in response. Then it was that suffragists felt, as at no other time, the poignant difference between the appeal of a just claim and a clinging vine. However, even this experience stirred a new suffrage zeal, so was not without its uses.

Whatever value women anti-suffragists may have placed upon their own efforts in campaigns, neither their opponents, the organized suffragists, nor their unacknowledged allies, the liquor forces, as evidenced in the secret minutes, credited them with decisive influence. A letter, already quoted in part, is illustrative of the attitude of the liquor forces on the subject. Wrote Hugh Fox, Secretary of the United States Brewers' Association, to the Fred Miller Brewing Company: "We are in a position to establish channels of communication with the leaders of the anti-suffrage movement for our friends in any State where suffrage is an issue." To those who erroneously thought of the anti-suffrage women as the leaders of the anti-suffrage movement this seemed conclusive proof of collusion, but the next sentence absolved the anti-women and threw this telling light on the situation: "I am under the impression that a new anti-suffrage association has been organized in Illinois and is a retail liquor dealers' affair." It is clear that Mr. Fox had no thought of the women antis at all, but pointed his correspondent to the only force he recognized as anti-suffragists. As a matter of fact there had been no organized women antis in Illinois for years.

Probably the worst damage that the women antis did was to give unscrupulous politicians a respectable excuse for opposing suffrage, and to confuse public thinking by standing conspicuously in the lime light while the potent enemy worked in darkness. The anti-suffragists were probably as neutral toward the prohibition vs. liquor campaign as were the suffragists, but there was this difference: the women antis and the liquor men worked for a common aim; the suffragists and the prohibitionists had two entirely different aims. The campaigns of the anti-women and the liquor men supplemented each other; the campaigns of the prohibitionists and suffragists were often in conflict and each regarded the other in those instances as a decided handicap. Very many persons accused the women antis and liquor opponents of collusion; suffrage field workers had the habit of sending affidavits in support of such a contention to headquarters. In the closing years, well known counsel for the liquor forces appeared at hearings in several States with the anti-women, and not only spoke for but sat with them and wore their red rose insignia.

A representative of the anti-suffrage association sent to Montana, in 1914, attempted to arrange a basis of co-operation with the Montana liquor men whereby the women would do the public work and the liquor men keep out of sight. The *National Forum,* liquor organ at Butte, published the whole story. The *Liberal Advocate,* official organ of the Ohio liquor league published at Columbus, ran a series of articles by the Secretary of the Cincinnati Association Opposed to Woman Suffrage, and many liquor papers carried general material sent out by the women anti-suffragists. Street cars in Stark County, Ohio, 1914, carried advertisements for the liquor amendment which urged the reader to "see the card on the opposite side of the car." On the opposite side was the women's anti-suffrage advertisement, asking for votes against the suffrage amendment. In Warren, Ohio, pieces of literature issued by the women antis and literature issued by the liquor organization, folded in the same package, were left at the doors of all houses by professional bill distributors. In Nebraska, the conspicuous "right-hand man" of the women antis was the well-known publicity agent for the brewers.

The Macomb County Michigan Retail Liquor Dealers' Association addressed the following letter to newspapers—one of which turned the copy over to suffrage headquarters:

"Macomb County Retail Liquor Dealers' Association,
Office of the Secretary,
Mt. Clemens, Michigan   March 31st, 1913.

To the Publisher:

I enclose herewith copy for an advertisement which I wish you would insert in this week's issue of your paper. . . .

I will thank you to see that this is done, and mail statement of charges and also marked copy to me and we will remit for the same. . . .

Joseph Matthews

Enclosure   Secretary"

The enclosure, for the publication of which the Macomb County Retail Liquor Dealers' Association guaranteed payment, read:

"AN APPEAL TO MEN!

You should vote against woman suffrage for ten thousand reasons.

We mention but six.

As women, we do not want the strife, bitterness, falsification and publicity which accompany political campaigns. We women are not suffering at the hands of but fathers, husbands and brothers because they protect us in our homes. We have women's greatest right—to be free from political medley. We do not want to lose this freedom. We have refrained from protest heretofore, depending upon men to protect women from the ballot. We now ask the men of Michigan to defend us and vote NO on suffrage.

* * * * * * *

Keep mother, wife and sister in the protected home. Do not force us into partisan politics. Put a cross before the word 'No' on April 7th, and win our gratitude."

The appeal was issued by the Michigan Association Opposed to Woman Suffrage and signed by its women officers.

In many States, posters or placards issued by the women antis were hung both outside and inside saloons. Usually they were hastily removed when photographers appeared, yet photographs were taken and are on file.

To hints in the press that their association was supported by liquor money, anti-suffrage women made loud disclaimers, as did also the liquor men. Certainly there was no need for anti-suffrage women to go outside their own group for funds, for most of their leaders were among the wealthiest of American women.

One interesting affidavit, filed at National Headquarters was that of Frances Belford Wayne, a clever, well-known newspaper writer of Denver. A Mr. Maling of Denver, long the antis' chief field man, tried to persuade her, as he had other Colorado women, to engage in the service of the antis:

> "If only you would drop your silly convictions and look after No. 1, I could take you down to these anti-suffragists and put you in a position to make as much money in six months as you can make here in two years. You could have a trip to Europe, live on velvet and line your pockets merely by boosting against suffrage instead of boosting for it!" . . . "Better let me lead you to the trough" was Mr. Maling's final word. (The *Woman's Journal*, October 31, 1914.)

Although the antis were able to finance themselves and seemed to be well supplied with campaign funds, and although the officers and members of the organization probably knew of no collusion, suffragists believed that a trail led from the women's organization into the liquor camp and that it was traveled by the men the women antis employed. The anti-women usually sent a man and woman manager to each State, the man working among the men and the woman among the women. These men were observed in counsel with the liquor political managers too often to doubt that they laid their respective plans before each other so far as co-operation could be of advantage. One evidence of this understanding came in the last years when the prohibition campaign was waxing exceedingly hot throughout the nation. By then the liquor men were exerting their utmost strength to vote, not only all living sympathizers, but also names on tombstones in suffrage referenda. They had waged a deadly anti-suffrage campaign among labor men, but in response to the appeals of suffragists the Federation of Labor and most labor unions had resolved for woman suffrage and labor leaders had long been sincere advocates of the cause. Union men were therefore engaged by the liquor interests to go among the local unions and by the reiterated declaration that women would vote prohibition, and thus not only take away the working-man's beer but also throw thousands out of employment, they succeeded in turning large numbers of organized labor men against suffrage.

Even this additional force did not suffice, for they apparently felt the need of still greater numbers. There followed an organized attempt to alienate from suffrage support a class less easy to reach, the men who were supposed to be supporting woman suffrage because they believed women voters would in turn support prohibition. To this task the women antis set themselves with definite intent and great zeal. A pink leaflet entitled, "Woman Suffrage and the liquor question—Facts show women's votes have not aided prohibition," was widely distributed by them in the 1915 campaigns and thereafter. At least one speaker at every meeting devoted time to this plan and tried to prove that women had not supported prohibition. At times the speech got a bit misplaced, as at Plattsburg, New York, where to a small audience, conspicuously sprinkled with well-known saloon men, an anti discoursed upon the positive disinclination of women voters to aid prohibition.

At one and the same time, many trade papers were desperately entreating the liquor men to work early and late to defeat woman suffrage because women voters here and there and everywhere had voted dry. "It behooves all saloonkeepers and brewers to get busy early in the campaign to oppose the suffrage amendment by organized effort. It is the only way to save your business," urged the *National Forum* in the Montana campaign.

The combined plans are best described by the political colloquialism, "catch 'em goin' and comin'."

Throughout the suffrage campaign suffragists were constantly making accusation that votes were being bought and returns were being juggled. They did not, however, accuse the women antis even of possessing knowledge that these things were being done, yet the antis were continually diverting public attention from the guilty men to themselves, to the complete bewilderment of the public. Again and again when suffragists attempted to tell the people what they knew and to announce some new evidence of the criminal nature of liquor opposition, the lady antis would "rise to explain." Such public defense of the entire opposition was as exasperating to suffragists as it must have been gratifying to the liquor trade. This interpretation of the situation became so general that cartoonists found a fruitful theme in picturing ladies with widely spread skirts concealing the real anti-suffragists hiding behind.

The last group in the fighting forces, the Prohibitionists, included the Prohibition party and the Woman's Christian Temperance Union. The Anti-Saloon League, non-partisan and as strictly neutral on all other questions as the National American Woman Suffrage Association, assumed and held the leadership of the fight for prohibition during the decade preceding the ratification of the prohibition amendment. The relation between this body and the organized suffragists was admirably stated by L. Ames Brown in the *North American Review* (Suffrage and Prohibition 1916):

"Enmity against a common foe does not always result in an alliance between the two crusaders but it cannot fail to produce a feeling of benevolent neutrality."

Yet the woman suffrage struggle was vastly complicated by the prohibition struggle. Men indifferent to suffrage but hostile to prohibition were rendered impervious to the suffrage appeal, and men hostile to prohibition but in favor of suffrage were frightened by the continual insistence of liquor workers that woman suffrage meant the speedier coming of prohibition.

Mr. Taft, ex-President, in a magazine article in 1915 was representative of the first class:

> "It is said that women will vote for prohibition and that, therefore, if they are given the vote we shall be rid of the saloon evils. To those of us who do not think that the saloon evil can be abolished by general prohibition, either national or statewide in States with large cities, and that the result of the effort would be worse than present conditions, this argument does not appeal. The lack of experience in affairs and the excess of emotion on the part of women in reaching their political decisions upon questions of this kind are what would lower the average practical sense and self-restraint of the electorate in case they were admitted to it now."

Upon these two parallel reforms, each propelled onward by men and women whose souls were afire with a "holy zeal," a vast part of the population at first looked indifferently. Eventually all the intelligent members of society were listed for or against one or both. Had there been no prohibition movement in the United States, the women would have been enfranchised two generations before they were. Had that movement not won its victory, they would have struggled on for another generation.

CHAPTER 19

The Decisive Battle

To even a casual observer at the close of 1916 it must have been clear that the long-continued strategy of the National American Woman Suffrage Association in the forwarding of the suffrage cause was nearing its crucial test. Eleven States had been won to full suffrage and the argument that was bearing down with most force upon the passage of the Federal Suffrage Amendment was the number of western women who were voting for the President of the United States and for members of the Congress. Even those suffragists who belittled the State method of securing suffrage were proudly advertising the four million voting women of the West—whose suffrage had been won by State referenda—as the main reliance of their argument at Washington.

For its own part, from year to year and steadily, the National Suffrage Association had used the political dynamite in the victories gained in the States as a means of blasting through to success at Washington. How many more States must be added to the full suffrage column before the Congress of the United States would hear and be persuaded by that on-march of destiny?

When the day comes that we have enough States we shall know it, Miss Anthony had said. With the year 1917 the day drew close and its recognition flushed the Washington prospect rosily for suffrage workers. On one State hung all their hopes for winding up referenda campaigns and compelling federal action by the Congress. That State was New York. A suffrage referendum was scheduled there for November, 1917, the second to be held in two years. Certain factors made the situation thrilling. For one thing the campaign was in the Far East instead of the Far West. For another, in point of suffrage, New York had become the most intensively organized State in the Union. Then, too, New York is—New York, with more intricate problems of population and persuasions than any other State in the Union.

A tremendous amount of suffrage history had been packed into the State. From 1848 to 1876 it had been the recognized storm center of the woman's rights movement. Even after it became clear that no ordinary demand would persuade the New York Legislature to submit a suffrage amendment, the suffrage organization kept its flag flying and sought such suffrage rights as the Legislature could grant while asking continually for an amendment.

Meanwhile, the suffrage scene was shifted to the West and Eastern suffragists began staking work and money and hopes upon that region. Time demonstrated that there was something wrong with the West. It was not public opinion; that continued to be liberal toward woman suffrage. But suffrage victories came all too slowly. Western men suffragists gave their women political advice based upon their own experience in party contests. This advice was to the effect that the majority of voters were favorable, there being no known opposition, and that a small campaign with a watch over the election and the count was sufficient. No one seemed to know then that the sharpest political wits money could buy were surveying the field from secret watch-towers and reporting to their national chiefs that the Federation of Women's Clubs was not interested, that the Woman's Christian Temperance Union was absorbed in its own work, that the suffrage organization was small, and that the party managers "had been seen with gratifying results."—"Don't arouse the ignorant and vicious classes," advised the suffrage men, apparently quite unaware that these classes were always aroused and mobilized when men, unscrupulously intelligent and with sordid motives, needed their aid. Under this advice one Western campaign after another was defeated. By and by Eastern women lost faith in the investment of suffrage money and energy in the West. At the same time many Western women were persuaded that their failures might be due to resentment that in Western campaigns Eastern workers were on hand, telling Western people what to do. In no Western State where women were striving to gain submission of State suffrage amendments, but failing to understand the nature of the inevitable contest to follow, could they be persuaded to set themselves to the task of building up a suffrage organization big enough and strong enough to arouse public opinion to the point where it would overcome both blind traditional prejudice and wide-awake, if secretly directed, opposition.

It was at this point that certain New York City women determined to produce an example of efficient suffrage organization and to prove its value if possible. It was no easy stint. The City was the home of the foreign born, containing as many "Irish as the city of Dublin, as many Germans as the city of Munich, as many Italians as the city of Florence, as many Russians as Riga, as many Austro-Hungarians as Prague, as many Norwegians as Christiania," and the sum total constituted a larger population than that of all the thirteen colonies when they arose in revolution against their mother country. Many City suffragists questioned the merits of the experiment to be tried. "Up state" suffragists looked upon it with frank skepticism, for was it not a well-established fact that reforms might sweep the State from Buffalo to Harlem Bridge and inevitably be vanquished by the reactionaries and the vicious of the great city? Nevertheless from that moment New York State became again the storm center of the movement and proved in the end the political lever with which the final moves were successfully made.

The year was 1909. New York City, as the suffragists that year came painfully to know, is divided for government purposes, into sixty-three Assembly Districts, and these in turn into 2,127 Election Districts. City maps in hand, the few with the new idea laboriously classified the membership of all suffrage clubs, and also the names upon the Federal Suffrage Amendment petition that was then being circulated, into Assembly Districts with a temporary suffrage Leader in charge of each district. In districts where no suffragists were known women envoys were sent to interview all kinds of people and in this way find suffragists. Through many private meetings the membership of the old order of clubs was merged at last into the proposed organization.

Following the established custom of established parties, fifty-two assembly districts held conventions and organized and elected delegates to a city convention. From the remaining eleven districts delegates were appointed. On October 29, 1909, the "Woman Suffrage Party" was launched by a city convention at Carnegie Hall. The floor was completely filled by the 804 delegates and two hundred alternates, representing all the assembly districts of the city. It was the largest delegated suffrage convention yet held. The galleries were occupied by the general public, the boxes and platform by prominent women and men well known in politics and world affairs. The plan was there presented that the new organization should be modeled on that of the political parties, first adopted by Tammany Hall, and afterwards copied by all parties. The organization proposed to go farther than the parties and unite the five counties which constituted the big city under an elected Board of Officers, including a chairman for each county or borough, and announced its intention to have not only a Leader for each Assembly District but a captain for each of the Election Districts.

The Press found the undertaking unique and united in declaring it a genuinely political move. *The New York World* said:

"The Woman Suffrage Party is now to be reckoned with as a political force. It has a 'machine.' Given that the machine operates harmoniously, the Woman Suffrage Party will be in a position to make deals with the older parties and to exercise political influence. The suffragists are to be congratulated on their new tactics."

The new organization at once began search for 2,127 captains, holding Election District, Assembly District, Borough, and City meetings, and drawing upon a long list of city men and women speakers to make its plea to the uninformed. It established a City Headquarters with press, literature, organization and political departments. Every day bulletins were issued, "press parties" were received weekly or oftener, tons of literature were printed and distributed. While the perfecting of the organization moved forward, a systematic campaign to convert and interest *political* men formed the first main activity.

The next step was an attempt to convince the State Suffrage Association that the time had come to secure a referendum campaign. While the submission of an amendment had been a pending question for two generations, New York suffragists, convinced in later years that such an amendment could not be carried, had emphasized municipal suffrage and tax-paying suffrage for towns and cities which could be secured by act of the Legislature. They had won the school vote in 1880, tax suffrage in third class cities in 1901 and in 1910 they won township suffrage on bond issues. These were merely entering wedges. Still skeptical, upstate suffragists reluctantly yielded to the entreaties of the City suffragists. No sooner was the November election of 1910 over, than Assembly District suffrage leaders, accompanied by deputations from the elected Assemblyman's own District, waited upon him to plead for submission of a state suffrage amendment. The Leaders of the three Assembly Districts that composed each Senatorial District, heading deputations from all three, called upon the Senators. The deputations followed each other in succession and were often accompanied by reporters, the press being actively interested in the result,—often to the annoyance of the member.

Special cars carried the New York Woman Suffrage Party representatives to Albany, and a wealthy, intelligent society woman whose interest had been greatly stirred, took upon herself the self-appointed task of securing the co-operation of the Speaker of the Assembly who was a relative of hers. She came from the interview much chagrined and surprised. "Something holds him; it is not prejudice and I do not know what it is," she reported.

The Legislature of 1910 did not act but its failure to do so was not received, as in the earlier days, with silent resignation. Instead, in New York a procession and open-air protest meeting were held on May 21st. Ten thousand people in Union Square listened to the speeches the suffragists made and furnished the largest suffrage demonstration ever held to that date in the United States. It was also the beginning of the long line of huge American processions for woman suffrage.[100] Ninety automobiles were in line, each decorated in yellow, and behind them came marching on foot the College Equal Suffrage League in cap and gown, the Women's Political Union and the women of many trades. Many suffragists gathered upon the streets with the crowds, too timid as yet to join in the procession, but among them were some who became the boldest leaders of the spectacular campaign that was to follow.

The City Party method did not immediately convert up-state suffragists nor attain its aim of securing a captain in each Election District, but the city membership grew from twenty thousand in 1910 to over five hundred thousand in 1917 and its work had grown more intensive each year.

Each Leader was instructed to gather her Captains for frequent meetings and to teach them how to make a survey of their districts. On their maps every church, settlement, school, factory, saloon, house of prostitution, store or shop was indicated, and every moral agency was enlisted in the Election District campaign. Mothers', school, and church meetings were held, at which the suffragists talked with the women. Thirteen thousand public school teachers became members and workers. Street meetings were held in every Assembly District for both men and women, Captains uniting to take charge of them. "Rainbow fliers," printed in ten colors and seven languages, carrying the suffrage evangel in big type and simple terms, were distributed at these meetings. More formal meetings were held in such churches, halls and hotels as were available, an especial effort being made to place such meetings in the District Headquarters of the Democratic and Republican parties. Every club, church and organization was asked to grant space on its regular program for suffrage speakers and an occasional great City meeting was held in Carnegie Hall or Cooper Union, always crowded to the doors.

To secure money for these campaigns, bazaars, rummage sales, teas, theatre parties, plays, picnics, card parties and dances were constantly in progress. A suffrage school was held to teach workers how to work by the new methods, and so unquestioned became the results of the system that students attended from twenty-eight States. This school was followed by many others.

By this agitation the suffrage question was soon lifted within the State to the acknowledged status of a political issue. Although the Legislature of 1910–1911 took no action, that of 1912–1913 passed a suffrage amendment by a vote of 40 to 2 in the Senate and 125 to 5 in the House. This overwhelmingly favorable vote followed logically upon the suffragists' systematized campaign to show legislators the strength of women's demand for the vote. One member publicly announced that the women of his district did not want to vote, whereupon the suffrage leader of that District asked him if he would meet the women who did. A large American basement house was selected as the place and the lone Assemblyman was not a little abashed at the sight of an overflowing first floor, second floor, stairs filled and crowds below, striving to come up. The next day he announced to the Legislature that however the men of his District might feel, he was convinced that the women *did* want to vote. Still another announced to the public through the press that he had caused a canvass of his own block to be made and his man canvasser had reported five women only who wanted to vote. The Leader of his district read the statement in her morning paper, called up her helpers and the following morning the names of 189 women who wanted to vote in that block were printed in the daily press. The organization was proving practical!

What could the Legislature do? "After all a submission is only passing the responsibility to the voters," said the members. The 1913–1914 Legislature voted for submission the required second time without a dissenting vote and the election was fixed for November, 1915.

The State Suffrage Association transformed itself into a Woman Suffrage Party in 1915. What was called the Empire State Campaign Committee, combining all suffrage associations in the State and working through the chiefs of twelve campaign districts, was organized and took charge of the campaign. Plans for simultaneous action for the workers in all parts of the State were formulated and executed with such precision that every woman engaged in suffrage stint or stunt, knew that she was companioned by hundreds of other women who on that day were doing the same thing. There were "canvassing squads," processions with banners and music, meetings of every kind, peripatetic headquarters, gaily decorated and supplied with speakers and workers who went the rounds of each county visiting every town and post office. On Mother's Day, hundreds of churches had ceremonies and appeals for the new order, and on the Fourth of July, the Woman's Declaration of Independence was read from the steps of fifty court houses, New York City conducting its ceremonies of the day at the foot of the Statue of Liberty on Bedloe's Island. For the first time in suffrage history there was a strongly organized press department with an auxiliary body, the famous "Publicity Council," the two together devising and spreading broadcast suffrage publicity in the twenty-six languages in which newspapers were published in New York State.

The City campaign was more intensive than in any other part of the State, as its political unit organization had been established longer and therefore worked more smoothly. There were barbers' days, days for firemen, street cleaners, bankers, brokers, business men, clergymen, street car men, factory workers, students, restaurant and railroad workers, ticket sellers and choppers, lawyers, ditch diggers and longshoremen. No voter escaped. Each one of these days had its own literature and attractions and called forth columns of comment in the newspapers. Evening demonstrations took place daily and brought interested and thoughtful crowds. There was a bonfire on the highest hill in each Borough, with balloons flying, music, speeches, and tableaux illustrating women's progress from the primitive campfire to the council of State. Torchlight processions were formed upon twenty-eight evenings with Chinese lanterns, balloons, banners and decorations in yellow and ending in a street rally at some important point in the City. There were street dances on the lower East Side, in honor of political leaders; there were Irish, Syrian, Italian, Polish rallies; there were outdoor concerts, a series of small ones culminating in a big one given in Madison Square Park where a full orchestra played, opera singers sang and many distinguished orators spoke on a platform erected for the purpose. There were open air religious services on Sunday evenings, with the moral and religious aspect of suffrage discussed; there was a fête in beautiful Dyckman Glen; there were flying squadrons of speakers from the Battery to the Bronx; there was an Interstate Rally where the suffragists of Massachusetts, New Jersey and New York met publicly in picturesque formation; there was the New York to San Francisco trip of the dancer Joan Sawyer to whom a letter was given at Times Square from Eastern suffragists for Western suffragists. Bottles containing suffrage messages were consigned to the waves from boats and wharves with appropriate speeches. Sandwich girls advertised meetings and sold papers. Sixty playhouses had theatre nights, many with speeches between the acts. There were innumerable movie nights with speeches and suffrage slides; "flying canvass wedges," "hikes" and automobile tours. The entire State was stirred by the activities. Many things easy to do won widest publicity, as when college women in cap and gown visited naturalization courts where hordes of ignorant men, anxious to escape conscription in Europe where the great war was now raging, were being speedily manufactured into American citizens and voters. There were other things that helped the agitation which had no publicity value, such as traveling libraries and the correspondence classes of the Equal Franchise Society. There were German and French Committees, and Committees to work with the Protestant and Catholic Churches.

"What rot!" said some. "What ingenuity!" said others. "Surely the women have gone stark mad," said others.

A woman physician who had been chief of a hospital in India for thirty years returned home to Great Britain to find English women in the turmoil of campaign for the vote. She joined one of the great London processions and as she marched past the sidewalks lined with curious thousands, she cried, "What fools men are!"—"What do you mean?" asked her fellow marcher. "Why, to make us do all these ridiculous things to get that which rightfully belongs to us."

Just so New York women were deliberately doing the ridiculous thing in order to challenge men's attention and so make men think. The campaign of 1915 thus kept itself before the public on the plane of the public every hour of every day.

Suffragists themselves were passing through an unforgettable experience. To this day they close their eyes and hear again the thrill of martial bugles, the tread of marching thousands, and see the air once more ablaze with the banners of those spectacular years. Just before election day a great procession possessed Fifth Avenue, the entire suffrage forces of the State uniting in it. Every Assembly District in the State sent its women. Twenty-five bands made music for thirty thousand marching men and women. The streets and windows of the buildings on both sides were filled with lookers-on and there were more tears than jeers in that contemplation. In the Union League Club a group of the great men in City affairs somewhat cynically watched the procession. A break caused a lull in the interest, then another band marched forward and behind it came five thousand of the public school teachers of the city. They were soberly garbed in dark gowns with white hats and gloves. Their banners were blackboards and on them their mottoes and messages were penciled in chalk. They knew American history and they were telling it to the public. As the endless line moved on, one of the great men jumped to his feet and exclaimed, "My God, men, I never understood the menace of this woman suffrage campaign as I do now. Here is a hundred dollars to defeat it. Who will join me?"[101] And the dollars came plentifully, for the politically great find democracy troublesome.

The procession was to close with street meetings, but the end did not come until long past the time set. Henry Allen, afterwards Governor of Kansas, had come to New York to make a few suffrage speeches for the campaign. He had made one, but it had not satisfied him nor his audience. He sat on a hotel balcony through the hours of the passing of the procession, waiting to join in the street meetings which were scheduled to follow. The next morning he came into the suffrage headquarters and with big, honest tears in his eyes, exclaimed: "I came to help in a campaign, but this is not a campaign, it is a crusade. I understand now." That day in a "Marathon speech" beginning at 10 a.m. and closing at 10 p.m., he spoke continuously all day with only intervals enough to rest his voice. And they were speeches which gripped the heart and compelled understanding.

No political party had endorsed the amendment, but in New York women could serve as watchers at the polls, because a special law to that effect had been passed. It was estimated that 2,500 women had held official positions in the organization of the Empire State Campaign Committee, that two hundred thousand women had aided the campaign, and on election day 6,330 women served as watchers or workers at the polls, some serving from 5 a.m. until midnight. The total cost of the campaign was about ninety-five thousand dollars.

Headquarters filled with anxious men and women on election night. A few of the younger workers wept as adverse returns kept coming in, but the older heads counseled, "Don't give up. Forward march," and when at midnight it was certain that the amendment was lost a group of young State and City women went forth to a public square, where suffrage rallies had been a familiar sight, called together the late street crowd, homeward bound from theatres, announced the result and declared that gathering the first meeting of the *new* campaign.

On Friday night, three days later, an overflowing meeting was held in Cooper Union where one hundred thousand dollars was pledged for the new campaign. Every campaign district in the State offered its quota and no note of surrender was heard.

The New York amendment of 1915 was lost by a majority of 194,984. The yes vote was 553,348. The no vote was 748,332.

In that year of 1915 there were three other campaigns in the neighboring States of Massachusetts, New Jersey and Pennsylvania. The opposition centered upon New Jersey, where the vote came on registration day, October 19th. James R. Nugent, Democratic boss and reputed the ablest political maneuverer in the State, led the opposition. The Democratic machine and the liquor interests worked openly against the amendment. President Wilson came home to vote for suffrage in Princeton, and the higher class of men of both parties espoused suffrage. Anti-suffrage "ladies" campaigned against it, decrying government by the ignorant; and on election day, drunken rowdies and saloon henchmen marched up to the polls in solid phalanx to do what those ladies wanted done. Hundreds of men who came to register were allowed to vote at once on the amendment. In one single district over five hundred names of men who attempted to register but were refused cast their votes against the amendment and those votes were not thrown out. "How could this happen?" the political novice may ask. The answer is: it happens. The amendment was lost by a majority of 51,108, there being 133,282 yes votes, and 184,390 no votes.

When two days later, the great New York suffrage parade closed the New York suffrage campaign, a doughty section of New Jersey women was a conspicuous feature in it. With heads erect and firm step they marched forward, their banners flying such mottoes as "We're still fighting," "No surrender," "Victory merely postponed," "Defrauded but not defeated."

The Pennsylvania campaign had the most effective single publicity feature of any of the campaigns. A replica of the Independence Bell was carried on a motor truck throughout the State and attracted great crowds to hear the accompanying suffrage speakers. While Independence Hall and the Independence Bell are American,

Pennsylvanians hold them in particular reverence and more closely their own. The Pennsylvania vote was proportionately the largest polled in any of the four States, 385,348 for and 441,034 against.

Massachusetts had been a lively suffrage center from the early days and had probably given more money to Western campaigns than any other State, but it was also the center of that form of conservatism which created the woman's anti-suffrage movement. The Republican party had been in continuous power in the State and its organization had been unmoved by the suffrage appeal. The amendment received 162,615 ayes and 295,702 nays, barely 35.5 per cent of the total vote, whereas New Jersey had polled for suffrage 42 per cent, New York 42½. per cent, and Pennsylvania 46 per cent of the total vote on the suffrage question.

Massachusetts suffragists considered that another campaign would be futile, and the admirable advantage and fine spirit of the New Jersey and Pennsylvania suffragists were blocked by provisions in their State constitutions which precluded the resubmission of a defeated amendment until the lapse of five years. At the national suffrage headquarters the responsible representatives of the four campaigns met a few days after the election to discuss the causes of failure and how to overcome them. Separate ballots used in New York and Massachusetts and the acceptance of votes of men whose registration was refused in New Jersey had given advantage to corrupt agencies which had unquestionably used them to the full. The fact that the Pennsylvania amendment had been printed on the main ballot, where corruptionists had no means of checking the results of mobilized voters, might easily explain its higher per cent. The New York workers, already projecting their second campaign, contended that the Pennsylvania campaign had not gone far enough to awaken the full opposition, and that the New York campaign had gone far enough to do that but not far enough to overcome opposition. With that view, they proceeded towards the next campaign.

The four amendments of 1915 had, altogether, polled 1,234,593 votes for suffrage. That million and a quarter of favorable votes insured from the nation a vastly increased consideration of the cause. The New York Legislature of 1916 voted to resubmit the amendment, the Assembly by a majority of 79, the Senate by a majority of 23. The opposition to resubmission had so far disappeared before the Legislature of 1917 met that the Assembly passed it the second time by a vote of 117 ayes, 10 nays; the Senate, 39 ayes, 7 nays. The last vote was taken in March, 1917.

In April, the nation entered the great World War. The New York State Woman Suffrage Party, following the National Suffrage Association, offered its organization for war service, the State organization to the Governor of the State and the City to the Mayor. War Service Committees were promptly organized. These committees served as registrars in the Governor's Military Census, enrolled volunteered women for all sorts of war work, sold bonds in each Liberty Loan and Thrift Stamp Campaign, and raised money in all the numerous drives for funds for foreign or home relief or helps to the soldiers. "Knitting teams" supplied thousands of woolen garments for the Red Cross. There were war gardens to produce food, canning demonstrations to preserve food, and the distribution of food pledge cards designed to economize food. A recreation hut at Plattsburg for white soldiers and one at Yaphank for colored troops was maintained and money was raised for the Oversea hospitals that had been organized and were being maintained by the National Suffrage Association.

But the suffragists of 1917 had read history; they knew how prone men were to accept the help of suffragists in the hour of need and forget women's case for suffrage in the hour of calm. So while working loyally and energetically as special war organizations in support of the needs of the nation in its time of crisis, the New

Yorkers did not lay aside their campaign. In the 1915 campaign one of the stock insistences of the indifferent and opposed had been "New York women do not want to vote." To meet it the Empire State Campaign Committee had dared claim "A million New York women want to vote." The claim had been laughed at and pooh-poohed but it had had enough vitality to pass into campaign history in the form of a slogan. But, unsupported, the claim was not conclusive. Even in 1915 the need of supplying incontrovertible evidence had been encountered on every hand, and the close of the campaign had found a plan of proof well-matured. This plan, covering no less an undertaking than the assembling of the personal signatures of the million women of the State who wanted to vote, was the heavy heritage of the workers of the 1917 campaign. With dogged endurance, they canvassed door to door in an effort to secure the signatures of women to a petition to voters to vote for suffrage on election day. They climbed stairs, descended into cellars, found their way into the homes of the rich and the incredibly poor, walked country lanes, left no section untouched. In the result they piled up the largest individually signed petition ever collected, 1,030,000 names, all of New York State women appealing to men for the vote.

Next in order was the problem of how to make the public realize the enormous force of that petition. In the City a ceremony was arranged and the Mayor and other prominent officials came to the City Headquarters to verify the numbers. Then all the petitions went to Albany to allow the Governor and State officials to verify them. "Press parties" in New York and Albany gave opportunity to newspaper correspondents and the Associated Press to verify them. At the State Headquarters the petitions were pasted upon huge pasteboards and the general public allowed to inspect them. In the great procession that closed the suffrage campaign the chief feature was the display of these petitions. Each of the placards was borne by two women, marching four abreast in a special section, with banners giving the totals in all the "up state" districts. The City section displayed its petitions in sixty-three ballot boxes, one for each Assembly District, resting upon a decorated platform, and each borne by four women. The "Procession of the Petitions" alone covered more than half a mile and was the most conspicuous feature of those thousands who went marching by to the music of forty bands.

Meanwhile ten million leaflets were distributed, schools for training women watchers were conducted and ten thousand watchers and poll workers were enrolled. Hundreds of newspapers were served with daily news, including twenty-four foreign language papers. The voters were circularized. Friendly windows were filled with posters, silent speeches and printed appeals; and, as a climax, advertisements announcing the number of women petitioners for the vote and carrying various appeals to the voters were placed in the leading newspapers of the State. Huge billboards advertising suffrage lined the railroads, and street cars and electric signs in the cities emphasized the women's appeal.

Meanwhile the women antis were busy and working hard. In the subway stations they put up advertising billboards carrying false and misleading statements. The suffragists wishing to answer them, asked for space of the advertising company in control of the advertising privileges of the stations. No space could be begged or bought. The company was advocating the other side. The election was coming in a few days and every available woman was already engaged in campaign work, yet from a hasty conference emerged a plan and the necessary pledges of service. The answers to the offending billboards were printed upon small posters, together with the statement that advertising space had been denied the suffragists. Women, turning themselves into living billboards, and calling themselves the lapboard brigade, paid their fares and rode up and down the subway lines all day long, carrying the posters.

Every day millions of passengers looked upon the fashionably gowned society women who performed the mission, and read the lapboard messages with astonished enlightenment.

A few days before election, the Executive Committee of Tammany Hall met. There were members there whose wives were now suffrage Captains and Assembly District Leaders, for the Woman Suffrage Party had carried its organization from palace to tenement, from schoolhouse to church. These men pleaded with the directors of the great political machine to give the amendment a chance, and it was finally voted to keep "hands off" in the election. Orders to this effect were passed to Tammany Leaders and Captains, and the good news found its way by the "grape vine" route to the City Chairman of the Woman Suffrage Party.

The Up-State Republicans were divided. Governor Whitman, seeking re-election, was opposed by the "regular" organization and had been forced to form an organization of his own. This he urged to use its best offices for the suffrage amendment, and this word, too, passed down the lines, but in the camp of the "regulars" the same old instructions were given.

Outside the City the amendment was lost by 1,510 votes, but in the City it carried by 103,863 majority, so that the Tammany "hands off" injunction won the State by a majority of 102,353. Up-State Republican regulars peevishly chide the Tammany leaders for this traitorous act with a, "Why didn't you tell us you were going to let it through?"

The women antis and their allies immediately published the charge that the State had been won by German, pro-German, pacifist and Socialist votes, each class being at that time anathema. The charges set the suffragists and the press upon the task of analyzing the vote. It was found that the strongly Republican and Democratic districts had polled a larger suffrage vote proportionately than the German and Socialist Districts, and that the uptown residence sections of the city had exceeded the radical downtown districts in approving the amendment.

In truth all parties, races, nationalities and religions supported the amendment. The intensive campaign which had carried the appeal direct to every man and woman, black and white, educated and ignorant, and to each in the language of his nationality, with the supplementary campaign of reminder through the press and in hundreds of spectacular ways, had won the day. Every suffragist who had worked throughout the campaign was convinced that the intensive plan of organization which covered and took cognizance of every block and emphasized in every procession and banner, press interview or advertisement, the political character of the organization was the great factor which had won the victory.

In the City, the cradle of the Party, suffrage work had never paused from October, 1909, to November, 1917. Thousands of women had come into the campaign and gone out again, too tired to continue, but there were hundreds who worked every day for the eight years as hard as men work in a campaign for a few weeks to find themselves exhausted at the end. Ten thousand women, all trained in watcher's schools, worked at the polls. This ceaseless insistence had been supplemented by the liberal spirit of a war period and the daily account of the crucial service women were rendering overseas. Then, too, the backbone of the liquor opposition had been broken by the winning of the federal prohibition campaign.

Political leaders pronounced the suffrage victory in the Empire State a political miracle. The bosses from ocean to ocean "listened in," and recognized that the coming of woman suffrage could no longer be postponed. Supplementing the great New York victory had come other victories. The delegates to the Atlantic City suffrage convention who went home to put through that program of getting presidential suffrage in every available State had been indeed putting it through. During the year 1917 the Legislatures of five States,—Ohio, Indiana, Rhode Island, Nebraska and Michigan—had given women the right to vote for the President of the United States, and Arkansas had given them the right to vote in the primaries—which in Arkansas, a one-party State, had all the force of voting at the elections. The number of presidential electors for whom women were entitled to vote had been increased over 150 per cent by legislative grant in the twelve months. Instead of ninety-one it was now 232. The mandate from the country to Congress, which earlier suffragists had sought from the States, had been given and the way was opened, after forty years of "wandering in the wilderness" as Miss Anthony had called it, for the submission of the Federal Suffrage Amendment.

CHAPTER 20

More Victories and More Defeats

As a consequence of the adoption of suffrage resolutions by the two major political parties in the conventions of 1916, friends of the suffrage cause in many State Legislatures proposed amendments to State constitutions providing for the enfranchisement of women by referenda. In some States these resolutions passed one house only, but from 1916 to 1919 there were submissions in seven States besides New York: West Virginia, Maine, Michigan, Oklahoma, South Dakota, Louisiana and Texas.

It so happened that in West Virginia, when the campaign opened in 1916, the same woman was president of the State Woman's Christian Temperance Union and the Suffrage Association, a connection never made before in the life of the two organizations. There was some rejoicing in the ranks of the Woman's Christian Temperance Union that the leadership of the campaign had fallen to one of their number who could thus command the aid of their organization and through it reach the churches in behalf of suffrage. So many State suffrage campaigns had been lost that it was natural that the Woman's Christian Temperance Union should have come to distrust somewhat the ability of the suffragists to conduct winning campaigns.

Ever since 1882 the Woman's Christian Temperance Union had had a Franchise Department which aimed to educate its following to a belief in woman suffrage. Addresses made by Woman's Christian Temperance Union speakers, presenting the faith that "the ballot in the hands of women would destroy the rum traffic," contributed much to the fears of the wet interests. Woman's Christian Temperance Union women believed that the church vote, which was the main support of prohibition, would follow their lead in suffrage campaigns. Yet often when they had desired to initiate suffrage campaigns on their own account these same women had magnanimously given way to the suffrage organizations whose sole object was to secure the enfranchisement of women.

The West Virginia campaign became, then, the Woman's Christian Temperance Union's suffrage opportunity. The State had had a Prohibition campaign the year before and the question had carried by a majority of one hundred thousand. The wets were infuriated by the Prohibition victory and especially incensed by the stringency of the enforcement law, and they determined at any cost to defeat the suffrage amendment. They did defeat it, too, by a majority of 98,067, nearly as large as the majority the year before for Prohibition.

Yet the campaign was a good one. Not one recognized means of campaigning was overlooked and several features were remarkably well done. A "flying squadron" of prominent men and women speakers was sent to thirty points in the State; an ex-Governor, Judges and members of the State Legislature were among the speakers. Twenty organizers were in the field; the voters were thoroughly circularized with general literature, and two hundred thousand congressional speeches on suffrage were mailed them. There was advertising in all of the rural newspapers.

At both Democratic and Republican State Conventions there were evidences of the attempts of the wets to organize the opposition. Resolutions passed, endorsing the amendment, were ineffective because of this wet control. To this opposition were added the many church drys who still adhered to ideas of woman's sphere outworn in Northern States. Moreover, no State campaign ever quite so completely rallied the "drunks" and the "ne'er do weels" of all kinds on election day as did West Virginia's. The vote was ayes, 63,540; nays, 161,607.

While the campaign for votes for women was going on in New York, another was in progress in Maine. Here the suffrage strength was limited to small groups in a few of the large cities. However, the Woman's Christian Temperance Union had been for many years a thoroughly well-organized and highly influential body. Their members were chagrined at the failure in West Virginia and welcomed the opportunity of another trial of their forces. An officer and prominent worker in their organization acted as chairman of the campaign committee. The campaign was a short one, lasting only five months and closing with the election in September, 1917.

The argument for suffrage was never put before the voters of any State more thoroughly. They were circularized with a suffrage speech made in the United States Senate by William Shafroth, and again with "Have You Heard the News?" which carried the latest statement of the suffrage gains the world around. The same envelope, which was mailed to each voter of the State, carried a printed petition over the signatures of the women of the county in which he resided. In these petitions there was better proof than any State had yet given that the women wanted the vote. House-to-house distribution of fliers was made in several communities. A million and a half leaflets were distributed—ten to every voter in the State. The clergy were circularized three times, the State Grange, the committees of the political parties and members of the Legislature, twice. About five hundred meetings were held. An ex-chairman of the Democratic State Central Committee talked and worked for suffrage. The President of the United States appealed to the Democrats by letter. The Republican Governor, a popular man, spoke for it.

Yet the amendment was defeated, nays 38,838; ayes, 20,604. The vote was one of the smallest in the State's history. One hundred thousand men who voted the year before did not go to the polls. Thirty-eight thousand women petitioned for the vote and only twenty thousand men answered, "Yes."

It was at least clear that men do not vote as "their wives tell them to" nor, put to the acid test of numbers, could the result be taken as "the voice of the people."

The campaigns of Colorado in 1893 and Idaho in 1896 cost $1,800 each, that of California in 1896, where all the large cities carried except San Francisco, Sacramento and Oakland, cost $18,000. The campaign in Maine cost the National Suffrage Association $15,268. What then was wrong with Maine? A worker in the campaign gave these reasons for defeat, "Natural conservatism, the picketing of the White House, the War, but of far greater influence the antagonism of the two political machines and the pronounced wet opposition, which was in evidence from the first."

No outsider would believe there was wet opposition in the supposedly dry State of Maine, but the truth was the brewers had never entirely given up Maine. In 1911, after several attempts, they secured a referendum on the question whether the Prohibition amendment should be resubmitted, the vote resulting in a majority against resubmission. Representatives of the brewers' association were sent to the State in 1915 to make a secret survey. Writing in February of that year to the President of the United Brewers' Association, Percy Andreae said: "The press of Maine has obtained knowledge of the investigation now proceeding. . . .

Fortunately our men have nearly completed their work but they have had to go back into the State under another guise."[102] In a report printed later these men stated that all of Maine was for prohibition but only a small part for enforcement.

In 1918 there were seven State suffrage campaigns, three of which were successful—South Dakota, Michigan, and Oklahoma—all conducted under the most difficult and distracting conditions. The handicaps of war and an influenza epidemic affected all States equally. As a preliminary to the campaigns the National Suffrage Association contributed suffrage schools to these States for the purpose of instructing the workers. Later it supplied eighteen organizers, press helps, one hundred thousand posters, 2,528,000 pieces of literature, eighteen street banners and fifty thousand buttons. One requirement for assistance from the National Suffrage Association was that each State should secure signatures of women on petitions for suffrage. The combined number obtained by the three States was 310,687. The cost of these campaigns to the National Suffrage Association was $30,720, in addition to expenses borne by the States.

In South Dakota, as in nine other States in 1918, the foreign-born could vote on their "first papers" and citizenship was not a qualification for the vote. Six prior campaigns for suffrage had been defeated, each time by a mobilization of this alien vote by American-born political manipulators. In 1918 the tables turned. The war had created a feeling of caution concerning voting privileges in the hands of the aliens, and South Dakota was aroused to make a change in its laws in this respect. The South Dakota women, smarting under the defeat of 1916, at which time their amendment had been last lost by the foreign vote, mainly of German-Russians in nine counties, saw their opportunity and urged a bill which would combine woman suffrage and the qualifications of citizenship for all voters.

Suffragists were willing to forego the opportunity offered because of the pressure of war work, but members of the Legislature said: "We look to the women to wage the best campaign they have ever waged." So the women went to work to such purpose that the suffrage majority was 19,286. The cost of the campaign was $7,500, the small cost being due to the absence of the organized opposition that usually entered a campaign State from the outside, this absence being due in turn to the alien clause in the amendment, a State official having pointed out early in the campaign that should outsiders attempt to come into the State to work against the amendment, they would be turned back on the grounds that they were unpatriotic, undemocratic, un-American.

The campaign in Michigan was unique because of its cooperative basis. The National Suffrage Association's State auxiliary had the assistance of both political parties and their representatives. Professional and business men formed themselves into a federation to give more effective aid. All three States acknowledged that the petitions of women to the voters were a determining factor in the victory. Michigan obtained 202,000 names on these petitions. One State suffragist said, and her letter was typical of many others: "We decided that our last shot should be the publication of fourteen thousand signatures of women who had asked the men in our town to vote 'Yes.' The names filled three newspapers and was the talk of the town." The amendment carried by a majority of 34,506, ayes—229,790; nays—195,284.

The Oklahoma campaign of 1918 was not the first in that State. The story of 1899 has already been sketched. In 1910 suffragists obtained forty thousand signatures on an initiative petition and forced the submission of the question to the voters. This was defeated at the polls that year, ayes—88,808; nays—128,928. In 1917 some members of the Board of the Suffrage Association of Oklahoma and the Legislative Committee of the Oklahoma State Federation of

Women's Clubs jointly secured the passage of a bill providing for a State referendum on woman suffrage in November, 1918.

Oklahoma is one of the States whose constitutions require a majority of the highest number of votes cast in the general election to carry an amendment. Every ballot cast in the election which fails to record an opinion on the amendment is termed a "silent vote" and is counted as a negative vote. It is a task to arouse the voter to such a degree of interest that he remembers to mark his ballot on amendments. Suffragists were pessimistic and said: "It can't be done." The severe heat of the summer and a third successive drought, with crop failure, made local handicaps many and difficult.

Both Democratic and Republican parties gave assistance, their State conventions passing strong resolutions for suffrage. During the campaign one and one-half million pieces of suffrage literature were distributed and during its last week 126,000 copies of a suffrage supplement went out through the newspapers of the State. The National Suffrage Association gave eleven organizers to the State and spent eighteen thousand dollars in the campaign.

The National Suffrage Association's representatives responsible for the campaign were able from the first to locate the center of opposition in Oklahoma. It lay in what was called the "Capitol Ring" and included the Governor, Robert L. Williams, the Lieutenant-Governor, Edw. Trapp, the Attorney General, S. P. Freeling, and the Secretary of the State Elections Board, who was also a Senator, W. C. McAlester. These four men had the reputation of holding in their hands the power to defeat any measure in the State. All of them openly opposed the amendment, but the first evidence of effective hostility was revealed in August, 1918, when it was generally alleged that the Secretary of the Elections Board had told the women antis from the North to go home, as the failure of the Secretary of State to supply the official wording of the suffrage amendment to the Elections Board ninety days before election would keep the question of woman suffrage off the ballot. An appeal was made to Judge Ledbetter of Oklahoma City who had become the legal adviser of the suffragists, and to Mr. Lyons, Secretary of State. To the persistent work of these two men was due the fact that this obstacle was finally removed, and the amendment was printed.

As it was necessary to obtain a majority of all the votes cast at the election, the suffragists desired the amendment to be on the regular ballot. If it were not there, the old tricks which had so often defeated suffrage amendments would probably be repeated. The Elections Board could do as it chose, and its members decided to use a separate ballot. A large part of the campaign was necessarily devoted to educating the electorate to the task of marking the separate ballot. The most successful device was the printing of a million red, white and blue leaflets showing a separate sample ballot with the amendment and the correct way to mark it, with a reminder that if a man forgot to vote he was recorded as voting "No."

The next bumper was the discovery that the Elections Board had printed only half as many suffrage ballots as regular ballots. To offset that local workers were informed they could legally have extra ballots printed at State expense wherever there was a shortage, and they were also urged to have sworn statements of any fraud detected sent to the suffrage headquarters.

On October 16, Oklahoma soldiers voted in seven camps, Bowie, McArthur, Logan, Travis, Cody, Norman and Dix, and presently it was discovered that suffrage amendment ballots had not been furnished for them. The evidence was collected as speedily as possible and turned over to Judge Ledbetter, and an appeal was made to Governor Williams, who finally agreed to see that suffrage ballots were sent to Ft. Sill where, too, the soldiers were to vote in a few days. Later he suggested that two representatives from the Campaign Suffrage Committee go, at State expense, to the cantonments where elections had already been held and take the vote on the amendment, adding, "I must also send two from the Anti-Suffrage organization." He went so far as to give the representatives of the National Suffrage Association letters to the commanding officers at the camps. These letters read:

October 28, 1918.

From: The Governor of the State of Oklahoma.

To: The Commanding Officer of Camp Bowie, Ft. Worth, Texas.

Subject: Matter of soldiers voting on constitutional amendment.

1. It has been brought to my attention that in some of the Army Camps ballots were not furnished to the soldiers so that they had an opportunity to vote on the constitutional amendment relating to Woman Suffrage in Oklahoma. I see no objection where the soldiers were furnished with the proper forms for affidavit and ballot to separately cast their votes through the mails on this constitutional amendment. Where the soldiers desire to qualify for this purpose, by making the affidavit, I see no objection to the proper officers taking their affidavit for such purpose although they have heretofore voted for national, State or county offices. I suggest, however, that the soldier mail his ballot on the constitutional amendment to the same person to whom he mailed his vote to be cast for him in his home precinct for national, State or county officers.

In order that my meaning may be made clear, I see no objection to the soldier voting separately on the constitutional amendment and sending the same separately to the same person to whom the vote was sent on national, State or county officers to be cast. And I would be very glad to see this done so that every soldier should have an opportunity to vote on this constitutional amendment.

R. L. WILLIAMS.

This sounded well but it was now October 28 with the election scheduled for November 5. It was impossible for the suffragists to send workers to seven widely separated camps. Besides, they were suspicious of a trap. Warned by previous experiences, they had made an exhaustive study of the election law and they knew that the soldier was entitled to return only one sealed envelope. If he had already sent one containing his vote for State officials he could not legally send another with his vote on the suffrage amendment.

In the meantime, to prevent a repetition of what had happened in other camps, instructions had been given to the suffrage captain at Lawton, near Ft. Still, to prepare for the election. The Democrat sent by the Board of Elections arrived the night before the vote was to be taken. The suffragists were on the watch and at 11 p.m. they found he had no suffrage ballots. This possibility had been anticipated and met by the printing of four hundred ballots. The next morning at eight o'clock suffragists went to the tent where the voting was to take place. Neither voters nor officials appeared. There was a deluge of rain, the women tramped from one military post to the other, and at last discovered that the Democratic and Republican representatives were in a motor car taking the vote at the different regimental headquarters. A colonel, taking pity on the women, agreed to send the suffrage ballots to the various headquarters, and at 5 p.m., drenched and fatigued, the suffragists started for home.

But the soldiers did not get their ballots.

Signed statements to this effect were obtained from the representatives of both parties who had conducted the elections at the camps, and from the soldiers themselves, many of whom wrote home to suffrage mothers, to ask why they had not been allowed to vote on woman suffrage. The number of votes thus lost was estimated at 4,197, that being the number of soldiers in the camps who voted for State officials.

From the beginning those responsible for the campaign had emphasized the necessity of women at every precinct on election day to act both as watchers inside the polling booth and outside to remind the men that woman suffrage was to be voted on. When in any town one political party denied the women the privilege of watching, the National Suffrage Association's representatives made a point of securing appointments as regular watchers for the other party. When the list of watchers was completed, printed slips were sent them with spaces for name of County, Town, Number of Voting Precincts, and the For and Opposed, Blank, Void and Total Vote with space for Name of Chairman of Elections Board and name of Watcher with the statement, "I certify that the above is correct." Watchers were asked to telephone returns to Suffrage Headquarters as early as possible election night, but if for any reason the count was delayed the women were told to remain at their posts and mail the tally slips as soon as possible.

To this precaution the women of Oklahoma owe the fact that they were able to keep their vote after it had been won.

The work of the suffragists was so well done that although the polls did not close on election day until seven o'clock, returns from all precincts in Oklahoma City except three were in by nine o'clock and showed that thirty-nine of the fifty-one precincts had been carried for the amendment. Oklahoma County had been considered the most difficult in the State and it was predicted that the result in that county would indicate the returns from the State at large. By midnight returns were in from fifteen counties and all indicated majorities in favor. But workers were everywhere cautioned not to claim victory publicly, for if they did the familiar trick used in other States would undoubtedly be practiced. That is, returns' from districts under control of unscrupulous election officials would be held back until the favorable majorities had been reported and then an adverse vote would be piled up out of these delayed returns sufficient to overcome the favorable majorities.

The morning after election the *Daily Oklahoman* printed returns showing that twenty-three counties had been carried for suffrage. The State Elections board began to show signs of worry. Two days later the suffragists caused the publication of a statement by a member of the State Elections Board declaring that the Suffrage Amendment had carried in twenty-three counties. Local workers were instructed to procure at once the returns from a list of thirty-three counties.

Two members of the Elections Board frankly admitted that an effort was being made to count out the amendment and gave suffragists a list of counties where work to this end had been begun. Returns from certain counties were being held back. There were unaccountable discrepancies in the figures of the State Elections Board and those received by the suffragists. In 1916 Attorney-General S. P. Freeling had made a ruling, in the case of Murray vs. McGowan asking for a recount, "that the Elections Board could not go behind the returns certified to it by the County Elections Boards." It was clear that if the suffragists could secure the returns on their slips, signed by the Chairmen of the County Election Boards, and have them printed in as many city, county and local newspapers as possible, there would be less chance of the figures being changed at the Headquarters of the Elections Board. All day Saturday and Sunday women remained at the telephone, confirming and checking returns, and on Monday were ready with a report of sixty-three out of seventy-seven counties. Of these only six had lost, one by one vote, two by three and one by six.

During this time the suffragists were told that the Secretary of the State Elections Board had been asking officials in certain counties to open the sealed boxes and give returns from the stub books which would include all mutilated and spoiled ballots. This would have been to repeat old election history in Oklahoma. After the Oklahoma election of 1916 just such fraudulent procedures had been charged and, in the opinion of many, proved. It made the watching suffragists tremble to consider the possibilities but, trembling, they stayed steadfastly on guard at their posts.

Meantime the State was greatly aroused. Many men who had winked at election fraud in the old days now assured the suffragists that they wanted the women to get a "square deal." A campaign of letters, telegrams and telephones to the Governor was begun and he, as well as the Chairman of the Elections Board, was informed that the suffragists held affidavits of attempts at fraud. The Governor was a candidate for a federal judgeship and when prominent men over the State telephoned him and Congressmen from Washington wired him to know what the Elections Board was trying to do, it was plainly seen that he wished he were out of it.

On Thursday, November 14, the *Daily Oklahoman* printed a statement that the Governor and the members of the State Elections Board admitted that the returns showed that the suffrage amendment had carried. But the joy of the suffragists was short-lived. The Governor and the Elections Board had made the statement to relieve themselves of public criticism, but at the instigation of Attorney-General Freeling a protest against certification by the Elections Board was entered. This was signed by the officers of the Oklahoma Association Opposed to Woman Suffrage and members of the Advisory Board. These officers were Mrs. T. H. Sturgeon of Oklahoma City, President; Miss Alice Robertson of Muskogee, Vice-President;[103] and Mrs. Eugene Lorton of Tulsa, Secretary. There was little public sympathy for this eleventh-hour effort of the antis to block the amendment. Most people believed the measure had carried and all believed that the antis were attempting to base hopes for defeat of the amendment upon slim technicalities. The newspapers very generally condemned the protest and pronounced it flimsy. It was based on the fact that the returns from counties had not separated the soldier from the civilian vote. The totals included both votes and separation could have no bearing on results. The aim was to increase the "silent vote." The well-laid plans of the opposition to count out the soldiers had not brought a sufficient number to defeat the amendment.

After much dallying Governor Williams called for the election returns and, without certification by the Elections Board, proclaimed on December 3 that woman suffrage had carried. At the time it was agreed by the attorneys representing both sides, in a formal hearing before the Governor, that the actual filing of the document should be withheld for three days in order to give the anti-suffrage attorneys an opportunity to institute proceedings against the Secretary of State, or through some other avenue of attack. They stated at that time that the validity of the adoption of the amendment would be contested.

The three days expired December 6, and no notice having been served in injunction proceedings, the document was made a matter of record. Thus was carried and recorded the second amendment to the State constitution of Oklahoma. The vote was ayes 106,909, nays 81,481. The majority on the amendment was 25,428; the majority of the amendment on all votes cast at the election was 9,791. The tricksters had been defeated.

While this campaign was going on in Oklahoma another was in progress in Louisiana, the first referendum on Woman Suffrage in the South. It had the support of Governor Pleasant, who in his message to the Legislature had urged the great importance of the South's realizing the danger from the proposed submission of the Federal Woman Suffrage Amendment. A bitter three-cornered Senatorial fight being under way, the women were asked to postpone their activities until after the September primaries, which they did. Full preparations for a "whirlwind campaign" for October had been made when an influenza epidemic broke out and the people were not allowed to assemble in any section of the State. A deluge of rain and the consequent impassable condition of the roads prevented any work in outlying districts. Thus there could be little campaign of personal appeal to the voters. Notwithstanding these adverse conditions, the majority against the amendment was only 3,500, nearly all of it in New Orleans. In that city Mayor Martin Behrman, through the ward "bosses" of a well-controlled machine, issued direct orders for defeat. Many parishes gave reports of precincts not opened at all on account of the epidemic and the weather.

The last referendum in any State on woman suffrage before the ratification of the Federal Woman Suffrage Amendment came in Texas on May 24, 1919. The Texas Legislature had already given women primary suffrage. The vote was taken on enfranchising women and requiring full citizenship as a qualification for the vote. There were only three months in which to reach the voters in 253 counties, and partially naturalized aliens were to be allowed to vote on the question while soldiers and women were to be debarred.

Four hundred woman suffrage leaders and 1,405 speakers were the medium through which three million fliers and two hundred thousand copies of *Texas Democrats,* edited and managed for this occasion by Dr. A. Caswell Ellis, of the faculty of the University of Texas, reached the voters. The press, both rural and urban, gave magnificent support. More than ninety small papers issued a four-page suffrage supplement, while some of the most noteworthy editorials ever appearing in the pages of the big dailies were written in behalf of woman suffrage.

On the other hand every nook and corner of the State was flooded with anti-literature, much of it mailed from Selma, Alabama. This literature was of such a vilely insinuating character that the day it was put upon their desks the Representatives put aside all other business and passed a resolution, with only five dissenting votes, condemning its circulation.

Despite the fact that press, pulpit, educators, professional and laboring men and the organized Democrats of the State and nation stood behind the amendment, it failed by twenty-five thousand votes. The impeached ex-Governor, James E. Ferguson, who was at war with all stable influences in the State, was alleged to have been one of the chief manipulators of this vote. After the defeat in May he said in a public statement that he never felt better in his life. "My crops are fine, my cattle are fat and my crowd beat woman suffrage."

Thus eight State referenda in two and a half years foot up four victories and four defeats. The total number of fully enfranchised women was now over seven and a quarter million in fifteen States. And so successful had been the work for presidential suffrage that these seven and a quarter million full-fledged voting women were flanked by eight million more who could vote for President in twelve other States—thirteen, if Vermont, where the legislative grant of Presidential suffrage was in question, be included. Moreover, Texas, another one-party State, had followed the lead of Arkansas and granted primary suffrage to women. All told, the number of electoral votes affected by the fact of woman suffrage was 326, out of the total electoral college of 531. It meant the end of State referenda. No more educating the public to believe that the vote would not in some mysterious way throttle women's maternal instincts, no more climbing to topmost tenements and descending to bottom-most basements to plead with illiterates and foreign-born. The day of triumph of the Federal Suffrage Amendment was at hand.

CHAPTER 21

The Congress of
the United States Surrenders

It is doubtful if any group—men or women—who ever kept ward and watch over legislation at Washington ever came to know the true inwardness of the Congress of the United States as suffragists came to know it. For one thing, the suffrage vigil was so long maintained. For another, it engaged the energies of so many different women with so many different points of view from so many different parts of the country, all flashing in their reflections of the congressional body like so many mirrors held up to nature, man's nature, at every conceivable angle. Toward the end of the vigil they were coming and going from the headquarters of the National American Woman Suffrage Association at Washington from every State in the Union, in relays of dozens, of fifties, of hundreds. They constituted the largest lobby ever maintained at the national capital, the "Front Door Lobby" as the press called it, in tribute to its above-board methods and policy.

They learned Congress through and through, those women. Its way of work, its machinery; its tricks; the men in it, their pet foibles, their fundamental weaknesses, their finer abilities, their human quality. Quietly sitting in the galleries of House or Senate, listening to floor speeches, or watching floor tactics, they learned. They learned talking across desks, in animated discussion with those same men in private Senatorial and House offices. Pleading at public hearings, before committees of House or Senate, they learned.

They learned the cheap bi-partisanship that dominates the Congress; its insensate capacity to block justice for party advantage. They learned that the State's rights cry of the Southern Congressman voiced a great principle—to be used as expediency dictated, now hushed into self-righteous acquiescence in federal control of the liquor question, now raised in uproar against federal interference in the suffrage question. They learned that Massachusetts Republicans could find it in their hearts to be stern State's righters when it came to the point of defeating suffrage, though determined federalists on all other scores. They learned that, as in the State Legislatures, so in the federal Congress, there was the imprint of something dark and sinister, something that suggested and interfered and often controlled—the old trail and the old invisible enemy.

And, finally, they learned that here and there in the Congress were men who stood up like mountain peaks, as unswerving in their devotion to the principle of self-government as they were intelligent in their understanding of it. It was on these men that suffragists banked their hopes as they went forward with their final program to secure the submission of the Federal Suffrage Amendment, a program that, after January, 1917, had to be shaped at every step by the impending exigencies of war.

Early in 1917 the National American Woman Suffrage Association called its Executive Council to meet in Washington prior to the opening of the Special War Session of the Congress scheduled for April of that year. By its authority, at a great theatre meeting packed to the doors, it pledged the loyalty of its organization to the country in the event of war and offered its services at command. The offer was received in person by the Secretary of War.

The Association, keenly alive to the fact that idealism was aroused by the crisis of war, urged its constituency to unite at once in a stupendous appeal to Congress for the immediate submission of the amendment. The appeal followed. Letters, telegrams and petitions poured in on the Congress by hundreds and thousands. Men were talking in that day and hour of democracy, of liberty and justice, as they had talked after the Civil War, yet in the light of past experience suffragists had little faith in any real change in the reactionaryism of Congress. So little faith that in a conference on the congressional campaign a resolution was adopted to the effect that if the Sixty-fifth Congress should fail to submit the Federal Suffrage Amendment before the next congressional election, the suffrage association should select a sufficient number of Senators and Representatives for replacement to insure passage by the Sixty-sixth Congress.

In the War Congress five Senators introduced the suffrage resolution in the Senate and six members in the House, one being Miss Jeannette Rankin of Montana, the first woman member of Congress. Hearings followed in quick order. The Senate Committee, for the first time, voted unanimously to recommend its passage.

In the House an incredible amount of work had been put into an attempt to secure a suffrage committee, the Judiciary Committee systematically opposing and blocking its consideration. But on September 24, 1917, the House voted itself a suffrage committee, by a vote of 180 to 107, with three answering present and 142 not voting. It had taken four years of ceaseless agitation to secure this result. Of the favorable votes eighty-two were Democratic, ninety-six Republican; of the unfavorable, seventy-four were Democratic and thirty-two Republican. Of those not voting fifty-nine were Democratic and eighty-one were Republican.

In November came the decisive suffrage victory in New York. Forthwith up and down and across the nation resistance began to crumple. Inevitably the effect reacted upon Congress.

In December the National American Woman Suffrage Association held its annual convention in Washington. During this convention each senior Senator was asked to invite the junior Senator and the House membership of his State to his office on a fixed morning and to allow the suffrage delegation from home to address them. Thirty such get-together meetings were held, congressional delegations from the smaller States combining to receive their suffrage delegates. In the afternoon the suffrage delegates met again in convention, and the roll of States was called, the president of each responding with a brief account of the morning's experience. A thrill of approaching triumph possessed the big convention when, to the call of Arkansas, the clear-cut tones of its president responded: "The Arkansas congressmen, with two exceptions, say they will be *pleased* to vote for the Federal Amendment!" If the border States were coming in, all would be well. As the sense of that fact penetrated, a glad shout went up, which none present who did not know history would have understood. State after State followed, with such favorable reports of pledges that none could doubt the approach of victory. A speech in the form of an address to Congress was later made by the president of the National American Woman Suffrage Association at a great public meeting, and adopted by the convention, and a deputation of suffragists from each State handed a printed copy to their Senators and Representatives.

Yet the road to victory was not to be strewn with roses. The chairman of the Congressional Committee of the National Suffrage Association reported that the new Congress had brought three sharp surprises: (1) The discovery that, because there was likely to be a struggle over the Chairmanship of the new Committee on Woman Suffrage, many of the Democratic leaders were inclined to defer indefinitely the appointment of members of the Committee; (2) The announcement by Democratic leader Kitchin that the

Suffrage Amendment would be voted upon on December 17, a most unpropitious date, being the day before that assigned for the vote on the Prohibition Amendment; (3) the determination of Chairman Webb, of the Judiciary Committee, to have his Committee report the Suffrage Amendment. In spite of the fact that the Woman Suffrage Committee had been created late in the previous session for the specific purpose of dealing with the suffrage question, Mr. Webb held that his committee alone possessed the right to deal with constitutional amendments. To offset these plans of opposed members required work every day and all day and most of the night on the part of the Association's Congressional Committee.

But all the obstacles were finally overcome and the Woman Suffrage Committee was put in operation December 15, with Mr. Raker of California as Chairman. The Suffrage Amendment, being extricated from the vexatious contest over jurisdiction, was transferred to it from the Judiciary Committee, and the date for voting on the amendment was postponed to a more propitious date, to be set in the future.

The new Suffrage Committee, with energy before unknown, gave five entire days to suffrage hearings, and at last committee smiles, of old reserved for the antis, were turned toward the suffragists. The Rules Committee settled the date for the vote as January 10, 1918.

Fifty-three members of Congress were secured as a Steering Committee to organize the friends of the suffrage measure in the House. The month before the vote was tense with work and hope. A far-flung yet intensive publicity campaign drove the question of the Amendment into every nook and cranny of the nation. From home constituencies the pressure on Congressmen became tremendous, while on the ground, in Washington, suffrage representatives of those constituencies besieged Capitol and Senate and House office buildings. When the day of the vote, January 10, finally arrived capital and nation were awaiting the day's roll-call with taut interest. The moment the House galleries were opened suffragists and general public, packed for hours in the foyers, surged eagerly forward. Every available seat was occupied and remained occupied throughout a dramatic session that lasted until seven o'clock in the evening.

The suffrage question was labored and re-labored. Men rose to make interminable speeches on man's God-given right to tell woman what she must and must not do, sentimental speeches, speeches that put all womanhood to blush by the reflection of womanhood in some man's mind. They rose to speak with force and fire in an effort to make other men forsake old fashions of autocratic thought and feeling and espouse fundamental democracy. They rose to score a party advantage. They rose to points of order. They rose merely to get into the picture, the Congressional Record. The hours were packed with incident, with suspense. The intensity of suffragists had long ago communicated itself to many House members who by now were as strongly committed to the success of the measure as the heart of suffragist could wish. Down on the floor and out in the cloak-rooms tottered men so ill that they should have been in bed, but on hand at any hazard to vote for suffrage, Enthusiasm could not be repressed when the Republican leader, James R. Mann, of Illinois, walked feebly to his seat. Everybody knew that he had left a hospital in Baltimore to answer to the suffrage roll-call. Another man, who was in such pain from a broken shoulder that he wandered about cloak-rooms and corridors like a soul possessed, was in his seat on the Democratic side, just the same, when his name was called. This was the Southerner, Representative Sims, of Tennessee. Another sick man, Representative Barnhart, of Indiana, was brought in from a hospital bed to remain long enough to vote. Another who thrust aside illness to vote was Mr. Crosser, of Ohio. Still another case of suffrage loyalty that deeply moved the few who knew among the waiting women was that of Representative Hicks, of New York, who came from the death-bed of his wife to cast his vote, and returned home for the funeral.

Down the roll-call, name by name, droned the voice of the clerk. Yes—No—name by name, came the answering vote. It was close indeed. Of the 410 votes polled, 274 were aye and 136 were no, a two to one vote being necessary to carry. But it was enough. Just forty years after the introduction of the Amendment in Congress it had gone over the top with the required two-thirds.

The vote over, the corridors filled with women from the galleries, relaxed, smiling, happy women. On the way to the elevators a woman began to sing "Praise God, from whom all blessings flow," and the surging throng stood still to join in the expression of gratitude that was rising spontaneously from many hearts. From pillar to pillar the triumphal notes reverberated; they mounted to the dome of the old Capitol, a sound never heard there before; they floated out into the upper air. Many a member who had voted no was seen with hat pulled low over his eyes, listening as he hastened toward the exit— perhaps comprehending that on that day a new thing had come to the nation.

In that House vote was evident again the influence of the New York victory in 1917. Of the thirty-nine New York Representatives, there being four vacancies, 35 voted aye. Without New York the vote would have been lost and without the preceding victory in November the aye vote of New York would have been mainly a no vote.

One thing that the House debate did was to bring into sharp relief the competition by now existing between Republicans and Democrats for whatever credit and advantage should accrue from suffrage successes. A ludicrous but complicating instance of this was developed out of the National Suffrage Association's effort to express the gratitude of suffragists to Republicans and Democrats alike for help given. With punctilious care letters of appreciation were sent to all the sick men who had come to the Capitol at such sacrifice, and a statement was issued to the press covering a copy of the letters and mentioning by name the leaders of both parties, President Wilson, Colonel Roosevelt and others, who had notably helped the suffrage cause. Thereupon the Republican papers published the letter after carefully eliminating the Democratic names, and Democratic papers published it after eliminating the Republican names. Both Republicans and Democrats forthwith angrily charged the suffrage association with partisanship and a special call upon all the gentlemen mentioned had to be made, with suitable explanations. The non-partisan attitude of the suffrage association never varied but from this date forward there was continual difficulty in convincing partisans that it was not favoring their rivals.

By chance, on the date of the House vote the British constitutional suffragists won their full enfranchisement through the vote of the House of Lords, and cabled congratulations to their American sisters, with the suggestion that January 10 be made a holiday for both countries.

While the debate had been in progress in England, hundreds of women waiting in the corridors, because there was no place for them within, anxiously queried each passing policeman for news. Said one of these, "Lord Cromer's hup but ee won't do ye much 'arm." In the United States there is no House of Lords but the Senate is this nation's citadel of fixed opinion, and it was "hup," and all the efforts of the suffragists, massed now on it, failed to secure a vote. Women came from all parts of the country to plead with the Senators of their States—Southern women with petitions, and with evidence of the popular change of sentiment in that section. Nothing availed. President Wilson attempted to influence the situation. He was supported in his effort by a number of the most influential Southern newspapers. One of the publicity activities conducted for the National American Woman Suffrage Association was a department of editorial correspondence devoted to correcting the errors of editorial statements and opinion and to the conversion of newspaper editors to the Federal Suffrage Amendment. This work had borne fruit in the South as elsewhere. In September a deputation of Southern women called upon the President and urged his more active help, and he frankly promised it.

At this eleventh hour certain Democrats conceived the idea that another form of amendment might prove more acceptable to the Southern Senators and as many sheets of paper were wasted in the attempt to write one as Charles Sumner had used in his efforts to avoid the word male in the Fourteenth Amendment. Senator Williams, of Mississippi, on June 27, proposed to make the amendment read "the right of *white* citizens of the United States to vote, etc." Three others were proposed.

The Prohibition Amendment had been submitted December 17, 1917, and the spirit of fair play was beginning to arouse widespread resentment against the discrimination shown to the woman's amendment. Editorial writers and cartoonists put forth pungent comment worthy of the historical crisis. A national petition signed by the one thousand "best known men" in the United States, a list of imposing quality, was secured, which called forth a large number of editorials and, in printed form, was presented to Senators. The date for a vote was at last set for October 1, 1918.

As the day drew near the poll indicated that two more votes were needed and the National Suffrage Association appealed to the President. In laying the poll, 62 for to 34 against, before him, the appeal said: "You who have proved yourself a miracle worker on many occasions may be able to produce another on Monday, the miracle of putting vision where there was none before."

But the miracle was beyond the President's power to achieve, though he labored by day and by night with Southern Democrats, urging them by letter and by interview to give way. On September 30 he delivered in person his memorable message to the Senate urging its favorable action. In part he said:

"I had assumed that the Senate would concur in the amendment because no disputable principle is involved, but only a question of the method by which the suffrage is to be extended to women. There is and can be no party issue involved in it. Both of our great national parties are pledged, explicitly pledged, to equality of suffrage for the women of the country.

"Neither party, therefore, it seems to me, can justify hesitation as to the method of obtaining it, can rightfully hesitate to substitute federal initiative for State initiative, if the early adoption of this measure is necessary to the successful prosecution of the war and if the method of State action proposed in the party platforms of 1916 is impracticable, within any reasonable length of time, if practical at all.

"And its adoption is, in my judgment, clearly necessary to the successful prosecution of the war.

* * * * * * *

"They (the people of Europe) are looking to the great, powerful, famous democracy of the west to lead them to the new day for which they have so long waited; and they think, in their logical simplicity, that democracy means that women shall play their part in affairs alongside men and upon an equal footing with them.

"If we reject measures like this in ignorant defiance of what a new age has brought forth, of what they have seen but we have not, they will cease to believe in us.

"They have seen their own governments accept this interpretation of democracy—seen old governments like that of Great Britain, which did not profess to be democratic, promise readily and take action."

But October 1 dawned with the suffrage measure still short one vote. Responsibility for failure to get the extra vote needed was laid by each party upon the other. Friendly Republicans every day had passed the opinion to suffragists that "any President can get the votes necessary to put over a question if he wants to when it lacks so few. The fact is the President is not sincere." And every day friendly Democrats had expressed the conviction that the Republicans could get those needed votes if they wanted to. "Their party is not opposed to federal action. The truth is the Republicans do not want the Amendment to pass at all and certainly not while Democrats are in control of the Congress, because that would be almost sure to line up the new women voters as Democrats."

Those suffragists who knew just what the President was doing knew that he was not only sincere but using the full extent of his influence with his party. On the Republican side, William Wilcox, Chairman of the National Committee, went to Washington to urge the Republican minority to give way. The suffragists knew that Mr. Wilcox was sincere and that the pro-suffrage Republicans were sincere. They knew that the obstacle was a minority bloc led by the Senators of Massachusetts and South Carolina. They knew that on the Republican side the opposition would be over-ridden just as soon as the success of suffrage could accrue to the benefit of a Republican administration. They knew that on the Democratic side the minority was but using the Republican opposition to protect its own deep sectional bias on the woman question and the Negro question, ever looming behind the blind of the State's rights question.

When on October 1, 1918, after five days of debate, the vote was at last taken, the Amendment was defeated, as expected, by a vote of 62 to 34. So narrowed had the struggle become that the death of two favorable Senators, one in New Hampshire and one in New Jersey, and the appointment of anti-suffrage Senators to the vacancies created, caused the adverse vote. The Amendment would also have passed had two Republican Senators from suffrage States voted aye, one Senator Borah of Idaho, a suffragist and a Republican who clung to the State's rights method; the other Senator Wadsworth of New York, the husband of the president of the national association of anti-suffragists. Again, it might have carried if two northern Democrats, outside the State's rights area, had voted aye, Senator Hitchcock of Nebraska and Senator Pomerene of Ohio, but each of them represented a State wherein the controlling factor in politics, as has already been shown, was opposing woman suffrage to the bitter end.

The grim facts disclosed by the vote pointed the way inexorably to a disagreeable task. If there were not men enough in the Senate who could change their minds it had become the inescapable duty of suffragists to change the men. According to the announced agreement of the Executive Council in April, it was decided to conduct campaigns against four men in the coming autumn elections. Two were Republicans in Republican States, Senator Weeks of Massachusetts and Senator Moses of New Hampshire; one a Democrat in a Democratic State, Senator Saulsbury of Delaware, and one, Senator Baird, a Republican in the two-party State of New Jersey. The prospects were unpromising, as many other issues were involved in the campaign.

When a representative of the National American Woman Suffrage Association announced to an executive session of the Massachusetts Suffrage Association that the only hope for the Federal Suffrage Amendment lay in the defeat of Senator Weeks, the announcement was received with a gasp of dismay. "We can never do it," the women ejaculated; "he is the very heart of the Republican machine." But an Anti-Weeks Committee was formed and it laid before the voters his reactionary votes in the Senate. A Democrat replaced him.

When the women of Delaware were told in the same way that the Amendment depended upon the defeat of Senator Saulsbury, they exclaimed: "Impossible! he is the Democratic leader of the State and this is a Democratic State." But they began a campaign and were able to score heavily against him with the argument that he was a representative who wouldn't represent. Everybody knew that suffragists had made a town-to-town canvass in Delaware before the United States Senate vote in October to secure signatures to a petition to Senators Saulsbury and Wolcott asking their support for the Amendment, and knew, too, that 11,111 signatures had been obtained. And everybody knew, too, that though this petition was enormous for a State of three counties only, it had had no appreciable effect, for both Senators had voted no. Delawareans showed their resentment of this fact by voting to put Mr. Saulsbury's rival in at Washington.

In New Jersey Mr. Baird was re-elected with a much reduced majority, and in New Hampshire, where large Republican majorities are usual, Mr. Moses was elected with only 1,200 majority.

The success of the Amendment in the Sixty-sixth Senate was assured, provided death or disaster did not take away a friend, for there was not a vote to spare. But the suffragists decided to try for earlier action without waiting for the convening of the Sixty-sixth Congress. The chairman of the Suffrage Committee, Senator A. A. Jones of New Mexico, had changed his vote, on October 1, from yes to no, in order to move a reconsideration, so that the way was clear for another chance with the Sixty-fifth Congress, still in session. All the clearer because the large vote of women in the November elections had so impressed political leaders that it was hoped that two men in the Sixty-fifth might be in repentant mood and change their vote on reconsideration.

Many additional events had strengthened the suffrage position. In the elections of the year over forty thousand women in Arkansas and 386,000 women in Texas had voted in the primaries. This showing, surprising to the South, had been achieved despite the fact that the women of Arkansas had voluntarily paid a poll tax to gain the privilege and that the women of Texas had had but seventeen days in which to register. Ex-Governor Ferguson, who had presented the minority resolutions report in the 1916 National Democratic Convention, had been effectively disposed of at the Texas polls and the women's vote was credited with this result. In New York, where women went to the polls for the first time, the estimated number of women voters was one million, and the November press recorded a large vote of women in all States.

The 1918 elections had also brought three more States into the full suffrage list, Michigan, South Dakota and Oklahoma, the last a section of former slave territory. The Vermont Legislature had broken the record of New England's staid conservatism by extending the municipal vote to women in 1917; the Legislatures of North Dakota, Michigan, Nebraska and Rhode Island in 1917 had extended presidential suffrage to their women and in 1919 Indiana and Missouri had followed suit. The managers of political parties were finding a vexatious situation in the task put upon them of enlisting and organizing the new voters in these States while men and women were charging each party with responsibility for the failure to secure the vote for the women of all States.

Large honorary committees of prominent men, including many contributors and workers in party campaigns, had been organized and were compelling party leaders to sense the responsibility for delay. These leaders were nettled by the Senatorial impasse and far more actively interested than ever before. On February 11, 1918, the Democratic National Committee, and, on February 12, the Republican National Committee, had resolved for the passage of the Amendment. Through the spring and summer this action had been seconded by the action of many State party conventions and by the Congressional Committees of both parties. So the two National Party Chairmen and their immediate predecessors all went to Washington to labor with their respective minorities. At last the women heard the cracking of the party whip.

For their own part the suffragists were leaving no stone unturned in the search for the needed votes. Both the hopeful and the doubtful Senators were being bombarded with home petitions, letters and telegrams. Deputations of women and men called upon them. The daily telegrams, carefully listed on disconcertingly long sheets of paper, were laid by secretaries on their desks. Scrap books, in which were neatly pasted the favorable editorials from their State press, were handed them. Public opinion was vastly on the side of action by the Senate, so it seemed not too much to expect that at least two Senators would yield their obstinacy to the overwhelming public demand.

The details of one campaign to secure a Senatorial vote are worthy of record, since it was typical of many like efforts to lose woman suffrage in a thicket of conditions. When Senator Gallinger of New Hampshire died, an Amendment vote and a working friend were lost. The Republican Governor was urged by the National Republican Chairman to appoint a man to the vacancy who would vote for the amendment. The National and State suffragists supported this request by earnest and continued effort; while Senators Lodge and Weeks of Massachusetts made appeals for an appointee who would vote against suffrage— and were probably supported by those mysterious forces which had long controlled politics in New Hampshire. Mr. Drew was appointed ad interim and was polled in opposition. Mr. Moses had been elected at the next election and had voted against the Amendment on October 1.

Immediately after his election a Republican woman was sent to interview him. The campaign against him had not left him pleasantly disposed toward suffragists but he was made to understand that the women's opposition had been directed toward his suffrage attitude only. He promised the interviewer to support the Amendment should he be asked to do so by a resolution of his Legislature. As the New Hampshire Legislature would not convene before January, 1919, the National Suffrage Association proposed a still stronger mandate and sent three workers into the State, who with New Hampshire women made a canvass of the legislators in their own homes for signatures to a petition to Senator Moses. The Legislature is the largest in the United States (426 members) although the Senate is small. The signatures of two-thirds of the total membership were secured as petitioning Senator Moses to vote for the Federal Suffrage Amendment and a deputation of suffragists took the petition to Washington, emphasizing the fact that a resolution required only a majority vote, whereas the petition carried the names of two-thirds of the Legislature. Senator Moses made reply that the petition would not serve the purpose expected and that he would insist upon the resolution. The Legislature met the first week in January and a public hearing before both Houses was granted to suffragists, after which by a majority of seventy-four the House passed the resolution endorsing the passage of the Federal Suffrage Amendment. The Legislature then adjourned for the week-end.

A hasty poll was made by personal interview with the State Senators to make "assurance doubly sure," and found the majority standing firm for the resolution. Andrew J. Hook, a Senator who had not been interviewed when the petition to Senator Moses had been in circulation, now said he would vote for the resolution if the women could bring him a petition from a majority of the members of the Republican town committees in his district asking him to do so. There was but a single day in which to do this work and there were ten towns to be covered, but it was done. The petition was presented to Senator Hook on January 14 when the Legislature again convened. The resolution came up at once and was disposed of by a vote of 6 ayes and 15 nays! Mr. Hook voted No!

An explanation of the way his mind worked was later revealed. After stipulating that he must have a petition from his district, he had gone to the suffrage headquarters and had said that if the women could get twelve Senators to vote for the resolution he would make the thirteenth. The women replied that the majority was already pledged and that they were already at work upon the petition he requested. When Senator Moses received the news of the action taken by the House, he had hastened to Concord to confer with Senators, apparently to urge them to save him from his rash promise, and when the Legislature reconvened three of the most powerful lobbyists of the State were in Concord and at work against the resolution. Mr. Hook, learning that enough men had been induced to fall from the poll so that twelve men would not vote for the resolution, ignored his first proposal, never withdrawn, and fulfilled with all conditions by the suffragists, and remembered only the second. Thus may a politician emerge from under a broken pledge with honor intact!

A group of New Hampshire Senators explained to a representative of the Manchester *Union Leader* why they had broken their agreements, which they readily acknowledged they had done. They had agreed, they said, to vote for the petition *in the full belief that it would be killed in the House* where it was likely to come up first and therefore would never reach them. But, one Senator had added, "You can't depend on this House; it is liable to do most anything."

While this campaign was in progress a letter appeared in the New Hampshire press declaring that the National Republican Committee had no right to dictate to Senators how they should vote. It was signed by Senator Wadsworth of New York who had actively and continuously sought to prevent a favorable vote on suffrage by the federal House and Senate. On January 3, two days before his death, Colonel Roosevelt had written Senator Moses a letter in which he said: "I earnestly hope you will see your way clear to support the National Amendment. It is coming anyhow and it ought to come. When States like New York and Illinois adopt it, it can't be called a wild-cat experiment." Mr. Moses considered his opposed attitude justified by the failure of the New Hampshire Senate to concur in the House resolution, overlooking the discreditable process of securing that result.

Once again the suffragists asked the perennial and always unanswerable question, why do men repudiate ordinary principles of honor in United States politics when to do so in business and private life would make them outcasts from all contact with decent people? This New Hampshire experience is illustrative of American legislative history rather than the record of an exceptional case. "Slippery politicians" has become, in consequence of custom, a term of good usage in political vocabularies.

In the general result the November elections changed the control of the Congress from Democratic to Republican. Americans, with their habit of finding the solution of political and economic problems by oscillation between the two major parties and being hard pressed by the aftermath of war, had repudiated the Democratic party at the polls. So that while the Sixty-fifth Congress had been Democratic the Sixty-sixth was to be Republican.

The Democrats who were friendly to suffrage, realizing that the Republican Congress would submit the Suffrage Amendment and thus win the loyalty of unknown numbers of new voters, now made desperate attempts to pass the measure before the session should close and put an end to the Sixty-fifth Congress. Open and private letters to Senators were sent by members of the Democratic Cabinet. Several caucuses of friendly Democrats were held, to try some new approach to gain the needed two votes. There were similar conferences of friendly Republicans. On December 2, on the eve of his sailing for Europe for the Peace Conference, President Wilson addressed a joint session of the Congress and included in it another earnest appeal to pass the Federal Suffrage Amendment.

On December 8 the National Suffrage Association held a Woman War Workers mass meeting in Washington from which hundreds were turned away for lack of room and an overflow meeting was held. At both meetings resolutions urging the submission of the Amendment were adopted and a copy was presented to each Senator.

The date of February 10 was at last fixed for the vote on reconsideration—and the Amendment was lost by a single vote, the record standing 63 to 33. Not a Senator had changed. The gain of one vote had come through the appointment of William P. Pollock of South Carolina to a vacancy. He accepted the President's advice and not only voted for the Amendment but spoke for it, a fact which threw his State into an uproar of controversy in which abuse was more often heaped upon him than praise.

Twenty States cast all their votes in Senate and House in favor; and three, Alabama, Delaware and Georgia, all their votes in both Senate and House against the Amendment. Only three Senators west of the Mississippi River voted against, Borah of Idaho, Reed of Missouri and Hitchcock of Nebraska. Both Senators in nine States voted against the Amendment: Massachusetts, Connecticut, Pennsylvania, Delaware, Virginia, North Carolina, Florida, Georgia and Alabama.

New York suffragists felt keenly that the one lacking from their majority was their Senator Wadsworth. And what is a representative for if not to represent, they asked? And what constitutes a mandate from a constituency? By a majority of more than one hundred thousand the State had enfranchised its women in November, 1917; in the winter of 1918 the Legislature had called upon him by resolution to vote for the measure. In September, 1918, his party, meeting in State convention, had called upon him to vote for the Amendment, and he was himself a member of the Resolutions Committee which presented the resolution. This action had been taken at the request of a majority of the Republican County Conventions of the State. In 1918 the National Republican Committee by resolution had called upon him and other Senators to vote for the measure and in 1919 his Legislature had again called upon him to support the Amendment. Women knew of no stronger expression of public demand that could be made. Turning to history, they found no mandate so complete given to any Congressman at any time to persuade him to sacrifice his individual inclination to the public demand.

Following the vote, the *Woman Citizen,* in an editorial, entitled "They shall not pass," said: "Men come and men go, but a truth goes marching on. Not a banner will be furled, not a marcher will break step, not a friend will desert, not a political party will falter, not a newspaper will lapse into silence. All the way down the lines leading from Washington to New England, to the Solid South and to the Great West, those with ears to the ground will hear the tramp, tramp of millions of feet, responding to the call, Forward, Forward March! And there will be men's feet, women's feet, soldiers' feet and children's feet in that mighty tramp! It is the tramp of the people. 'They shall not pass?' They *shall* pass and soon."

The Amendment having been voted down, could not again come before the Sixty-fifth Senate, but Democrats, convinced that the failure of the Democratic Senate to pass the amendment would prove a handicap in the coming election, were unwilling to give up. A serious effort was made to devise a slightly different form of the Amendment which would not only win the one vote needed but allow consideration. Men and women from the South went to Washington and attempted to unite their party Senators upon such an amendment. Most of the forms drawn were unacceptable to the suffragists, but one was finally approved. Two Senators of the opposition agreed to vote for it and the two-thirds vote was therefore assured. The resolution was introduced and referred to the Suffrage Committee where a favorable report was promptly secured.

The end of the session was approaching and owing to Senatorial procedure in the closing days unanimous consent was necessary to get the favorable report upon the calendar. Most, if not all, the Democratic opponents agreed to make no objection to unanimous consent. Optimistic Democrats claimed that a large additional Southern vote would be secured should the amendment come to vote, since the proposal was certain to pass. To this optimism was opposed the assurance of hostile Republican Senators that the House had agreed to find objection to the new form and would not agree to the amendment, even though the Senate should pass it. They further declared that there was no assurance that a suffrage amendment would *ever* pass, since House leaders had also agreed not to allow any form of the amendment to pass the Sixty-sixth Congress even though such provision should pass the Senate.

Both claims were false and in any event there were votes enough to pass the new amendment in the Sixty-fifth Senate. The Chairman of the Senate Committee was on watch day and night to find opportunity to ask unanimous consent for the presentation of the favorable report. At this point it was observed by many friends of the measure that Senators Wadsworth and Weeks spelled each other in a vigil so that one or the other could always be present to object whenever consent should be asked. This small incident aroused much additional acrimony, the friendly Democrats again contending that the Northern opposed Senators were merely postponing action in order to throw to the Republicans whatever political credit might accrue from the passage of the Amendment in the Sixty-sixth Congress, and Republican Senators accusing the Democrats of attempting to cover their years of opposition to federal suffrage action, by the appearance of support at the eleventh hour. Both accusations contained much truth, and the sorry fact was that the Sixty-fifth Congress adjourned with the Amendment not yet submitted.

From one of the earliest ships to bring soldiers from France, a lively boy soldier ran down the gang plank ahead of his fellows and astounded the group of women, waiting to serve coffee and sandwiches, with the excited question, "Have you got it yet?" "Got what?" they inquired. "Why, the vote," he answered. "Not yet," replied the women, whereupon the young patriot ejaculated in a tone of scorn, "O hang, you ought to be ashamed. The German women have it."

The more intelligent people of America had come to much the same opinion. The President's war message to the Congress and the one hundred congressional speeches that followed had implied that entrance into the World War was necessary to prevent the recrudescence of an autocracy ruled world. "Making the world safe for democracy" had become the text of sermons, speeches and appeals pronounced on behalf of conscription, food conservation, extra production, liberty loans, and loyalty pledges. Though an American Ambassador said to an English audience in 1921 that "the United States had gone to war to save its own skin," this was not the interpretation given in the midst of the contest. On the contrary, the moral aims of the war were more and more stressed in all the allied nations as the campaign to uphold the home defenses proceeded. The leaders everywhere seemed in accord with General Smuts of South Africa when he said that the war was a great crusade for human liberty. "It began," said he, "as a great military war, but all that has happened has transformed it into a great moral and spiritual crusade."

During the years of the war the story of the unexpected and heroic services of women had been inextricably interwoven with all reports of the war for democracy. Mr. Balfour said in the United States: "Behind every man in the trenches there are ten persons making it possible for him to stay there. In 1917 seven of the ten were women." General Joffre said: "We have two armies, one in the trenches and one behind the trenches. The one in the rear is composed largely of women."

In the United States the women were not lagging behind those of Europe in heroic war services. A Woman's Council of Defense with Dr. Anna Howard Shaw as Chairman had united the women of the nation in the home defense work and various organizations were sending hundreds of women overseas. The National Suffrage Association was itself maintaining a hospital in France.[104]

It was after the women of Great Britain, Canada, Germany and many other countries had been enfranchised that the Senate, on February 10, 1919, again refused to allow the Federal Suffrage Amendment to go to the Legislatures. The contrasting generosity of the British Parliament had been shown January 4, 1919, when "in seventy-eight minutes it passed a bill of seventy-eight words," making women eligible to sit in the House of Commons. American leaders of both political parties were by then battling hard with their respective reactionary minorities, for it was by then clear that there might be an enormous advantage accruing to the party that should finally enfranchise women. The spirit of these leaders had come to resemble that of an omnibus conductor in London during one of the great suffrage processions. After a vain attempt to make headway through the surging crowds, he shouted: "O sy, give wimmen the vote and let's get on with the traffic!"

The armistice came, bloodless revolutions erected republics where kaiser and emperor had once reigned, and elections were held for Reichstag and State assemblies in which all men and all women were permitted to participate. The press carried the news to the farthest corners of the earth that millions of German women had not only voted but that thirty had been elected to the Reichstag.

This was the spirit and these the events of the world while in the United States the willful thirty-three, as the press quite generally designated that bi-partisan minority of the Sixty-fifth Congress, refused to budge. They showed no comprehension of the changed thought of the world, nor were they characterized by that party loyalty which demands that men yield personal prejudice to the superior claim of party advantage.

In accordance with the plan adopted in 1916 at the Atlantic City Convention, the National American Woman Suffrage Association's State auxiliaries had continued hard at work during the winter of 1919, and before the end of the legislative session twenty-four State Legislatures had petitioned Congress to pass the Federal Suffrage Amendment, and five of these, New York, Idaho, Nebraska, Ohio and Missouri, had called upon an opposed Senator to change his vote.[105] Before May 1, 1919, the number of States in which presidential suffrage had been extended was fourteen.[106] One of these, Michigan, had entered the full suffrage list in 1918 and in one, Vermont, the Governor had vetoed the presidential suffrage bill. Inclusive of Arkansas and Texas where women had the right to vote in the primaries, women would vote for presidential electors in thirty States, a fact which was still proving the most persuasive of all arguments for extending full suffrage to women in all States.

The President called a special session of the new Congress to meet May 19, 1919. On May 21 he addressed it and again recommended the passage of the Federal Suffrage Amendment. The Amendment was introduced by six members in the House, promptly reported by the Suffrage Committee on the twentieth, and placed on the calendar for the twenty-first.

James R. Mann was now the chairman of the Suffrage Committee in the House and to his organizing abilities the quick work of getting the vote was due. The Amendment was brought up almost immediately on the twenty-first and after two hours of discussion it was passed by a vote of 304 ayes, of which 200 were Republicans, 102 Democrats, 1 Prohibitionist, 1 Independent; 89 nays, of which 19 were Republicans and 70 were Democrats. Forty-two votes more than the required two-thirds had been secured. Seventy-one of the affirmative votes were cast by Representatives from the Southern States. The Democrats polled 54 per cent of their membership, the Republicans 84 per cent of theirs for the Amendment. Of 117 new members elected in November, 103 voted for the Amendment, fifteen returned members changed from negative to affirmative and no affirmative changed to negative.

The Democratic National Committee, not waiting for the Senate to act, called on the Legislatures of the various States to meet in special session and ratify the Amendment.

On June 4, 1919, after a two days' debate, the measure again came to vote in the United States Senate.

Four amendments were submitted, all by Southern Democrats for the obvious purpose of securing delay. One by Senator Underwood of Alabama proposed to refer the ratification of the amendment to State conventions. One amendment to this amendment was offered by Senator Phelan, of California, defining the character of such conventions. One was proposed by Senator Harrison, of Mississippi, introducing the word white as defining citizens, one by Senator Gay, of Louisiana, providing that enforcement of the amendment be left to the States. All were lost.

Three times the galleries violated the rule against demonstrations. There was applause when Senator Spencer, of Missouri, defended Missouri suffrage sentiment against his senior colleague, Senator Reed. Laughter when Senator Underwood, who shared dishonor with Senator Reed as the chief obstructionist in the debate, absentmindedly gave a loud "aye" when his name was called on the main amendment and then hastily changed to "no." And a great wave of rejoicing when from the chair the voice of the presiding officer, Senator Cummins, rang out more clearly than the galleries had ever heard it as he announced the victory. Sixty-six Senators had voted aye; thirty had voted no.

The crowds of women issuing from the Senate Chamber that day did not sing as they had done on January 10, 1918, the day the amendment had first passed the House. To their weary senses the only meaning of the vote just taken was that the Senate had at last surrendered, given over its stubborn resistance, given in to the people it represented. "The ayes were the ayes of Congress, but the voice was the voice of the people" *(Woman Citizen).*

That afternoon, in the presence of representatives of the National Suffrage Association and many friendly Senators, Speaker Gillette, and, on the following day, Vice-President Marshall signed the Federal Suffrage Amendment with a gold pen, christened "the victory pen," now in the archives of the National American Woman Suffrage Association at the Smithsonian Institution in Washington.

"I join with you and all friends of the suffrage cause in rejoicing over the adoption of the suffrage amendment by the Congress. Please accept and convey to your association my warmest congratulations," cabled President Wilson from Paris.

A parting reception was held at the big suffrage house, before it was closed forever as a suffrage headquarters, the thanks to men who had helped were spoken, and many a hearty handclasp of suffrage workers and faithful friends in the Congress marked the close of the long battle. The Association thanked the political parties for their help and asked the continuance of their support; the parties congratulated the Association and promised that support.

Only a few weeks earlier the suffrage association had finished with State referenda. Almost coincidentally, it had come to the end of its work with the Congress. It faced now a new era of suffrage work, the work for ratification.

CHAPTER 22

Campaigning for Ratification

L ong before the Federal Suffrage Amendment passed the
Congress, the National American Woman Suffrage Association
had its ratification campaign formulated to the last detail.

Every Legislature had been polled, Governors had been
interviewed, the press kept informed of the necessary procedure
of the campaign, and an expectant, eager army, thoroughly well-
equipped and trained, was waiting for the next move. Before
the sun set on June 4, telegrams had been sent to all Governors
where special legislative sessions would be necessary, urging
that such sessions be called. Instructions for still more intensive
campaigns with Governors, legislators and the press were wired
to State auxiliaries to the National Suffrage Association, and
when the sun rose on June 5 the campaign was already under
full speed.

The situation was complicated by the fact that only six State
Legislatures meet annually (those of New York, New Jersey,
Massachusetts, Rhode Island, South Carolina and Georgia) and
these, with five others (Kentucky, Virginia, Maryland, Louisiana
and Mississippi) whose regular sessions would be held in 1920,
were the only ones that would have an opportunity to take action
before the Presidential election of 1920, unless it were possible

to catch Legislatures before adjournment in some States and to secure extra sessions in others.

The response to the National Suffrage Association's effort to catch these adjourning Legislatures and to secure the extra sessions was immediate and, to the uninitiated, of happiest augury for quick and complete success.

All the next day, and for many days to come telegrams poured into the Association's office from Governors. The first answers were from Alfred E. Smith, Democratic Governor of New York, and Henry J. Allen, Republican Governor of Kansas. Fourteen Governors answered yes definitely, and several others answered that they would call special sessions provided a sufficient number of other Governors would do so. Thereupon the National Suffrage Association, on June 9, sent telegrams to twenty-four Governors, which read, "Ten State Legislatures now in session, or meeting in called session, are expected to ratify the Federal Suffrage Amendment. Four meeting January, 1920, are certain to do so. Would you be willing to agree to be one of twenty-two Governors to call a special session in order to complete ratification before Presidential election?" This telegram brought immediate answers from several Governors, pledging special sessions, and on June 10 came the first ratification.

The Legislatures of Illinois and Wisconsin being on the eve of adjournment, the Suffrage Amendment was wired to both from Washington for ratification. Thereupon started a lively contest between the two States for first place. Illinois newspapers helped by calling loudly upon the Legislature to be "First"; her Governor, Frank O. Lowden, helped by sending a spirited message to the Legislature; and her Assembly helped by introducing into the Senate a resolution for ratification twenty-four hours after the passage of the amendment and before the receipt of the official notification. Action was taken on June 10.[107]

Two letters in the alphabet came near losing Illinois first place. A sentence in the joint resolution transmitted from the federal Secretary of State's office to the Illinois Governor read "which shall be valid for all events and purposes as part of the constitution." "Events" should have been "intents." Legal authorities said that ratification was not invalidated, but to be safe the Illinois Legislature re-ratified June 17.

Wisconsin ratified on the same day—in spite of Senator Herman Bilgrien, who, for reasons good and sufficient to himself, voted no. Pressed for these reasons by reporters, he objected to telling them because he feared that he would not be quoted correctly, so he carefully wrote out a statement which was carefully printed in the Wisconsin *State Journal* Thursday, June 12, 1919, and is carefully reproduced below:

Why I Voted against Women Suff

1 I and my Wife agree on point 1, a hous Wife belongs to home near her children and to keep hous, and not in open public Politic.

2ond. it is only for the city Women in larger Cities that want to vote and to get the controll of the Country vote, to Elect State officers and President of the U.S. because a Country Women wont not go to Vote they have all they wont to do to take care of their children and House Work garden and etc.

3th a Danger that the men will not go to the poles if the Women get Elected to any state Legislature, the big Danger will be that some hair pulling will going on if there will be Women Elected in the State Legislature they will be worse as the Attorneys at present.

The classic quality of the Bilgrien argument was not lost on the general public, which gasped with surprise at this evidence that such a grade of male intelligence and literacy should be allowed to sit in high places and pass judgment on women of brains and culture in their appeal for justice. There was no surprise in it, only grim humor, for suffragists. They had had to present their case before the tribunal of just such a grade of intelligence and literacy all too often.

The gallant competition for first place between Illinois and Wisconsin led a Wisconsin officer of the National Suffrage Association to obtain an appointment from the Wisconsin Governor for ex-Senator David G. James, an old-time suffragist, to carry Wisconsin's ratification in person to Washington. Mr. James allowed himself to be pressed into the service, rushed out to buy extra clothing, arranged his business over the telephone, and left on the first train. Thus Wisconsin had the distinction of filing her certificate first.

Commenting on the ratification, the Wisconsin *State Journal* said: "This Legislature is free, at least, which is something that cannot be said of all former sessions. For many years the brewers of Wisconsin were the political power in the State and the brewers of Wisconsin would not have allowed the ratification of the equal suffrage amendment."

Michigan was the third State to ratify. Kansas the next, then Ohio, then New York, each ratification having some drama of its own and all being received with loud acclaim by the public.

New York might reasonably have offered an excuse for delay in ratifying, inasmuch as its Legislature was to meet in regular session in January, 1920, but Governor Alfred E. Smith called the Legislature in special session June 16. After the Assembly had approved the Amendment unanimously, Mrs. Ida Sammis and Mrs. Mary B. Lilly, Republican and Democratic Assemblywomen respectively, were appointed to carry the notification to the Senate, "an event unprecedented in the history of New York State." In three and one-half hours the historic scene was over. In both Houses action was unanimous.

Six ratifications had now taken place in as many days. The State auxiliaries of the National Suffrage Association continued to send delegations to their Governors with appeals for ratification and the Association itself continued to press for more and still more special sessions. After consulting with the representatives of the National Suffrage Association four State Governors sent letters to all other Governors to suggest unity of action. The four were Governors J. A. A. Burnquist, Minnesota; Samuel B. McKelvie, Nebraska; James E. Goodrich, Indiana; and William D. Stephens, California. The results of these polls were sent later to the National Suffrage Association's office. Governor Burnquist reported twenty-eight favorable replies. In the meantime the Legislatures of three States in regular session—Pennsylvania, Massachusetts and Texas—ratified, and special sessions with ratification followed in Iowa and Missouri.

In Pennsylvania the cause of ratification was greatly forwarded by the steadfastly favorable attitude of Governor Sproul, Republican. In his inaugural address he said that he would be "gratified and proud" if the State should be among the first to ratify, and it was very generally alleged that had it not been for his determined action, which compelled party leaders to respect their promises, the General Assembly, inherently hostile to woman suffrage, never would have gone on record for ratification.

Pennsylvania's ratification campaign was marked, too, by the withdrawal of U.S. Senator Boies Penrose from the active opposition. True, he took his time to get out of the way, and sidetracked all appeals until he could go fishing. Evidently the fishing was good, for get out of the way he did.

With the ban of the Penrose influence lifted, the joint resolution passed the Pennsylvania Senate, on June 24, was rushed to the House, referred to the Judiciary special committee, and in less than three minutes reported out by a vote of 16 to 1. Speeches occupied three-quarters of an hour. Then came the roll-call. Half way through the women who were polling said, "We have enough votes now." Before the Speaker could announce the result, one enthusiastic legislator leaped to his feet and shouted "It's gone over, Mr. Speaker, it's gone over!" Whereupon the men burst into song.

Then the House took occasion to express its appreciation of the Pennsylvania State Suffrage Association, State auxiliary to the National American Woman Suffrage Association, and to credit the victory to its tactics and personnel. The State president was given opportunity to address the House from the Speaker's rostrum, the first time in Pennsylvania's history that the honor had been accorded to a woman.

Perhaps no ratification aroused more rejoicing among suffragists than the victory in rock-ribbed old Massachusetts, the State where the first shot was fired in the Revolution against taxation without representation; the first State to send a regiment to the front in the Civil War and a fully equipped regiment to Europe in the World War; the home of the oldest and strongest anti-suffrage association in the United States, whose workers had been sent all over the country to flood it with misleading literature; the birthplace of Lucy Stone and Susan B. Anthony, the seat of the first National Woman's Rights Convention in 1850, and eighth State to ratify the Federal Suffrage Amendment.

In Texas, first among Southern or Southwestern States to ratify, filibustering, threats, heckling, fervid oratory on woman's sphere, and women antis were used by the opposition in every conceivable way to defeat, deflect or delay the ratification. In vain. The suffrage men stood firm. A concurrent resolution providing that the members of the Senate and House resign immediately and go before the voters for re-election in order to obtain an expression on the question was referred to committee. Suffrage gained votes in the Senate with every substitute proposal. Finally, the effort to defeat ratification became so vehement that six Senators agreed to resign if ten more would do so, sixteen defalcations being necessary to break the quorum. That failed, Then on voting to pass the resolution to third reading three Senators (Alderdice, Suiter and Wood) changed their vote from "no" to "yes," the opposition was broken, and Texas ratified.

Immediately after the ratification, one of the bitterest of wet and dry fights was precipitated in Texas. The impeached ex-Governor, James E. Ferguson, against whom the women had voted in the primary election, aided by the "wets," organized an anti-suffrage association. They began their work in the courts and attacked the primary law. Losing in the first decision, they announced their aim to prevent ratification in thirty-six States until after the next regular session of the Texas Legislature in 1921. Meanwhile they intended to make it an issue and elect an anti-suffrage Legislature which would repeal the ratification just secured.

In Iowa, Governor William L. Harding called the Legislature in special session on July 2, for the sole purpose of ratifying the Federal Suffrage Amendment. The Legislature convened at 10 a.m., at 11:40 the resolution had passed both Houses, and the struggle begun in Iowa in 1868 was triumphantly finished.

In Missouri the opposition to a special session which at first seemed formidable soon melted away, and both the representative who had called the movement "bunk" and the other who had favored giving women the "mallet instead of the ballot" found themselves sitting in their respective places one hot day, July 2, listening to the reading of Governor Frederick D. Gardner's message, which closed with the words, "I entertain an abiding faith that you will give the subject favorable consideration."

The Governor's faith was justified. Early in the poll it was seen that the ayes would have it. It was Charles P. Comer, an especially vehement opponent, who gave the key to the situation, after going on record with his aye. "I've played poker long enough to know when to lay down my hand," said he.

Eleven States had now ratified within one month. While not quite one-fourth of the United States, or one-third of the number required to ratify the Amendment, these States contained more than one-half the population of the whole country. The group included every large State entitled to eighteen or more Presidential electors in the Electoral College. The Amendment had therefore a clear majority of the American people in its favor, as attested by the ratifying votes of their representative bodies, a fact that went far to lay low the charge, still made by the opposition, that a small minority was seeking to impose its will on a large majority of the people.

CHAPTER 23

Hard Work for Special Sessions

There followed next a discouraging phase of the campaign, due to the failure of Western Governors to call special sessions. Not a State in the Far West had ratified. The National American Woman Suffrage Association's plan had been rapid action by Western full suffrage States first, ratification by the partial suffrage States second, and a concentration of forces on the Eastern States last, where women were not yet political factors. Western Governors and suffrage organizations, fully understanding the plan, had agreed to co-operate in carrying it out. But it was the East that took action first, while the West, instead of quick action, betrayed a baffling hesitation to act at all. Delays, excuses and messages not easy to understand were the only explanations offered.

In July, 1919, four envoys were sent out from the National Suffrage Association, two to visit the Republican States of Minnesota, North Dakota, Washington, Oregon, Idaho, and Wyoming, and the other two to the Democratic States of Nevada, Arizona, New Mexico, Utah, and Oklahoma. The mission of the envoys was to investigate the local political situation as it affected the call of a special session, to arouse favorable sentiment among politicians, editors and the people generally, and to secure definite statements from the Western Governors as to the conditions under which the Legislatures would be called and the probable date of calling.

The Northern envoys followed Governor Burnquist across the entire State of Minnesota. The Governor finally, by riding four miles bareback and thirty-six miles in a car from his ranch to a little town, met them and gave his pledge to call a session in September.

The Southern envoys, learning that Thomas E. Campbell, Governor of Arizona, was on a speaking trip and would not return to Phoenix until September, secured his itinerary and, in spite of assurances that they could never overtake him, surprised him in a country hotel at Flagstaff where they secured a pledge for a session.

Women in the enfranchised States had been absorbed into the political parties and, with their suffrage campaign organizations practically dissolved, were in no position to carry out independent political action. They counseled patience when Governors replied "the women of my State have the suffrage—it will not help us" or "an extra session will be too costly," although these reasons were serving to cloak the real motives which in many cases were petty politics. In some States the Governor was of one party, the Legislature of another, and the several Governors hesitated to call special sessions for fear such sessions might give a chance for discussion which would affect their candidacy or be harmful to their party in the coming November election. Two Governors, one a Republican and one a Democrat, had been threatened by factions of their own party with impeachment if their Legislatures were called.

After initiating various plans to secure sessions, the four envoys met in Salt Lake City where the annual conference of Governors was called for August 18–24, 1919. The formal appeal of the National Suffrage Association to the conference was delivered by the envoys and concluded as follows: "All that is required is early action in the fourteen favorable Western States. The West controls the fate of the campaign entirely. Upon the date of its action depends the date of completed ratification. The National American Woman Suffrage Association implores the Governors of the West, in conference asembled, to find some ground of common agreement, so that the ratification of their Legislatures may be secured in the months of September or October and thus insure final ratification by February 1."

In response several Governors publicly restated pledges they had made privately to the envoys. On August 21, the following telegram was sent to National Suffrage Headquarters signed by the four envoys: "Republican Governors in conference this afternoon declared in favor of special sessions to ratify the Suffrage Amendment so that women may vote in 1920." Public pledges were brought back from seven Governors and confidential pledges from three.

But while several Governors were taking favorable action, one Governor, Ruffin G. Pleasant of Louisiana, was making an effort to secure a union of thirteen states to prevent ratification. He asked Southern Governors to join an alliance to demand that suffrage be gained by State action. This in face of the fact that suffragists had conducted weary campaigns for many years with the aim of securing State action, and had met with such stolid opposition that it had become necessary to resort to the only other method, a federal amendment! Governors C. H. Brough of Arkansas, James D. Black of Kentucky, Sidney J. Catts of Florida, and Theodore Bilbo of Mississippi publicly declined the invitation. If any such compact was effected, it was never made public.

Meantime a special session of the Arkansas Legislature had been called for July 28. As in Texas, so in Arkansas, the prejudices of the South were violently played upon by the opposition. A woman anti from Yonkers, New York, was imported to explain Southern traditions to Southerners, and the bogie of Negro domination was kept on constant parade.

Legislative debate brought into glaring relief the struggle between old-time Southern prejudice and the new spirit of Southern progressiveness.

"I'd rather see my daughter in her coffin than at the polls," declaimed one legislator.

Whereupon another rose to point out that in the estimation of that self-same tenderly protective father cattle ranked far ahead of daughters, for he had voted for one hundred thousand dollars appropriation with which to fight ticks from the backs of Arkansas cattle and refused to vote one penny for the maintenance of an Industrial School for Arkansas girls.

The debate served also to bring into high relief the fact that, as in the far South, so also in Arkansas, a border State, Negro suffrage the bogie keeps Negro suffrage as a practice non-existent. Said one Senator, "If this Amendment is ratified there will be a domination of Negro rule in the South. Time will come when the people will wake up and find that women should not be enfranchised." Said another, "We'll attend to the Negro vote all right." Said the first Senator, "You say you'll attend to the Negro vote; well, how are you going to do it?"—Said the second, "Well, there may be several ways.— I remember one time I was in charge of a ballot box in which there were 319 Negro and only seventeen white men's votes. I was riding mule back. Just as I got about in the middle of the bridge, while crossing a creek, my mule suddenly became frightened, pitched me off and I accidently let the ballot box drop into the creek. Neither the box nor the votes have ever been seen since."

But neither the spectre of Negro rule nor the fear of contaminating women at the polls sufficed in the final analysis to stop the Arkansas Legislature. The long hard work of Arkansas suffragists reaped its reward in ratification.

The last days of July, 1919, proved a fecund season for ratifications. Besides Arkansas, two other States ratified. One was Nebraska, a State where the liquor interests had long made the suffrage going hard in the extreme,[108] the other was Montana, first of the "farther West" to get into line. "I shall be disappointed if the vote is not unanimous," said Nebraska's Governor to Nebraska's Legislature. The vote was unanimous. The Joint Judiciary Committee decided to put the resolution through with the same procedure as a bill in order that no attack could be made upon its validity. This action required five days.

By invitation the president of the State auxiliary to the National American Woman Suffrage Association, addressed both Houses. An interesting feature was the transmission of the resolution from the Senate to the House by Miss Schenck, the first woman who had ever served as Assistant Secretary of the Senate in Nebraska.

Came a lull through August. Then the September ratifications took the stage. Minnesota was first, and its Legislature wound up the task dramatically by singing the Battle Hymn of the Republic. New Hampshire came next.

In the latter State there had been only two special sessions in sixty-six years, and none at all for twenty-nine years; and to many minds that is always a cogent argument for not having any at all, whatever the proposition, for twenty-nine more years. So extreme and so curiously stressed was the opposition that Governor Bartlett made occasion to write: "It is said that if I dare call the Legislature together, with the consent of the Council,[109] they (the ring) will flay me alive, kill every reform measure passed last winter, the trustee bill, the school bill and so on. This is silly. I will risk all dangers that may come to me. Let us come together briefly and keep our pledges to give women the ballot. . . . No political or bodily fear will stop me for one second."

The special session was duly called for September 9, and the Legislature duly ratified on that date.

Another lull, and then Utah swung into line on September 30 with a unanimous ratification. During the passage of the resolution in the House Assemblywoman Anna T. Pierson was in the chair.

At this point ratification seemed to reach a veritable impasse. An inexplicable situation was presented. The West was still strangely hesitant. The political battle front had shifted from the East where most opposition had been expected to the Pacific Coast where none had been anticipated. Seventeen States had ratified. Eleven having full suffrage in the far West had not called their sessions, although, with the exception of Oklahoma and Oregon, all had agreed to do so. Never in the history of the country was the provincialism of the States more apparent. In popular estimate the question of ratification seemed bounded by State lines and there was little national point of view. Said the press of Oregon, "Oregon has a sympathetic interest in ratification of the National Equal Suffrage Amendment but it is a detached interest when practical results are considered. The women of Oregon will gain nothing by ratification before the next presidential election. They will have full franchise rights in any event." And again: "It would seem that having waited so long for suffrage it will do no harm to postpone ratification."

The entire country had conceded to the West the leadership in the movement for woman suffrage and expected that the generosity shown by Western men in extending the suffrage within their own States would be applied to the campaign to gain suffrage for the women of the nation. Their failure to do what was expected was a vast disappointment.

In order to arouse Western Governors to an understanding of the national aspects of the question, the National Suffrage Association now organized an appeal from the States which had ratified. This petition was signed by the presidents of the National Association's State auxiliaries, the members of the National

Republican and Democratic committees, the chairmen of the State Republican and Democratic committees, and the official women representatives of the two parties. They were forwarded to the Governors of twelve States—Arizona, California, Colorado, Idaho, Nevada, New Mexico, North Dakota, Oklahoma, Oregon, South Dakota, Washington and Wyoming, with a special letter of entreaty from the National Suffrage Association which read in part:

We are well aware that the lives of all Governors of States in these times of unrest and reconstruction are overwhelmingly full of duties and problems. It is not unlikely on this account that you may not have kept pace with the progress of the woman suffrage movement in war-torn Europe. I beg, therefore, to call your attention to the fact that all the Allied Countries of Europe have now not only granted the suffrage, but the women have actually exercised the right, with the exception of France, Portugal, Montenegro and Greece. The last of these to extend the suffrage to women was Serbia. The Italian House of Deputies has passed the measure and the Italian women assure us that the Senate will do so soon.

All the enemy countries, with the exception of Turkey and Bulgaria, have extended the suffrage to women. All the neutral countries of Europe, except Spain and Switzerland, have now extended the vote to women, the last of these being Luxemburg, Holland and Sweden.

The suffrage for women in most of these countries has come as an act of revolution or, as in Serbia, as a ukase from the Government.

Meanwhile, Rhodesia and British East Africa, whose governments stand in comparison to the self-governing colonies of Great Britain much as the territories do to our own government, have extended suffrage to their women.

In the face of these amazing developments it comes as a very depressing humiliation to American women that the heavy, slow-moving machinery of our democracy has delayed so long this simple act of democratic justice.

It doubtless is impossible for you, who have lived all your life in a State where women have had equal suffrage with men and where no comment is made upon the fact, to realize the feeling of hundreds of thousands of American women who have borne the brunt of the struggle in this country for their own enfranchisement. Women have lived long lives and have died in advanced years and yet have given their very all during their lifetime to this struggle. Women still living look backward over more than a generation of continued service of education and pleading with the political parties of this country to do them justice. Now these women look across the ocean and see this act of democratic justice achieved as one of the results of the great world war, while we in this country are still questioning as to whether there may be some political advantage gained or lost by one party or the other.

I do beg of you in honor of our Nation, in respect to the history which is now being made the world around, to see that................makes its contribution of ratification in such time that posterity will not blush at the hesitancy of our country to put this amendment into the Constitution.

Later in the month, to set forth the fact that special sessions were absolutely necessary in every Western State, and to get renewed confirmation of the pledges made and make clear to Western Governors that their hesitation was being interpreted throughout the country to mean opposition to the Federal Suffrage Amendment, the president of the National American Woman Suffrage Association went on a Western tour. Her schedule included sixteen conferences in twelve States with "Wake up America" as the key-note of each, and an appeal to each State to be *the one* to ratify. Calls for special sessions followed quickly in California, North Dakota, Colorado, Oregon and Nevada.

For weeks the attention of the entire country had been focused on California, the largest and most influential Western State which had gained woman suffrage during the last ten years. William D. Stephens was Governor, a man who had gained prominence as a suffrage advocate in 1910, when the issue was in doubt and other political leaders refused to speak.

Late in October he sent the following telegram to seven Western Governors: ". . . We can perform a worthy and effective act if the Far Western Governors and Legislatures will present to the women of the West and of the nation a Thanksgiving present by ratifying the amendment. I am asking the Governors of Idaho, Nevada, Arizona, New Mexico, Wyoming, Oregon and Washington to join me in a group calling extra sessions before November 27, 1919. Will you call if the others will do so?"

Colorado and Nevada returned favorable replies. Oregon was not heard from. Governors Carey of Wyoming, Campbell of Arizona, Lazzarola of New Mexico, and Hart of Washington gave reasons why to them a special session was not advisable, the latter saying, "I have no power to limit the duration of a special session and doubt the wisdom therefor unless the necessity clearly appears."

Nothing daunted, a week later Governor Stephens sent telegrams to Governors of fourteen Middle West and Eastern States saying: "California, Colorado and Nevada will have special sessions in November. Other Western States may also call. Will you not join with us to hasten the day that will give our nation the benefit of the vote of its women citizens? We realize how greatly the voting of the women has benefited California. We believe it will be of like value in the nation. I earnestly ask your co-operation."

California's special session was called for November 1, "for the exclusive consideration of the Federal Amendment." Five minutes after the resolution was read in the Senate it was adopted. In the House only two men voted against it—Carlton W. Green of San Luis Obispo and Robert Madison of Sonoma, the former because of the color question and the latter on account "of the expense of an unnecessary call for which we gain nothing."

In Maine almost insuperable obstacles were overcome before a special session could be called. There had been only six special sessions since Maine became a State in 1820. The woman suffrage amendment had been defeated in 1917 by a vote of two to one; the State Supreme Court had unanimously decided that the presidential suffrage given by legislative enactment of 1918 must be referred to the voters and the Governor had sent out a proclamation for the vote to be taken September 13, 1920.[110] Although the State Republican Convention had gone on record in March for immediate ratification of the Federal Suffrage Amendment, there was much opposition to action until after the result of the vote on presidential suffrage had been determined. In October it became apparent that other matters needed legislative action and Governor Carl E. Milliken issued the call for November 4. Thereupon the Men's Anti-Suffrage Committee of Maine circularized the Legislature in an effort to prevent action. They were "amazed that ratification should be considered while a referendum on presidential suffrage was pending" and asked "whether or not the law of this State is to be respected?"

The Kennebec *Journal* replied in part:

"We apprehend that the attempt of our anti-suffrage friends to suspend the functions of and dictate to the constitutional tribunal entrusted with the power and duty of settling this great question will not be taken very seriously. The world moves and Maine will move with it."

Maine moved. Both Houses ratified on November 5, but in the House there were only three votes to spare.

In December it seemed necessary to call upon the political parties to speed up again the campaign for ratification. Before the passage of the Federal Suffrage Amendment there had been decided opposition to suffrage action within the ranks of both major parties. After the passage each was determined that if woman suffrage had to come the other should not have the credit for it. Both parties had maneuvered against each other on this question for many years and the finish of the ratification campaign found them still maneuvering.

At the urgent request of the National Suffrage Association both Republican and Democratic National Committees passed resolutions recommending that special sessions be held in order that women might be assured a vote in the early spring primaries. Three ratifications followed in December—those of North Dakota, South Dakota and Colorado.

In North Dakota the chances of ratification were for a time imperiled because the dominant party, the Non-Partisan League, could not forget that North Dakota women, with their school suffrage, had elected to the superintendency of Public Instruction the only nominee who was not a League candidate. However, the suffragists were so successful in pleading the abstract justice of their cause that Governor Frazer called a special session for November 25. Both House and Senate approved the ratification resolution.

South Dakota's case was unusual. The State had had only two special sessions in thirty years. Governor Peter Norbeck, who intended to call a special session in 1920, did not feel justified in calling one in 1919 also. The conditions under which he was willing to act were that 51 per cent of the South Dakota legislators should agree to attend the session at their own expense and without the usual per diem; promise not to vote for reimbursement at the session; act only on ratification and that favorably. The women must secure the pledges. This was an enormous task, but the women undertook it. Answers to their poll were slowly coming in when the president of the South Dakota auxiliary of the National American Woman Suffrage Association discovered a better way. The Richards Primary Law, carried November, 1919, provided that on the second Tuesday in December so-called proposal men, representing the parties in the various counties, should meet at the State capital to prepare platforms and to propose candidates to be voted on at the March primaries. The public announcement indicated that many legislators would act as proposal men. The Republican, Democratic and Non-Partisan Conventions were also called on that date. The suffragists recognized this as a psychological moment when almost the whole Legislature would be on hand in Pierre, and readily obtained the consent of the Governor to call a special session if it could be done with no expense to the State. The suffragists then interviewed legislators and entreated them to go to Pierre at their own expense. Pledges to do this were signed by a majority, and, to comply with the three-day time limit, the call was issued on Saturday, November 30, at three o'clock for Tuesday, December third, at 7 p.m.

For thirty-six hours telegraph and telephone lines hummed as the effort was made to reach legislators in the remotest parts of the State. The snow was heavy, the roads almost impassable, but the men came from all directions. One legislator used up three automobiles getting to the train from his home, many miles from the railroad; while another rushed from Minneapolis to Huron, called to his wife to send his grip and just caught the train for Pierre. South Dakota had a unique ratification. It was the only State to hold a midnight special session and ratify between supper and breakfast.

In Colorado, as in so many other States, the question of the expense of an extra session was paramount. Colorado women did not intend that this should serve as an excuse for failure to ratify. The Colorado auxiliary of the National American Woman Suffrage Association told Governor Oliver H. Shoup that if he would call an extra session their members would furnish all the necessary clerks and pages. The Governor replied that unless the suffragists would raise fifteen thousand dollars for the entire expense of the extra session it would not be called. However, as in other States, reluctance was overcome by continued agitation, and the discovery that the cost of special sessions was not so exorbitant. The Governor finally called the session for December 8. The resolution passed both Houses unanimously, having been introduced in the Senate by Senator Agnes Riddle.

Six months had gone by since the submission of the Federal Suffrage Amendment and twenty-two States had ratified. The inevitable legal tests now began.

CHAPTER 24

The Legal Tests Begin

With the era of State referenda left behind, with the fight for the submission of the Federal Suffrage Amendment by the Congress triumphantly finished, with the ratifications of twenty-two States already to the amendment's credit, and with the women of a majority of the States qualified to vote for the next President, ratification or no ratification, it might have seemed to the unwary that the rest of the suffrage struggle would be easy. But nothing in connection with the suffrage struggle was ever allowed to be easy. In that auspicious appearing autumn of 1919 two of the most menacing hazards of all suffrage history lay just ahead; one, the legal tests to which the constitutionality of both the suffrage and the prohibition amendments was to be subjected; the other, the determination of the opposition to prevent the thirty-sixth ratification. It was not twenty-two ratifications, nor thirty, nor thirty-five that that opposition feared. It was exactly thirty-six. Toward these hazards the suffrage struggle now moved irresistibly.

By Election Day (November 4, 1919) both the prohibition and the suffrage amendments were deep in the maelstrom of legal contention which awaits all controversial legislation. Law in the United States is exceedingly elaborate, consisting of a federal and forty-eight State constitutions, and a federal and forty-eight codes of statutory law. The most accomplished of legal minds is incapable of holding the details of so diversified a system, and the laity, prone to confuse statutory and constitutional provisions, simply dismisses the whole subject of law as quite beyond the realm of comprehension.

To make the entire system one constructive whole, every State law must be in agreement with the federal constitution, which is the supreme law of the land. Inconsistencies between newly made laws and constitutions of State or nation are not infrequently discovered, and, upon suitable action being brought, the courts declare such laws nullified because of their unconstitutionality.

Opponents of disputed measures usually transfer their activities from legislative halls to courts, as soon as the law they oppose has been passed by a Legislature or the Congress, anticipating that what has been done by the "will of the people" may be undone on the strength of some neglect or loose construction of legal procedure. Until they have set their lawyers to make a thorough search for unconstitutionalities and brought to the courts any flaw they allege has been discovered, no campaign on any issue is considered at an end. As any law to be tested proceeds upon its snail-like course from minor to higher court, from higher court to State Supreme Court, and thence to the Federal Supreme Court, its path is frequently obscured in the fog of contention, and long before its final destiny is determined the fact that an action has been begun has been forgotten by the masses of the people who were interested at the beginning. Only those who have endured it can comprehend the agony of uncertainty which is the portion of friends and foes of every measure during "the law's delay."

Before the suffrage amendment had been submitted to the Legislatures by the Congress, a group of prominent lawyers had been for some time engaged in a study of the possibilities of invalidating the prohibition amendment. Among them was the well-known Elihu Root, accounted one of the ablest constitutional lawyers in the United States. Although many suggested loop-holes, through which the nation might hope to escape from its dry fate, were used as a basis for legal tests, only one of the methods of attack upon the Eighteenth Amendment affected the Nineteenth. This method was one which, in the early months of the agitation, brought out widespread differences of legal opinions, with eminent lawyers arrayed upon both sides. It sought an affirmative answer to the following question:

Can a federal amendment be referred to the voters of a State, after ratification by the Legislature, under State initiative and referendum laws?

Twenty-two States had such laws.[111] The initiative and referendum was an undreamt of procedure when the federal constitution was written, and since its introduction its application to federal legislation had never been tested. It became the point around which for several months the hopes of anti-prohibitionists and anti-suffragists mounted with comforting anticipation, and likewise the point which presented to prohibitionists and suffragists the most gloomy uncertainty.

The Suffrage Amendment had three distinct advantages over the prohibition amendment and one important disadvantage. The advantages were, (1) A time limit of seven years for ratification had been fixed by the Congress for the prohibition amendment; no limit was attached to the Suffrage Amendment. (2) The prohibition amendment treated of absolutely new matter and consequently every phrase invited legal examination and interpretation concerning its agreement with other parts of the federal constitution. A considerable number of the legal attacks made against that amendment were based upon claims that inconsistencies existed; the Suffrage Amendment had been drawn in the exact form of the Fifteenth Amendment which had been held to be constitutional against every possible mode of attack. (3) The liquor forces threatened a referendum by petition in at least eighteen of the referendum States on the prohibition amendment. Twelve of the twenty-two initiative and referendum States were full suffrage States, and woman suffrage had passed so far beyond the controversial stage as to render a proposal for a referendum improbable in any of them. Two other initiative and referendum States, Louisiana and Mississippi, were certain to reject the Amendment in any event, thus leaving eight States only where there was any likelihood of a referendum, should the Federal Supreme Court declare State laws applicable to federal amendments.

On the other hand, these three advantages were offset by, first, the certainty that nine States of the far South, in obedience to tradition concerning the Negro vote, would reject the Amendment, thus leaving thirty-nine States only from which to draw the necessary thirty-six ratifications; second, suffrage referenda were already scheduled in three States for 1920. If the courts held that a State had the right to dispose of a federal amendment by referendum instead of by action of the Legislature, ratification in the three States was sure to be postponed for the referenda. That meant until after the presidential election; and should the referenda result adversely, the suffrage struggle might be indefinitely prolonged.

The liquor forces repeatedly announced through the press that they intended to defeat prohibition on referenda in ten States if possible, thus reducing the total number of States ratifying prohibition below thirty-six.[112] Failing to achieve this expectation, they relied upon other legal action either to invalidate the Amendment, or at least to keep the question pending in the courts beyond the seven years' limit. In support of this program they had either filed petitions on the prohibition amendment in eighteen States or publicly advertised their intention of so doing.

Two State Supreme Courts, Ohio with one dissenting judge, and Washington with four dissenting judges, had declared such referenda constitutional. Two State Supreme Courts, Maine and Oregon, had unanimously declared them unconstitutional. Under the Ohio decision, and pending action by the Federal Supreme Court, a referendum had actually been held on the ratification of the prohibition amendment, and the "wets" had won. Cases were pending in the Supreme Courts of Nebraska, New Mexico, Michigan, Colorado, California and Arkansas, and were on their way to State Supreme Courts in others. The opponents of both amendments were issuing widely published statements to the effect that ratification was not reflecting the "will of the people." In consequence not a little importance attached to the result of the Ohio election, as it seemed to furnish a practical illustration of the truth of their claim.[113]

The anti-suffragists announced anew that their plan was to defeat ratification of the Suffrage Amendment in thirteen States (and suffragists in private counsels always conceded nine such rejections) and to secure a Proclamation of Defeat. Although certain opinions rendered in connection with the Fourteenth and Fifteenth Amendments by the Secretary of State have lent weight to the theory that no Proclamation of Defeat can be promulgated, the fact remains that the Supreme Court, which is the sole authority to decide questions of that import, has had no occasion to express itself on this still undecided point. In support of this program of the antis two States had rejected the Amendment, and the eleven which would follow were confidently named. A petition for a referendum had been filed in Ohio on ratification of the Suffrage Amendment and also on presidential suffrage. Petitions were announced as in circulation in Missouri, Nebraska and Massachusetts. Other referenda were threatened should thirty-six States ratify. A referendum petition had been filed on presidential suffrage in Maine, and the State Supreme Court, which had declared a referendum on ratification of prohibition illegal, had declared such a referendum legal on presidential suffrage. As the authority for presidential suffrage was drawn from the federal constitution, this decision would probably have been overturned had the case gone up to the Federal Supreme Court. It happened that the Governor had signed the bill in each State where this privilege had been extended to women, a fact that gave the general impression that it was distinctly a State measure. An attack had been made upon the validity of the Woman's Primary Law in Texas and it had been upheld in the lower courts.

The state of legal confusion was now sufficiently perplexing to make it of use for campaign purposes. Suffrage opponents promptly organized a drive upon national and State Republican and Democratic party committeemen with the purpose of convincing the leaders that the Suffrage Amendment was caught in such a tangle of legal uncertainty and of threatened referenda that further efforts to secure ratification before the presidential election would be futile. As the Republican party was in control of the majority of the Legislatures that were expected to take action, the campaign was more forcefully aimed at the leaders of that party.

The group of Eastern Senators who had for so many years prevented the submission of the Federal Suffrage Amendment, and who were as obdurate if less publicly outspoken opponents as ever, listened to the anti-pleas and with fresh courage took up the appeals for delay. A public and private effort was made to persuade contributors to Republican campaign funds to make their gifts contingent upon promises quietly to withdraw the party from the ratification campaign. Whether these efforts met with any success only those in private charge of Republican affairs knew and they made no public confessions. Women anti-suffragists as callers at the National Republican headquarters became an insistent and daily feature. Constant official announcements, widely published by the newspapers of the country, were issued by the opponents to the effect that woman suffrage in 1920 was impossible.

"If ratification cannot be completed in time for women to vote in 1920, why disturb the even tenor of State politics by calling unnecessary special sessions?" they asked. This question was put in every conceivable form by the official publicity issued by the opponents and was revamped and put forth editorially by every State paper which for reasons of its own opposed a special session of its State Legislature.

This campaign began to tell. National party leaders began to betray a coolness in noticeable contrast to the warmth of their co-operation at an earlier period. When people do not know what to think, they pause. With a State press warning the public that action by the State would be useless, many State suffragists caught the general alarm and relaxed their efforts to secure early action. The success of the campaign in the suffrage States was particularly perplexing. In most of them, not an active opponent of woman suffrage could be found, and none objected to ratification. Yet press and public, while denouncing anti-suffragists, picked up the excuses found on legal ground as put forth by them to get delay and joined in forwarding their argument. Governors felt the effect of the gradual lessening of the demand for special sessions and began to return evasive replies to plain questions. All along the line of campaign a disconcerting hesitation made itself manifest.

CHAPTER 25

Adding Up the Ratification Column

The year 1920 opened with the National Suffrage Association wrestling with a difficult problem in arithmetic: Twenty-two States had ratified; three more, Rhode Island, Kentucky and New Jersey, were expected to ratify at regular sessions, and the Governors of eight more, Oregon, Wyoming, Indiana, Nevada, Idaho, Arizona, New Mexico and West Virginia had promised special sessions in order to ratify. But twenty-two and three and eight to do not make thirty-six. It was believed that the two enfranchised States of Washington and Oklahoma would not hold out against the appeal of their parties for special sessions when so many States should have been won that only the mysterious unknown thirty-sixth must be found. But twenty-two and three and eight and two do not make thirty-six. The Governors of Vermont and Connecticut, both anti-suffragists but with Legislatures favorable to suffrage, might succumb to party appeal and thus bring the last State without a battle. If their hostility should continue, there was still Delaware to offer hope of completing the sum in suffrage addition.

On the other hand, there was the possible Supreme Court decision which might make State referendum laws apply to federal amendments, in which case ratification by November, 1920, would undoubtedly be prevented. With this very object in view the fight

359

of the wet forces was still going on. The president of the National Association Opposed to Woman Suffrage sent frequent wires to the Governors, one of which read:

"In behalf of this organization of women determined to uphold the constitution of the United States and the federal principle embodied in State's Rights doctrines upon which our government rests, I express profound respect to you for withstanding the pressure to which suffrage leaders boldly proclaim they are subjecting you and to which they boast you must eventually accede. We infer, you understand, that ratification cannot stand the legal tests bound to ensue in the courts, and that these cases, should ratification be obtained in time for women to vote this year, would hold up the election result and throw the country into political chaos, possibly necessitating a second election."

In the meantime to show that the predictions of "political chaos" were not taken too seriously, five States ratified in rapid succession in January—Rhode Island, Kentucky, Oregon, Indiana and Wyoming.

In Rhode Island the State auxiliary of the National American Woman Suffrage Association had asked for a special session as soon as the Federal Amendment was submitted. Governor R. Livingston Beeckman objected to a special session because of expense and because other issues might be presented, but he agreed to do as Republican leaders of the State should decide. On June 27, 1919, these leaders had met in Providence and by an overwhelming majority had voted to recommend to the Governor that no session be held. The Governor had then issued a statement containing the following: "The calling of a special session is a power that should be used in a most careful manner and only at a time of grave necessity. . . . Within the short period of six months the resolution will come before the General Assembly in regular session and I believe there is no public necessity of calling a special session at this time or that the cause of woman suffrage will be in any way delayed or hindered by this course. Personally I am earnestly in favor of ratification."

By coming out for early action two influential Rhode Island Republicans, Colonel Colt and ex-Senator Lippitt, threw consternation into the ranks of the leaders. Moreover, to remove the Governor's objections the Providence *Journal* twice offered, in writing, to defray the expenses of an extra session, while the Democratic State Central Committee agreed not to press the property qualification for voters and the soldiers' bonus if the session were held. Through July and August of 1919 suffragists had worked on the State indefatigably. Interviews were held with the Governor, and the Governor in turn had conferences with the Republican State Central Committee, all apparently to no purpose. On September 29, seventy women, representing various State organizations, visited the Governor. While admitting that offers had been made to meet his two objections, he professed not to see any difference between an early session and one in January.

By this time women all over the country had become suspicious of the good intent of the major parties to put ratification through quickly, and in none of the States more so than in Rhode Island. Rhode Island papers began to discuss "the hidden forces" that were lined up against ratification. The good faith of Mr. Will Hays, chairman of the National Republican organization, was impugned by the Providence papers. Women in the political organizations were warned editorially to be on guard against putting party before principle if they wanted suffrage to win.

At all events there was no special session in Rhode Island, and the date of the regular session, January 6, found the women keyed up to press hard for ratification on the first day, lest there be some *contretemps*. When Senate and House came together to receive the Governor's message on that first day, he said to them: "I unqualifiedly approve the ratification of this amendment and urge that it be accomplished without a day's delay."

One of three dissenting votes in the House was cast by the Speaker, Hon. Arthur P. Sumner, a life-long enemy of woman suffrage, who asked the privilege of casting the first vote against. In the Senate Lieut.-Governor Emery J. San Souci, a friend of suffrage, was in the chair and within a few moments, with no speeches and only one vote against, that of John H. McCabe, Democrat, of Burrillville, ratification was accomplished.

Few knew that when the measure was submitted to the Senate only a last minute compromise prevented its going to committee overnight. Fifteen Senators were bent on delaying action for a day in order to show the Governor that "the Senate was not a rubber stamp for his office." Such petty jealousies of authority had crippled the giving of suffrage from the beginning—and would cripple it to the end. In the Rhode Island case fortunately the leader of the insurgents gave up his plans and voted with others under suspension of rules.

In Kentucky the president of the State auxiliary of the National Suffrage Association had polled members of the Legislature at the time that they were up for election, and enough favorable replies had been then received to insure ratification. As early as June 6, Governor James D. Black publicly stated that he would *not* call a special session. He did not change his mind. September 3, the Democratic State Convention met in Louisville. It had been rumored that an effort would be made to ignore the amendment and substitute a plank favoring a State referendum. President Wilson sent the following telegram: "Both as the leader of the party and as a student of existing conditions throughout the world, I venture to urge with the utmost earnestness that the State Convention include in its platform a plank in favor of the Suffrage Amendment. It would serve mankind and the party by so doing."

Attorney-General A. Mitchell Palmer, later candidate for President of the United States, wrote to Senator W. A. Perry of Louisville earnestly urging "early favorable action on the ratification resolution." The only fight in the adoption of the entire platform was whether to. call on the coming Legislature to ratify the Federal Suffrage Amendment or to submit suffrage to a State referendum. As finally passed the plank read: "We favor the ratification by the Legislature of Kentucky at its next session of the amendment to the Constitution of the United States extending to women this right of suffrage and we urge our representatives in the Legislature of Kentucky and all executive or other officers to use their votes and influence, in every legitimate way, to bring about the ratification of same. We pledge ourselves to support in the next General Assembly, if the Federal Amendment has not become operative by that time, the submission of an amendment to the State Constitution granting suffrage to women on the same terms as to men and when the amendment is submitted to support it at the polls as a party measure."

Ratification was completed January 6, 1920, during the regular session of the Legislature. There was little debate in the lower House, but Senate action was delayed until a proposition to submit the question of ratification to a statewide referendum was rejected.

In Oregon, from June to September of 1919, letters from legislators, organizations and individuals flowed into Governor Ben W. Olcott's office, to urge a special session which he persistently refused to call. It was on July 25 that the Governor named the conditions under which he would call a session as follows: "In offering to call a special session in the event that a majority of members of both Houses request it and with the understanding that they pay their own expenses, I am taking into consideration the fact that the matter of ratification is one lying solely within the province of the Legislature. The executive officers have power neither to veto nor approve a resolution of ratification. . . . For this reason I feel if a majority of the members wish it they should be given an early opportunity to act upon the question, but in so doing they must act at their own expense and not at the expense of the State." And, he added, "no other legislation must be considered." With these terms, which no other Governor had yet imposed, ratification met more serious difficulties in Oregon, a full suffrage State, than those presented by any other State.

The excuse of expense did not seem valid. As the legislators were paid only three dollars a day and mileage the entire cost would be within five thousand dollars. Members of the Oregon auxiliary of the National American Woman Suffrage Association promptly agreed to raise six thousand dollars, and proceeded with the roll of the legislators according to the Governor's demands. That they did not secure the required number of pledges was due to the fact that members resented the Governor's requirements to pay their own expenses and not take up other legislation. Mrs. Alexander Thompson, the only woman member of the Legislature, wrote the Governor at once, offering to waive her per diem and expenses, pointed out that if the Western Governors continued to say that they would call a special session "if needed to complete ratification" no headway would be made, and concluded, "By prompt action on your part we will help to inspire other States and pave the way for the settlement of this question." The Governor's answer was an announcement in the press that he would call an extra session at State expense when and if Oregon was needed to make thirty-six ratifications.

On November 5, the president of the National Suffrage Association, who was making a western trip in the interest of ratification, speaking at the Multnomah Hotel, Portland, with reference to action in Oregon, said: "One of the unfortunate things about our forty-eight States is the fact that each is so ignorant and so uninterested in the problems of each other. . . . The effect of your indifference is this: Our people are saying, 'These Western women don't care anything about the vote or they would see that we get it too.' Do you see the responsibility? I don't blame your Governor who says there is no demand. I ask you to create this demand, not boisterously, not bitterly. Don't try to force a special session but find out why he objects, and then meet conditions. If he doesn't want other legislation then let legislators confer with him." Following this meeting a special committee interviewed the Governor appealing for a special session on the ground that they wanted women of non-suffrage States to receive whatever moral support there might be in early ratification.

It was just after this call on the Governor that there developed "other and more important reasons" for calling a session than to approve the Suffrage Amendment. The provisions of the Roosevelt Highway Bill, as it had passed the previous State Legislature, were in conflict with those of the Government Road Aid Bill. With this discovery newspapers urged Senators and Representatives to use their influence to induce the Governor to call the session, which he finally did for January 12, 1920. Within twenty minutes from the time the two branches met, each had adopted unanimously a joint resolution to ratify the Suffrage Amendment.

When Governor James P. Goodrich of Indiana was importuned to call a special session early in June of 1919 by members of the Indiana auxiliary of the National American Woman Suffrage Association he replied that if thirty-five other States would call their Legislatures he would do so. He submitted a plan to the president of the National Suffrage Association, which she approved, and on June 13, he wired the Governors of thirty-one States as follows: "The sentiment here is for ratification but before deciding upon the advisability of calling the Indiana

Legislature, I am anxious to obtain the sentiment of other States whose Legislatures do not meet in ordinary session this year. . . . Are you willing to call a special session of your General Assembly in the event that a sufficient number of other States decide to take the same action in order to insure early ratification?" On June 28, the Governor wrote Indiana legislators regarding a special session for the first week in September and asked whether by proper resolution or by general agreement action could be limited to matters contained in the call.

Uneasiness immediately began to manifest itself among State officials and Republican leaders. They feared efforts would be made to amend or repeal the new tax law, that other questions would be injected, that it might be difficult for the Republicans to organize satisfactorily, since half a dozen candidates for Speaker of the House had appeared, and so on.

No public statement followed as the result of the Governor's correspondence and when, July 30, it was found that he had postponed the call indefinitely suffragists in turn became uneasy and then indignant. To all demands he replied, "There is no need for a session at this time. Further than that I have nothing to say." Women all over the State held indignation meetings and the Governor was deluged with protests from all kinds of Indiana organizations. July melted into August, August had been replaced by September and in turn by October, November and December. Still no action. On December 30 the Governor gave a plan to the officers of the Indiana auxiliary of the National Suffrage Association. It was: if the women could pledge two-thirds of the members of both Houses to come for a day and to consider nothing but ratification he would call the session.

Public sentiment was tremendously aroused over the Governor's proposal, and press and people commented freely and often fiercely on it.

Yet what was demanded the women did, and on January 13, 1920, they presented to the Governor written pledges from thirty-six Senators and seventy Representatives, and the session was called for January 16. The Senate and House met that day in joint session to hear the Governor's message. In the Senate, action was delayed for two or three hours by the final wails of three antis, Oliver Kline, Huntington; Charles A. Hagerty, South Bend; and Franklin McCray, Indianapolis. The vote silenced them. As soon as the House passed the resolution a waiting band struck up "Glory, Glory, Hallelujah."

Robert D. Carey, Governor of Wyoming, polled the Legislature himself for a voluntary session, although no one but suffrage leaders knew that it was being done and that on the result depended the call. The session was held January 26, and the vote was unanimous in both Houses.

When the envoys sent by the National American Woman Suffrage Association had called upon Governor Emmet D. Boyle of Nevada they had found him opposed to a special session because of expense. One of the envoys suggested the plan, which was afterwards put into effect, of securing the consent of the entire Legislature that only a quorum of members from nearby communities should be assembled, to consider ratification only, the women to serve as clerks. The Governor agreed to write the members and assured the women that if the one-day plan was not feasible, another would be made. Again at a meeting held in Reno in November, 1919, attended by the president of the National Suffrage Association, the Governor publicly announced that he would call a session.

Finally the call was issued and the Legislature met February 7, 1920, after an agreement to which the women were a party that the cost was not to exceed one thousand dollars. To, meet the expense the women of Carson City arranged to give legislators free room and board during the session. In his message to the Legislature the Governor said: "While no certainty exists that the favorable action of Nevada will in 1920 assure to the women of the United States the same voting privileges which our women enjoy by virtue of our State law, it does appear certain that without our favorable action the cause of national suffrage may be delayed for such a time as to withhold the right to vote at a Presidential election from millions of the women of America."

In the Senate the vote was unanimous. In the House Mrs. Hurst, the one woman member, introduced the resolution to ratify and presided during roll call. Representative W. O. Ferguson cast the one vote against, announcing that he "was opposed to having the people of Nevada tell the women of the Union whether or not they should vote."

By the hardest sort of addition the ratification column now footed up twenty-eight—and only twenty-eight.

CHAPTER 26

Last of All Suffrage Conventions

With February of 1920 the suffrage program reached its interorganization climax—the annual suffrage convention scheduled for Chicago February 12–18. Not only was this to be the last of all suffrage conventions; far and wide it had been heralded as the Victory Convention. Although the end of the suffrage struggle had not yet come, everybody felt sure it would come in 1920, and the National American Woman Suffrage Association was forehanded enough to go part way to meet the final victory.

Far from side-tracking the ratification campaign to make way for convention activities, those activities were but used to point and push the campaign.

"Suffragists hear this last call to a suffrage convention!" so read the call that was to assemble the suffrage hosts. "Of all the conventions held within the past fifty-one years this will prove the most momentous. Few people live to see the actual and final realization of hopes to which they have devoted their lives. That privilege is ours. . . . Let us tell the world of the ever-buoyant hope born of the assurance of justice and the inevitability of our cause which has given our army of workers unswerving courage and determination which has at last overcome every obstacle and attained its aim."

From Maine and from Florida; from California and from Texas, and from all the States between the women streamed into Chicago in the wintry February weather. The city, the whole country, was ice-locked and snow-banked, but spring was in the hearts of the suffragists. Never where women had come together had there been a gathering so gay—and never one so feelingly motivated by the sense of solidarity that holds organizations together. Handclasps seemed to mean more that February than they had ever meant before. Women looked into each other's eyes and saw old, endearing memories of long, hard work together leap to life. They were facing new things, new affiliations, separate ways, but the recognition of what the old things, the old supreme affiliation, the old way together, had done for them, singly and collectively, rested on them with a poignant inner compulsion. They could not shake it off. It dominated their merrymaking. It made them stop one another in corridors and in corners to whisper, "To think that we shall not meet again like this—not next year, not ever!"

"Ours has been a movement with a soul," said the president of the suffrage association to the assembled delegates, "a dauntless, unconquerable soul ever leading on. Women came, served and passed on, but others came to take their places, while the same great soul was ever marching on through a hundred, nay, a thousand years; a soul immortal, directing, leading the woman's crusade for the liberation of the mothers of the race. That soul is here today and who shall say that all the hosts of the millions of women who have toiled and hoped and met delay are not here today and joining in the rejoicing that their cause has at last won its triumph.

"Oh, how do I pity the women who have had no share in the exaltation and the discipline of our army of workers. How do I pity those who have felt none of the grip of the oneness of women struggling, serving, suffering, sacrificing for the righteousness of woman's emancipation.

"... be glad today. Let your voices ring out the gladness in your hearts. There will never come another day like this. Let your joy be unconfined and let it speak so clearly that its echo will be heard around the world and find its way into the soul of every woman of any and every race and nationality who is yearning for opportunity and liberty still denied her sex."

She closed with a parody on Kipling's poem, "If," which read:

> We kept our heads when all about us
> Were losing theirs and blaming it on us;
> We made allowance for the doubts of men
> And kept our faith though they were scornful then.
> We were lied about yet did not deal in lies,
> We were hated yet did not give way to hating;
> We did not look too good nor talk too wise,
> We waited and were not tired by waiting.
> We heard the truths that we had spoken
> Twisted by knaves to make a trap for fools;
> And watched the cause we'd given our life to broken,
> Yet bravely built again with poor cheap tools.
> We held on when there was nothing in us
> Except the will which says Hold on;
> Thus for sixty years marched on the suffrage soul
> And felt no doubt to reach the final goal.
> Thus filled we up each fleeting minute
> With sixty seconds' worth of distance run;
> And now ours is the Earth and everything that's in it,
> Rejoice, applaud, be glad—you've won!

A ribbon, attached to the clapper of a bell hung in the middle of the convention hall, was pulled by a woman holding the other end of the ribbon. Other women with other ribbon ends pulled. The bell pealed forth. The woman's hour was striking. At the sound old staid traditions were flung to the winds. Cheering and singing, delegation after delegation got to its feet and began marching. Women were sowing their political wild oats. They seemed suddenly to discover what men long since discovered—that the true purpose of a political convention is to make a noise. The high hall rang with their racket. For a long time it was a question whether they would ever be quiet again.

While convention celebrations and festivities were mounting to high tide there came, one by one, the announcement of ratifications in New Jersey, Idaho, Arizona and New Mexico, bringing the total number to thirty-two. The Washington League of Women Voters wired: "The women of Washington send greetings to the Victory Convention. We were a pioneer State, the fifth to be enfranchised. Therefore we resent the disgraceful humiliation put upon us by the stubborn refusal of our Governor to listen to our united demand for a special session to ratify the Suffrage Amendment." Immediately a telegram was sent by the convention to Louis A. Hart, Governor of the State, which read: "Washington is now the only enfranchised State which has taken no action toward ratification of the Federal Suffrage Amendment. Thirty-five ratifications are assured in the immediate future. The nation has been informed for many years that Washington approves woman suffrage. It therefore looks to you to call an immediate session of your Legislature and once more announce Washington's endorsement of woman suffrage by ratification of the Federal Amendment." Through the Associated Press the telegram went to the newspapers of Washington.

The Governors of Connecticut, Vermont, Delaware and West Virginia were also urged by wire to call sessions. And there was a lively exchange of telegrams with the Ratification Committees in these States. The convention ordered telegrams of thanks sent to the Governors who had called special sessions and to the chairmen of the National Committees of the two dominant parties,

Will H. Hays, Republican, and Homer Cummings, Democrat, who had rendered continuous and able support to the campaign. Telegrams were also sent to Governors who had not called special sessions urging the call.

A ratification banquet on St. Valentine's evening filled to overflowing the largest banquet hall in Chicago. Banquets had long been a feature of suffrage campaigning but never had there been one to tell a story like this. High upon a balcony was a huge old-fashioned Valentine with lacy frills and a big red heart in the middle. Two little maids upon signal pulled back the red silk curtains, leaving a space large enough for a person to stand in and make a half-length portrait with the heart for a frame. Then in verse the States which had ratified were introduced one by one and a prominent State suffrage leader appeared in the frame and, in humorous verse, told the story of the victory. There were salvos of applause and sudden bursts of State songs as Illinois's gaily attired State delegation sprang upon chairs after the State's story had been told by its living valentine. Tears of joyous happiness glistened in many an eye as incidents in the long struggle were brought to mind, or half-forgotten memories awakened. Eloquent speeches thrilled, flags waved, cheers and unexpected bursts of song reverberated through the vast hall.

Outstanding among the convention's features was a beautiful and solemn service in memory of Dr. Anna Howard Shaw, whose magic voice, now stilled forever, had been the inspiration of every previous convention for thirty years.

The one-hundredth anniversary of the birthday of Susan B. Anthony, greatest of all suffrage leaders, was especially commemorated by a program of brief speeches which collectively told the whole wonderful story of the emancipation of women from 1840, "The Age of Mobs and Eggs," to 1920, "A Portent of Victory." Another program told the suffrage story in pictures. Another in a Living Procession of Victories, a simple, beautiful and effective pageant. At a Pioneers' Luncheon the reminiscences of the workers of early days were told and many a woman whose name was familiar to all suffragists, but whose face was unknown to later workers, was there to share in that last organized tribute.

But in spite of such programs the convention did not expend all its energies on looking backward, nor its time in enjoying the triumph of the moment. It carefully planned for every emergency in the uncompleted ratification campaign, and it effected the organization of the "League of Women Voters" with a new national board distinct from that of the suffrage association. To this new body the National American Woman Suffrage Association's auxiliaries in all the ratified States were transferred by their representatives, and a program of education in citizenship for new voters and legislation for the protection of women, children and the home was adopted. Before the convention ended the phoenix of a new organization, with fresh ideals, aims and program, had arisen from the old.

Pronounced the most wonderful of all suffrage conventions during the seventy-two years of the struggle, the convention came to an end. The women who had worked side by side for a generation separated and went to their homes in the forty-eight States, some to throw themselves with ardor into political party organization work, some into the legislative program, some into citizenship education. But the National Suffrage Association's officers and the members of the Association's auxiliaries in those States whose Legislatures had not yet ratified the Federal Suffrage Amendment, bent anew to the suffrage task.

CHAPTER 27

The Opposition Grows Grimmer

No observer accustomed to judge popular opinion could have failed to recognize by March, 1920, that the fifty years' war for woman suffrage was won and that no opposition could now do more than delay the final triumph. That women would vote was already an accepted fact. Suffragists from all parts of the country reported this acceptance. Yet the directors of the campaign knew that although the war for woman suffrage was won, the fighting would go on and on, and that in all probability the bitterest conflict of the half century was scheduled for somewhere between the close of the last national suffrage convention and the proclamation of the Federal Suffrage Amendment by the federal Secretary of State.

It will be recalled that mention has been made of the fact that during the Chicago convention four State Legislatures ratified, those of New Jersey, Idaho, Arizona and New Mexico. One of these, New Jersey, served to emphasize for suffragists the mounting intensity of the opposition.

In August, 1919, Mr. James Nugent, the Democratic "boss" in the State, had declared himself a candidate for the New Jersey governorship and was quite frank in giving his reasons for so doing. He said: "The only reason that I got into this campaign as a candidate for the gubernatorial honors was that the State needed at least one man with the courage to stand four square against prohibition and woman suffrage." He was defeated at the primaries September 23, 1919.

The "bosses" of both political parties were avowedly anti-suffragists and, with the liquor interests, worked openly against the Amendment. To co-operate with the National Suffrage Association's New Jersey auxiliary a Men's Suffrage Council was organized which contained the names of leading Democrats and Republicans. They united in the demand for political recognition of women. Everett Colby was chairman and the honorary chairmen were Governor-elect Edward I. Edwards, United States Senators Joseph S. Frelinghuysen and Walter E. Edge. The list of vice-chairmen included legislators, judges and other public officials, editors, lawyers, business and professional men from both major political parties and from all parts of the State.

When the Legislature convened in 1920, the resolution for ratification was the first measure introduced. A public hearing was held February 2, and the Senate ratified that same day. The opposition then concentrated its efforts upon the Assembly. Attorney-General A. Mitchell Palmer had written to all the Democratic members urging support. By the evening of February 9, when ratification was to be voted on in the Assembly, it was clear that the stage was set by the opposition for an all-night "filibuster." Hugh Barrett of Essex, Nugent's special representative, led the opposition by making one motion after another, which, one by one, after a hot fight and much talking, were defeated. Outside, in the corridor, was Nugent himself, constantly sending messages to his representatives. Suffragists were there too, helping to steady their friends and firm in the determination to get the vote that night. For five hours the filibuster went on without abatement. Then the opposition gave up the fight and the resolution was passed.

In Idaho and Arizona, both full suffrage States, there was no delay in ratification once the special session was called. Governor D. W. Davis called the Legislature of Idaho February 11. The call requested the legislators not to take the full amount to which they were entitled but to confine the appropriation to an amount equivalent to their actual expenses only. The call further stipulated that no legislation should be considered other than ratification. The session came at the time of the meeting of the Republican State Committee and that of the Executive Committee of the Idaho Republican Press. Dr. Emma F. A. Drake, the only woman member of the House, introduced the resolution. The action there was unanimous but in the Senate there were six opposing votes, three Republicans and three Democrats.

Governor Campbell of Arizona, though not enthusiastic over calling a special session, because the majority in House and Senate were Democrats while he was a Republican, had, on August, 1919, at Flagstaff, promised the envoys sent out by the National Suffrage Association that he would call one if the women would poll the Legislature in order to learn if it would ratify and if the men would waive their per diem. He suggested the first week in November, 1919, but it was four months later, at noon February 12, 1920, when the first special session of the fourth State Legislature of Arizona ratified.

Attached to the House Bill were the names of the four women members—Mrs. Nellie Haywood, Mrs. Rosa McKay, Mrs. Westover and Mrs. O'Neill. There was little eloquence but much dispatch and the resolution went promptly to the Senate, which adopted the ratifying resolution at 9:15 p.m.

In New Mexico, owing to the large Mexican population, there was doubt from the first whether the Amendment could be ratified. Governor C. A. Lazzarola was opposed to ratification but as a Republican agreed to support it. In the Legislature the Democrats had worked for ratification and a poll of their members, taken immediately in both Houses, showed 20 out of 26 in favor.

At the Governors' conference in Salt Lake City the year before, the envoys of the National American Woman Suffrage Association had been assured by Governor Lazzarola that, although he was not for the Federal Suffrage Amendment, Republican support would be forthcoming and the Amendment would be ratified. It so happened that a Soldiers' and Sailors' Act, passed by the Governor's insistence at the last session, was faultily drawn and a special session was necessary to re-enact the measure.

The Legislature met in special session February 16, 1920. There was a determined effort on the part of one member, Dan Padillo of Albuquerque, to submit a referendum on the amendment to the voters of the State. Immediately the entire city protested—suffragists, prohibitionists, Y.W.C.A. and many men's organizations—until Padillo declared that he would vote for immediate ratification, which he did. The five "no" votes in the Senate and eight of the ten opposed in the House were Republicans.

The thirty-third ratification followed one week later. It was that of Oklahoma. At the Governors' conference at Salt Lake City in August, 1919, J. B. A. Robertson, Governor of Oklahoma, gave the great expense and the fear of untimely legislation as his reasons for not calling a special session of the Oklahoma Legislature, but he pledged that if the women could get the legislators to waive their per diem he would call the session at once. He added, however, "I do not think it can be done, as the women do not care enough." Thereafter he gave a telling exhibition of a chief executive dodging women who cared enough.

In September Miss Aloysius Larch-Miller, secretary of the Oklahoma Ratification Committee, assisted by a representative of the National Suffrage Association, secured signed pledges from a majority of the legislators that they would attend, serve without pay, consider no other legislation and vote for ratification. When these were presented, the Governor's answer was a refusal to answer. Several weeks later he addressed the State Federation of Women's Clubs at Edmond and again offered the same excuses—expense and State political problems. Meantime, the Republican State Organization, through the Republican National Committeeman, James A. McGraw, had offered to pay the expenses of the Republican legislators who could not pay their own. The Governor answered that by saying that the States which did not have the suffrage should assume the burden of ratifying the Suffrage Amendment.

In January, 1920, the Democratic State Central Committee called county conventions to select delegates to the Democratic State Convention. Many of these county conventions passed resolutions asking the Governor to call the session. Although she had been confined to her room for several days with influenza, Miss Larch-Miller attended the convention of her county—Pottawatomie—and spoke for the resolution in opposition to Attorney-General S. P. Freeling, one of the ablest orators of the State and also the strongest opponent of woman suffrage in Oklahoma. Her enthusiasm and eloquence carried the day for suffrage. The resolution was adopted. For her the price was her life. The exertion proved too heavy a tax and in two days she paid the supreme sacrifice for the cause she had served.

Interviewed again, the Governor said his action would depend on the action of his party convention. In the meantime Senator Robert L. Owen, who had a long record for woman suffrage, had become a candidate for Vice-President of the United States. Democratic women from many States had wired him to know why his State had not taken action on the Federal Suffrage Amendment, reminding him that he was the only candidate for Vice-President whose State had not ratified. At the Democratic State Convention at Muskogee, February 5, Governor Robertson finally agreed that, because of his interest in the candidacy of Senator Owen, he would call the session. This he did for February 23. A majority of the legislators were pledged to ratify, the Governor sent a favorable message and there was a telegram from President Wilson to the Speaker of the House: "May I not take the liberty of expressing my earnest hope that Oklahoma will join the other suffrage States in ratifying the Federal Suffrage Amendment, thus demonstrating anew its sense of justice and retaining its place as a leader in Democracy."

In opposition was the activity of Attorney-General Freeling, who used the State's Rights argument to influence some members, but the sacrifice of Miss Larch-Miller, coupled with the fact that Oklahoma was a suffrage State, overwhelmed all opposition. The resolution to ratify was passed February 27, 1920. Then Attorney-General Freeling added one more chapter to his record against suffrage by immediately starting the circulation of a petition to refer this action to the voters. The decision of the United States Supreme Court that there could be no referenda on federal amendments ended this effort.

Governor John J. Cornwell of West Virginia, a Democrat, was known to favor ratification. A letter from the National Suffrage Association in December, 1919, brought word from him that as soon as there was a court decision on the public utilities question, which was to be voted upon with the Suffrage Amendment, the call would be issued. The Democratic Governor called his Republican Legislature in special session Friday, February 27, 1920.

President Wilson wired members of the Senate as follows: "May I not urge upon you the importance to the whole country of the prompt ratification of the Suffrage Amendment and express the hope that you will find it possible to lend your aid to this end." The Democratic and Republican National Committees urged ratification, The State's delegation in Congress used its influence and the Governor's message was in favor. The outlook was promising, when opposition broke from two unexpected sources, due to the contest over the Governorship and to influences from outside the State. The Maryland Legislature sent a committee to urge rejection of the amendment. They arrived February 28, Senator George Arnold Frick and Representatives Willis R. Jones and Daniel P. Joseph, who said they had come to say that "West Virginia had no right to help put something over that was not wanted by other States." Two other members, Ellis R. Grimes and Senator Charles H. Gibson, came independently as former West Virginians, to say that the entire Legislature of Maryland was *not* opposed to ratification and that they believed "West Virginia capable of settling her own affairs without interference from Maryland."

A vote was rushed through both Houses and stood, House, ayes, 46; nays, 41; Senate, ayes, 14; nays 14. A motion to reconsider in the Senate was lost on Wednesday by the same vote. In the meantime, Senator Jesse A. Bloch, who was in California, receiving tardy notice of the session, wired that he was in favor of ratification and asked for a pair. This was refused by the opposition with jeers. Secretary of State Houston G. Young immediately got into telephone communication with Senator Bloch and he agreed to make the race across the continent if suffrage members would hold the lines intact until his arrival. The situation was acute. A motion in the House to reconsider had been laid on the table and could be called up at any time. Many legislators wanted to go home and it was difficult to keep the necessary number of suffrage men on hand to defeat hostile attacks. The entire country watched and waited, the tie in the Senate held, and Senator Bloch sped across the country. The day he reached Chicago the opposition resorted to its most desperate expedient by producing a former Senator, A. R. Montgomery, who about eight months before had resigned, because he was leaving the State permanently. The Governor had accepted his resignation and he was living in Illinois. Arriving in Charleston, he demanded the return of his letter of resignation from the Governor, who refused it because of documentary evidence that Mr. Montgomery had given up his residence in West Virginia. But Mr. Montgomery appeared in the Senate that afternoon and attempted to vote. President Sinsel ruled that he was not a member. On an appeal from the ruling the vote was a tie and his case was referred to the Committee on Privileges and Elections. That committee sustained the President's ruling.

Upon his arrival in Chicago Senator Bloch was met by Mr. V. L. Highland, National Republican Committeeman from West Virginia and Captain Victor Heintz, in charge of the National Republican headquarters in Chicago. He was given the choice of completing his journey by airplane or by train. Senator Bloch chose the airplane; Mrs. Bloch chose the train; they came by train. The trip was made with a record-breaking speed and the Senator arrived on March 10, taking his seat in the Senate amid cheers from crowded galleries. Men who were sick have gone into Senate chambers and Assembly halls to cast their votes for suffrage. Those who saw Representative Mann of Illinois, Sims of Tennessee, Barnhart of Indiana and Crosser of Ohio come into the House of Representatives in Washington on that historic day, January 10, 1918, when the Federal Suffrage Amendment won its first great House victory, will never forget it. Similar sacrifices have been made at heavy personal expense in many a State capitol. To the list of loyal men suffragists who have not only believed in suffrage but proved it was now added the name of Senator Bloch. A debate of several hours followed his appearance, each side fencing for the advantage. At 6 p.m. the vote was taken, ayes, 16; nays, 14; one opponent changing his vote when he saw that the resolution was going to pass without him.

After the Senate vote, a second vote was secured in the House by the opponents on the motion to reconsider. This resulted in a larger favorable majority than the first. On March 10 West Virginia completed ratification.

Thirty-four ratifications now; and ever more persistent grew the opposition as it saw that its time was short. On March 17 Joseph Holt Gaines and W. E. R. Byrne, counsel for the West Virginia Anti-Suffrage League, sent telegrams to the Governors of the States of Delaware, Connecticut, Vermont, Washington and North Carolina, which read: "We beg to inform you that the report that the proposed nineteenth amendment was ratified by the Legislature of West Virginia is not the fact, but on the contrary, the Legislature refused to ratify the amendment. The facts are that the Senate having refused to ratify, afterwards undertook, in violation of its own rules, to take action ratifying the amendment. That action, we claim, is absolutely void and we are taking legal steps to enjoin any official certification or promulgation to the effect that West Virginia is one of the States ratifying. We have taken the liberty of giving you this information, because there has been an effort to suppress the full facts with reference to West Virginia's action."

While they were notifying these Governors that steps would be taken to prevent the certification of the West Virginia ratification, the certificate had already reached Washington, making West Virginia thirty-fourth in the ratification list received by the Secretary of State.

Although the Governor of Washington, Louis F. Hart, in August, 1919, telegraphed his pledge to call a special session to the Governors' conference and requested the other Governors to join with him, it was not until March 22, 1920, that the Legislature of Washington, last of the full suffrage States, met in special session and ratified the Federal Suffrage Amendment. The session was called to provide funds for the maintenance of State Schools. It was summoned after a conference with State regents and legislators who had supervision of appropriations for educational institutions, because of a crisis in finances which might result in closing the University of Washington, the State College at Pullman, and several State normal schools.

Both Houses met in joint session to hear the Governor's message. There was a tense expectation throughout the proceedings, since at any moment the wires might flash the news that Delaware, known to be meeting in special session, had ratified, in which case Washington would be the thirty-sixth State to ratify, and would put the final seal on the full enfranchisement of the women of the entire nation.

The ratifying resolution was introduced in the House by Representative Frances M. Haskell from Pierce County, who the year before had introduced the memorial to Congress for the passage of the Federal Suffrage Amendment. Rules were suspended and the resolution to ratify was adopted unanimously.

Twelve minutes after the resolution reached the Senate it had been passed by another unanimous vote.

Thirty-five States had now ratified. Many of them had done so only because of the unceasing, intensive ratification campaign waged by the National American Woman Suffrage Association. Again and again the Association had had to work its way through State situations of extreme complication. Continually it had had to spur political leaders and political parties to further the struggle. Its representatives had had to fly from end to end of the country untiringly. It had had to agitate and educate and placate. Steadily the work had grown harder. State by State, through all the later ratifications, step by step, the opposition had grown grimmer. But the Association knew and the opposition knew that whatever had gone before, whatever success in the result, however hard the work, the real fight was now at hand. Everything else paled into insignificance before the opposition's final attitude. Before it every resource that suffragists possessed was going to be drained dry, every reliance be leaned on to the breaking point.

Suffragists might have thirty-five ratifications till the crack of doom. But the thirty-sixth they should not have. That was the final attitude of the opposition.

CHAPTER 28

The Struggle for the Thirty-Sixth State

The National Suffrage Association now called upon the two chairmen of the Republican and Democratic National Committees to secure the one ratification needed. The Republican leaders were determined that their record should not be blackened at the eleventh hour, and Democratic leaders were equally sincere in the decision that defeat of final ratification should not be laid at their door. So both national chairmen again issued statements and vied with each other in efforts to influence lagging States. The Democrats considered four States which had not yet taken action, Tennessee, North Carolina, Louisiana and Florida, from which they hoped to secure one ratification; while the Republican party looked to Connecticut, Vermont and Delaware and felt sure of one ratification out of the three chances. In May, the Democratic National Committee and the National Democratic Convention in San Francisco passed strong resolutions. The one adopted by the convention called specifically upon Tennessee, North Carolina and Florida to ratify the amendment. In Chicago, at the National Republican Convention, June 8, correspondingly strong resolutions were passed.

In July the *Woman Citizen,* the official organ of the National American Woman Suffrage Association, carried an open letter to Senator Harding, the Republican nominee for President of the United States, in which the fact was cited that he now, as the executive agent and mouthpiece of the Republicans, became responsible if the party failed to complete ratification in time for the women to take part in the 1920 elections. At the same time an urgent appeal was made to the Democratic nominee for President, James M. Cox. President Wilson was asked for co-operation in securing a special session in Tennessee and for assistance in North Carolina and Florida.

One more State! Which would it be? Governors Marcus A. Holcomb of Connecticut and Percival W. Clement of Vermont, both anti-suffragists and anti-prohibitionists, were known to have entered into some kind of compact not to call their Legislatures. They had been visited by deputations from the State auxiliaries of the National American Woman Suffrage Association in these States early in the summer of 1919, and petitions for special sessions had been refused. In all these months of ratification activity neither Governor had receded from the position then taken. The pressure brought to bear from within and without the States was unprecedented. Committees of men and women brought unquestioned evidence of popular demand, but interviews, petitions, resolutions of political conventions and appeals of party leaders went unheeded. In both States the Legislatures had been polled and would have ratified by large majorities, if called. In Connecticut the petition, signed by a majority of both Houses asking for the special session, was waved aside by the Governor, and by the chairman of the Republican party in the State, John Henry Roraback. These men had not only opposed the Presidential Suffrage Bill proposed in the last Connecticut Legislature, but in the days when suffragists had begged for opportunity to get the question before the voters of the State by a referendum, they had exerted all their efforts to prevent action.

In Vermont, the women secured pledges from a majority of the legislators to agree to pay their own expenses and give their time at a special session. Governor Clement still refused to call the session. In both States the Governors were in absolute control of the situation.

In Connecticut, Governor Holcomb masked his opposition to the special session with the contention that the suffrage problem did not present the circumstances of "special emergency" under which he was authorized by the State Constitution to convene the General Assembly in special session.

In Vermont, Governor Clement disguised his opposition with the argument that "If the electors of this State are not to be allowed to vote upon the Federal Suffrage Amendment it seems only fair that it should be acted upon by a General Assembly selected with knowledge that it is to be acted upon by them."

Over and over again these men, urged by their party, the Republican, and arraigned before the bar of public opinion by the press, were given to understand that full responsibility rested upon them for their policy of obstruction. Why was it so difficult to get the thirty-sixth State? Why? Why? The political machine that could make a President certainly could easily whip a reactionary or determined Governor into line. The National Suffrage Association and all its State auxiliaries bent every energy to secure the sessions. When the Governor of Connecticut announced that he was ready to receive proof of the existence of an emergency, the Association offered its co-operation for a demonstration of nationwide strength to furnish the proof as a protest against the blocking of woman suffrage for the whole country. It organized, at a cost of five thousand dollars, an "Emergency Corps" of forty-eight women, one from each State, doctors, lawyers, scientists, business and professional women, professors and public officials, a group of women which in size, prominence and ability had never been equaled in the United States. They met in New York May 2, and received their instructions from the president of the Association. At Hartford they held a meeting. Then, separating into four groups of twelve each, they spoke in the chief cities of the State. Dividing again into groups of four each, they visited many of the smaller towns. With Connecticut women, they interviewed most members of the Legislature. After a tour of thirty-six towns with forty-one meetings at which resolutions were passed unanimously calling upon the Governor to convene a special session, they came, on May 7, at eleven-thirty in the morning, to the Capitol. In short speeches they answered the Governor's objections and emphasized the national significance of their request. The Governor replied that he would reserve his decision until he had carefully considered their arguments. Four days later he announced that "while the arguments proved a strong desire for a special session they did not prove the existence of a 'special emergency' and he must decline."

As time passed on the situation became more and more exasperating. It seemed that these Governors could not realize how the nation with its millions of people regarded their attitude and the position into which this "emergency" had thrust the political parties of the country, so a campaign was organized by the National Suffrage Association to get the voice of the people and the voice of the party into written form. In the result hundreds of letters went to both Governors from prominent Republicans all over the country. The appeal was made from the standpoint of national emergency and all reference to the presidential campaign was eliminated.

In order that the country in general might have the facts regarding the delay in calling the session, the president of the Connecticut auxiliary to the National American Woman Suffrage Association issued a manifesto which read in part:

"Who is responsible for the delay which may keep ten million women from the vote for President and about twenty million from the vote for members of Congress, State officials, etc. Both great political parties, but the Republican in greater degree. . . . It lies in the power of this party to speak the word that will fully enfranchise the women of this country and where there is power there is responsibility. . . . You have withheld that one State which would make just the difference between our voting or not voting. . . . An emancipator is not the man who takes the prisoner all the way to the door and lets him look out but the man who actually unlocks the door and lets him go free. . . . At the time of the State Republican Convention the Hartford *Courant* obligingly explained that the suffrage resolution it passed was a pretense and really meant nothing—a statement, it is only fair to say, repudiated by many honorable Republicans. Now it is Chairman Roraback who, with happy unconsciousness that he is exhibiting his party in a 'yellow light', tells the public that the national Republican platform should not be taken seriously. . . . 'The leaders of the party,' he says, 'put the suffrage plank in to please women in the voting States, but they meant nothing by it!' Are the men who are to lead a great party as double-faced and untrustworthy as Mr. Roraback paints them? Were they laughing in their sleeves as they wrote the solemn pledges in the rest of the national platform? We wonder if Connecticut Republicans will let Mr. Roraback smirch the party honor unchallenged. The course for the State Suffrage Association is clear. We must play our part in this sector of the national suffrage struggle and we must let our opponents see that they cannot keep American citizens out of their fundamental rights with impunity."

In the meantime Republican women in the State organized a movement which pledged its members not to give money or work

for the Republican party as long as women remained unenfranchised; three Republican women went to Columbus, Ohio,
and impressed upon the Republican Executive Committee there
assembled that the sincerity of the party in regard to woman
suffrage was being questioned. Another group waited upon Senator
Harding and asked him to request the Governor of Connecticut
to call a special session. Senator Harding declined, on the ground
that it would be improper for him to make any suggestion to a
fellow Republican on a great moral question.

In August, when it was found that the Republican party was
taking credit for most of the ratifications already secured but
not bringing effective pressure on the Republican Governors of
Connecticut and Vermont, thirty women requested an audience
with Mr. Will Hays, chairman of the National Republican
Committee, to ask him what the party was doing to secure
ratification in Connecticut. He received them in the National
Republican Headquarters, New York City. The chairman of the
Connecticut auxiliary to the National American Woman Suffrage
Association spoke for the deputation. She said in part:

> "What the women want is to vote in November. What the
> parties apparently want is a good record as a talking point in
> the coming campaign. What to the women is the supremely
> important thing is that thirty-sixth State. What to the parties
> seems to be most important is to exact their full due of grati-
> tude from women who have not yet received the gift that was
> promised. . . . In our own State where the Republican party is
> responsible the women are actually being called upon to aid
> its campaign while it is repudiating the policy and promises
> of the National Party in regard to ratification. . . . From the
> time when suffrage became an issue it has had the opposition
> of the leaders of the Republican Party in this State. Since

the Amendment passed Congress they have resisted every expression of public opinion, every plea for ratification on grounds of justice and fair play. For a year the suffragists have tried sincerely and patiently to work in and with the Republican Party to overcome this opposition and have been co-operating with a Republican Men's Ratification Committee formed for this purpose, but we are apparently no nearer a special session than we were a year ago. During all this time we have had no evidence that the National Republican Committee was really working in the State. We found it very difficult to reach you personally and our appeals for specific help were ignored. Mr. Roraback and Major John Buckley, secretary to the Governor, have stated that they have never been asked by you to call a session. They evidently feel and wish the public to understand that the National Republican Committee has given them a free hand to pursue their obstructionist course. And to confirm this comes President-elect Harding's refusal to attempt to persuade Governor Holcomb. In the meantime, we women are being told that the Republican party cannot be held responsible, because the Governor stands alone in his opposition! We submit that so long as the official leaders of the party in the State are in entire harmony with him in opposing us, and the National Party keeps hands off, they are accomplices in his opposition and must be held responsible accordingly. And we further submit that if a national party is to come before the voters on the basis of its policies and promises, then it must be held responsible for making those promises good through its State branches. . . . If the Connecticut Republican leaders can play a free hand without interference from the National Party, then that Party faces the alternative of either admitting powerlessness and disintegration or of being an accomplice in the State's attitude of repudiation."

Governor Holcomb still refused to call the session.

In the meantime Vermont women had not been idle. There the same vigorous efforts were put forth. The women conducted a remarkable campaign, providing new and ingenious methods of reaching Governor Clement, the last of which was made possible by the help of the National American Woman Suffrage Association at a cost of one thousand dollars. It was the organization of such a deputation as had never before been attempted by men of the State for any cause. Twelve of the fourteen counties were represented by four hundred women who went to the State Capitol, overcoming the obstacles of long distances, almost impassable roads and poor train service. Many came from towns remote from railroads, one woman walking five miles to the station. Others plowed through deep snow and over muddy and rocky roads before daylight. Reaching the Capitol they marched, a silent army of loyal soldiers, through a cold drenching rain and took their places before the Governor's chair. One by one, in a sentence or two, they presented Vermont's case. His response was that he "did not care to make a decision at once." In addition to this demonstration, a campaign of letters and telegrams had been arranged to precede and follow the visit of the delegation and 1,600 communications from all parts of the State went to the Governor's desk.

On June 29 Governor Clement went to Washington and both press and people believed that at last he would give way. Senator Harding, candidate of the Republican party for President of the United States, and the Governor both acknowledged that the calling of a special session in Vermont had been discussed. Senator Harding said he told the Governor he would be very glad to see this done but made plain his desire not to interfere with the Governor's prerogative. On July 12 an official proclamation was issued by the Governor in which he stated that the federal constitution in its present form threatened the foundation of free popular

Government. He said: "The Sixteenth Amendment, providing for a Federal Income Tax, was lobbied through Congress and State Legislatures by Federal agents, and the Eighteenth Amendment, for Federal Prohibition, was forced through by paid agents of irresponsible organizations with unlimited funds." Concerning what he called the proposal to "force through the Nineteenth Amendment for Woman Suffrage in the same manner," he said: "I will never be a party to any proceeding which proposes to change the organic law of the State without the consent of the people." "The Constitution," he said, "threatened free popular Government alike as it stood and as it was interpreted by the Supreme Court. This decision leaves the people at the mercy of any group of men who may lobby a proposal for a change in the Federal Constitution through Congress and then through the Legislatures of the States."

The President of the National Suffrage Association issued an open letter to the Governor in the course of which she said:

"A careful perusal of your proclamation refusing to call the Legislature of Vermont into special session impresses the most casual reader with the conviction that you have doubtless told the truth, but not the whole truth. In order that this generation of your fellowmen and posterity may not misunderstand your position, the National American Woman Suffrage Association urges you to supplement your proclamation with replies to the following questions: Do you acknowledge that the Federal Constitution is the supreme law of this land and supersedes all State Constitutions wherever the two are in conflict? Do you challenge this fact that has stood unchallenged for 131 years? Do you know that on January 10, 1791, Vermont ratified that Constitution, although she had one of her own, and by so doing accepted the precedence of the Federal Constitution over it and by that act was admitted into the Union as a member of the United States of America? If you do know these facts of common knowledge, why did you throw over your refusal to call a special session the camouflage of a dissertation about the alleged conflict between the Vermont and Federal Constitutions which has nothing whatever to do with the calling of a special session of your Legislature? . . . Do you not know that when a Legislature acts upon a Federal Constitutional Amendment, it draws its authority from the Federal and not the State Constitution, and that the Governor has no responsible part in the transaction, except as custodian of the amendment when it comes from the Federal Secretary of State and returns to him with the Certificate of Ratification? Then why profess such a burden of personal responsibility in the matter? You profess to fear 'an invasion of State's Rights and take upon yourself the responsibility of preserving the foundations of free popular Government.' Then why did you veto the Presidential Suffrage Bill passed by the Legislature of Vermont in 1919, which was strictly a State action and conferred the vote upon the women of Vermont alone?

Your National Party Convention in 1920 called for completion of ratification in time for women to vote for the next President. Your Party's National Committee in the interim of conventions took action three times, once asking the Congress to submit the Suffrage Amendment, once favoring early ratification and once calling upon Republican Governors to call special sessions in order that ratification might proceed. Your State Party Conventions, your Party's State Committee, your State Legislature, hundreds of Vermont women, the chairman of the National Republican Committee and the chairman of your State

Republican Committee, the candidate for President of your Party, all have asked you to call a special session. This is a very distinguished and notable group to be dismissed with the implication that your people are at their mercy. . . You owe it to the Republican Party and to the world to explain your assumption of an authority that belongs to your party leaders. By what right do you make this assumption? Governor Clement tell it all."

But Governor Clement did not call the session in Vermont.

While the Governors of Connecticut and Vermont persisted in their refusals to call the special sessions, attention was turned to Delaware where there was hope. The history of Delaware on constitutional amendments had been unusual and strikingly irregular. Delaware was the first State to ratify the Constitution. It refused to ratify the three amendments proposed in the Reconstruction period after the Civil War and did not reconsider its action until 1901 when its Legislature accepted them. Delaware ratified the Income Tax Amendment but the Seventeenth Amendment, providing for direct election of United States Senators, did not meet with the approval of the Legislature, although the State of Delaware, because of the attempt of rival candidates to influence the Senatorship, had kept one of its seats vacant one entire Senatorial term. Delaware was the ninth State to ratify the Eighteenth Amendment.

This record did not tend to a favorable forecast of the fate of the Nineteenth Amendment; but there were other things which did. Delaware was now a Republican State. In the Senate there were twelve Republicans and five Democrats; in the House twenty-three Republicans and twelve Democrats. If the Republicans would adhere to their expressed party policy the Amendment could be ratified the first day of the session—and the Republican leaders did not minimize the ratification by the Legislature of Delaware as a party asset. If Delaware failed to ratify, leaders argued their party would be held responsible for the defeat of the Amendment and reprisals at the polls might follow in the coming campaign from the women of the thirty-one States in which they now had presidential suffrage, exclusive of Vermont and inclusive of Kentucky, which in 1920 had been added to the list of States whose Legislatures had given presidential suffrage to women. But Delaware, governed by provincial interests, failed to see the party importance of favorable action on the Amendment. She was in the midst of a factional fight. The Republican party in the State was divided into two groups led by rival members of a single family. One of these was the National Committeeman. The State Republican Chairman was a follower of the other faction. The National Republican Chairman, perceiving that the only probable chance of a Republican ratification was in Delaware, sent favorable instructions to the Republicans of the State through the National Committeeman instead of the State Republican Chairman, which at once turned one faction against the Amendment because the other was charged with its responsibility. It should also be said that had the message reached the State chairman the other faction would probably have turned against it.

Governor Townsend had delayed calling a special session because he feared action against the school code. A large sum had been offered to the State by Pierre Dupont for a much needed extension of Delaware's public school facilities, contingent upon a like sum being raised by the State. The gift had been accepted by the Legislature and the necessary taxes had been assessed. The Governor was fighting hard to raise the State from its thirty-second place in educational ranks, but when it became apparent that Delaware was needed to complete ratification he laid aside his fears for the code and issued a proclamation calling the session for March 22.

Since the anti-Saulsbury campaign a campaign for ratification had been waged continuously in the State. The State auxiliary to the National American Woman Suffrage Association had secured resolutions from all kinds of State organizations favoring suffrage and immediate ratification, and had interviewed the legislators and found a majority to be favorable. The State Democratic Committee endorsed ratification on January 22 and the Republican State Committee at a later date. Indications were so favorable that the women were unprepared for the weeks of intrigue that followed immediately upon the convening of the Legislature.

The people of Sussex, the most southern county, were particularly hostile to the school code and to suffrage. It was these county representatives, led by Daniel Layton, chairman of the Republican State Central Committee, former Governor Simeon S. P. Pennewell, U.S. Senator Wolcott and former Senator Saulsbury, who eventually blocked ratification in the House. Daniel Layton had always been known as a suffragist, but because of his personal opposition to the Governor he publicly announced that he would defeat ratification.

In his message to the two Houses in joint session the Governor said, "Woman suffrage has been a subject of public discussion for over half a century. It is not an agitation of the moment, it is a world-wide question of right and wrong. Your supreme duty is to think and act for the good of your State and the nation. The responsibility is yours." Hundreds of telegrams from outside the State poured into Delaware daily. They came from the President of the United States, from Secretaries Daniels, Houston and Meredith and Attorney-General Palmer of his Cabinet, from Republican Governors, State party chairmen and interested party leaders throughout the country.

Governor Townsend was one governor who did everything possible to secure ratification. He was a candidate for the National Republican Convention and antagonism to him took the form of opposing his nomination as delegate. When he was given to understand by the opposition that ratification could be obtained only at the cost of his individual political humiliation, he called a meeting of Republican members of the Legislature and withdrew his candidacy. The opposition, however, after making this proposal, failed to fulfil its part of the agreement and now signed a "round robin" letter declaring against ratification, which was circulated by the president of the Women's State Anti-Suffrage Association.

John E. McNabb, the Democratic floor leader, boldly ignored the telegrams from President Wilson, members of the Cabinet, Homer Cummings, chairman of the Democratic National Committee, and from other party leaders. He said that not twenty-five persons in his district favored ratification and refused to retreat from his position even though two days later a petition from five hundred men and women of his district was handed to him.

The small town of Dover was soon filled to overflowing with parties interested in the defeat of ratification. Among them were all of the notable wet and railroad lobbyists of the State, reinforced by legislative workers and brewers' representatives from other States. Prominent men in high positions worked with them. Henry P. Scott of Wilmington, chairman of the State Republican Ways and Means Committee, widely circulated a statement which read: "If the Legislature will refuse to ratify the proposed Amendment and thus prevent the hysterical rout of the politicians of the country to make shreds and patches of our sacred Constitution, the State of Delaware will receive in the near future the greatest possible glory."

On March 30 word was received that the Mississippi Senate had ratified the Suffrage Amendment. This was followed by a telegram to the anti-ratificationists of Delaware that the Senate vote was only a flash in the pan and would be reconsidered. The Republican opponents in Delaware telegraphed to the Speaker of the House in

Mississippi, "Stand firm against ratification. Delaware Legislature still firm for doctrine of State's Rights and will not ratify. We refuse to be stampeded and whipped into line by any party lash."

The date for the House vote was fixed for March 31 and defeat there seemed certain. But Assemblyman Hart to whom, as the introducer, belonged the responsibility of bringing up the bill, left the capital for his home, thus making it impossible for action to take place. After a conference with anti members, Representative Lloyd introduced an exact copy of the Hart resolution, so that its opponents might control the measure. Mr. Hart brought up his resolution the next day, April 1, and it was defeated. Days passed. No further action was taken.

The Republican convention met in Dover April 20 and the Delaware auxiliary to the National Suffrage Association made a remarkable demonstration. Hundreds of suffragists arrived on every train and in decorated automobiles. In themselves they constituted the best argument that could be made for ratification. Long petition sheets were exhibited with the names of twenty thousand Delaware women asking for ratification. In the convention speech of its permanent chairman, a staunch suffragist, Robert Houston of Georgetown, Sussex County, was a strong appeal for ratification, and it called forth the great outburst of enthusiasm of the day.

Two weeks later, May 5, the resolution to ratify the Amendment was called up in the Senate and a referendum to the voters which was offered as a substitute was defeated by a solid Republican vote of ayes, 4; nays, 13. The resolution to ratify was adopted, ayes, 11; nays, 6; ten Republicans and one Democrat voting for and two Republicans and four Democrats against it. The expectation was that action would be taken in the House on Friday, but on Thursday morning a clear intention to defeat the resolution was revealed and the bill was therefore placed under lock and key in the Senate. For in Delaware bills were known to have been stolen.

Senator Gormley (wet) attempted to offer a motion ordering its delivery to the House, but was ruled out of order by the President *pro tem*. In the House "Bull" McNabb launched an attack on those who were withholding the resolution and freely used the words "bribery," "cajoling," "threats," interspersed with much profanity. The president of the anti-suffragists called out encouragement to him, and the Republican floor leader, William Lyons, had to ask her to stop in order that he might make his own speech.

The Senate refused to send the resolution to the House and an adjournment of the Legislature was secured until May 17, in the hope of bringing about a change of sentiment. Republican leaders interested in ratification met at the capitol that day and pleaded with members to stand by their party, but to no avail.

On May 28, three days after the resolution had passed the Senate, it was sent to the Lower House, read twice, and a motion was unanimously carried that the House resolve itself into a Committee of the Whole. A motion was next put to adjourn until twelve-thirty, June 2, and it was carried. On June 2 Representative Lyons offered a motion that a vote be taken on the resolution. It was defeated by ayes, 10; nays, 24. The House thus placed itself on record against the Amendment and ended all further legislative action on it in Delaware.

The causes for defeat in Delaware were personal quarrels between party leaders, augmented by contests over local issues. This rendered the Legislature particularly susceptible to the overwhelming appeals of the well-organized and powerful wet and railroad lobbies. The women antis, as usual, served to hide from the public the real character of the opposition.

The failure of the Legislature of the State of Delaware to ratify filled party leaders with such exasperation that suffragists saw hope that out of it one or the other of the parties would yet find the thirty-sixth State.

CHAPTER 29

The Supreme Court Speaks

Many eminent lawyers were convinced that even should the Federal Supreme Court declare referenda on federal amendments in general invalid, such decision would not apply to the State of Ohio, whose voters had amended the State constitution especially providing for referenda after ratification of all federal constitutional amendments. It was held that a decision declaring a referendum in Ohio unconstitutional would apply to all other States, but that the reverse would not be true—a viewpoint that lent additional interest and significance to the Ohio case.

The Ohio Supreme Court had handed down its opinion on September 30, 1919, that a referendum on the ratification of the prohibition amendment was valid. Although an appeal was promptly taken to the Federal Supreme Court, the drys of the State recognized that there was no time to secure an opinion before the November election, and therefore proceeded to wage a campaign of preparation for the election contest. After they had lost by less than five hundred votes, they called for a recount, and opinion among their forces seems to have been divided as to whether to expend the time and money necessary to secure a statewide recount, or to wait for the Federal Supreme Court decision, which they believed would declare the referendum void. It was not generally believed, however, that this appeal of the Ohio drys was going to bring the much anticipated Federal decision, because the election it was supposed to prevent had already taken place; and whatever damage the Ohio taxpayer who brought the suit might suffer, on account of an unnecessary election, had already been suffered and the decision could give him no redress.

When the petitions were filed for a referendum on ratification of the suffrage amendment, George S. Hawke of Cincinnati, the man who had taken similar action in behalf of the prohibition amendment, filed a motion in the Court of Common Pleas, Franklin County, to enjoin the Secretary of State from putting the question on the ballot. By agreement he secured prompt action in the minor courts so that the case had passed through to the Supreme Court in the record-breaking time of one month. On November 11, 1919, that court announced its opinion as upholding the Franklin County Courts in refusing to enjoin the Secretary of State. Mr. Hawke promptly appealed his case to the Supreme Court of the nation.

Although there were a bewildering number of cases much advertised as on their way to the Supreme Court, and although all the appeals from the referenda decisions of State Supreme Courts were supposed to be on the calendar of the Federal Court, the facts were that when the Supreme Court took recess on November 21, 1919, the only cases involving the referenda which were actually on the federal calendar were the two Hawke cases from Ohio. The one, prohibition, was regarded as mooted; the other, suffrage, as premature, since in the eyes of the law the suffrage amendment had not been ratified and might never be.

Meanwhile the presidents of the National American Woman Suffrage Association and the Ohio auxiliary of the Association held a conference with Mr. Hawke in Cleveland on December 9, 1919.

Mr. Hawke was a young attorney connected with a group of the Prohibition party wing of the prohibition movement which had never come into unison with the Anti-Saloon League, the organization that was in control of the main campaign in Ohio and the nation. He had attempted to enjoin the Secretary of State on the prohibition amendment case without the consent or knowledge of the Anti-Saloon League, as he had attempted to enjoin in the suffrage case without the consent or knowledge of any suffrage association. He had allowed the National Anti-Saloon League to join with him in the argument on the referendum of the prohibition ratification before the State Supreme Court, but he had done so through courtesy, not choice. When asked why, without consultation with the suffrage leaders of Ohio, he had challenged the anti-suffrage petitions, he replied that the prohibition case which he had appealed to the Federal Supreme Court was weak, since the election had taken place, and he wished to strengthen it. He was not, however, averse to taking the National American Woman Suffrage Association into partnership on his undertaking, and an agreement was made that this would be done provided the counsel of the Association so advised.

The Hon. Charles E. Hughes had been engaged as the Association's Counsel—and no more able constitutional lawyer had the country produced. Mr. Hughes, Mr. Wayne Wheeler, the chief counsel for the National Anti-Saloon League, and the Federal Department of Justice, all advised that the Hawke case stood small chance of bringing forth the much coveted decision, but that that decision would come soon on some one of the numerous and seemingly far more important cases. Mr. Hawke was, therefore, informed that the tentative agreement would not be carried out. Mr. Hawke had neither money of his own nor many supporters who could provide the costs of the appeal to the Supreme Court, but he had faith in his case and that most valuable of American traits—stick-to-it-ive-ness. He took the matter up with J. Frank Hanley, one time Governor of Indiana, and for some years a fearless advocate of prohibition. He too had not yielded the prestige of the Prohibition Party leadership to the Anti-Saloon League. A small group had established "The Flying Squadron Foundation" which played an independent part in the prohibition drama. Mr. Hanley was an able lawyer and to him Mr. Hawke—young, unknown—made his appeal. There was no money to reward him, perhaps none for printing unless it could be gathered from friends, an always difficult task made more difficult by the fact that all the nation knew that the decision must soon be forthcoming anyway from one of the many cases coming up from other States.

Yet Mr. Hawke persuaded Mr. Hanley to join him, and on February 7, 1920, their briefs were filed with the Court. On February 25, reply briefs were filed with Attorney-General Price of Ohio as Counsel, and on June 2, 1920, to the amazement of all the most interested lookers on, the Supreme Court selected the Hawke cases upon which to send to the waiting nation the great decision, long expected and crucial. That decision was that there could be no State referenda on federal amendments.

The entire question was involved in the single query, "What is a Legislature?" Is it the small legislative body elected by the people or may the legislative function be extended to the people themselves as the initiative and referendum act extended it. The briefs of the Kentucky Distillers and Warehouse Company, the Liquor Dealers of New Jersey and, later, the State of New Jersey, the State of Rhode Island, and the appeals from State Supreme Court decisions, now wet, now dry, had all expended much time and space on the referendum proposition. Charles E. Hughes, on behalf of the twenty-two States (Rhode Island, Delaware, North Carolina, Kentucky, Louisiana, Indiana, Alabama, Maine, Arkansas, Michigan, Florida, Oregon, Kansas, West Virginia, Nevada, Nebraska, Montana, North Dakota, South Carolina,

Wyoming, Utah, and Arizona) which as *amici curiae* filed briefs on the Rhode Island case, summed up the whole matter in masterly fashion.

The chief points of argument *for* the right of referendum on federal amendments were:

1. The Initiative and Referendum was unknown when the constitution was written, but it is the establishment of an enlarged Legislature created by the "will of the people."

2. In the words of Attorney General Price of Ohio: "The voters of the States have the power to abolish their General Assemblies and to take into their own hands all matters of legislation. Such authority as the Legislatures have to ratify amendments to the Federal Constitution is not mandatory but permissive."

The State of Ohio did take from the Legislature some of its authority and vest it with the people when it established the Initiative and Referendum.

The chief points in the argument *against* the right of referendum on federal amendments were:

1. The Federal Constitution is the supreme law of the land and supersedes all State constitutions and State statutory laws in authority.

2. The Federal Constitution clearly indicates the method of its own amendment and this provides that an amendment must first be submitted by a two-thirds vote of the two houses of Congress and then must be ratified by the *Legislatures* of three-fourths of the States.

3. A vast amount of evidence has been gathered to show that the Federal Constitution clearly indicated the elected body known as Legislatures when it said Legislatures. The

discussion which resulted in the adoption of the Federal Constitution made that point quite clear.

4. While the States have full authority to change their own constitution and laws in any manner they choose without consulting the Federal Government, they have no power to change the meaning of the Federal Constitution and since the Federal Constitution has never been amended so as to give authority to any State to choose a different method of ratification of a Federal Amendment than that prescribed by the constitution itself, the interpretation of the meaning of the word *Legislature* today is precisely the same as that in existence when the Constitution was written.

5. In the opinion rendered by the U.S. District Court of New Jersey is the following:

"In Article V two methods are authorized for the ratification of amendments, one by convention and the other by Legislatures. If the method by convention had been chosen, would the ratifying action by the convention have been subject to a referendum vote by the people? Manifestly not, if the express language of the Constitution is conclusive. And if not, where is the warrant for holding that ratification by the Legislatures requires such a referendum vote?"

6. To those who hold that the Initiative and Referendum laws may be held as having control over the Federal Constitution, the question is directed as to whether the people of any State could initiate a Federal Amendment. By common consent it is agreed that this was not within the intent of the law. If one part of the law fails in application to federal matters, how can the other be held to be applicable? "The Federal Constitution, and not the constitutions of the several States, controls the method by which the U.S. Constitution may be amended."

The decision was announced in glaring headlines from ocean to ocean, and followed by editorial comment by all the leading newspapers of the country. Mr. Hanley's own paper, *The National Enquirer* (Indianapolis), said:

"The Supreme Court of the United States has spoken, and its words were double-charged; charged with life and death, life for the two great amendments to the Federal Constitution—the Eighteenth, the prohibition amendment, and the Nineteenth, the woman suffrage amendment—and death to every State referendum endeavor—legislative or constitutional—having for its purpose the change of the method of amendment of the Constitution or the placing of a limitation upon the ratifying power of a State Legislature.

"In the judgment it has rendered in the two cases of George S. Hawke vs. Harvey C. Smith, Secretary of State of Ohio, it has written 'Finis' upon the grave of the hopes of the wet interests so far as they were based upon State referendums of legislative ratification of either of these amendments.

"The decision is of vast importance, not only because of its conclusiveness as to these amendments, but as to all future amendments which may be submitted, and because of its reiteration of the supremacy of the National Covenant. . . .

"The decision blasts the most substantial hope the wet interests had. The cases were defended by a great array of able counsel especially employed by the liquor interests, and the litigation contested with stubborn determination and by the exercise of every resource and skill of learning and experience they possessed. . . .

"Eminent counsel had advised that no decision could be had on the merits of the cases for lack of jurisdictional facts. The law officers of the Government, when invited to appear and assist in the presentation of the cases, had declined to do so because of what, in their judgment, was lack of jurisdiction.

"All in all, it is a signal victory for Mr. Hawke, the plaintiff in error; for counsel; for the causes whose fate was so intimately involved; for the American people, and for their unborn posterity."

At last the threatened referenda on the suffrage amendment were no longer legally possible. Maine had not filed petitions, as its own State Court had declared them illegal. The petition in Massachusetts was thrown out because of insufficiency in number of names. Missouri let the time limit for filing petitions pass and it is uncertain whether they were ever circulated. In Texas the primary law had been declared constitutional by the Supreme Court, as had been the presidential suffrage law in Nebraska. With ratification completed, the referenda filed on presidential suffrage in Ohio and Maine became futile, and even aside from ratification, the Supreme Court of the nation would without doubt declare referenda on presidential suffrage unconstitutional, as the authority for it was likewise drawn from the federal Constitution. One by one, the legal attacks fell away from the amendments like barnacles from a ship in fresh water. The opponents sent forth more publicity, in which they angrily warned the nation that should another State ratify and the women be thereby allowed to vote in the coming election, the entire presidential election would have to be thrown out, since they were still prepared to invalidate the amendment. As the method for so doing was not clearly revealed, the threats, although widely published, were accepted as expressions of temper on the part of supporters of a fast losing cause.

The decision of the Supreme Court did more than clear the suffrage field of legal entanglements, it pointed to the door of the thirty-sixth State and toward this door suffragists turned with hurrying feet.

CHAPTER 30

Tennessee

When on June 2, 1920, the United States Supreme Court rendered that, to suffrage, momentous decision that State referenda were not permissible, thirty-five States had ratified the suffrage amendment; eight had defeated ratification. The final decision therefore rested with the remaining five States that had not yet taken any action. These States were the Northern States of Connecticut and Vermont and the Southern States of North Carolina, Florida and Tennessee.

The poll of the Legislatures of North Carolina and Florida indicated an adverse majority so of course these States were expected to take adverse action, in accord with the remainder of the South. This limited the immediate prospect of the thirty-sixth ratification to Connecticut, Vermont, and Tennessee. None of the Legislatures of these States was in session, so none could ratify unless its Governor called a special session. Responsibility thus narrowed down to the Governors of the three States. Temporarily, the case of Tennessee was dismissed from consideration because of an amendment in its State constitution which read:

"Article III, Section 32: No convention or general assembly of this State shall act upon any amendment of the constitution of the United States proposed by Congress to the several States, unless such convention or General Assembly shall have been elected after such amendment is submitted."

(Florida's constitution also contained this provision.)

This provision of the Tennessee constitution had stood unchallenged for half a century and was accepted as prohibiting a special session for tie purpose of ratifying the Suffrage Amendment.

There was no longer any doubt of the ratification of the Amendment if it could be put before any one of the three Legislatures of Connecticut, Vermont, and Tennessee. All were favorable to ratification and the general sentiment in these States was not only very friendly, but the Republicans in the one-party Republican States of Connecticut and Vermont, and the Democrats in the one-party Democratic State of Tennessee, were pledged to aid ratification. Yet the presidential election of 1920 was coming nearer and nearer, with women's chance to vote in it hanging upon a thirty-sixth ratification and that ratification hanging upon a special session. It was believed that the Governor of Tennessee could not call such a session. As has already been shown, the Governors of Connecticut and Vermont would not.

Feeling was tense and irritable throughout the country. Suffragists regarded the situation with the amazed irascibility of a plaintiff given a verdict by a jury but with the judgment mysteriously and suspiciously withheld. A more surprising manifestation came from hundreds, if not thousands, of women who had taken no part and had shown no especial interest in the campaign for suffrage, but who now developed a more raucous attitude toward the delay than did the better disciplined suffragists. Women whose sympathies with the suffrage struggle had never been apparent, now, because the thirty-sixth State was not more speedily achieved, even went so far as to throw bitter invective at suffragists who had given the whole potentiality of their lives to the cause.

There were other causes of irritation. After the ratification of the thirty-fifth State on March 22, political leaders had concluded that there would be a thirty-sixth State and that millions of women would vote in November. The prediction had been widely heralded that these new voters might turn the scale in the coming election, and in consequence a hectic effort to enroll them in advance had been made by all parties. Suffragists, non-suffragists and anti-suffragists had been appointed to official posts and the first duty assigned them had been the organization of the coming women voters. Although hosts of women flocked to the organizing meetings, many declined to be organized as voters before they had attained that dignity. National chairmen of the political parties were harassed on the one hand by suffragists and their State party organizations, who entreated them to use every possible effort to find a thirty-sixth State; and on the other by women anti-suffragists and a powerful party minority, threatening a variety of disasters were that State found. Two considerations tipped the scale suffrageward, one that the politics of the thirty-sixth State might easily be a determining factor in the coming presidential election; the other that if there should be no thirty-sixth ratification each dominant party would be held blamable and the premature organization of women might prove a boomerang.

It was in the midst of this impasse that the Supreme Court handed down its decision. It validated all the ratifications already effected, cleared the Amendment of legal doubt and emphasized the fact that completed ratification required the action of only a single State. Immediately a fresh campaign to persuade the two Northern Governors to action was begun, and the Republican party left no stone unturned to persuade them to call special sessions, but neither would budge. It left the Republicans, whose majorities in Congress had submitted the Amendment and whose proportion of the State ratifications was the larger, seemingly unable to deliver the thirty-sixth State.

Meanwhile Democratic hopes had turned slowly but steadily to Tennessee. Colonel Joseph H. Acklen, general counsel of the Tennessee Suffrage Association, on May 11, had published an opinion in the Nashville *Banner* declaring that should the Supreme Court of the United States hold that ratification of federal amendments may be accomplished only by the exact procedure outlined in the federal constitution, then Section 32 of Article III of the Tennessee constitution would be abrogated and a called session could legally ratify the Suffrage Amendment. The opinion attracted little attention at the time but it convinced the women of the State auxiliary of the National Suffrage Association. (That auxiliary was now known as the Tennessee League of Women Voters. Its old title was the Tennessee Equal Suffrage Association.) At their annual convention a week later they discussed the situation and determined to be on watch. The decision clearly recognized and applied the principle that no State possessed the authority to alter or modify in any way whatsoever the method of amending the constitution, and Colonel Acklen urged the Tennessee League of Women Voters to agitate the question of a special session.

This the League lost no time in doing. Telegraphing to the headquarters of the National Suffrage Association for help, it turned its forces to the problem of converting the State press, the Governor and the Legislature to the idea that the Supreme Court decision had made ratification in Tennessee possible. Its first appeal was made to the State Democratic convention. The convention, with enthusiastic applause, carried a hearty resolution endorsing ratification of the Amendment and recommending a special session. Armed with this resolution, the women requested the Governor to call the Legislature. The National Suffrage Association added its request, but he gave them no encouragement.

"There will be no extraordinary session of the sixty-first General Assembly," said he. . . . "I am forbidden by the constitution of Tennessee to call an extra session of the Legislature to act upon any amendment to the constitution of the United States. That matter is delegated to the succeeding General Assembly."

The agitation proceeded nevertheless. The *Tennesseean*, the Chattanooga *News* and the Tennessee League of Women Voters were simultaneously taking a poll of the Legislature and from time to time publishing interviews with the legislators. On June 20 the Governor, still believing that Tennessee had no authority to ratify, again declined to call a session. The newspapers were timidly discussing the possibilities of the session, the suffragists alone being confident. It was then that the chairman of the Tennessee Ratification Committee wrote the National Suffrage Association:

"Our only hope lies in Washington. In Tennessee all swear by Woodrow Wilson. No one here believes he has clay feet. The Democratic State Convention on the 8th of June exhausted every adjective in our voluminous Southern vocabulary to approve, praise and glorify his every word and deed. If he will but speak, Tennessee must yield."

Inspired by her faith, the entire State Board of the League of Women Voters, thirty-two women, signed a telegram to the President, urging him to ask Governor Roberts to call the session and assuring him that the Legislature would ratify if called. A copy of the telegram was sent to national suffrage headquarters and with it a plea for more help. Through its Washington representative, the National American Woman Suffrage Association secured the intercession of President Wilson, who asked the United States Department of Justice to render an opinion to the Tennessee Governor concerning the application of the Supreme Court decision to the constitution of Tennessee. This was done within an hour by Assistant Attorney-General Frierson, a citizen of Tennessee, and the following was made public by the White House in the afternoon, fifteen hours after the telegram had been sent from Nashville:

> "The ruling of the Supreme Court in the recent Ohio case, and the consideration which I gave to this question in preparing these cases for hearing, leaves no doubt in my mind that the power of the Legislature to ratify an amendment of the Federal Constitution is derived solely from the people of the United States through the Federal Constitution and not from the people through the Constitution of the State, The power thus derived cannot be taken away," limited or restrained in any way by the Constitution of a State. The provision of the Tennessee Constitution, if valid, would undoubtedly be a restriction upon that power.
>
> "If the people of a State through their Constitution can delay action on an amendment until after an election, there is no reason why they cannot delay it until after two elections, or five elections, or until the lapse of any period of time they may see fit, and thus practically nullify the article of the Federal Constitution providing for amendment."

On the same day President Wilson telegraphed Governor Roberts:

> "It would be a real service to the party and to the nation if it is possible for you, under the peculiar provision of your State Constitution, having in mind the recent decision of the Supreme Court in the Ohio case, to call a special session

of the Legislature of Tennessee to consider the Suffrage Amendment. Allow me to urge this very earnestly."

Governor Roberts had no prejudices *per se* against a special session, for on March 11 he had announced that he would call a special session of the Legislature when and if the Amendment should be ratified by thirty-six other States, in order to preclude the possibility of contesting elections in which women had voted "without previous enactment of State laws relating to payment of poll tax and registration." With the proposal of the President, supported by the Frierson letter, a new light was thrown on the political screen. The next day, June 24, an elaborate opinion was handed the Governor, at his request, by State Attorney-General Frank M. Thompson, which declared that ratification of the Suffrage Amendment by a special session would be legal. The National American Woman Suffrage Association on June 25 gave to the public the opinion of Hon. Charles Evans Hughes, its counsel. In part it said:

"The provision of the Constitution of Tennessee attempts to take away from an existing Legislature of that State the authority to ratify the amendment as proposed by Congress for ratification by the Legislature, and to place this authority in a Legislature subsequently chosen. This, in my opinion, is beyond the power of the State. In the adoption of the Federal Constitution, the State assented to the method of ratification by the State Legislature without any such qualification and the. State Legislature sitting as such after the amendment has been duly proposed by Congress has, in my judgment, full authority to ratify."

Chief Justice Clark of the North Carolina Supreme Court volunteered a similar opinion. The widely published opinions of these high legal authorities of both dominant parties instantaneously changed the direction of expectation throughout the nation. Democratic presidential candidates sent drastic telegrams to the Governor urging that Tennessee put an end to the uncertainty of the woman's vote. In response to combined entreaties, the Governor announced that he would call a session—whereupon a long-drawn breath of relief swept over the nation. Newspapers carried the news that the Democratic State of Tennessee had come forward as the gallant rescuer of the befogged Suffrage Amendment. Cartoonists discovered a wide diversity of humorous features with which to carry the same message; and Tennessee, "the perfect thirty-six," became the talk of the hour. Democrats were exultant; Republicans exceedingly generous.

The relief and joy in suffrage and political party headquarters were not, however, universal. The opposition had not given up hope and it now gathered its forces for the most terrific battle it had ever waged. That battle might have been a mere flurry had it not been for two unfortunate facts: First, the political situation within the State was the worst possible for united action on any measure, and second, the Tennessee League of Women Voters was ill-qualified at that particular date to take care of so serious a campaign.

Tennessee had been a Democratic State since the Civil War, although one-third of its Legislature was Republican. The Republicans came mainly from the eastern mountain regions which had remained loyal to the Union in the Civil War and loyal to the Republican party ever after. They were regarded by the majority party with frigid tolerance and the only time that there were Republican victories in the State was when there were rifts in the Democratic forces. In one-party States the normal party antagonisms practically cease, but the instincts for division reappear as factions in the majority party. In Tennessee, these factions within the Democratic party were now at each other's throats. Staid citizens anxiously shook their heads, remembering a similarly bitter occasion when a shocking murder had resulted from a factional political quarrel. The prevailing fear that a tragedy might ensue, or that the State might be thrown into the hands of the Republicans, tended to widen the breach as each group laid the responsibility for the gravity of the situation upon the other. A persistent rumor, untraceable to any definite source, ran through each faction to the effect that the Republicans, provided with unlimited funds, were making a deal with the leaders of the opposing faction. Suspicion, animosity and uncompromising hate possessed the entire State.

The Governor was a candidate to succeed himself against two rival candidates. A whispering campaign of scandal involving the Governor was traveling fast. Every person in the State was classified as for or against him. No neutrals were permitted and when workers sent by the National Suffrage Association entered the State they were regarded with suspicion, each side accusing them as favorable to its rival. The Governor, obviously indifferent in his own feelings toward the question of woman suffrage, now found it an exceedingly troublesome issue. His political opponents alternately charged that he did not intend to call the extraordinary session; or if he did, that he and his friends could be depended upon "to dish the Amendment." Whatever the harried Governor's personal impulse may have been, he was certainly much disturbed by these opposing conditions and weighed the question to call or not to call each day, with varying conclusions.

Many Tennessee women had been anxious to vote in the primaries on August 5, and might have done so had the session been called at once. The rival candidates' forces therefore scolded, threatened, ridiculed and dragooned the Governor in the effort to get him to call a special session; and were without doubt not a little moved in their anxiety for early action by the hope that the scandal afloat would drive the new women voters into their camp. On the other hand, the Governor's friends, recognizing that possibility, assured him daily that enfranchising the women before August 5 would be equivalent to putting a weapon in the hand of his enemy with which to slay him. So suffragists and the opponents of suffrage in State and nation watched, waited and grew wroth, while embittered Tennessee fought her way to and through the primaries.

Most unfortunately of all perhaps, some of the leading Democratic women suffragists of the State had yielded to urging from the men and become involved in the political quarrel, some being arrayed on the Governor's side, some on the other. Although the active and efficient chairman of the Ratification Committee of the State auxiliary to the National American Woman Suffrage Association was strictly neutral, the Governor refused to deal with her on the ground that she belonged in the enemy camp. He appointed his own Committee of Women to work for ratification, with a former president of the Tennessee Suffrage Association as its chairman. Then he announced that he would call the special session for August 9, four days after the primaries.

Meanwhile the chairman of the Governor's Committee of Women hurriedly began to organize and to take a poll of the Legislature. At the same time she appealed to the National Suffrage Association for official recognition of her committee. The Tennessee League of Women Voters had no objection to its one-time president, but she was not, at the moment, an officer. Other women were officers and responsible to their constituency for the success of ratification. These women found themselves in the curious position of having their official duty taken from them by the Governor. He had summarily waved aside the organization which had produced the conditions that made ratification possible. As the Equal Suffrage Association it had blazed the trail through the early gloom of Tennessee prejudice, and later had conducted without pause the agitation, education and organization which had so largely converted the State to the justice of woman suffrage. At the moment the local groups of the League, under direction of their Congressional Chairmen, were engaged in getting the poll of the Legislature. It was the usual routine with all auxiliaries of the National Suffrage Association, the principle being applied that the legislator was responsible to his constituency, and that they alone should solicit his voting pledge. Without the League and its many connections, ratification was dubious.

The National Suffrage Association, dismayed at this unexpected tangle within its own forces, sent a representative to reconnoiter. A call upon the Governor's staff confirmed the rumor that the chief executive was surrounded by a hostile group, who not only did not want the session called but would prevent it if they could. From both friends and foes of the Governor it was learned that the session was considered doubtful. The Governor's tactical mistake in appointing an independent woman's committee was recognized by his enemies at its full value, and the *Tennesseean*, the leading newspaper in Nashville, had a series of editorials and cartoons in readiness with which it intended to lampoon him in relentless fashion. Perceiving that such an attack would arouse the Governor's friends to urge the withdrawal of the promise of a session, the representative of the National American Woman Suffrage Association pleaded for delay in the publication. This was reluctantly granted. The Governor was campaigning afield but a doubty Leaguer, driving her own car, took the representative to the place of his next meeting. In a brief midnight interview she pleaded for a compromise which would enable the recognition of both committees by the National Suffrage Association and by the Governor. The plea was graciously granted and she returned to Nashville, with the signed compromise in her pocket, at five o'clock in the morning, having motored all night. The *Tennesseean* would not accept the agreement. Then further delay was begged until the president of the National Suffrage Association could reach Nashville. This plea, too, was granted and a hurry telegram was sent to New York. On June 15 the president of the Association, after a twelve hours' notice, started for Tennessee, expecting to remain less than a week. But it was not until the comedy-tragedy of the Tennessee ratification passed into history, more than two months later, that she was able to return.

The *Tennesseean* reluctantly withheld its planned attack upon the Governor and in an interview with the chief executive on Sunday, August 18, between trains, the president of the National American Woman Suffrage Association assured him that the Association recognized that ratification would be accomplished only by his aid and the aid of his followers in the Legislature; that it was not interested in the local politics of any State; that it recognized the Governor's right to appoint any committee he chose but that it could not repudiate its own auxiliary. She pointed out that there were Republicans in the Legislature and also Democrats of the opposing faction. She undertook to guarantee that the officers of the League of Women Voters would neither work for nor against him but would give their undivided attention to ratification. From that moment the national suffrage president served as liaison officer between the Governor and the suffragists—and found the position most delicate and difficult.

The National Suffrage Association knew one thing that Tennessee did not know, and that was that the opposition meant to wage a desperate, and probably unscrupulous, battle to prevent ratification in the thirty-sixth State. It knew that every weak man would be set upon by powerful forces, and that every vulnerable spot in the campaign would be discovered and attacked in its vulnerability. It knew that the chances of success depended upon preparedness to the "last buckle on the last strap." It was no easy task to arouse either men or women to comprehension of the dire need of the hour. All factions professed to stand for ratification. Both the National Democratic and the National Republican Committees had urged the Governor to call a special session and the Legislature to ratify. Both Democratic and Republican national platforms had confirmed this request. Both Democratic and Republican State conventions had urged a special session and ratification. The Legislature about to be called had extended presidential and municipal suffrage to women, and more than a majority of its members were pledged to ratification.

Suffrage men were inclined to pooh at any expression of doubt as to the result. Yet there was not long to wait before warnings against false security began to materialize. The opposition began its work with an old campaign device. In order that legislators might "save their faces" when they should repudiate their pledges, a plausible excuse must be found. Suddenly there appeared in the press and, directly after, in every street-corner conversation the remarkable claim that those legislators who voted for ratification would violate their oath of office. It was held that though ratification might be legal if secured by the Legislature called into special session for the purpose, that fact did not free men from their oath to uphold the State constitution as it read, even if it included an invalid provision!

Every wheel in the opposition machinery was set in motion to spread this idea and to fix it indelibly in the minds of Tennessee. The anti-suffrage press hammered it home in daily editorials. Anti-suffrage lawyers, surprisingly ignorant of the relation of the federal constitution to State constitutions, contributed further confusion to the situation by labored opinions on the inviolability of the oath of office. Men who had never been credited with political virtue came forward to warn legislators of the wickedness of voting for ratification under such circumstances. The Bar Association, in session, contained so many members who held this remarkable view that the friends of suffrage present did not introduce an intended resolution favoring ratification, lest it be rejected. With amazing docility, intelligent men fell into the trap and for three weeks this device of the opposition threatened defeat of the Amendment in the special session.

It was obviously the first duty of suffragists to destroy this legal contention. An invitation to address a luncheon of the Kiwanis Club of Nashville gave the president of the National Suffrage Association an opportunity to discuss it. An excerpt was published in all leading papers of the State and for the first time the answer to the claim, which had already gained widespread and distinguished support, was put squarely before the people of the State. She said:

"Those who are urging that legislators who vote for ratification will be violating their oath to support the State constitution forget that every legislator takes an oath of loyalty to two constitutions. The oath is no more in support of one than of the other. In fact the obligation to take an oath to support the constitution comes from the federal constitution (Article VI, Section 3). The possibility of conflict between the two was foreseen and the federal constitution (Article V, Section 2) declares that to be the supreme law of the land, and 'the judges in every State shall be bound thereby, anything in the constitution or laws of any State to the contrary notwithstanding.' The legislator does not vote to nullify the Tennessee constitution when he votes to ratify the Federal Suffrage Amendment. Any part of a State constitution is already nullified when it conflicts with the federal constitution. His oath first supports the federal constitution, which is the supreme law of the land,

and, second, such portions of the Tennessee constitution as are in agreement with the federal constitution, for all others, including the provision in question, would be held to be nullified and to all intents nonexistent should the question of their legality ever reach the Supreme Court."

Committees were hurriedly appointed in all the chief towns and cities and suffragists were given instructions to visit all influential lawyers and secure either an opinion upon the mooted point, or their signature to an opinion on the question: When a legislator takes a joint oath to support the federal and the State constitutions, does he violate his oath when voting in accord with the provisions of the federal constitution? As fast as these opinions were secured, they were printed by the favorable press. After a two weeks' vigorous campaign in this direction a large majority of the important lawyers of the State were publicly recorded against the assumption.

A tour of the chief cities of the congressional districts was next planned and a hurry call issued to the local groups in each district to send their leaders forward for conference with State and national officers of the National American Woman Suffrage Association. There were public meetings, newspaper interviews, talks with political leaders, and a private conference with workers at each point. At the conferences the poll of all legislators from the District was carefully reviewed, and arrangements were made for deputations of constituents, or a succession of them, if needed, to wait on every member not already pledged to vote favorably on ratification in the special session.

To every conference the question was put: "Are there any known bribable legislators from your district?" Sometimes the entire group ejaculated a name in unison, so well established was some legislator's ill repute in this connection. The same question was put to all political leaders in private talk, and was often met by a surprised look of suspicion, to be quickly covered by an expression of canny determination not to reveal any names. However, further discussion usually secured the names. All such names were checked by a secret mark on the poll list. Several names were checked as bribable by eight different persons, each thoroughly acquainted with practical politics and each having given his opinion without the knowledge of the others.

The women of Tennessee, alarmed by the unexpected development of hostility, and now understanding the false grounds for their belief in prompt action, laid aside their political differences and worked together in a manner worthy of imitation by the men of the State. The Southern summer heat was merciless, and many legislators lived in remote villages or on farms miles from any town. Yet the women trailed these legislators, by train, by motor, by wagons and on foot, often in great discomfort, and frequently at considerable expense to themselves. They went without meals, were drenched in unexpected rains, and met with "tire troubles," yet no woman faltered and there was not a legislator who had not been visited by his women constituents before the Legislature met. In many instances, members were visited by deputations of men, or by joint delegations of men and women. Each day the poll was corrected in Nashville as the reports of interviews were received by wire and by mail. Each day the prospects were carefully estimated. Although several men under suspicion as bribable had signed pledges to vote for ratification they were never included in the private estimate. It was intended to make the poll so safe that it would not be endangered if the bribable fell from it.

The problem of arriving at an exact account of the ayes and nays was embarrassed by the fact that ten vacancies existed and by the further fact that there was a question of the eligibility of certain other members to serve at the special session, since they had been appointed to public office after the regular session.

Meanwhile the need of added political influence was not forgotten. The Democrats having announced that the National Committee would meet in Columbus on July 19 in connection with the ceremonies of notifying Governor Cox of his nomination for the presidency, the National Suffrage Association appointed a committee of Democratic women to be present, under the leadership of a director of the Association who was also a proxy member of the Committee, This committee presented a memorial from the Association and made three definite requests. (1) A resolution of endorsement; (2) an expression from Mr. Cox; (3) the appointment of a representative of the Democratic Committee to go to Tennessee and North Carolina to work for ratification.

Representatives of the National Suffrage Association further advised the Democratic National Committee that suffragists were surfeited with resolutions and that what the women of the country desired was that the Democratic Committee should use its full power to bring about ratification in States like Tennessee and North Carolina and not content itself with the mere adoption of a resolution.

All that was asked was done. The Committee resolved its hope for Tennessee ratification, two Tennesseeans were privately appointed as national representatives of the party to work for ratification, and Candidate Cox gave a frank and urgent request for Tennessee's ratification. At his own request two private conferences with the National Suffrage Association's committee were held and he agreed that he would come to Tennessee on his campaign trip if needed to urge ratification. As an additional expression he wired the president of the National Suffrage Association:

"I am gratified over the news that you are to remain in Nashville for the ratification campaign. It gives me added reason for expressing confidence that the Tennessee Legislature will act favorably, which will greatly please the Democratic party."

The Republicans unexpectedly called their National Committee to meet at Marion on July 21 in connection with their notification ceremonies. The National Suffrage Association thereupon hastily appointed a committee of Republican women, and provided it with a memorial similar to that sent to the Democratic Committee and instructed it to make the same requests. The Committee passed the following resolution:

"Resolved, That it is the sense of the Executive Committee of the Republican National Committee that the Republican members of the Tennessee Legislature should be and hereby are most earnestly urged and requested by this resolution to vote unanimously for ratification of the woman suffrage amendment in the special session of the Tennessee Legislature which is to be called, and the chairman of the Republican National Committee is hereby authorized to communicate this resolution to each Republican member of said Legislature."

This was wired to each Republican member of the Tennessee Legislature and confirmed by letter. The National Suffrage Association's Committee then called upon Mr. Harding, who declared that he was ready to throw the full weight of his influence for ratification, and the news was sent broadcast by the many correspondents then in Marion. Mr. Harding also wired the president of the National Suffrage Association and gave the message to the press himself:

"I am exceedingly glad to learn that you are in Tennessee seeking to consummate the ratification of the equal suffrage amendment. If any of the Republican members of the Tennessee Assembly should ask my opinion as to their course, I would cordially recommend an immediate favorable action."

The opposition had been at work for several weeks upon a plan to defeat ratification by a solid Republican adverse vote, on the ground that should Tennessee ratify, "the Democrats would get the credit." The rumor of this had been persistent and disconcerting. The action of the National Republican Committee at Marion and the endorsement of Presidential Candidate Harding checked that effort, but did not eliminate it from the possibilities. Representative Fess, chairman of the National Republican Congressional Committee, now urged each Republican member of the Legislature by telegram to join in a solid vote for ratification. Several State Committeemen and Harding clubs wired the Republican chairman of Tennessee, H. H. Clements of Knoxville, urging a solid vote for ratification. He publicly announced that he did so urge the Republican members of the Legislature and added, "I feel safe in pledging every Republican member of the Senate and House for the immediate ratification of the Amendment." Later the National Republican Committee sent a member, Mrs. Harriet Taylor Upton, to Nashville to join Republican legislators in the counter-campaign to secure a solid party vote for ratification. The combination of these influences secured nearly all the Republican votes for ratification; without them ratification would have failed.

Although the public announcement had been made a month before that the special session would be called for August 9, the official call was not issued until August 7. The ratification resolution went before the Legislature with the strongest political support it had had in any State or at any time. The preparations were complete. When, on July 25, the poll had shown a certain majority, the announcement had been given to the public, while deputations continued to visit the doubtful members and meetings were still held. A. L. Todd, presiding officer of the Senate, and Seth Walker, Speaker of the House, had agreed to introduce the resolution to ratify. Most of the best known lawyers of the State, including the Attorney-General, had given opinions not only upon the constitutionality of ratification by the Tennessee Legislature but upon the specific question as to whether men would violate their oath of office if they should vote for ratification, so that the argument which three weeks before had threatened to send the resolution to defeat had been largely eliminated from the field.

The League of Women Voters, the Governor's Committee of Women, the Democratic Woman's Committee and the Republican Woman's Committee had all been at last united under the leadership of Miss Charl Williams, Vice-Chairman of the National Democratic Committee. With all these influences on the side of ratification and with a majority of the Legislature pledged in writing to vote for ratification *in the special session* the prospects to onlookers seemed uninterestingly obvious, and the effort to accumulate further evidence of demand for the Tennessee ratification appeared to them a senseless waste of energy. Yet experienced suffragists faced the coming events with anxiety, and each congressional chairman to whose workers the legislators' pledges had been made was urged to be present when the Legislature met.

On Saturday evening, August 7, the great foyer of the Hermitage Hotel was packed with men and women bedecked with suffrage yellow and anti-suffrage red and the "War of the Roses" was on. The "anti" women had made an eleventh-hour attempt to show numbers and had brought women from all parts of the country, especially from Southern States. All the women who had become familiar figures in anti-suffrage contests were there, and many more. Mysterious men in great numbers were there, taking an active part in the controversy, while in and out through this crowded "third house" moved the bewildered legislators.

That very day the ominous possibilities of the "invisible government" were made manifest. Seth Walker, Speaker of the House, who had willingly joined the Men's Ratification Committee and had not only pledged his vote verbally and in writing to several persons but had accepted the invitation to introduce the resolution, sought out the president of the League of Women Voters and announced a change of mind. By evening it had become clear that he would assume the floor leadership against the Amendment. Before midnight, suffragists had other worries. During the evening groups of legislators under escort of strange men had left the foyer and gone to a room on the eighth floor. As the evening grew late legislators, both suffrage and anti-suffrage men, were reeling through the hall in a state of advanced intoxication—a sight no suffragist had before witnessed in the sixty years of suffrage struggle.

Sunday passed and Monday, August 9, came. The Legislature met at noon. The Governor's message recommending ratification was delivered and both Houses adjourned for the day. With nothing to do, members again accepted the invitation to the eighth floor, where a group of anti-suffrage men dispensed old Bourbon and moonshine whisky with lavish insistence. Tennessee had been a prohibition State before the Eighteenth Amendment had been submitted, and the State had also ratified that amendment. Why was not the law enforced, asked the women. "Now see here," was the answer, "in Tennessee whisky and legislation go hand in hand, especially when controversial questions are urged." Denial of this traditional license when a great issue was at stake would be resented as an interference with established custom by suffragists and anti-suffragists—"This is the Tennessee way." Suffragists were plunged into helpless despair. Hour by hour suffrage men and women who went to the different hotels of the city to talk with the legislators came back to the Hermitage headquarters to report. And every report told the same story—the Legislature was drunk! "How many legislators?" was the abashed query. No one knew. "Are none sober?" was next asked. "Possibly," was the answer.

In agony of soul suffragists went to bed in the early morning, but not to sleep. The members of the Tennessee Legislature, however, largely slept themselves sober during the night and hope revived.

Presiding Officer Todd introduced the resolution in the Senate on the tenth, according to agreement, and the entire Shelby County delegation introduced it in the House. At the request of the antis the Senate and House Committees to which the resolution had been referred granted a hearing on the evening of the twelfth. Mean time the opponents tested their strength in the House by introducing a resolution referring the Amendment to county conventions in order "to hear from the people." Suffrage legislators promptly tabled it by a vote of 50 to 37. The suffrage men also tabled another resolution declaring ratification of any amendment in that session to be in violation of the spirit of the State constitution.

One of the largest crowds ever assembled in the Capitol attended the suffrage hearing. The suffragists entrusted their side to a group of brilliant and distinguished Tennessee lawyers. The evening furnished the suffrage side with two disagreeable surprises. Major Stahlman, of the Nashville *Banner,* who had faithfully promised support to suffragists at the Kiwanis Club, spoke for the antis. Later it was learned that he had assumed direction of the opposition lobby. His sudden change of position was regarded as another ominous sign.

The other incident that startled the suffragists was this: A man arose and read a letter from Presidential Candidate Harding:

"I beg to acknowledge your esteemed favor of August 4th. Your letter is the first bit of information I have had concerning the provision in your State constitution. I have heard something about a constitutional inhibition against your Legislature acting upon the Federal Amendment, but I did not know of the explicit provision to which your letter makes reference. I quite agree with you that members of the General Assembly cannot ignore the State constitution.

"Without having seen the document myself I should be reluctant to undertake to construe it.

"I have felt for some time that it would be very fortunate if we could dispose of the Suffrage Amendment, and I have done what I could in a consistent way to bring about the consummation of ratification. I have tried throughout it all to avoid trespassing upon the rights of State officials.

"It has not seemed to me a proper thing for a candidate on the federal ticket to assume an undue authority in directing State officials as to the performance of their constitutional duties.

"I did say and I still believe it would be a fortunate thing for Republicans to play their full part in bringing about ratification. I should be very unfair to you and should very much misrepresent my own convictions *if I urged you to vote for ratification when you hold to a very conscientious belief that there is a constitutional inhibition which prevents your doing so until after an election has been held.* (Italics ours.)

"I hope I make myself reasonably clear on this subject, I do not want you to have any doubt about my belief in the desirability of completing the ratification but I am just as earnest about expressing myself in favor of fidelity to conscience in the performance of a public service."

Candidates Harding and Cox had both been fully informed of the alleged technical obstruction in the Tennessee constitution and of the campaign among the lawyers of the State to offset it. In the flood of impressions circling around a presidential candidate, the explanation had apparently slipped away in Mr. Harding's case, and the effect of this letter upon the campaign was to hand a cudgel to the opponents. It opened the way for Republicans to creep out of their pledged obligations with a pose of extra conscientiousness and for a return of the argument which had been largely eliminated by intensive effort. To watching suffragists that letter came like a bolt from a blue sky, and again there was no sleep.

The anxiety was stilled for a time by the prompt and generous action of the Tennessee Senate. The Senate Committee met immediately after the hearing on the twelfth and voted to report the Amendment favorably by a vote of 8 to 2. The two dissenters made ready to present a minority report. Although the debate in the Senate on the thirteenth had been awaited with anxiety, only two speeches were made in opposition. One of these was so vituperative and vulgar that it not only aroused the fighting qualities of the friends of suffrage but called forth denunciation from the entire State. Many were the letters of apology sent to suffrage headquarters from prominent men on behalf of the State for this attack upon individual suffragists. Senator Collins, who had been brought from a sick bed to cast his vote for ratification, stood tremblingly clinging to his desk, as with shaking voice he eloquently defended women against the attack.

Senator Monroe, who was carried on the anti-poll, created a sensation when he announced that he had been reminded of the Fourteenth and Fifteenth Amendments and requested in that connection by Northern women antis to vote against the Amendment. "But," said he, "I am going to vote for ratification in order to give back to the North what the North gave to Tennessee when it ratified the Fourteenth and Fifteenth Amendments." Others for various reasons announced changes of attitude. The minority report was promptly rejected and ratification passed August 13, 25 ayes and 4 nays. To the outside world, watching, this result was an expected and normal action. To the suffragists on guard in Tennessee, it meant a reversal of the usual policy—the opposition had centered on the House instead of the Senate.

The political fate of the women of the nation now rested in the hands of a minority of a single legislative chamber. From day to day the House ominously postponed the date of the vote. Though the postponement meant that the pledged majority was still standing fast, in vain did the suffrage members try to get the resolution on the calendar. Meanwhile the male anti-suffrage lobby, from early morning of each day until the wee small hours of the next, threatened and cajoled the embattled sixty-two who had signed pledges. They were baited with whisky, tempted with offers of office, loans of money, and every other device which old hands at illicit politics could conceive or remember. An alleged attempt to kidnap a suffrage member was made. Various schemes were started to get rid of enough suffrage legislators to allow the opposition a chance to act, a favorite proposal being that men might conveniently get messages calling them home.

Engaged in this nefarious intrigue was what old-timers recognized as the former "whisky lobby" in full force, the one-time railroad lobby which was alleged to have directed Tennessee politics for years, and a newer manufacturer's lobby. All pretense was thrown aside and all three worked openly as one man, although who paid the bills the public never knew. Every day men dropped from the poll. In some cases the actual consideration was noised about. One man who had written nine letters in which he declared that he would be on hand "to vote for woman suffrage until I am called up yonder" had fallen early. Before the end all men checked as bribable on the poll, taken before the Legislature met, fell from it.

The American Constitutional League, Everett P. Wheeler, president (formerly the Men's Anti-Suffrage League), formed a branch in Nashville, and its members, mainly politicians, joined in the bombardment of legislators friendly to suffrage. The Maryland Legislature sent a memorial, which was read at the opening of the Tennessee Legislature, urging rejection of ratification, and representatives of the Maryland League for State Defense (formerly the Men's Anti-Suffrage League of Maryland) joined the lobby. Women antis pressed the sharp point of Negro woman suffrage into Southern traditions; the men antis bore hard on the alleged illegalities of ratification by the Tennessee Legislature; all of them quoted Mr. Harding's sympathy with the oath-violating theory. Men and women, as organized anti-suffragists, issued daily press bulletins assuming the responsibility for the campaign of opposition, while, as usual, other men, whose presence in Nashville was unannounced to the outside world, were applying the "third degree" in a hotel bedroom.

The House Committee met on the evening of the sixteenth and reported favorably on the seventeenth. The vote on the resolution having been set for that day, the debate was opened by T. K. Riddick of Memphis (Shelby County), a distinguished lawyer who had allowed himself to be elected to a vacancy for the sole purpose of aiding ratification. Said he:

> "I have in my pocket the pledges of sixty-two members of this House which the people of Tennessee will have the opportunity to read. If those men fail to keep faith I shall go from this chamber ashamed of being a Democrat, ashamed of being a Tennesseean."

Seth Walker made what the mountaineers called "a bear cat of a speech," saying that it had been charged that his change of attitude was due to a certain railroad which he named; this he resented, but he conspicuously failed to give an explanation of his strange *volte face* which was amazing the entire nation. The antis brought the debate to a close by a motion to adjourn, passed by a vote of 52 to 44. The previous tests had indicated that suffragists were in control of the House, but this one gave evidence that the position had been reversed. Suffrage anxiety was intense.

That night the suffrage leaders with heavy hearts confessed their despair to each other. "There is one thing more we can do," said the president of the National Suffrage Association, "only one, we can pray."

In the interim representatives of a group of newspapers called upon the Governor and threatened to defeat him at the election if he did not "pull off his men." He stood firm. On the eighteenth the House was again packed and hundreds of would-be onlookers were turned away. The debate continued. "What is a greater crime than for interests, from New York to San Francisco, to send lobbyists here to break your pledges, or for certain newspapers connected with railroads to threaten you as they have been doing for the last ten days," demanded Joe Hanover, floor suffrage leader. L. D. Miller of Chattanooga closed with a ringing speech in which he said:

> "When the special interests made an attack on this Legislature in January they had a gang of lobbyists to put over their infamous bills. I recognize in the lobbies these same special interest servers. You have an opportunity on this occasion to rid this State of an incubus that has had its claws in this Legislature for fifty years. Let us show by our votes that the special interests are done in Tennessee."

The moment had become intensely dramatic; every onlooker knew that the fate of the question might depend upon a single vote. Of the ninety-nine elected members of the House, ninety-six were present. One had resigned and his place was vacant. The other two, both suffragists, were kept at home by serious family illness. Dr. J. Frank Griffin had hastened home from California to cast a suffrage vote. R. L. Dowlen, who had just undergone a serious operation, was brought from his bed to the capitol to vote for the resolution. Seth Walker, in a last effort to rally the weakening lines of the anti-ratificationists, at the end of the debate shouted in melodramatic manner, "The hour has come. The battle has been fought and won"—and moved to table the resolution. But the vote on tabling stood 48 to 48! The room rang with the cheers of the galleries. One more vote had been won for suffrage. The roll call showed that Banks Turner who was carried on the anti-poll had dropped into the suffrage column. Unwilling to believe the roll-call, Mr. Walker demanded a second and it was taken. He left his Speaker's seat and, with arms thrown around Banks Turner, whispered insistent entreaties in his ears as the names were again called. Shivers ran down suffrage backs as Mr. Turner passed his call without response. Heads stretched forward and every eye centered on the legislator and the Speaker, while a breathless silence pervaded the room. The fans ceased to wave. Even the overpowering heat was forgotten. At the end of the roll-call Mr. Turner threw off the Speaker's arm, drew himself up proudly and shouted a defiant no. Cheers and shouts burst forth again and the galleries would accept no discipline from the chair. The vote still stood 48 to 48 against tabling.

A motion to ratify the Amendment was then made and the vote was taken in a tension that was well-nigh unbearable; 49 ayes, 47 nays. The House broke into an uproar, and the cheers of triumph that rang through the old legislative chamber were heard far down the street.

The second additional vote that had been won for suffrage was that of Harry Burn, a twenty-four-year-old Republican, who forthwith became a hero to the suffragists and a traitor to their opponents. He had been placed on the suffrage poll as conditioned, for he had promised to vote for the resolution only if his vote should be necessary for ratification, otherwise he was going to vote against it, as he believed his constituents were opposed. From the vote on the motion to table he saw that his vote *was* necessary and so changed his attitude on the ratification motion.

Although 49 was a majority of 96, the number of members present and sufficient for legal ratification, Tennessee was accustomed to consider 50 the majority of 99, the total elected membership, as a "constitutional majority." Seth Walker, in order to move a reconsideration, changed his vote from no to aye, which made the final record 50 ayes to 46 nays, thus giving the constitutional majority.

Thus, by a freak of politics, the last vote needed by the Tennessee standard to enfranchise the women of a great nation was cast by a man who was clearly staking heavily to defeat it.

According to the printed rules of the House in Tennessee, a motion to reconsider any ordinary measure may be made by any person voting on the majority side, and that person controls the right to bring the motion up at any time within three days; no other person may bring it up. On each one of these three days the House met with full quorum present, but the Speaker did not bring up his motion to reconsider. The two suffrage absentees had returned and there were suffrage votes to spare. During that three days' period the opposition again worked desperately. One suffrage member was called every half hour through two nights, each time with a different appeal to change his vote. Another was urged every half hour all night to come downtown to see an important man. A man who was laboring day and night in the midst of the anti-forces to break the suffrage majority finally implored his daughter-in-law to renounce publicly the suffrage side and come out in opposition. With tears in his eyes he entreated: "It will mean a great deal to you and your daughter in the future if this amendment is defeated."

Whereupon the spirited seventeen-year-old daughter, present at the interview, spoke for her mother: "Mother and I would rather live in poverty all the rest of our lives than get money by treachery to our sex. We will not desert the suffragists and we are not proud of the work you are doing." A man who was carried on the suffrage poll was reported by suffrage men as wavering, and was boldly claimed by the opposition. A confession was secured by U.S. Senator McKellar that he had been offered a position under the Excise Commissioner for his vote. A telegram to the President of the United States brought prompt rebuke to the Commissioner, who left town at once. And the man ceased to waver. Young Harry Burn was the chief object of persecution. He was threatened with exposure of an alleged bribe if he did not remain out of the Legislature until the vote on reconsideration was over. Men declared they had affidavits to prove that he had been bribed by suffrage floor leader Hanover and the Governor's secretary between the vote on tabling and that on ratification. The presentation of affidavits disproved that charge. The efforts at intimidation led Mr. Burn to make a statement to the House:

> "I desire to resent in the name of honesty and justice the veiled intimation and accusation regarding my vote on the Suffrage Amendment as indicated in certain statements, and it is my sincere belief that those responsible for their existence know there is not a scintilla of truth in them. I want to state that I changed my vote in favor of ratification first because I believe in full suffrage as a right; second, I believe we had a moral and legal right to ratify; third, I knew that a mother's advice is always safest for her boy to follow and my mother wanted me to vote for ratification; fourth, I appreciated the fact that an opportunity such as seldom comes to a mortal man to free seventeen million women

from political slavery was mine; fifth, I desired that my party in both State and nation might say that it was a Republican from the East mountains of Tennessee, the purest Anglo-Saxon section in the world, who made national woman suffrage possible at this date, not for personal glory but for the glory of his party."

A few hours later the president of the League of Women Voters received a telegram from Mrs. J. L. Burn, the young man's mother. The telegram read:

"Woman was here to-day, claims to be wife of Governor of Louisiana, and secured an interview with me and tried by every means to get me to refute and say that the letter I sent to my son was false. The letter is authentic and was written by me and you can refute any statement that any party claims to have received from me. Any statement claiming to be from me is false. I stand squarely behind suffrage and request my son to stick to suffrage until the end. This woman was very insulting to me in my home, and I had a hard time to get her out of my home."

An amusing indication of the state of suffrage nerves occurred when during this three-day period Harry Burn was reported as having left Nashville. His hotel said he had gone and the clerks did not know where. There was consternation again among the suffrage forces. Had he deserted after all? Had he been kidnapped? An hour later his name appeared upon the register of another hotel to which he had moved.

Men were found listening at the transoms of suffrage doors, a telegram between the receiving and operating telephone desk was stolen and given to the press. Men, whom nobody seemed to know or what they represented, mysteriously appeared and joined the opposition forces. All day and all night suffrage lines were guarded. Suffrage women picketed the hotel floors where suspicious incidents had taken place and suffrage men polled the suffrage members every two hours during the day and watched over them at night.

On the 18th the opposition held a mass meeting where two things of note occurred. In a speech, Seth Walker confidently announced that three men had deserted the suffrage side and that in consequence the defeat of the Amendment was certain. The other incident was a letter from Presidential Candidate Cox surprisingly similar to that of Mr. Harding and dated on the same day. More doubt and confusion. Again the public did not know whether to believe that the two candidates were playing politics or were sincere in their desire to see the Amendment ratified, and the opposition made the most of the situation. Again the oath loyalty argument was revived and made to work. Could it be true that three men had deserted, suffragists asked. Faithful suffrage men did not sleep until they had sounded every pledged man, and when they found the sterling forty-nine still standing firm they recorded Seth Walker's claim as a political "bluff."

The vote on reconsideration was expected hourly on Friday, and the galleries were again packed. A manufacturer had given a holiday to his women employees and sent them red-rose bedecked to help fill the galleries and swell the anti-numbers. It was clear that every vote might be needed. T. A. Dodson had received a message that his baby was dying and had just taken his train when it was discovered that his vote might prove crucial. A suffragist drove her motor on a flying trip to the station, taking two suffrage men with her. They reached the train just as it was moving out and the men promised the legislator a special train which would get him home as soon as the regular one if he would come back. He returned, remaining while needed, was given the special train, paid for by Newell Sanders, a Republican and ex-State Senator, and reached home to find the baby happily recovering. The hours passed, the quorum was present, the suffrage voters were all there, but Mr. Walker, perceiving the futility of so doing, did not bring up his motion to reconsider. At the end of the session the suffrage majority carried a motion to meet on Saturday morning, the 21st. According to the custom, but not the printed rules of the House, it was possible after the three days for any member to call up a motion to reconsider, and the suffrage members intended to bring it up on Saturday morning and vote it down.

The city of Nashville looked forward to another exciting session, but before Saturday's breakfast the news was all about town that thirty-eight anti-ratification House members had ignominiously fled in the dead of night. They had gone in small groups to a station near Nashville where they boarded an L and N train which carried them across the border into Alabama. This move of last resort was intended to prevent any further action by destroying a quorum and to give time to anti-suffrage workers to break down a suffrage member.

The House met on Saturday morning with fifty suffrage men and nine antis present and with women suffragists occupying the seats of the absentees. The anti-suffrage chaplain added a bit of irony to the situation when he prayed that "God's richest blessings be granted our absent ones." The suffrage garrison prepared to enjoy itself and harassed Speaker Walker by overturning every ruling and voting down every decision of the chair. Speaker Walker announced that an injunction against forwarding the certificate of ratification to Washington had been issued that morning by Judge Langford of the Supreme Court and that the injunction had been served upon the Governor, the Secretary of State and the Speaker of both Houses. The ratificationists went on with the legislative program. The pending motion to reconsider was called up and voted down. The ratified Amendment was ordered returned to the Senate and it was returned. It was common knowledge that the Governor could not be enjoined by the laws of the State and lawyers now begged him to ignore the injunction and forward the certificate, but the Governor was non-committal while neither the Attorney-General nor any of his assistants could be located! The Attorney-General's office mysteriously professed no knowledge of their whereabouts. After a two days' absence, however, Attorney-General Thompson emerged from his hiding place, brief in hand, supporting a plea which was heard by Judge Lansden, Chief Justice of the Supreme Court, on August 23. The plea was for a *writ of certiorare et supersedeas* and it was issued, thus dissolving the injunction of the lower court, and clearing the way for the Tennessee certificate to be sent to Washington.

During this time the Attorney-General issued two opinions which were seconded through the press by many other equally prominent lawyers throughout the State.

1. When a Legislature has taken favorable action on a federal amendment, it has exhausted its power to act and no motion to reconsider is applicable even for the limit of three days.

2. Had a motion to reconsider been applicable in the case of a federal suffrage amendment, that power was exhausted according to the printed rules of the House when three days had passed; for no contrary custom of the House could be held to have legal value.

On Tuesday, August 24, at 10:17 a.m., Governor Roberts, in the presence of interested suffragists, signed the certificate and sent it by registered mail to the Secretary of State. It was delivered at 4 a.m. on the 26th, and was at once referred for examination to the Solicitor who had been sitting up all night in order to be on hand when it should arrive. An open threat to secure an injunction to prevent the issuance of the Proclamation certifying to the ratification of the Amendment had been continually made by the opposition. In July Justice Bailey of the District of Columbia Supreme Court had declined to issue such an injunction upon action brought by Charles S. Fairchild and the American Constitutional League. On August 25, Justice Seddons of the same court had refused the same application. The Secretary of State, Bainbridge Colby, however, took no chances and arose early on the morning of the 26th. At eight o'clock, without ceremony, he signed the Proclamation.

The group of workers of the National Suffrage Association, returning from Tennessee, arrived in Washington the morning the Proclamation was signed and found a great victory celebration awaiting them. In the evening, to a packed theatre audience, they told the story of the Tennessee campaign. The Secretary of State was there to represent the Administration, and on behalf of the nation congratulated the suffragists upon their freedom.

On August 27 the Tennessee suffrage group returned to New York city, the home of the national suffrage headquarters. The Governor of the State and representatives of the Republican and Democratic National Committees were at the station to welcome them and so were the "old guard" suffragists. With the 71st Regiment Band at the head and with the old familiar banners waving, they marched together for the last time to the Waldorf Astoria, where all made speeches of self-congratulation. Mrs. Harriet Taylor Upton, National Chairman of the Republican women, told how the Republicans carried Tennessee, and Miss Charl Williams, National Chairman of the Democratic women, told how the Democrats did it. Others told how resourceful and fearless the Tennessee women had been, how heroic were the faithful forty-nine in the midst of the whirlwind of opposition and how the victory was everybody's victory who had labored in the cause.

A hurry call had been sent to all the mayors of Tennessee, urging them to join the women's celebration by ordering the ringing of bells and blowing of whistles. And the whistles did blow and the bells did ring merrily and sincerely in most Tennessee towns, for the people in the main stood by the ratifying Legislature. From ocean to ocean, from "Canada to the Gulf," the celebrations continued. Meetings, processions, flag raisings, transformations from suffrage associations into Leagues of Women Voters were the order of the day for the month that followed. None was more significant than the draped flag over the tablet that marked the site of the chapel where the world's first woman's convention had been held in 1848, in Geneva, New York; none more significant than the wreaths of flowers hung on the old building where the world's first woman's jury had sat in 1870 in Cheyenne, Wyoming.

Here the story of woman suffrage in the United States should appropriately end, but there was more to come—and come in Tennessee—before the long suffrage campaign was permitted to pass into history as a closed issue.

The Tennessee Legislature recessed from day to day, as there was no quorum. The call had included 132 bills as needing attention by the Legislature. The majority of the anti-ratificationists stubbornly remained in Alabama or at their homes and awaited the call of their masters. The ratification members, unwilling to remain in Nashville without a quorum, had gone home also. Anti-ratification mass meetings were still in progress and the speakers were defiantly threatening to undo ratification in the Courts. Meanwhile the Governor and the Sergeant-at-Arms were striving to get a quorum of the Legislature. It was publicly announced that on August 30 the "red rose brigade" would return. Four hours were spent on that day in an effort to secure the quorum of sixty-six members, but at no time could more than sixty-three be found. The filibusters had returned with "a great show of being ready for business." The full suffrage majority was not in Nashville and the ratificationists who were there feared to help compose the quorum lest some unfriendly act be passed. Ratification legislators, arrested and brought into the House, escaped by other doors while the forty-six anti-ratificationists held their seats.

Finally it was announced that the ratificationists would all be in their seats on the 31st, whereupon the antis failed to appear, lest they could not muster a sufficient vote to overthrow the suffrage action of August 21. The scene had lost its attraction for both suffragists and anti-suffragists, who now deserted the balconies. Without the yellow and the red, the place looked lonesome. Even Mr. Walker absented himself on this date.

On September 11, however, the anti-ratificationists won the game of hide-and-seek and got control of the House, many suffrage men being absent. Amid shouts of glee, by a vote of 47 to 37, they passed a motion to expunge from the record all that had taken place on the 21st except the record that there had been no quorum. Mr. Riddick, on behalf of the ratificationists, contested every step with points of order. The entire controversy raged around the question of a quorum. By the rules of the Legislature two-thirds, sixty-six, of the elected number constituted a quorum in the House. There was a quorum when the House ratified. There was a majority but not a quorum by Tennessee rules when the House voted down the motion to reconsider and returned the ratified Amendment to the Senate. Mr. Riddick contended that the authority for procedure was drawn from the federal constitution and that no rules of the House could supersede. He claimed that the authority for a quorum composed of a majority was drawn from parliamentary usage. In these views he was sustained by the Attorney-General whose opinion he quoted. The anti-members refused to accept this interpretation. A resolution to reject the Suffrage Amendment as a substitute for the one to ratify, which the antis held to be pending on reconsideration, was voted on, 47 to 24, with 20 not voting. This rejection resolution was sent to the Senate with instructions that it be forwarded to the Governor. The suffrage House members now enjoined the Chief Clerk of the Senate from receiving it. On September 12, the Senate was in a turmoil of indignation as it discussed the resolution received from the House and resented "attempts to control its business." By a vote of 17 to 8 it refused to accept the resolution and returned that message, whereupon House members volubly informed Senators that if their resolution was not received there would be no passage by the House of the *per diem* for Senators nor other Senate legislation. The threats proved persuasive and on September 13, the Senate, having turned a somersault overnight, accepted the resolution by a vote of 21 to 4. Then the Senate forwarded the resolution of rejection to the Governor, who in turn sent it to the Secretary of State.

With the suffrage question thus disposed of to the satisfaction of each contending faction, the Legislature settled down to business, and remained in session until September 6, when it adjourned after passing—over the Governor's veto—the Appropriation Bill which gave to each member one hundred dollars extra for expenses incurred in remaining longer than the twenty days of the special session allowed by the constitution. Although the laws of the State of Tennessee declare desertion of a legislative post to be a felony, this law was not enforced and the fleeing opposition members of the House drew their *per diem* and extra allowances without protest!

On September 12 Speaker Walker and a group of anti-men appeared in Washington to entreat the Secretary to withdraw the Proclamation. Failing in their mission, they went on to Connecticut with the avowed purpose of persuading the political group which had so stubbornly resisted all efforts to secure a special session in that State to continue that policy in order that the legality of the ratification of the Amendment might rest upon the case of Tennessee. They returned to Washington and again sought an interview with the Secretary of State in order to renew their appeal. Interviews in the press widely announced that they had not surrendered and would contest the ratification of Tennessee in the Courts.

The American Constitutional League (formerly the Men's Anti Woman Suffrage League) and the Maryland League for State Defense (formerly the Maryland Men's Anti-Suffrage Association) were still declaring through numerous press communications that ratification would be proved invalid. The women antis still continued their publicity service, announcing with frequency that litigation would be started not only to invalidate the Amendment but the entire presidential election.

None of the threatened litigation alarmed the nation, but it doubtless served to convince political leaders that another State was desirable to make assurance doubly sure.

Governor Holcomb of Connecticut, although still unyielding, now called a special session to provide for registering women. When calling it he warned the legislators that they must confine themselves to the business contained in the call—and omitted the Suffrage Amendment from the list. No such restriction had ever been put upon a Connecticut Legislature and the Governor himself had said, two years before, that he had no power to prevent the transaction of any business when once the Legislature had been called in special session. The members, a majority of whom had long been pledged to ratification, determined to show independence and to ratify.

As soon as the special session opened, Governor Holcomb appeared and asked that it adjourn without action, as it was his intention to issue another call to meet a week later to ratify the Amendment and to enact other necessary legislation. Both Houses refused, and by unanimous vote in the Senate and with only eleven voting in opposition in the House, ratified the Federal Suffrage Amendment, even though the Governor had failed to transmit the certified copy. In further defiance of the Governor they passed several bills, none of which was included in the call. They then adjourned until September 21.

When the Legislature again met, the Governor appeared and asked the members to ratify the Amendment. Many refused, as it seemed an acknowledgment that their former action was invalid, but reason conquered tempers and, as the Connecticut auxiliary to the National Suffrage Association strongly recommended a second action to make legality absolutely certain, the Amendment was again ratified. The same day, to placate the members who wished the first record to stand, a motion was made to reconsider and confirm the action of the first session. Thus terminated a continuous struggle of fifteen months to secure ratification from a Legislature which all that time had been ready to act favorably, and which finally ratified the Amendment not once but three times. The ratification of Connecticut stilled any restless questioning of the validity of Tennessee and forever established the Amendment as a part of the federal constitution.

Governor Clement of Vermont retired from office December 31, 1920, and was succeeded by Governor James Hartness. The Vermont Legislature met in regular session in January, 1921. The resolution to ratify the Federal Suffrage Amendment was read in the House for the third time on January 28 and passed, ayes 202, nays 3. On February 8 it was passed unanimously by the Senate.

The threats of the Tennessee antis had died of inattention and the threatened invalidation of the Amendment had by now narrowed down to two cases. One—the Leser vs. Garnett case, claiming that thirty-six States had not legally ratified the Amendment, the ratifications of West Virginia, Missouri and Tennessee being cited as invalid—brought a decision from the Maryland Court of Common Pleas that thirty-six had duly ratified. The case was carried to the Court of Appeals (Maryland) where on June 28, 1921, the Judge affirmed the decision of the lower Court that these ratifications were valid. It was then appealed to the United States Supreme Court, where a decision sustaining the two prior opinions was handed down. The other, a similar contention, known as the Fairchild case, which had been pending in different form since July, 1920, was also dismissed by the Supreme Court of the United States. Thus all efforts to declare the Amendment invalid came to an end.

The final announcement of these decisions appeared in small paragraphs in obscure corners of the newspapers. Hardly anyone noted them. Woman suffrage was already everywhere recognized as an established fact.

CHAPTER 31

The States That Did Not Ratify

It is doubtful if any man, even among suffrage men, ever realized what the suffrage struggle came to mean to women before the end was allowed in America. How much of time and patience, how much work, energy and aspiration, how much faith, how much hope, how much despair went into it. It leaves its mark on one, such a struggle. It fills the days and it rides the nights. Working, eating, drinking, sleeping, it is there. Not all women in all the States of the Union were in the struggle. There were some women in every State who knew nothing about it. But most women in all the States were at least on the periphery of its effort and interest when they were not in the heart of it. To them all its success became a monumental thing. The action of their respective Legislatures in ratifying the Federal Suffrage Amendment was greeted by the women of every State with a vast State pride and gratification because that commonwealth stood forth before the world as an upholder of the American ideal of democracy.

To the women of ten States of the Union this pride and gratification were denied. The men of ten States left it to the generosity of the men of other States to enfranchise their own wives, mothers, sisters, daughters. One of the ten was Delaware—the only one north of the Mason and Dixon line. The other nine were Virginia, Maryland, North Carolina, South Carolina, Georgia, Alabama, Louisiana, Mississippi and Florida.

In preceding pages it has been set forth that the original plan of the opposition was to secure thirteen refusals to ratify. This was later modified into a plan to secure the adoption of forthright rejection resolutions in thirteen States. If this had proved successful it would have been next in order to ask for a Proclamation of Defeat. By the use of this rejection resolution, it was hoped, too, to raise the question whether a succeeding Legislature could adopt an amendment that the preceding Legislature had formally rejected. The rejection resolution read: —

Resolved, by the General Assembly of the State of............... the House and the Senate concurring, That the proposed amendment to the Constitution of the United States be, and hereby is, rejected as an unwarranted, unnecessary, undemocratic and dangerous interference with the rights reserved to the States or to the people in both State and Federal Constitutions, and be it further,

Resolved, That a copy of this resolution be filed with the Secretary of the United States as the expressed will of the people of...............as registered in their constitution and by their elected representatives in the General Assembly to retain the fundamental rights of local self-government vested in the States or in the people; and be it further,

Resolved, That we call upon our sister States of the Union to uphold and defend the right of each State to decide who shall vote for its own officers, and to oppose and reject any amendment to the Constitution of the United States that would transfer control of State franchises to the Federal Congress without the consent of the people themselves as duly exercised under their several State Constitutions.

The resolution used was practically the same in all States except that the words "unwarranted," "unnecessary," "undemocratic" and "dangerous" were used interchangeably.

The keynote of the opposition that was to be directed against ratification of the Federal Suffrage Amendment by the Southern States had been struck as early as June 10, 1919, just six days after the submission of the Amendment, in a statement issued by Senator Lee S. Overman of North Carolina. The prominence of Senator Overman in Administration councils, his long service in the Senate and his prestige throughout the South made an indelible impression upon those to whom his message was directed.

"In my opinion," said he, "the Woman Suffrage Amendment just adopted by Congress is a reaffirmation of the Fifteenth Amendment. I wonder if this is appreciated throughout the South? This latter amendment simply goes a step further than the Fifteenth Amendment. In addition to saying that the right of suffrage shall not be abridged by reason of race, color or previous condition of servitude the new amendment adds the word 'sex.' The language is not identical, but it is evident that the Woman Suffrage resolution is a postscript to the former amendment, which we have always opposed in the South. . . . The illiterate colored woman, for instance, irrespective of her non-conception of the duties of citizenship, may vote and pair with the most intelligent woman of the Caucasian race. Congress reserves the right of 'appropriate legislation' to enforce this mandate, regardless of the State. That is the condition in a nutshell. I wonder if woman suffrage advocates in the South have taken into consideration all the embarrassing features possible under such legislation."

Through the years since the "Force bill" had ceased to be operative there had been talk of its revival and the dread of that possibility ever hung over the heads of Southern legislators like the sword of Damocles. Coincident with the passage of the Federal

Woman Suffrage Amendment had come the demand for "self-determination" on the part of the black people of the Southern States. A dispatch from Paris the last week of June, 1919, had carried the story of the appearance there of an American Negro, William Trotter, who was seeking to have the Negro question taken up by the Peace Conference along with the Irish, Jewish and other "racial" questions. This demand created a further disturbance in the minds of representatives from Southern States.

There was also the occasional question whether Southern representation in Congress should be reduced in accord with the federal constitution. There had been threats of this in political conventions. Threats might become an actuality. Damaging figures could be arrayed against the South. In 1916, 159,749 votes cast in Georgia elected twelve members of Congress, while 999,781 votes in California elected eleven members of Congress. In other words, 13,312 votes in Georgia had as much power as 90,889 votes in California.

Spread out on the record this precarious position of justice in the South was a menace to the whole Democratic party at each election. The leaders of that party were not blind to the danger. Every effort was made by them to persuade Southern Legislatures to ratify the Federal Suffrage Amendment. They prophesied that the rejection of the Amendment in these States not only meant certain defeat for the Democratic Party at the polls in 1920 but that the hostility of Northern women voters might be aroused to the extent of insisting on enforcing the Fifteenth Amendment, "with all the horror of racial strife and loss of self-government."

President Wilson wired the Governors of all the Southern States urging ratification from the viewpoint of expediency and warning them that the National Democratic party's success was at stake. Secretary of the Navy, Josephus Daniels, Attorney-General A. Mitchell Palmer, and the Chairman of the National Democratic

Committee, Homer Cummings, also sent urgent requests to party leaders and to members of the Legislatures. The only outcome was the condemnation of the President, who was called a "meddler," and resentment against the national chairman for what was termed "outside interference."

The press in many of the Southern States was favorable. It scored the legislators for their ignorance and unprogressiveness. The *Press* of Savannah, Georgia, said: "The majority of the Legislature is opposed to suffrage. Of course we can't blame them for that. The fault is not theirs that their intellects are limited or their consciences dwarfed. We, the people, have elected them. We are to blame, not they. No rational person hopes to defeat the Amendment. All that can possibly be done is to write down Georgia as one of the few, if not the only State, that opposes right and justice with her own feeble bulk."

Georgia, the "Empire State" of the South as she is self-styled, was the first to reject the Federal Suffrage Amendment. In well informed circles there was no great surprise over this action. Before the session convened members of the Georgia auxiliary to the National American Woman Suffrage Association and their friends in the Legislature realized the impossibility of ratification and decided to wait a year in the hope of a growing suffrage sentiment. Usually when the advocates of a measure withhold it, the opponents make no objection. Not so in Georgia. The opposition introduced ratification resolutions in Senate and House for the announced purpose of defeating them. "Never in any legislative body have the opponents of a measure shown themselves so bloodthirsty and vindictive" declared a Representative on the floor. In both Houses these resolutions were referred to the Committees on Constitutional Amendments, one of which had five bills proposing to amend the State Constitution so as to enfranchise women, on which no action had ever been taken. When the joint hearing was held, a rejection resolution was substituted. In both committees the vote was unfavorable to suffrage.

In the Senate the report was unexpectedly called a few days later and a motion to disagree with the Committee report was lost. As ratification was considered hopeless, friends in the Senate attempted to postpone action indefinitely by a filibuster which lasted for several days and was the means of recommitting the entire suffrage question to the Committee on Constitutional Amendments, with the understanding that it would remain there the balance of the session. But July 24, the same day that this agreement was made, a rejection resolution was introduced in the Senate, reported favorably by the Committee and, after several hours' debate, was carried. The Senate also voted down a proposition to submit a suffrage amendment to the State Constitution. On the same day the rejection resolution was carried in the House.

During the debate in the Senate a bitter attack was made on the Amendment with many acrimonious and personal references. It was called "a vicious piece of legislation." Susan B. Anthony was declared "the worst enemy the South ever had." One Senator affirmed, "we opponents of the Amendment are trying to save the women of Georgia from a repetition of reconstruction days. It is not a question of woman suffrage but of protecting Georgia womanhood." Another said: "It would deprive the South of every right to control its own suffrage and place it forever under the dominant North." He "cared not what position the Democratic Party took in the matter," he "would insist on Georgia recording what she believed to be a vital matter of right even if her action ends the life of what was once the Democratic Party." Still another said: "Women should not be allowed to vote. Their privilege and obligation is to bear children . . . the sole intent of this voting privilege is to equalize white women with Negro women . . . these suffragists, men and women, are out with a propaganda for race suicide. Women are now refusing to bear children because of the policy of woman suffrage; women who vote came here to induce Georgia women to refuse to bear children which was the sole aim and end for having women at all, according to Bible doctrine."

In the House the final period of debate was one of the most tempestuous since the reconstruction days. At times there were a dozen Representatives on their feet at the same time, clamoring for recognition. The grant of unanimous consent gave opportunity for a parliamentary battle exceeding in interest anything that the Georgia Legislature had ever indulged in. During the debate one proponent of suffrage said: "I heard it stated that a very high official in the Democratic Party in this State has publicly announced that if the suffrage is given to women he will quit the Party. But where will he go? The Republicans are for it. The Socialists stand upon it. Even the Bolsheviks are on this platform. If we take the wings of the morning and fly to the uttermost parts of the earth, we will find it in Russia, in Germany, in England, in Scandinavia, in Switzerland and the islands of the sea. It would be interesting to see the eminent gentleman, like Noah's dove, finding no place for his foot till with wearied wing he comes back to the ark of his fathers."

Both Senate and House passed resolutions rejecting the Suffrage Amendment, the subject-matter of both being practically the same, but neither resolution was passed by both Houses. As there was no joint resolution no resolution ever reached the Governor, so the action was null and void. By over-reaching itself Georgia's virulence was, officially, as if it had not been. If the President of the Senate and the Speaker of the House had been less anxious to send the official notice of the rejection of the Federal Suffrage Amendment to the Congress they might have remembered that they had failed to sign a joint resolution.

According to one newspaper, "Alabama craved the privilege of being first to reject the Federal Suffrage Amendment without a technicality." She was. From the beginning of the ratification campaign there was evidence of a determination on the part of Alabama's United States Senators that the adverse vote they had registered against the Federal Suffrage Amendment in Washington should be vindicated by their State Legislature. The defeat of ratification in Alabama can, therefore, be laid squarely at the door of the Democratic Senators Oscar W. Underwood and John H. Bankhead. Governor Kilby and Lieutenant-Governor, Nathan L. Miller, both maintained neutral attitudes. The liquor opposition worked openly. The national Democratic leaders urged ratification on the grounds of party expediency, all the more because the Republicans were claiming credit for nine of the eleven ratifications already secured at that time. The State Democratic Committee, 20 to 13, adopted a resolution which read, "We pledge our support in every proper way to accomplish the result desired." But the opposition machine was well-oiled and not a cog in a single wheel failed to turn. Governor Kilby transmitted the resolution without recommendation. By joint resolution the Senate and House were to act simultaneously on July 17, but the House broke the agreement and the Senate alone took action. After defeating a motion to defer action and one to postpone indefinitely, the Senate passed a resolution to reject the Amendment.

The women hoped for postponement in the House, as the rejection resolution carried the provision that a message should be sent to the federal Secretary of State, the President of the Senate and Speaker of the House before the State of Alabama could be recorded as rejecting the Amendment. On August 13, the Republican minority in the Legislature, five members in the House and one in the Senate, issued a statement declaring that they intended to vote in favor of ratification in accordance with the mandate from their party. But on September 2 the Senate defeated the ratification resolution and on the 17th the House adopted the rejection resolution.

No one had expected Mississippi to ratify, though members of the Mississippi auxiliary to the National American Woman Suffrage Association pointed to the statement of Senator John Sharp Williams as indicating encouragement. He favored "a white woman's primary in which the women of the State might say whether they wanted the ballot or not." He was "inclined to woman suffrage" and thought that "with safeguards it might be made a bulwark of white supremacy in the State." There was also the favorable attitude of State officials. Retiring Governor Theodore G. Bilbo had replied to Governor Burnquist of Minnesota, when he took the poll of Governors, that the Mississippi Legislature would be called in the autumn and he expected ratification. His farewell message, delivered in person, closed with the words "Woe to that man who raises his hand against the onward march of this progressive movement." The newly elected Governor, Lee M. Russell, in his inaugural address January 20 devoted more time to the question of ratification than to any other topic. Mississippi women argued that their legislators could not consistently urge State's rights as a reason for not ratifying, because the same legislators had ratified the prohibition amendment in fifteen minutes' time, and the same principle was involved. They did not know the elasticity of a Mississippi legislator's logic. The men who did not hesitate to ratify a federal amendment under which it was made a crime for a man to buy a bottle of beer in New York, refused to ratify a federal amendment which placed the white women of their State on the same constitutional level as the colored men.

Without warning to the friends of suffrage a rejection resolution was offered in the House on January 21. It was not referred to a committee but rushed to a vote and, amid cheers and laughter, after ten minutes' debate it was carried. The resolution was sent to the Senate and by it referred to the Committee on Constitution. A new resolution ratifying the Amendment was then presented and failed of adoption. Then the rejection resolution was re-committed to the Constitution Committee, where it rested until March 30, when in Committee of the Whole a ratification resolution was substituted. The vote in the Senate was ayes 22; nays 22, the Lieutenant-Governor H. H. Casteel, breaking the tie and casting an affirmative vote. News of this favorable action spread all over the country and the suffrage center of interest was suddenly shifted from Republican Delaware to Democratic Mississippi. Telegrams came pouring into Mississippi, offering congratulations and appealing to the House to make Mississippi the thirty-sixth State.

When the substitute resolution to ratify was presented to the House the next day, March 31, a motion was made that the House "do not concur with the Senate resolution of ratification." Hoots, catcalls and jeers drowned the words of speakers. In the midst of the confusion calls for the vote became loud and insistent. The author of three State suffrage bills introduced at this session attempted to speak against ratification. Representative R. H. Watts of Rankin County interpolated, "I would rather die and go to hell than vote for woman suffrage." And the press said, "The boys cheered nearly a minute."

The substitute resolution was read at three o'clock, at 3:15 the vote had been taken; the resolution to ratify announced as defeated, and the clerk was reading another bill. A curious incident of the suffrage action in Mississippi was that the Legislature later passed bills making provision for the women to vote in primary and general elections, both contingent upon the ratification of the Federal Suffrage Amendment!

The same Legislature passed a suffrage referendum bill which was voted on in November, 1920, after the enfranchisement of women, and received ayes 39,186; nays, 24,296. Even in Mississippi the people were for suffrage, more than three to two. But the bill was not adopted, as the law requires a majority, not a plurality, of all the votes cast on an amendment. By then, however, women had already been enfranchised under the Federal Suffrage Amendment. Unfortunately for Southern women, the State law in Mississippi required registration four months and in Georgia six months before election. Since ratification was not completed until August, 1920, the women in these two States were barred from voting in 1920, the only States where women were not allowed to participate in the election.

South Carolina women had no illusions about ever securing the vote from South Carolina men through ratification or otherwise. Their experience in 1917 with a State referendum bill, defeated by the Senate and withdrawn at the women's request from the House, because they knew it would fail, had given them a realization that their legislators did not favor votes for women by any method whatsoever. One newspaper made it plain from the beginning that "the electorate, and the General Assembly of South Carolina representing it, will never vote for woman suffrage for no better reason than that other States vote for it. Nor will the State be governed by the exigencies of the National Democratic party or any other party when it considers the matter of limiting or expanding its electorate."

On January 14, 1920, the joint resolution to ratify was introduced and referred to the Judiciary Committee which reported it unfavorably. In the House on January 22 a concurrent resolution to reject the Amendment was carried. This House action of voting on a measure without referring it to a committee or placing it on the calendar was unprecedented. In debate a speaker wanted "a joint resolution which will kill the infernal thing now and forever." Another said he had told some of the women lobbyists that "more hell and the devil would be raised over this thing than anything else." On January 29 the rejection resolution was carried in the Senate.

The Virginia Legislature assembled on August 13, 1919, in special session and the Federal Suffrage Amendment was submitted by the Governor without recommendation. As the session was called specifically for good roads and as answers to a questionnaire submitted to members showed that it would be impossible to obtain ratification, the Virginia auxiliary of the National American Woman Suffrage Association intended to wait for the regular session of 1920 to press for action. However, the opponents of suffrage hurried through a rejection proposal in the House without debate ten minutes before the 1919 adjournment. The Senate voted to postpone action until the next session.

In 1920 conditions in Virginia were not greatly improved for, although there were sixty-one new members in the two Houses who had been elected since the last Legislature, it was acknowledged to be not only a reactionary but a very wet body. These men resented the ratification of the prohibition amendment and it had crystallized their sentiment against the approval of any federal legislation.

The Federal Relations Committee reported in favor of the rejection resolution. In both Senate and House a ratification resolution and another to refer ratification to the voters were substituted for the rejection resolution.

In the Senate on February 6, after a debate of twelve hours, the rejection resolution was adopted by a vote of 24 to 10 and on February 12 the House also adopted it by a vote of 62 to 22.

Although the Virginia legislators voted against the Federal Suffrage Amendment, they knew that it would be ratified and on March 12 a Qualifications Bill to enable Virginia women to vote contingent on ratification of the Federal Amendment and a resolution to submit to the voters a woman suffrage amendment to the State Constitution were adopted by both Houses. This action was intended to appear magnanimous. But it appeared only futile.

In Virginia a referendum amendment must pass two consecutive Legislatures and then be submitted to the voters for their decision before it becomes a law. As only three States were then needed to complete ratification, Virginia women would be enfranchised under the Federal Suffrage Amendment long before the Virginia referendum could reach the voters.

All the Republican Senators in the Virginia Legislature voted for ratification, but most of the Democratic Senators and members of the Lower House ignored the request to ratify that came from the head of their own party, the President of the United States. They publicly declared that as far as they were concerned their party "could go to smash," "that Democracy could go down," that "it makes little difference in Virginia who has control of the Government in Washington." They scorned the hundreds of telegrams and letters from their own constituents and the thirty-two thousand State petitioners requesting ratification. As one Senator said, "They set their minds in defiance of justice and fair dealing. They didn't get the pulse of the times."

In Maryland, as in other States, the women had tried for many years to get some form of suffrage from their Legislature but without success. When the Federal Suffrage Amendment was submitted in June of 1920 pressure was at once brought by the Maryland auxiliary to the National American Woman Suffrage Association to induce Governor Harrington to call a special session, but he advised waiting until the regular session because the Legislature had not been elected with the question of the Amendment before the people. After the regular session convened January 7, 1920, the ratification resolution was introduced in the Senate and sent to the Committee on Federal Relations, while in the House it was sent to the Committee on Constitutional Amendments. A hearing was set for February 11, but when informed that the date was inconvenient for speakers and suffrage leaders who would be in Chicago attending the convention of the National American Woman Suffrage Association, the chairman of the Senate Committee agreed to postpone the hearing until the 18th. The surprise of the suffragists was therefore great when on February 10, at the reconvening of the session, the chairman of the House Committee on Constitutional Amendments insisted on the hearing for February 11. A canvass of the Committee showed a majority in favor of the date being February 18, so the suffragists returned to their homes.

Next morning Baltimore papers announced that the hearing would be held Feb. 11. The suffragists learned that the preceding night the Speaker had transferred the Suffrage Amendment from the Committee on Constitutional Amendments, which was favorable, to the Committee on Federal Relations, which was hostile! None of the members of the Suffrage Ratification Committee spoke at the hearing. The House Committee refused a hearing; the Senate Committee granted one for February 17. Early that morning, suffragists gathered from all over the State and at 10:30, led by a band, they marched into the State House. They presented resolutions and petitions representing over 125,000 residents of Maryland. The women made their appeal to Governor Ritchie, successor to Governor Harrington. Answering, he said that the platform of the Democratic party of the State on which he was elected opposed suffrage and that he could not ask the legislators to repudiate their platforms. Early in the afternoon the rejection resolution was reported favorably and carried in both Senate and House. In the House 33 of the 45 Republicans and 2 of the 56 Democrats, and in the Senate 7 Republicans and 2 Democrats voted against the rejection resolution.

As a visible demonstration of its belief in State's rights, on February 24, the Senate and House voted to send seven anti-suffrage members to West Virginia to urge that Legislature to reject the amendment. The next day two resolutions were introduced in the Legislature. One was to "repeal, rescind and recall the resolutions ratifying the so-called Eighteenth Amendment to the Constitution of the United States." The other authorized and requested the Governor of Maryland to call on the national government, in behalf of the State of Maryland to "have the so-called Eighteenth Amendment and the Volstead Act declared null and void."

On March 30, by a vote of 20 to 7, the Senate passed a joint resolution "authorizing and directing the Attorney-General of Maryland to bring suit or suits to prevent the Secretary of the United States from proclaiming the Federal Suffrage Amendment prior to the holding of a referendum thereon in certain States, and to test the validity, should the same be ratified by the elected Legislatures of three-fourths of the States."

In September, just before the Legislature adjourned, it was discovered that the resolution of rejection had not been sent officially to the Governor of the State and by him to the Secretary of State in Washington. It was brought before both Houses again on September 22, at which time the ratification resolution was voted down.

There was great expectation in Democratic circles that North Carolina would ratify. Democratic leaders emphasized that the Republican States of Connecticut, Vermont and Delaware having failed, it would be of strategic value if the Democratic party could get the glory of the thirty-sixth ratification. Furthermore, it was maintained that if the North Carolina Legislature defeated the Suffrage Amendment it would defeat the Democratic candidate for President in November; while if it ratified it would virtually assure success to the Democratic party in November.

Of all the Southern States North Carolina now presented the greatest hope, not only because of the number of prominent men in federal and State positions in favor of ratification, but because the North Carolina press was almost a unit for it. The

Republican State convention in March had for the first time seated two women delegates and had put a woman on the ticket for State Superintendent of Public Instruction; in April the Democratic State convention had seated forty women; United States Senator Simmons and Governor T. W. Bickett, always opponents of suffrage had announced themselves in favor of ratification. The only discouraging symptom was the attitude of United States Senator Overman who said, "I have been and still am opposed to woman suffrage. It is fundamental with me, deep and inborn . . . but I recognize the fact that it seems inevitable."

Could the Democratic convention which was held in April of 1920 have dodged the question and deferred action, undoubtedly it would have. But the friends of ratification were there in force. The suffrage plank as it came from the Committee recommended that the Federal Suffrage Amendment should not be ratified but that a State amendment should be submitted to the voters. Two minority reports were offered, one to present to the convention the question whether the platform should contain a plank for ratification, and the other to eliminate all reference to woman suffrage. Men said that never in the history of the Democratic party in North Carolina had there been such a contest over a platform. Finally a substitute was presented for all the reports which read: "This Convention recommends to the Democratic members of the General Assembly that at the approaching special session they vote in favor of the ratification of the proposed Nineteenth Amendment to the Federal Constitution." This was carried 585 to 428.

The attention of the whole country thereupon focused on North Carolina and many people believed that this convention majority, though small, forecast favorable action in the Legislature. Early in the summer, in response to an appeal by President Wilson, Governor Bickett had replied in part, "I hope the Tennessee Legislature will meet and ratify the Amendment and thus make immediate action by North Carolina unnecessary. We have neither the time nor money and such action on the part of Tennessee would save this State the feeling of bitterness that would surely be engendered by debate on the subject that would come up in the Legislature. I have said all that I intend to say on the subject of ratification. While I will take my medicine, I will never swear that it tastes good, for it doesn't."

The North Carolina political situation was further complicated by an exciting Gubernatorial primary. There were three candidates in the field for Governor. Two of them opposed ratification and one made defeat of the Federal Suffrage Amendment his chief issue.

On August 10 the Legislature met in special session to consider questions of taxation. The enemies of ratification had been busy; on August 11 a round-robin signed by sixty-three House members was sent to the General Assembly of Tennessee, which read: "We, the undersigned members of the House of Representatives of the General Assembly of North Carolina, constituting the majority of said body, send greetings to the General Assembly of Tennessee and assure you that we will not ratify the Federal Suffrage Amendment interfering with the sovereignty of Tennessee and other States of the Union. We most respectfully request that this measure be not forced upon the people of North Carolina."

The news of this statement, as it flashed over the country, caused consternation in Democratic ranks. The fact that such action had been taken before the Legislature had really organized showed party leaders that a force determined to defeat ratification was at work. The ratificationists decided to make a sudden and decisive coup, and pursuant thereto on August 13, the Governor appeared before the joint Assembly. He said in part: "It is well known that I have never been impressed with the wisdom of or the necessity for woman suffrage in North Carolina. . . . But, gentlemen, in the words of Grover Cleveland, a condition not a theory confronts us. Woman suffrage is at hand. It is an absolute moral certainty that inside of six months some State will open the door and women will enter the political forum. No great movement in all history has ever gone so near the top and then failed to go over. . . . We may just as well realize, gentlemen, that this country is no longer an association of States but a nation. Whatever a majority of the people of the nation want is going to be the supreme law of the land. . . . I realize more keenly now than ever before that State's rights have passed away. . . . The very most this General Assembly can do is to delay for six months a movement it is powerless to defeat. This being true, I am profoundly convinced that it would be the part of wisdom and grace for North Carolina to accept the inevitable and ratify the Amendment."

There was pathos in this courageous but reluctant recognition of and capitulation to the new order. It could not have been an easy task to stand before a Legislature representing two and one-half millions of North Carolina people and tell them that the political faith handed down by their fathers and grandfathers and treasured by them as fundamental bases of government were but musty relics of bygone days.

The Governor was severely criticized for asking the Assembly to ratify for party reasons without urging on members the sanctity of convention obligations. Republicans declared they were obeying the behests of their State and national conventions, even as Democrats should be expected to live up to theirs. The Republicans in Senate and House were resentful. The result of the Governor's message was to leave the Democrats unmoved and to incense the Republicans.

In the afternoon news came from Tennessee of the Senate victory and on the same day the resolution to ratify was introduced in the Senate of North Carolina, referred to the Committee on Constitutional Amendments and, within fifteen minutes, reported favorably, 7 to 1. Simultaneously the resolution was introduced in the House and referred to the Committee on Constitutional Amendments.

August 17, amid scenes which had not been witnessed since the days of the Civil War, the North Carolina Senate began consideration of ratification. Great crowds surged through the Capitol, the east wing being assigned to ratificationists and the west wing to rejectionists. For five hours a heated debate raged, with charges and counter-charges. When agreement to vote was reached a resolution was unexpectedly made to defer action until the regular meeting of the Legislature in 1921, and was carried 25 to 23. It is quite possible that when this resolution to block immediate action was introduced it took the friends of suffrage unawares, but it is also true that there were suffrage Senators who were glad to make use of any excuse to avoid a vote on the direct issue before the election.

The opposition forces planned to bring the ratification up under special order in the Lower House in the meantime and dispose of it quickly. "Call it up and kill it right" was the way the anti-suffrage floor leader described it. The ratification resolution was called up in the House on August 18 and defeated. A rejection resolution was immediately reported by the Constitutional Amendment Committee. It was tabled in the House without a dissenting voice. Thus closed the North Carolina chapter on ratification.

The attention of Democratic leaders next turned to Louisiana. The women there had early strengthened their position by uniting all organizations under one head called the Ratification Committee and there were many favorable assets. All of the newspapers in the State except four advocated the Federal Suffrage Amendment; Martin Behrman, Mayor of New Orleans, who had killed the State suffrage amendment in 1918, had not only become converted to woman suffrage but to ratification; the New Orleans Democratic Association and the State Central Committee were in favor.

The opposition centered in New Orleans where certain elements, mainly the liquor interests, aroused in the campaign of 1918, opposed woman suffrage in any form. And there was other opposition. On reaching Baton Rouge in April, suffragists from the National American Woman Suffrage Association saw women who had worked for suffrage for twenty-five years and more lined up on the side of the anti-suffragists, because of their State's rights belief.

On May 10, the General Assembly convened and on the 11th the joint resolution for ratification was presented in both Houses, while a State amendment and a bill providing for the payment of poll taxes by the women, in case the State amendment became a law, were introduced in the House. On May 13, Governor Pleasant submitted the Federal Suffrage Amendment to both Houses with a message of many pages urging the Legislature not to ratify it but instead to submit a State amendment. On the same day arrived two anti-suffrage representatives from Maryland. They appealed to Louisiana to join hands with Maryland and kill the Federal Suffrage Amendment, and entered no protest against State suffrage if Louisiana should desire to adopt it.

On May 17, John M. Parker was inaugurated Governor. It had been expected by people throughout the country that Governor Parker would be of great assistance in the ratification campaign. As a Progressive, in 1916, he had been a candidate for Vice-President of the United States on a platform that endorsed suffrage by national amendment. In his campaign speeches in the autumn of 1920, while running for Governor, Mr. Parker had repeatedly said, "I am for suffrage; it is almost here and we must have it." Yet there appeared mysteriously, with or without his knowledge, in many parts of the State copies of his platform containing a State's rights plank, presumably designed to placate those who were opposed to the Federal Suffrage Amendment. This was not known to the women and they were totally unprepared when, shortly after his inauguration, he announced that he "was going to keep hands off the suffrage fight; it was a matter for the Legislature anyway," and even refused to receive a deputation of women from the Louisiana auxiliary to the National American Woman Suffrage Association. In answer to a telegram from President Wilson, urging his "interest and influence," he answered that he found a great difference of opinion among the legislators, large numbers opposed to any kind of woman suffrage and, all being Democrats, any dictation on his part would be unwise.

Early in June a hearing was held in the House chamber. The hour was eight-thirty in the evening. One of the suffrage speakers reported to the National Suffrage Association: "I will never face anything more thrilling or more fearsome. I stood on the press platform just below the Speaker's desk, with the press people sitting all about me; legislators on the floor and on the aisle steps, the president and members of the National auxiliary in the seats with the legislators, or perched on the tops of the desks. . . . They were all over the place where they could be conspicuously seen and heard, especially heard. The audience was terribly near. I could touch the first of them and away up to the roof was a sea of faces. . . . I could not write my speech beforehand. It had to be born out of the inspiration of the day's events, the occasion and the other speeches. . . . When I looked at the men, most of them crouching behind an old tradition of State sovereignty and a pitiful make-believe fear of Negro domination, I was filled with such indignation that my speech came tumbling out. . . . I challenged the quality of their democracy and said they voted with their party only because of one issue—the Negro question, but that in everything else they were more spiritually akin to Henry

Cabot Lodge and the other Tories. The women raised one great shout and many of the men joined them. I told them that in the Mississippi Valley, on the border of the great West and out through all the reaches of the great West itself, no such word was known as the one reiterated over and over again in the Legislature of Louisiana and on the streets, and that was the word "sovereign" prefixed to the name of their State; that we knew no sovereign States, we knew only the United States, the Union, where more and more the selfish interests of sections were being merged in the common good of all people."

Ex-Governor Pleasant, in his argument against ratification, said: "The South never has stood for the Fifteenth Amendment. It is true that seven Southern States are recorded as having ratified it, yet it was done by carpet-bag rule. It was ratified in these halls with Negroes sitting as legislators and a carpet-bag Governor in the office below. Ratification of the Nineteenth Amendment not only would give suffrage to the white women but to the Negro women of the State. If we ratify the Nineteenth Amendment we ratify the Fifteenth and give suffrage to the Negro man."

Reviewing these arguments, Mr. Phanor Brezeale cried that he did not believe "that any law can be enacted that will let you, red-blooded as you are, stand by and let the Negro vote. The death knell of force bills was sounded in '78 and you know it. I know it, too, because I was there in my parish with a gun, and the only reason that I was not imprisoned is that a friend furnished me a fast horse, and today there is a federal indictment pending against me up there. . . . I can promise you one thing and that is that if the Federal Amendment is ratified there'll be no Negro women voting in the parish of Natchitoches."

That sentence caught the fancy of the crowd. "No, nor in Red River, either," roared a deep voice. "Nor in Plaquemine." "And they won't vote in Sabine, you can bet!" "Neither anywhere." J. Y. Sanders,

United States Congressman, appealing for ratification and answering the Negro argument, said in part: "There ain't but one thing—and you might as well remember it—that keeps Louisiana, Mississippi and Alabama white and that is this: that we have decreed that the palladium of our liberty and the cornerstone of our civilization rests for all time in the white Democratic primary and that once the primary is over there is not, nor, under God's providence shall there ever be, any general election."

From May 27 to July 8, Senate and House played football with the ratification, State suffrage and poll tax resolutions. In the meantime Champ Clark, former Speaker of the House of Representatives, addressed the General Assembly and urged ratification. In answer to an appeal from members of the National's auxiliary, Homer Cummings wired Mr. Behrman to help on the grounds of party advantage and James M. Cox, Governor of Ohio, Democratic nominee for President of the United States, wired members of the Legislature to act favorably, saying, "the Legislature owes such action to the Democratic Party."

It was clear from the first that the State amendment was only a subterfuge, and as such it was killed. Ex-Governor Pleasant, its chief sponsor, was reported to have said that he did not care whether it went through or not, all he wanted was to kill ratification. With the resolution to let the voters of the State decide the question of woman suffrage by vote at the polls defeated, the poll tax resolution was withdrawn. The ratification resolution was defeated in the House and action indefinitely postponed in the Senate. The Legislature then completed its record before' adjourning July 8 by passing the rejection resolution in the House and withdrawing it from the Senate files.

The Florida Legislature was still in session when the Federal Suffrage Amendment passed Congress, and on June 5, 1919, Sidney J. Catts, Governor, sent a message to the Legislature, pointing out that Florida could be the first State to ratify if it chose. "Move that the Governor's message be referred to the Committee on Unfinished Business," yelled a chorus of voices. This was met with loud guffaws of laughter, as that is a committee that never reports. "Suffrage lost by skylarking in the House" read the newspaper headlines next day and under them was this: "The suffrage amendment resolution would no doubt have passed, as earlier in the session a resolution proposing submission of a State suffrage amendment had carried, but that the spirit of fun had permeated the House and practically killed all business." The Legislature adjourned on June 6 without taking action on the Governor's message asking for ratification.

The constitution of Florida regarding ratification of federal amendments reads: "No convention or Legislature of this State shall act upon any amendment of the constitution of the United States proposed by Congress to the several States, unless such convention or Legislature shall have been elected after such amendment is submitted." It was later that this same provision in the Tennessee constitution was held to be outruled, but even at this time it was known that the Legislature of Florida had ratified the federal prohibition amendment, though half of the members composing it were elected before the amendment was submitted.

To the request of the National Suffrage Association, for a special session, the answer of the Governor was a most emphatic "no," bolstered up with a statement which read: "I have no intention of calling the Legislature to consider the woman suffrage amendment. I did my best to pass the same at an extra and a regular session. The legislators were very much opposed and it would do no good to call them together again for the same purpose."

There was, just the same, a continuation of appeals all through the year. Legislators were interviewed and no stone was left unturned to secure a session. Florida, as well as Tennessee, was affected by the decision of the United States Supreme Court regarding the Ohio referendum case, and when this decision came in June, 1920, and legal obstructions were by it set aside, it was hoped that Florida, where many towns had given municipal suffrage, would break the shackles that bound her to tradition and take her place as one of the ratifying States. But she did not. Florida was the only State in the Union that successfully evaded action.

During the last year of the campaign there hung on the wall at the national suffrage headquarters a large map of the United States which recorded the suffrage history of each State by a system of differently colored stars. When the campaign was completed, thirty-eight of the States bore an additional star to show that they had ratified the Federal Suffrage Amendment while nine had a black star to show that they had failed to ratify it. Florida had none. These black-starred States were in a row along the Atlantic seaboard from Delaware to Louisiana, the majority constituting the heart of what was once the Southern Confederacy.

But was the black record really made in defense of State's rights against federal dictation?

Not a bit of it. The proof? It was the South that led the campaign for prohibition by federal amendment. The measure was introduced in the Senate by a member from Texas, and of the nineteen Southern Senators who voted against the submission of the Federal Suffrage Amendment, fourteen voted to submit the federal prohibition amendment. Fifteen ratifications of the prohibition amendment took place the year following its submission. Eleven of them were those of Southern States. Every State that failed to ratify the woman suffrage amendment on the alleged ground of federal interference ratified the federal prohibition amendment.

An argument which claims that it is a violation of State's rights for New Jersey, Connecticut or Rhode Island to ratify woman suffrage and impose it upon South Carolina, Alabama or Georgia, which rejected it; but that it is no violation of State's rights for Southern States to ratify federal prohibition and impose it upon New Jersey, Connecticut or Rhode Island, which rejected it, is more ingenious than convincing.

To summarize: Of the ten States that did not ratify the Federal Suffrage Amendment, Florida took no action in either House; Georgia's vote was null and void as Senate and House did not act on a joint resolution; Delaware ratified in the Senate and refused to take action in the House; Mississippi ratified in the Senate and defeated ratification in the House; North Carolina voted to postpone action on the ratification resolution in the Senate and tabled the rejection resolution in the House; South Carolina passed a concurrent instead of a joint rejection resolution and each House voted on a different measure; Louisiana passed a rejection resolution in the House but the Senate Journal shows the rejection resolution to have been withdrawn from the Senate files; Maryland discovered just before the Legislature adjourned that its rejection of February 17 had not been officially conveyed to the federal Secretary of State and on September 22 voted down a ratification resolution, but did not present the rejection resolution, as the Federal Suffrage Amendment had been proclaimed a month before. Alabama and Virginia adopted joint rejection resolutions in both Houses. These two States, therefore, represented the total tally of States that were actually scored in the rejection program of the anti-suffragists.

CHAPTER 32

Conclusion

We have brought together the evidence that the answer to our question in the foreword to this book is—politics. The evidence that it was politics that made America, the cradle of democracy, twenty-seventh instead of first on the list of countries democratic enough to extend the right of self-government to both halves of their respective populations.

That evidence tends to make clear, too, how slowly men as a whole retreated from the "divine right of men to rule over women" idea, and how slowly women rose to assume their equal right with men to rule over both. Long after men's reason convinced them that woman suffrage was right and inevitable the impulse to male supremacy persuaded them that the step would be "inexpedient." The lower types of men have always frankly resented any threatened infringement of the rights of the male and although the higher classes of male intelligence defined the feeling toward woman suffrage in other terms, at source the highest and lowest were actuated by the same traditional instinct.

Men believed what they wanted to believe in believing that women did not desire the vote. In 1916, thirty-eight thousand women of Maine signed petitions to the electors asking for the vote; but when the question was put to the men voters at the election, only twenty thousand responded with "aye." In 1917, 1,030,000 women in New York said, over their signatures, that they wanted to vote; but only 703,000 men voted affirmatively on the question at election time. These examples, were there no others, bring into high relief the fact that in the suffrage struggle there were more women who wanted to vote than there were men who were willing to grant them the privilege.

Superimposed upon this biological foundation of male resistance to female aggrandizement was the failure of political leaders to recognize the inescapable logic of woman suffrage in a land professing universal suffrage. On top of this, and as a consequence of it, lay the party inaction which gave opportunity to men who were far from inactive on the suffrage question, because they feared that their personal interests would suffer should the evolution of democracy take its normal course.

Had not the Republican party enfranchised the Negro by whip and bayonet it would have been easier for women to gain their enfranchisement without party endorsement, but suffragists, left to make their own appeal to majorities accustomed to be told how to vote, found that the lack of political endorsement was as effective as a mandate to vote against. Lax election laws and methods often opened doors for corruption, and by, and with, the assistance of party officials, suffrage elections were stolen.

The damage thus wrought to the woman suffrage cause, and the nation's record, was far more insidious than the loss of any election would imply. The alleged rejection of suffrage became to the unknowing public an indication of an adverse public sentiment, and tended to create rather than correct indifference, for the average man and woman move with the current of popular opinion. The inaction of the public gave a mandate for further political evasion of the question to party leaders, some of whom were certainly cognizant of and others working factors in the criminal schemes which produced the misleading result. Around and around the vicious circle went the suffrage question. "Get another *State*," said President Roosevelt, excusing national inaction. "*Congress* has given no indication that it wants woman suffrage," said Governor Pierce of Dakota, as he vetoed the Territorial Bill which would grant suffrage to women. The Congress looked to the States for its cue, the States to Congress, both to the parties and the parties to the various financial interests, which in turn were responsible for the election of a picked list of members of Congress, of Legislatures and of the party leadership.

Had more statesmen and fewer politicians directed the policies of parties, women would have been enfranchised in the years between 1865 and 1880 and American history, along many lines, would have changed its course. Party suffrage endorsement was won in the United States after forty-eight years of unceasing effort, but when the final victory came women were alternately indignant that it had been so long in coming, and amazed that it had come at all. Many men expressed disappointment that women did not at once enter the party campaigns with the same zeal and consecration they had shown in the struggle for the vote. These men forgot that the dominant political parties blocked the normal progress of woman suffrage for half a century. The women remembered.

The Republicans found that the Negro fresh from slavery knew too little to play the "game of politics." All parties may find in the years to come a still more formidable problem in the woman vote, but for a different reason. If women do not make docile partisans, it will be because through the long weary struggle they have learned to know too much. "Wars are not paid for in war time, the bills come afterwards," said Franklin, and so it may be said of the cost of political blunders. American women who know the history of their country will always resent the fact that American men chose to enfranchise Negroes fresh from slavery before enfranchising American wives and mothers, and allowed hordes of European immigrants totally unfamiliar with the traditions and ideals of American government to be enfranchised in all States after naturalization, and in fifteen States without it, and be thus qualified to pass upon the question of the enfranchisement of American women.

The knowledge that elections can be controlled and manipulated, that a purchasable vote and men with money and motives to buy can appear upon occasion, that an election may be turned with "unerring accuracy" by a bloc of the least understanding voters, that conditions produce many politicians but few statesmen, began long ago to modify for Americans the fine pride in political liberty still the boast upon the 4th of July. That this knowledge should have made conservative types of men and women hesitant to extend the suffrage is not strange, nor is it to be held against conscientious men that they had to struggle with real doubts as to the wisdom of adding women to the electorate.

On the other hand, in spite of all weaknesses of the American government, no conscientious man or woman should ever have lost sight of four counter facts, (1) The United States will never go back to government by kings, nobilities or favored classes. (2) It must go forward to a safe and progressive government by the people; there is no other alternative. (3) Women have had a corrective influence in department after department of society and the only one pronounced "a filthy mire" is politics where they have not been. (4) The problem of leading government by majorities through the mire to the ideal which certainly lies ahead is one which women should share with men.

Looking backward, however, it is not resentment at the long scroll of men's biological inhibitions and political blunders unrolled in the suffrage struggle that is, for suffragists, the final picture. The final picture fills with the men and the groups of men, Republican men, Democratic men, with a vision of real democracy luring their souls, who in the political arena fought the good fight for and with suffragists. Their faith in and loyalty to the suffrage cause, their Herculean efforts, their brilliant achievements, their personal sacrifices, leap out from the record compellingly, riding down all else.

On the outside of politics women fought one of the strongest, bravest battles recorded in history, but to these men inside politics, some Republicans, some Democrats, and some members of minority parties, the women of the United States owe their enfranchisement.

And if we have made here a case for our assertion that American politics was an age-long trap for woman suffrage, we hope that we have not failed to make, as well, a case for these higher-grade American politicians who rescued woman suffrage from that trap and urged it forward to its goal.

Chronological Record of the Winning of Woman Suffrage by Federal Amendment

TEXT OF THE AMENDMENT

"Section 1. The right of citizens of the United States to vote shall not be denied or abridged by the United States or by any state on account of sex.

"Section 2. The Congress shall have power, by appropriate legislation, to enforce the provisions of this article."

HISTORY OF AMENDMENT

First introduced in the Senate, January 10, 1878, by Senator A. A. Sargent, of California.

Reported from Committee:

In the Senate:

1878, Adverse majority.
1882, Favorable majority, adverse minority.
1884, Favorable majority, adverse minority.
1886, Favorable majority, adverse minority.
1889, Favorable majority, adverse minority.
1890, Without recommendation.
1893, Favorable majority, adverse minority.
1896, Without recommendation.
1913, Favorable majority.
1914, Favorable majority.
1916, Favorable majority.
1917, Unanimously.

In the House:

1883, Favorable majority.

1884, Adverse majority, favorable minority.

1886, Adverse majority, favorable minority.

1890. Favorable majority.

1894, Adverse majority.

1914, Without recommendation.

1916, Without recommendation.

1917, Sept. 24, Woman Suffrage Committee created, yes, 181, no 107.

1917, Dec. 15, Reported from Judiciary Committee without recommendation.

1918, Jan. 3, Reported favorably from House Suffrage Committee.

Voted Upon:

In the House:

January 12, 1915; yeas 174, nays 204 (378 voting).

January 10, 1918; yeas, 274, nays 136 (410 voting).

May 21, 1919; yeas 304; nays 89 (393 voting).

In the Senate:

January 25, 1887; yeas 16, nays 34 (50 voting).

March 19, 1914; yeas 35, nays 34 (69 voting).

October 1, 1918; yeas, including pairs, 62; nays 34.

February 10, 1919; yeas, including pairs, 63; nays 33.

June 4, 1919; yeas, including pairs, 66; nays 30.

Notes

1   Australia, Austria, Belgium (municipal), British East Africa, Burmah (municipal), Canada, Czecho-Slovakia, Denmark, Esthonia, Finland, Germany, Great Britain, Holland, Hungary, Iceland, Isle of Man, Latvia, Littonia, Luxembourg, New Zealand, Norway, Poland, Roumania (municipal), Rhodesia, Russia, Sweden.

2   Mrs. Russell Sage.

3   Lucretia Mott, Sarah Pugh, Abby Kimber, Elizabeth Neal, Mary Grew, Mrs. Wendell Phillips, Emily Winston, and Abby Southwick.

4   "History of Woman Suffrage," Volume 1, page 475.

5   "History of Woman Suffrage," Volume I, page 515.

6   1850 and 1851, Worcester; 1852, Syracuse; 1853, Cleveland; 1854, Philadelphia; 1855, Cincinnati; 1856, New York; 1857, none; 1858, 1859 and 1860, New York.

7   "History of Woman Suffrage," Volume I, page 567.

8   Thorpe, "Constitutional History of the United States," Volume 3, page 459.

9   *Thirteenth Amendment,* Sec. i. Neither slavery nor involuntary servitude, except as a punishment for crime whereof the party shall have been convicted, shall exist within the United States, or any place subject to their jurisdiction.

Sec. 2. Congress shall have power to enforce this article by appropriate legislation.

10   *Fourteenth Amendment,* Sec. i. All persons born or naturalized in the United States and subject to the jurisdiction thereof, are citizens of the United States and of the State wherein they reside. No State shall make or enforce any law which shall abridge the privileges or immunities of citizens of the United States; nor shall any State deprive any person of life, liberty, or property, without due process of law; nor deny to any person within its jurisdiction the equal protection of the laws.

Sec. 2. Representatives shall be apportioned among the several States according to their respective numbers, counting the whole number of persons in each State, excluding Indians not taxed. But when the right to vote at any election for the choice of electors for President and Vice-President of the United States, Representatives in Congress, the Executive and Judicial officers of a State or the members of the Legislature thereof, is denied to any male inhabitants of such State, being twenty-one years of age, and citizens of the United States, or in any way abridged, except for participation in rebellion, or other crime, the basis of representation therein shall be reduced in proportion which the number of such male citizens shall bear to the whole number of male citizens twenty-one years of age in such State.

Sec. 3. No person shall be a Senator or Representative in Congress, or elector of President and Vice-President, or hold any office, civil or military, under the United States, or under any State, who, having previously taken an oath, as a member of Congress, or as an officer of the United States, or as a member of any State Legislature, or as an executive or judicial officer of any State, to support the Constitution of the United States, shall have engaged in insurrection or rebellion against the same, or given aid or comfort to the enemies thereof. But Congress may by a vote of two-thirds of each House, remove such disability.

Sec. 4. The validity of the public debt of the United States, authorized by law, including debts incurred for payment of pensions and bounties for services in suppressing insurrection or rebellion, shall not be questioned. But neither the United States nor any State shall assume or pay any debt or obligation incurred in aid of insurrection or rebellion against the United States, or any claim for the loss or emancipation of any slave; but all such debts, obligations and claims shall be held illegal and void.

Sec. 5. The Congress shall have power to enforce, by appropriate legislation, the provisions of this article.

11   "History of Woman Suffrage," Volume 2, page 354.

12   "Life of Frederick Douglass," page 463.

13   A referendum on Negro suffrage in 1865 had resulted in 6521 votes in Washington, and 812 in Georgetown against; and 35 votes in Washington and 1 in Georgetown in favor.

14   Negro suffrage had been twice submitted before, once in 1846 when it was rejected by a vote of 223,834 to 85,306; again in 1860 and rejected by a vote of 337,984 to 197,150; again in 1868 and rejected by 282403 to 249,802. (Thorpe's "Constitutional History of the United States," page 173.)

15 Negro suffrage was carried twice only on referendum. It was submitted in 1865, 1867 and 1868 in Minnesota and at the last date was carried. There were only 246 Negroes in Minnesota as late as 1870. Iowa submitted Negro suffrage in 1868, there being less than one thousand Negroes of voting age in the State, and it was carried.—A. Caperton Braxton, "Fifteenth Amendment."

16 "Biography of Susan B. Anthony," Volume 1, page 295.

17 "Constitutional History," Volume 3, page 450.

18 "Fifteenth Amendment," Virginia Bar Association, page 4611.

19 "A search through the editorials and news columns of the leading newspapers of the country issued during the presidential campaign of 1868, fails to reveal a single direct reference to any proposed Fifteenth Amendment. . . . Four days after the election, however, a Senator and also Wendell Phillips on the same day announced the forthcoming amendment forbidding disfranchisement on account of race or color."—Matthews, page 20.

20 "Twenty Years in Congress," Volume 2, page 412.

21 Braxton, "Fifteenth Amendment," page 45.

22 Richardson's "Life of Grant," page 527.

23 *Fifteenth Amendment, SEC. 1. The right of citizens of the United States to vote shall not be denied or abridged by the United States or by any State on account of race, color, or previous condition of servitude.

SEC. 2. The Congress shall have power to enforce this article by appropriate legislation.

24 "Eighty Years and More," Stanton, page 289.

25 The Fifteenth Amendment had been submitted in February, 1869, and although not yet ratified Negroes had the right to vote under the law granting Negro suffrage in territories to be organized.

26 "The First Woman Jury," Grace Raymond Hebard, *Journal American History,* 1913, No. 4.

27 "The First Woman Jury," Grace Raymond Hebard, *Journal American History,* 1913, No. 4.

28 "History of Woman Suffrage," Volume 4, page 998.

29 "History of Woman Suffrage," Volume 4, page 1003.

30 Blaine, "Twenty Years in Congress," Volume 2, page 488.

31   "Legislative and Judicial History, Fifteenth Amendment," Matthews, page 95.

32   Blaine, "Twenty Years in Congress," Volume 2, page 472.

33   The Chinese were later denied citizenship by act of Congress at the instance of the Irish of California.

34   "Legislative History, Fifteenth Amendment," Matthews, page 126.

35   "Biography of Susan B. Anthony," Volume 1, page 421.

36   For copy of 14th Amendment see page 41 and copy of 15th Amendment, page 70.

37   New Hampshire, Michigan, California, Oregon, Pennsylvania, Illinois, Connecticut, Ohio, Missouri, New York, and the District of Columbia. The number of women who made the effort to vote was about 150.

38   "Legislative History, Fifteenth Amendment," Matthews, page 108.

39   *Atlantic Monthly*, 1875, page 665.

40   *Atlantic Monthly*, 1875, page 666.

41   For full account of these cases see "History of Woman Suffrage," Volume 2, pages 586 and 754.

42   "Biography of Susan B. Anthony," Volume 1, page 433.

43   In the year 1867 there was a suffrage referendum in Kansas, see p. 120, The Suffrage Referenda of 40 years, 1869-1909, inclusive; Michigan, 1874; Nebraska, 1882; Colorado, 1877-1893; Rhode Island, 1887; Washington, 1889-1898; Kansas, 1894; Idaho, 1896; California, 1896; South Dakota, 1890-1898; Oregon, 1884-1900-1906-1908; New Hampshire, 1902; the question, included in statehood constitutions, was referred to the voters in Wyoming in 1890 and in Utah in 1895.

44   South Dakota, 1890 and 1898; Colorado, 1893; Kansas, 1894; California, 1896; Idaho, 1896; Oregon, 1900, 1906, 1908, and Washington, 1898.

45   "History of Woman Suffrage," Volume 3, page 691.

46   House vote—34 ayes, 27 nays; divided ayes, 22 Populists, 11 Republicans, 1 Democrat; nays, 3 Populists, 21 Republicans, 3 Democrats. Senate vote—20 ayes, 10 nays; ayes, 12 Populists, 8 Republicans, no Democrat; nays, 1 Populist, 4 Republicans, 5 Democrats.

47   For 35,798; against, 29,451.

48   Anti-Saloon League Year Book chronology.

49 "Brewing and Liquor Interests and German Propagandas," Senate Investigation, pages 116-300.

50 "Brewing and Liquor Investigation," page 308,

51 *Ibid.*, pages 85 and 342.

52 *Ibid.*, page 79.

53 "Brewing and Liquor Investigation," pages 78 and 320.

54 † *Ibid.*, page 333.

55 ‡ *Ibid.*, page 77.

56 §*Ibid.*, Volume 1, Exhibit 1031.

57 *Ibid.*, page 417.

58 *Ibid.*, page 400.

59 In 1914 seven States had suffrage referenda and suffrage campaigns were in progress in four others in which the vote was taken the following year. There were also seven prohibition referenda campaigns.

60 Texas Brewers' Investigation.

61 "Brewing and Liquor Interests," Volume 1, page 1195.

62 Chief of a Brewers' Bureau and President of the Association of Commerce and Labor, an organization set up by the brewers to give the appearance of voluntary outside protest against prohibition. Percy Andreae was under contract to receive forty thousand dollars per year from the brewers. (*Ibid.*, page 1032, Exhibit No. 780.)

63 "Brewing and Liquor Interests," Senate Investigation, Volume 1, page 1170.

64 "Brewing and Liquor Interests," Volume 1, page 1173.

65 *Ibid.*, page 1179.

66 Page 1015, Exhibit No. 760, from Andreae's files by subpoena.

67 See story of Iowa.

68 "Brewing and Liquor Interests," Senate Investigation, Volume I, page 353.

69 "Brewing and Liquor Interests," Volume 1, page 862.

70 *Ibid.*, page 848.

71 "Brewing and Liquor Interests," Volume 1, page 344.

72 *Ibid.*, page 924.

73   Arizona, Oregon, Wisconsin, Kansas, Michigan and Ohio. See stories of States for part liquor interests played in their campaigns.

74   North Dakota, South Dakota, Nebraska, Nevada, Montana, Missouri, Ohio. See State stories for liquor activities in their campaigns.

75   "Exhibit No. 780"; from Andreae's files by subpoena, page 1032.

76   "Modern Democracies," Volume 2, page 475.

77   "Modern Democracies," Volume 2, page 479.

78   "Modern Democracies," Volume 2, page 485.

79   Yes—125,037; noes—121,450.

80   The no vote remained about the same as in the two preceding referenda, but the yes vote gained twenty-five thousand.

1884	Yes		11,223	No		28,176
1900	"	....	26,265	"	....	28,402
1906	"	....	36,902	"	....	47,075
1908	"	....	38,858	"	....	58,670
1910	"	....	36,200	"	....	58,800
1912	"	....	61,265	"	....	57,104

81   "Brewing and Liquor Interests," Volume 1, page 1170.

82   Senate—Republicans 25, Democrats 24, Progressives 2; House— Republicans 52. Democrats 73, Progressives 25, Socialists 3.

83   New York, Pennsylvania, Illinois, Wisconsin, in the order named exceeded Ohio in quantity of fermented liquor produced.

84   "Brewing and Liquor Investigation," Volume 1, page 836.

85   *Ibid.,* page 1191.

86   The total vote was 462,186—273,361 voting yes and 188,825 voting no.

87   Official report Ohio Woman Suffrage Association.

88   "Brewing and Liquor Investigation," Volume 1, page 462.

89   Total vote on suffrage amendment 853,685; against 518,295; for 335,390; lost by 182,905.

90   From suffrage petition to the court praying investigation concerning the affidavit that the man was unpaid.

91   Exhibit No. 758 from Andreae files, page 1014.

92   *Ibid,.* Exhibit 760, page 1015. Another conference was probably held in Milwaukee as was voted by brewers (B. & L. I. 1013), but the report of it does not appear in the papers on subpoena.

93   The plan of concentrating effort upon the Senate with its smaller membership in order to block its passage is not uncommon among the opponents of measures, and several times a single Senator had prevented the submission of the suffrage amendment in Iowa. When Senators were likely to find an explanation to their constituents embarrassing, the tactics changed to the House. It was now proposed to so constitute the Senate that a few men could block the submission of the prohibition amendment already passed by one Legislature.

94   Files of the National American Woman Suffrage Association.

95   "Third Party Movements," Haines.

96   Mrs. Millicent Garrett Fawcett, President of the National Union of Suffrage Societies of Great Britain, says: "It will ever be an open question on which different people with equal opportunities of forming a judgment will pronounce different verdicts, whether militancy did more harm or good to the suffrage cause. It certainly broke down 'the conspiracy of silence' on the subject up to then observed by the press. Every extravagance, every folly, every violent expression, etc., were given the widest publicity, not only in Great Britain but all over the world."

97   *Woman's Journal.*

98   Report of National Congressional Chairman.

99   James Ferguson, Governor of Texas, James Nugent, New Jersey, Stephen B. Fleming, Indiana, and former Representative Bartlett of Georgia. Upon investigation it was found that all of them were well known representatives of wet interests.

100   In 1913 the College Equal Suffrage League organized the first of all suffrage parades. It was small but it carried tremendous consequences.

101   This man, a Democrat, was completely converted when the women of California were alleged to have tipped the scale in the presidential election of 1916 and returned Mr. Wilson to the White House.

102   Senate Investigation; "Brewing and Liquor Interests and German Propaganda," Volume I, page 1048, Exhibit No. 838.

103   The second woman to be elected to Congress, coming into office with the Republican landslide of 1920.

104   For account of women's war service see Volume VI of the History of Woman Suffrage.

105 Legislatures that memorialized Congress on behalf of the Federal Woman Suffrage Amendment in 1919: Colorado Jan. 3; Michigan Jan. 3; Indiana Jan. 9; South Dakota Jan. 9; North Dakota Jan. 11; Washington Jan. 13; Arkansas Jan. 14; Oregon Jan. 14; Utah Jan, 14; New York Jan. 15; Wisconsin Jan. 16; California Jan. 17; Nebraska Jan. 17; Kansas Jan. 20; Texas Jan. 20; Arizona Jan. 21; Idaho Jan. 23; Minnesota Jan. 23; Missouri Jan. 23; Montana Jan. 23; Nevada Jan. 28; Illinois Jan. 29; Wyoming Feb. 1; Ohio Feb. 5.

106 Illinois 1913; Michigan 1917; Nebraska 1917; North Dakota 1917; Rhode Island 1917; Indiana 1919; Iowa 1919; Maine 1919; Minnesota 1919; Missouri 1919; Ohio 1919; Tennessee 1919; Vermont 1919; Wisconsin 1919. Kentucky's Legislature granted presidential suffrage in 1920.

107 A chronological table of ratifications will be found in the Appendix.

108 In December, 1919, the convention that was to rewrite the Nebraska constitution met in Lincoln. It was provided that women should vote on the acceptance of the amended constitution, and that a full suffrage clause which was inserted should go into effect as soon as the adoption of the constitution was announced by the Governor. Before the vote was taken on the constitution, September 21, 1920, the Federal Suffrage Amendment had been ratified. Thus Nebraska women, enfranchised by the Federal Amendment, went to the polls and voted on their own State enfranchisement. With their votes the constitution received 65,483 ayes to 15,416 nays.

109 The Governor and a Council of Five in New Hampshire have full power to call a special session at any time, "if the welfare of the State should require the same."

110 Although the Federal Suffrage Amendment was proclaimed as adopted on August 26, 1920, there was no way in which the Maine referendum on presidential suffrage could be legally omitted from the ballot. Therefore Maine women, possessed by then of full suffrage, went to the polls on September 13, 1920, and voted on this partial suffrage State measure. The official count showed ayes 88,080; nays 30,462—Maine women's answer to the question, "Do women want to vote?"

111 Arizona, Arkansas, California, Colorado, Idaho, Louisiana, Maine, Maryland, Massachusetts, Michigan, Mississippi, Montana, Missouri, Nebraska, New Mexico, North Dakota, Ohio, Oklahoma, Oregon, South Dakota, Utah and Washington.

112 Prohibition had been ratified by forty-five States; Connecticut, Rhode Island and New Jersey did not ratify.

113 The referendum to repeal the State prohibition amendment in Ohio had been lost by forty-one thousand majority, while the referendum to confirm ratification of the federal prohibition amendment had been lost by five hundred majority.

Index